SUNBELT CITIES

SUNBELT CITIES

POLITICS AND GROWTH SINCE WORLD WAR II

Edited by Richard M. Bernard and Bradley R. Rice

 University of Texas Press, Austin

Copyright © 1983 by the University of Texas Press
All rights reserved
Printed in the United States of America
First Edition, 1983

Requests for permission to reproduce material from this work
should be sent to Permissions, University of Texas Press,
Box 7819, Austin, Texas 78712.

LIBRARY OF CONGRESS CATALOGING IN PUBLICATION DATA
Main entry under title:
Sunbelt cities.
    1. Cities and towns—Sunbelt States.   I. Bernard, Richard M., 1948–   .
II. Rice, Bradley Robert, 1948–
HT123.5.A163S93   1983   307.7′64′0973   83-10222
ISBN 0-292-77576-8
ISBN 0-292-77580-6 (pbk.)

for
Benjamin and Emily Bernard
Travis and Vera Rice

CONTENTS

ACKNOWLEDGMENTS

Our first debt is to our ten fellow contributors. They have been patient and understanding of the demands and delays inherent in a collaborative project. We especially enjoyed the personal interaction with each other and the audiences at Sunbelt panels at the fall 1981 meetings of the Western Historical Association in San Antonio and the Southern Historical Association in Louisville. We want to thank Jo Ann Carrigan for chairing the SHA session.

For over two years we have had the opportunity to discuss our thoughts about the Sunbelt and particular cities in it with many scholars, but we would like especially to thank Blaine Brownell, Jim Cobb, Chandler Davidson, Lewis Gould, and Gene Hatfield. Carl Abbott was kind enough to supply the editors with a manuscript copy of his book *The New Urban America: Growth and Politics in Sunbelt Cities* prior to its publication.

Much of the background work for the introduction was done by Brad Rice while he was in attendance at a National Endowment for the Humanities Summer Seminar for College Teachers directed by Robert A. Divine of the University of Texas at Austin. Hardy Jackson of Clayton Junior College provided a twofold service for Rice. As a colleague he was a patient sounding board—no small task for a colonialist who thinks that any event after Appomattox is mere nostalgia. As a division chairman facing recession year budget crunches, he still managed to find little ways to help this project. Mamie Jeffries and Marie Mayfield remained cheerful when parts of this work demanded time from their overworked typewriters.

Marquette University was also cooperative and helpful. The Graduate School provided Richard Bernard with a research grant and a summer faculty fellowship and also underwrote the production of camera-ready maps. Bernard is also grateful to the American Philosophical Society for its financial support.

Arnold Hirsch would like to thank the University of New

Orleans Research Council, Martin Melosi wishes to acknowledge the counsel of Robert Calvert, Brad Luckingham is grateful to Arizona State University for a summer grant, and Howard Rabinowitz appreciates the financial support provided by the National Endowment for the Humanities and the comments provided by David R. Goldfield and Gerald D. Nash on an earlier version of his essay.

SUNBELT CITIES

1
INTRODUCTION

by Bradley R. Rice and Richard M. Bernard

A great migration is under way. It has, in fact, been going on since World War II. Between 1940 and 1980, the Sunbelt, which stretches from coast to coast below the 37th parallel, increased its population by 112.3 percent. Over the same period the combined northeastern and midwestern regions, often called the Frostbelt, grew by only 41.9 percent (Table 1.1). Most of the difference between these two rates of population expansion results from a mass movement of northern Americans to the emerging metropolitan areas of the Sunbelt. Within this region there are ninety-eight Standard Metropolitan Statistical Areas (SMSAs) comprised of central cities and one or more suburban counties (by 1977 definition). During the 1970s, all but eight of these exceeded the 9 percent growth rate for all SMSAs, and all but thirteen surpassed the 10.9 percent overall rise in national population. Of the thirteen large (250,000+) SMSAs that exceeded 40 percent growth, twelve are located in the Sunbelt as defined here. This demographic explosion has reversed the century-old movement of young people and blacks from the South to the North and represents one of the greatest population shifts in American history.[1]

The twelve metropolitan areas chosen for this anthology were singled out for their size, regional importance, and historical significance. Certainly others (Columbia, Winston-Salem/Greensboro/High Point, Jacksonville, Tulsa, Memphis, Nashville, Birmingham, Las Vegas, El Paso, Tucson) could have been included, but the editors believe that these dozen case studies (four in each of three subregions: Southeast, Texoma, and Southwest) exemplify the major characteristics of Sunbelt development. Although the particular organization and emphasis of each contribution was left to the individual author, all wrote from a common prospectus that called for careful attention to the causes of economic growth and the reasons for political changes. The essays are designed to be suggestive narrative

TABLE 1.1. Population of the Sunbelt, 1940, 1960, 1980 (in thousands)

State	1940	1960	1980	% Increase 1940– 1980	% Increase 1960– 1980
North Carolina	3,572	4,556	5,874	64.5	28.9
South Carolina	1,900	2,383	3,119	64.2	30.9
Georgia	3,124	3,943	5,464	75.0	38.6
Florida	1,897	4,952	9,740	413.4	96.7
Alabama	2,833	3,267	3,890	37.3	19.1
Mississippi	2,184	2,178	2,521	15.5	15.7
Tennessee	2,916	3,567	4,591	57.5	28.7
Louisiana	2,364	3,257	4,204	77.9	29.1
Arkansas	1,949	1,786	2,286	17.3	28.0
Oklahoma	2,336	2,328	3,025	29.5	29.9
Texas	6,415	9,580	14,228	121.8	48.5
New Mexico	532	951	1,300	144.8	36.7
Arizona	499	1,302	2,718	444.7	108.8
Southern Nevada[a]	16	127	461	2,781.2	263.0
Southern California[b]	3,841	9,399	13,803	259.4	46.9
Total	36,378	53,576	77,224	112.3	44.1
Northeast-Midwest[c]	76,120	96,927	107,986	41.9	11.4
United States	132,165	179,323	226,505	71.4	26.3

[a]Clark County (Las Vegas SMSA)

[b]San Bernadino, Kern, San Luis Obispo, Santa Barbara, Los Angeles, Riverside, Orange, San Diego, Ventura, and Imperial counties

[c]See Map 1.1 for definition.

overviews of the past forty years. They will provide readers with convenient and authoritative introductions to the histories of these major Sunbelt cities and their suburbs. Taken as a whole, the essays demonstrate significant comparisons and contrasts about what caused the Sunbelt's rise and what political impact it has had.

The very concept of a Sunbelt is a novel and somewhat controversial notion in American geography. Political strategist Kevin Phillips coined the term "Sunbelt" (often "Sun Belt") in his 1969 book *The Emerging Republican Majority*. He used the concept to focus attention on the increasing electoral strength of the region and how the Republican party could benefit from it. Ironically, the term caught on before the Republicans did. The election of southern

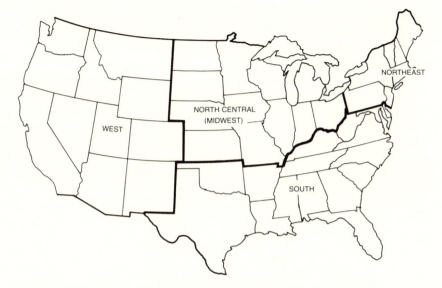

MAP 1.1. United States Regions as Defined by the Census Bureau

Democrat Jimmy Carter to the presidency in 1976 served as a catalyst for a mid-decade outpouring of journalistic and scholarly analysis of the South in particular and the Sunbelt in general. Both during
the campaign and after the balloting, the *New York Times, Nation's
Business, Business Week, Fortune, Saturday Review,* and numerous
other periodicals ran stories extolling the growth of the Sunbelt.
These articles had the effect of legitimating the term "Sunbelt" as a
part of the nation's intellectual as well as popular vocabulary.[2]

General usage, however, has not led to a common definition of
the American Sunbelt. Despite all the media attention accorded the
migration to the region, the concept remains hazy and ill defined in
the minds of many people. The Sunbelt idea is a mix of economics,
conservative politics, and demographic change generally associated
with the observation that the southeastern and southwestern sections of the country have been growing and prospering more than
the Northeast and Midwest in recent years. Geographers Clyde E.
Browning and Wil Gesler argued that the use of such an imprecise
term as "Sunbelt" constituted "sloppy regionalizing." For professional geographic use perhaps they are correct, but even these critics
were compelled to admit that the Sunbelt is "a notion whose time
has come." The Sunbelt, they conceded, "has become fixed firmly in
the minds of many Americans: *the image is the reality.*"[3]

The most widely circulated early description was probably that of freelance journalist Kirkpatrick Sale, who assailed the rise of the Sunbelt as a threat to the nation's progressive political tradition. Sale actually used the term "southern rim" rather than Sunbelt, but he discussed the same phenomenon. With some minor adjustment, his definition of the region's boundaries is still the best. "It hardly seems an accident," Sale wrote in his 1975 polemic *Power Shift*, "that there is indeed a cartographic line that sets off this area almost precisely: the boundary line which runs along the northern edges of North Carolina, Tennessee, Arkansas, Oklahoma, New Mexico, Arizona, or generally the 37th parallel." He extended the line to the Pacific to catch lower Nevada and Southern California.[4]

Subsequent writers, both those who agreed with Sale's alarmist tract and those who challenged him, have not been so confident about the Sunbelt's exact perimeter. Much of their confusion has its origin in the failure of the United States Census to recognize the Sunbelt as a separate region and to list statistics for it as a unit. The Census Bureau instead generates regional economic and demographic data for the Northeast, North Central (Midwest), South, and West (Map 1.1). In order to utilize the government's population schedules, the researcher must devise his or her own Sunbelt and then laboriously add up its people from the specific counts given for states, metropolitan areas, counties, or cities. Given this lack of official guidance, some authors have chosen one set of boundaries and others have redrawn them. The resulting lack of consistency in terminology has made it quite difficult for scholars, including the editors of the present work, to generalize about the findings of previous inquiries. Different writers have, in fact, written about different Sunbelts.

The areas that have caused the most definitional difficulty are the upper South, the Pacific Northwest, the Rocky Mountain states, and the state of California. A typical approach in the Sunbelt literature has been to generalize about the region by drawing figures from the Census Bureau's South and West regions. Writers who follow this pattern end up including the rainy Northwest and the snowy Rockies in the western half of what must surely then be misnamed the "Sunbelt." In the South, the use of census regions results in the addition of Kentucky, West Virginia, and the Chesapeake Bay region. With the possible exception of Virginia, however, none of this territory lies within the Sunbelt as popularly conceived.

Other observers eschew census regions and simply specify certain states for Sunbelt membership, adding and subtracting them from the region with little or no rationale. In *Fortune* magazine

(June 1977), Gurney Breckenfield included all of Virginia but split California along county lines in the vicinity of Fresno. About a year later, *Sales and Marketing Management* magazine prepared a Sunbelt map that included all of California but excluded Virginia. Two economics professors at the University of Texas at Dallas further complicated the matter in their book when they omitted northern California from the Sunbelt but admitted the entire upper South. One of the most thorough demographic studies of Sunbelt migration was prepared for the prestigious *Population Bulletin* by Jeanne C. Biggar, but the usefulness of this otherwise solid forty-two-page report is limited by its surprising inclusion of Missouri. Biggar's goal was not to miss a few thousand Ozark Mountain retirees, but in order to do that she ended up with a Sunbelt definition that also included most of the St. Louis and Kansas City SMSAs. In another interesting case, political scientist Thomas R. Dye published a Sunbelt map that excised oil-rich Oklahoma but included Colorado, Utah, and Nevada. The confusion is illustrated further by an unusual example in which Alfred J. Watkins, coeditor of *The Rise of the Sunbelt Cities*, published one article with Memphis in the Sunbelt and another with it in the Frostbelt.[5] These inconsistencies do not necessarily invalidate the findings of the authors, but they do bedevil readers and cloud their understanding of the Sunbelt experience.

Professor Carl Abbott of Portland State University produced one of the most comprehensive and unusual attempts to define the Sunbelt. Abbott fashioned an area composed of a "pair of regions oriented toward the southeastern and southwestern corners of the United States." He claimed that this approach "places more importance on the census than on sunshine," and indeed it does (at least through 1970). But it also places more emphasis on Abbott's particular manipulation of the census than it does on general public image. He correctly calls attention to variations in urban growth within the popular Sunbelt, but his new definition is at odds with all other scholarly or journalistic uses of the concept. He based his boundaries on metropolitan or state growth rates depending on what best suited his conclusions. Consequently he brings into the Sunbelt such questionable locales as Richmond, Norfolk, Denver, Seattle, and Portland but leaves out Mobile, Memphis, Nashville, and Little Rock—all of which grew faster than Portland. His definition also denies Sunbelt status to such tremendously important regional centers as New Orleans and Birmingham and to smaller cities such as Shreveport, Jackson, Baton Rouge, Chattanooga, and World's Fair host Knoxville.[6]

The present study concentrates on growth and political change, but it posits a definition of the Sunbelt based on public perception of the region. A few diehards continue to deny the existence of the Sunbelt. For example, Blaine Liner, executive director of the Southern Growth Policies Board, told a *Wall Street Journal* columnist that "the term is ludicrous and should be stricken from our vocabulary." In his provocative book *The Nine Nations of North America*, Joel Garreau called the Sunbelt a "spurious idea" and a "misleading confection." But for every such negative commentator, a chorus of others continues to find the concept useful. There are literally hundreds of references to the Sunbelt on television, in newspapers, in the major news magazines, and in other periodicals, including such middle-American standards as *Changing Times.*[7]

Measuring popular perceptions of the Sunbelt is a difficult task. One way is to look for the most common definition in journalistic accounts. This avenue leads to a conclusion that sticks pretty closely to the 37th parallel but occasionally includes Virginia and all of California. Many states are clearly within the Sunbelt so defined—Florida, Texas, and Georgia, for example—while others must work a little harder to attract media attention. Since being known as a Sunbelt state has considerable booster value, in 1982 Oklahoma officials redesigned their automobile tags to include a rising sun logo that would solidify the Sooner State's place in the Sunbelt. The press sometimes dubs certain cities as Sunbelt members in such titles as "Place in the Sunbelt—Phoenix Growth Machine" or "A Sunbelt City Plays Catch-Up" (New Orleans).[8] Every mythical belt—cotton or corn, Bible or borscht—must have a "buckle." Atlanta, Phoenix, Dallas, and Research Triangle Park, North Carolina, have vied for the title, but Houston usually wins.

One simple technique for measuring regional perception was demonstrated by sociologist John Shelton Reed, who sought a common definition for the South. Working with the assumption that the South is "that part of the country where people think they are Southerners," he used business entries in telephone directories to plot the geographic incidence of the terms "South," "southern," and "Dixie." Dixie turned out to be, in Reed's words, "more attitude than latitude."[9] A similar technique can be applied to the Sunbelt, assuming that it is that part of the country in which people believe that they live in the Sunbelt. The result is a fairly neat convergence of attitude and latitude that tends to endorse Sale's 37th parallel definition, with the exception of the San Francisco Bay area.

Business listings beginning "Sunbelt" (or "Sun Belt") were counted in the white pages for 1979 or 1980 (whichever was available in autumn 1980) for sixty cities that appeared in at least one

MAP 1.2. The American Sunbelt

Sunbelt definition. For control purposes, fifteen indisputable Frostbelt cities were also checked. As might be expected, Houston led the list with twenty-two entries, followed by Atlanta with eighteen. Other metropolitan areas with more than ten were Dallas, Oklahoma City, and San Diego. North of the 37th parallel only five cities had even one such entry. Those five included three possible Sunbelt cities (Sacramento, Lexington, and Baltimore) and two clearly in the Frostbelt (Columbus and Minneapolis). In the cases of Baltimore, Columbus, and Minneapolis, the "Sunbelt" businesses were transport companies probably named for their southern or southwestern destinations. No entries appeared for Norfolk, Richmond, Denver, Portland, San Francisco, or Seattle.[10]

Neither the broad use of census regions, the state-based definitions that stray north of the 37th parallel, nor Abbott's two-triangle approach gets much support from this admittedly simple device for measuring self-perception. What does emerge is a sort of consensual Sunbelt that generally follows the 37th parallel from the northern border of North Carolina through the lower third of California, including, of course, the twelve cities selected for this book (Map 1.2).

One factor that draws these particular cities together is substantial postwar growth. Among them, Phoenix's forty-year metropolitan growth rate of 1,137.8 percent was most impressive. San Di-

TABLE 1.2. Population of Major Metropolitan Areas in the
Sunbelt: SMSAs, Central Cities, and Outlying Areas, 1940–1980[a]

Metropolitan Area	1940	1950	1960	1970	1980
Southeast					
Atlanta					
SMSA	442,294	671,797	1,017,188	1,390,164	2,029,710
City of Atlanta	302,288	331,314	487,455	496,973	425,022
Outlying area	140,006	340,483	529,733	893,191	1,604,688
Miami					
SMSA	250,537	495,084	935,047	1,267,792	1,625,781
City of Miami	172,172	249,276	291,688	334,859	346,865
Outlying area	78,365	245,808	643,359	932,933	1,278,916
Tampa–St. Petersburg					
SMSA	209,693	409,143	772,453	1,072,594	1,569,134
City of Tampa	108,391	124,681	274,970	277,767	271,523
City of St. Petersburg	60,812	96,738	181,298	216,232	238,647
Outlying area	40,490	187,724	316,185	518,595	1,058,964
New Orleans					
SMSA	540,030	685,405	868,480	1,045,809	1,187,073
City of New Orleans	494,537	570,445	627,525	593,471	557,515
Outlying area	45,493	114,960	240,955	452,338	629,558
Texoma					
Dallas–Fort Worth					
SMSA	584,225	976,052	1,656,816	2,318,036	2,974,805
City of Dallas	294,734	434,462	679,684	844,401	904,078
City of Fort Worth	177,662	278,778	356,268	393,476	385,164
Outlying area	111,829	262,812	620,864	1,080,159	1,685,563
Houston					
SMSA	510,397	806,701	1,243,158	1,985,031	2,905,353
City of Houston	384,514	596,163	938,219	1,232,802	1,595,138
Outlying area	125,883	210,538	304,939	752,229	1,310,215
San Antonio					
SMSA	319,010	500,460	687,151	864,014	1,071,954
City of San Antonio	253,854	408,442	587,718	654,153	785,880
Outlying area	65,156	92,018	99,433	209,861	286,074
Oklahoma City					
SMSA	221,229	325,352	511,833	640,889	834,088
City of Oklahoma City	204,424	243,504	324,253	366,481	403,213
Outlying area	16,805	81,848	187,580	274,408	430,875

TABLE 1.2 (continued)

Metropolitan Area	1940	1950	1960	1970	1980
Southwest					
Los Angeles–Long Beach					
SMSA	2,904,596	4,367,911	6,742,696	7,032,075	7,477,503
City of					
Los Angeles	1,504,277	1,970,358	2,479,015	2,816,061	2,966,850
City of					
Long Beach	164,271	250,767	344,168	358,633	361,334
Outlying area	1,236,048	2,146,786	3,919,513	3,857,381	4,149,319
San Diego					
SMSA	256,368	556,808	1,033,011	1,357,854	1,861,846
City of San Diego	203,341	334,387	573,224	696,769	875,504
Outlying area	53,027	222,421	459,787	661,085	986,308
Phoenix					
SMSA	121,828	331,770	633,510	967,522	1,509,052
City of Phoenix	65,414	106,818	439,170	581,562	789,704
Outlying area	56,414	224,952	194,340	385,960	719,348
Albuquerque					
SMSA	69,391	145,673	262,199	315,774	454,499
City of					
Albuquerque	35,449	96,815	201,189	243,751	331,767
Outlying area	33,942	48,858	61,010	72,023	122,732

SOURCES: U.S. Census, 1940–1970, and *U.S. Department of Commerce News,*
"1980 Census Population Totals for Racial and Spanish Origin Groups [by states]
Announced by the Census Bureau." The 1980 data are taken from releases listing
the final population counts. There is one release per state.

ᵃWith the exception of Dallas–Fort Worth and Los Angeles–Long Beach, the
SMSA definitions used in this table are those in effect for the particular census year.
(For an explanation of this approach see chapter 1, note 11.) For the 1940–1970
census Dallas and Fort Worth were separate metropolitan areas, but the totals are
combined here. In the 1940 and 1950 census Long Beach was classified as suburban
Los Angeles rather than as a joint central city. Here we list the Long Beach city
totals and subtract them from the outlying totals for 1940 and 1950. All figures are
from U.S. Census publications.

TABLE 1.3. Growth Rates of Major Metropolitan Areas in the Sunbelt: SMSAs, Central Cities, and Outlying Areas, 1940–1980 (percentages)[a]

Metropolitan Area	1940– 1950	1950– 1960	1960– 1970	1970– 1980	1940– 1980
Southeast					
Atlanta					
SMSA	51.9	51.4	36.7	46.0	358.9
City of Atlanta	9.6	47.1	2.0	−14.5	40.6
Outlying area	143.9	55.6	68.6	79.7	1,046.2
Miami					
SMSA	97.6	88.9	35.6	28.2	548.9
City of Miami	44.8	17.0	14.8	3.6	101.5
Outlying area	213.7	161.7	45.0	37.1	1,532.0
Tampa–St. Petersburg					
SMSA	95.1	88.8	31.1	46.3	648.3
City of Tampa	15.0	120.5	1.0	−2.2	150.5
City of St. Petersburg	59.1	87.4	19.3	10.4	292.4
Outlying area	363.6	68.4	64.0	104.2	2,515.4
New Orleans					
SMSA	26.9	26.7	20.4	13.5	119.8
City of New Orleans	15.4	10.0	−5.4	−6.1	12.7
Outlying area	152.7	109.6	87.7	39.1	1,283.9
Texoma					
Dallas–Fort Worth					
SMSA	67.1	69.7	39.9	28.3	409.2
City of Dallas	47.4	56.4	24.2	7.1	206.7
City of Fort Worth	56.9	27.8	10.4	−2.1	116.8
Outlying area	135.0	136.3	74.0	56.0	1,407.3
Houston					
SMSA	58.1	54.1	59.7	46.4	469.2
City of Houston	55.0	57.4	31.4	29.4	314.8
Outlying area	67.2	44.8	146.7	74.2	940.8
San Antonio					
SMSA	56.9	37.3	25.7	24.1	236.0
City of San Antonio	60.9	43.9	11.3	20.1	209.6
Outlying area	41.2	8.1	111.1	36.3	339.1
Oklahoma City					
SMSA	47.1	57.3	25.2	30.1	277.0
City of Oklahoma City	19.1	33.2	13.0	10.0	97.2
Outlying area	387.0	129.2	46.3	57.0	2,464.0

TABLE 1.3 (continued)

Metropolitan Area	1940– 1950	1950– 1960	1960– 1970	1970– 1980	1940– 1980
Southwest					
Los Angeles–Long Beach					
SMSA	50.4	54.4	4.3	6.3	157.4
City of Los Angeles	31.0	25.8	13.6	5.4	97.2
City of Long Beach	52.7	37.2	4.2	0.8	120.0
Outlying area	73.7	82.6	−1.6	7.6	235.7
San Diego					
SMSA	117.2	85.5	31.5	37.1	626.2
City of San Diego	64.4	71.4	21.6	25.7	330.6
Outlying area	319.4	106.7	43.8	49.2	1,760.0
Phoenix					
SMSA	172.3	91.0	52.7	56.0	1,138.7
City of Phoenix	63.3	311.1	32.4	35.8	1,107.2
Outlying area	298.8	−13.6	98.6	86.4	1,175.1
Albuquerque					
SMSA	109.9	80.0	20.4	43.9	555.0
City of Albuquerque	173.1	107.8	21.2	36.1	835.9
Outlying area	43.9	24.9	18.1	70.4	261.6

[a] For boundary explanation see Table 1.2 and chapter 1, note 11. All growth rates are based on the figures in Table 1.2 and will differ in some cases from growth rates calculated on adjusted boundaries.

ego, Houston, Dallas–Fort Worth, Tampa, Miami, and Atlanta all showed better than fourfold increases. New Orleans grew slowest, but even this Sunbelt laggard more than doubled its size (Tables 1.2 and 1.3).[11]

Why have these metropolitan areas experienced such significant population growth? Some of the reasons are intangible and some overlap, so it is not easy to identify with precision just why these areas grew so rapidly, but four influences stand out: defense spending (especially that generated by World War II), other federal outlays, a favorable business climate, and an attractive quality of life. Certain sections of the region have also benefited from other economic activities, notably oil and gas exploitation in Texas, Oklahoma, and Louisiana; the building of retirement centers in Florida and Arizona; and the emergence of the recreation and tourism industries in Southern California, Florida, New Orleans, and Las Vegas. These factors and others have combined to make the Sunbelt attractive to migratory individuals and to the companies that employ them. In fact, across the southern rim of the United States, economic opportunities snowballed (pardon the expression) as postwar migrants moved westward and southward.

A common theme that runs through these twelve case studies, especially San Diego and Los Angeles, is the positive impact of World War II on metropolitan growth. Federal defense policy before the war had not been especially favorable to the South and the West when it came to the allocation of military installations and the letting of contracts for weaponry and other hardware. Most bases, and to an even greater extent most production contracts, had gone to the great industrial areas of the Northeast and Midwest. With war clouds overhead, however, the armed forces made deliberate efforts to relocate their personnel and training facilities around the country and to spread out defense contracts in order to make bombing and even invasion more difficult for the enemy.

The South and the West were the big winners in this policy shift. Warm weather coastal cities became centers of naval construction and land-based operations, causing such places as Mobile, San Diego, and Tampa to suddenly overflow with shipbuilders and sailors. Mobile, wrote John Dos Passos in 1943, looked like "a city that's been taken by storm." Inland cities of the South and Southwest offered wide-open spaces for ground force training and airplane production and maintenance and clear skies for airplane testing and flight training. New Orleans, Atlanta, Fort Worth, Oklahoma City, San Antonio, Albuquerque, and Phoenix were among the many locales to prosper thanks to the construction of aircraft production facilities and the location or expansion of military bases.[12]

It was the cities of the South and the West that experienced the greatest in-migrations as a result of the war effort. Between 1940 and 1943 defense contractors issued calls for massive numbers of new workers, and the military inducted and trained its first waves of fighting men. In those early war years the metropolitan counties of the South grew by 3.9 percent and those in the West expanded by 2.7 percent. In contrast, such areas in the North Central section were up by only 2 percent, and the metropolitan counties of the Northeast actually suffered a net loss of .6 percent.[13]

Immediately after the war, most of these burgeoning centers suffered predictable economic downturns, but usually only briefly. Military spending slowed down, but it certainly did not stop. One journalist remarked that only increasing cold war expenditures saved San Diego "from the ravages of peace."[14] Much the same could be said about San Antonio and to a lesser extent about most of the cities of the Sunbelt. Today Lockheed in Atlanta and General Dynamics in Fort Worth produce military aircraft in old World War II factories. In Oklahoma City the air force absorbed the wartime Douglas bomber facilities into Tinker Field, the primary installation for upkeep and modification of B-52s. In New Orleans NASA took over a big war plant. Through the efforts of southern, and to a lesser extent western, congressmen, the Sunbelt has continued to garner far more than its proportional share of defense dollars.

In 1980, Richard S. Morris, a New York City–based political consultant and writer, called the Pentagon "a five-sided building that faces South." He argued that

> the entire Sun Belt is incredibly dependent on defense dollars for its economic growth and survival. Without the defense budget, the Sun Belt simply could not sustain the economic boom of which it has boasted for the past decade. . . . The northeastern states, with 45 percent of America's people, get only 28 percent of the national defense spending while the states of the Sun Belt [including Virginia and all of California] with 38 percent of the population get almost half of the national defense budget.[15]

A recent study prepared by Employment Research Associates of Lansing, Michigan, quantified the drain on the Northeast and Midwest at $27 billion per year. They reported that while the Pentagon spent only $44 billion in the Frostbelt the region contributed over $70 billion in taxes toward the military budget. Defense spending, the report concluded, "is by far the most important factor in accounting for the now massive shift of resources from the Northeast and Midwest to the South and West."[16]

Nondefense federal spending has also stimulated Sunbelt development, although in this case the region's relative advantage vis-à-vis the Frostbelt is less pronounced. A 1976 article in the limited-circulation but influential *National Journal* clearly delineated the Sunbelt's advantages in federal allocations, including defense. The article's conclusions sparked such a hot debate between congressional, academic, and economic spokesmen of the two sections that *Business Week* labeled the exchange "The Second War between the States."[17]

The ten-year-old Southern Growth Policies Board has carried the Sunbelt banner in this war. Located in Research Triangle Park near Raleigh, North Carolina, the board supplies southern policy makers with statistical information and other reports about how economic development can best be promoted and how states of the region can best profit from federal policy. In 1976 Frostbelt congressmen escalated the war with the organization of a caucus called the Northeast-Midwest Economic Advancement Coalition. These northeastern and midwestern congressmen had been shaken from their complacency when they realized that a seemingly innocuous bill, for which most of them had voted, would shift millions of dollars to the Sunbelt by using annually updated population figures in grant allocations. The goal of the caucus was to redirect federal funds back to the North, and it gained its first victory in a 1977 revision of the funding formula for the Community Development Block Grant program. The Northeast-Midwest Institute supports the caucus with research and reports. Further Frostbelt successes, including some in the crucial area of defense contract awards, inspired southern and western congressmen in 1981 to form their own group called the Sun Belt Council.[18]

A 1981 update of *National Journal*'s original study revealed that the Frostbelt had indeed made inroads. The Sunbelt advantages found in fiscal year 1979 were "generally less" than they had been in fiscal 1975. However, the authors found that the Pentagon's love for the Sunbelt had not lessened, for "most of the inequities" that did remain between the regions could be traced to defense spending. Northeastern and midwestern members of Congress are worried now, however, because they not only face a better-organized Sunbelt bloc, but they must also contend with President Ronald Reagan's two-pronged approach of increased defense outlays and reduced social spending, which threatens to accentuate the Sunbelt's advantage in receiving federal largess.[19]

Although offering advantages to all sections of the country, some federal spending programs have proved especially helpful to the South and Southwest. Interstate highway construction and urban redevelopment, for example, came into being at a time that was crucial in the development of Sunbelt cities. The age of massive growth in most of the locales coincided with the age of the superhighway. The creation of these primary transportation routes with huge federal subsidies encouraged the outward sprawl of these cities as residential subdivisions, regional shopping malls, industrial parks, and office centers clustered around the off-ramps of the interstate legs and perimeters. These superhighways have solidified the regional leadership of such metropolises as Altanta, Dallas, and Phoenix by routing more people and products through these cities. But they have had the simultaneous effect of hastening the relative decline of the central business districts.

Urban redevelopment programs also arrived at an opportune time for cities such as Atlanta, Tampa, New Orleans, and Oklahoma City, which wanted desperately to build impressive downtowns, civic centers, stadiums, and universities that would signify their rising national importance. In Fort Worth, Dallas, and San Diego conservative civic leaders were troubled enough by their antihandout principles to drag their feet in the race for federal funding. Other Sunbelt leaders also distrusted these programs at first, fearing the strings that Washington attached to them. Most, however, soon came to welcome and seek them as effective means for enhancing business opportunities in the hearts of their communities.

Other federal programs stand out as important stimulants in particular examples. Without federal assistance, for example, Atlanta could not have built its impressive rapid rail transit system. The establishment of the Johnson Space Flight Center south of Houston and the location of the Federal Aviation Administration's training center in Oklahoma City illustrate how federal spending can boost local economies and images. Federal regional offices are especially important to Atlanta and Albuquerque. Without Social Security and other government retirement programs, the booms in Miami, Tampa–St. Petersburg, and Phoenix would probably have been smaller. In short, through a combination of deliberate redistributive policy, political clout, and plain happenstance, the Sunbelt owes much of its rise to money from Washington.

A third reason for the Sunbelt explosion is that amorphous but very real asset known as "a good business climate." State and local governments in the Sunbelt, especially in the South, have been willing, indeed anxious, to pass legislation that is designed to cut the costs and improve the efficiency of doing business. For example, South Carolina has constructed highways to serve new industrial sites; Texas has hamstrung efforts to limit the influx of cheap Mexican workers; California has established the nation's most elaborate system of junior colleges, including many with industrial training programs. The states and many localities have offered tax concessions to businesses seeking new locations. Some have used public financing to erect facilities that industry could lease on favorable terms. Although most studies have shown that such incentives are seldom the crucial factor in business site location, they are symptomatic of generally cooperative and supportive governments. Sunbelt states, with the partial exception of California, usually promise a bare minimum of governmental interference with the conduct of business, and some even offer to help cut through federal red tape. Sometimes states waive their already minimal environmental protection rules in order to attract industry. Area technical schools often offer start-up training tailored to the needs of new firms.

The Sunbelt's lower rate of unionization appeals to cost-conscious executives. Given the individualistic cultural heritage of much of the region, unionization rates might be low even without legal discouragement; but all of the states of the region except New Mexico, Oklahoma, and California have right-to-work laws. In recent years, the national rate of unionization has hovered at just under 30 percent of the nonagricultural work force, but in many Sunbelt states it is less than half that.[20]

Given this type of environment, it is little wonder that an article in *Fortune* could declare, "Business Loves the Sunbelt (and Vice-Versa)." John S. Hekman, University of North Carolina economist, put it succinctly. "In terms of the often-mentioned Sunbelt-Frostbelt competition for industry, the Southeast has been winning most of the battles."[21] Governments are generally cooperative and the costs of land, labor, and just about everything else are lower, especially in the Southeast. A number of researchers have attempted to quantify the advantages of a good business climate, and almost all have concluded that the Sunbelt rates high.

A 1975 survey by Fantus, the nation's largest industrial relocation assistance firm, listed seven Sunbelt states in the top dozen in terms of their business environment, and a 1981 study by Alexander Grant and Company for the Conference of State Manufacturers Associations ranked six Sunbelt states (Mississippi, South Carolina, North Carolina, Georgia, Arkansas, and Florida) in the highest twelve on the basis of twenty-two business-climate factors. Two geography professors quantified twenty business-climate factors, and their findings correlated highly with the Fantus and Grant rankings. "In general," they wrote, "the states placing in the lower two quartiles are found in the New England, Mid Atlantic, and North Central regions of the United States. With the exception of California, states ranking in the higher quartiles are generally in the South and West."[22] Even a report by the Northeast-Midwest Institute conceded that

> the Sunbelt undoubtedly enjoys an enviable reputation in business circles as being better suited to business needs than the Frostbelt. But perhaps more important than the pleasant lifestyle afforded by the "fun and sun" states is the attitude of local officials toward economic development. The South and West work hard to attract prospective newcomers to the business community. Until recently, the Northeast and Midwest appeared to shun such an aggressive stance.[23]

An official of Georgia's Department of Industry and Trade put it concisely, "The Sunbelt is not sunshine. It's an attitude . . . conducive to business. The North has lost that attitude."[24]

For the most part, studies reveal that the Sunbelt's growth has been due to the creation of new jobs rather than the pirating of firms directly from the Frostbelt. The results, however, are essentially the same: The Northeast and Midwest lose jobs and the Sunbelt gains. Firm closings are about equal in the two belts, but the birth of new companies and branch operations is much more frequent in the Sunbelt.[25]

A combination of state and local agencies and nongovernmental organizations carries out the task of spreading the good word about the Sunbelt to the nation's business leaders. At first the old families of New Orleans and the "geranium" forces in San Diego moved cautiously, but everywhere else the growth ethic, personified in the Chambers of Commerce, predominated. The Atlanta chamber's Forward Atlanta campaign of the 1960s was so effective that dozens of other cities sent observers to copy the Gate City's methods. In Dallas the Chamber of Commerce shares credit with the even more elite Citizens Council for cementing Big D's regional hegemony over merchandising and manufacturing. The Phoenix chamber sold Motorola on the desert city's assets of transportation, education, business climate, and warm weather. Few boosters could match the efforts of the Oklahoma City Chamber of Commerce, which not only instigated and carried out a major industrial and commercial development program, but also guided city hall through the nation's most ambitious municipal annexation program and a huge downtown redevelopment project.

When talking with industrial executives, Sunbelt boosters have been able to stress not only the superiority of their business climates but also the fourth major factor in the growth of the Sunbelt: the region's quality of life. As Biggar put it in her *Population Bulletin* article, "The Sunbelt offers both more 'sun' and more 'fun.' Outdoor living, informal entertaining, and golf the year round—all afford the new lifestyles which Americans have adopted."[26] For the more serious-minded potential migrant, the Sunbelt cities now offer a wide variety of educational, cultural, and entertainment facilities that rival those of the North. Over the last three decades state governments have either established or greatly expanded universities in each of the twelve metropolitan areas represented here. Symphonies, legitimate theaters, and even opera companies abound. At the end of World War II, big-league sports were confined to the Frostbelt; but by the 1970s local boosters had brought major franchises in baseball, football, and/or basketball to ten Sunbelt towns beginning with the Dodgers' celebrated trek to Los Angeles. These activities complement the Sunbelt's two preexisting specialties: stock car racing in the Southeast and college football everywhere.

Life in the Sunbelt can be not only more pleasant but also just about as remunerative. Between 1970 and 1979, every Sunbelt state increased its per capita income more rapidly than the national average. According to one Bureau of Labor Statistics economist, the South, which had the country's lowest per capita income (some 25 percent below the national average in 1950), had reached parity in *real* income by 1975. Actual income still lagged, but considering the lower cost of living in the region, the statistically average southerner had reached a standard of living comparable to that of the east of the nation.[27] Areas of prosperity like the Florida peninsula, most of Texas, and metro Atlanta help the southern figures. Problems persist and poverty lingers in many Sunbelt spots, but the strides in income and other quality-of-life indexes have been immense.

The southern renaissance, Texas chic, and the flowering attractions of the Southern California hot-tub lifestyle have demonstrated their appeal to both business executives and rank-and-file white- and blue-collar workers. The best-selling out-of-town newspapers in Detroit in 1981 were the Sunday *Houston Chronicle*, the *Dallas Morning News*, and the *San Antonio Light*, all filled with employment listings. Houston radio station KILT solicited listeners from among the ex-Mo-town residents by proclaiming, "If you're from Detroit . . . you've found your station in Houston."[28]

Occasionally North-to-Sunbelt migrants yearn for a return to the snow ("I miss the change of seasons down here"), but generally southern and western residents are more pleased with their environments than those who live in the Frostbelt. One survey discovered that between 21 and 31 percent of the people in the Northeast and Midwest desired to live elsewhere, but in the regions that include the Sunbelt fewer than 20 percent wanted to move.[29]

Recent detractors have insisted that the quality of life is worsening in the Sunbelt at a rate commensurate with the in-migration of millions of newcomers. More people mean more crime, and violent crime certainly does pose a serious actual and image problem for Miami, New Orleans, Houston, and Atlanta. Air pollution, long the scourge of Los Angeles, now afflicts Houston, New Orleans, Phoenix, and even Oklahoma City, "where the wind comes sweeping down the plains." Higher energy costs are making air conditioning more and more expensive, and refrigerated air, as a number of essays to follow indicate, was instrumental in making Sunbelt life bearable for many transplanted northerners. Severe water shortages threaten the western half of the belt. Ironically, the great gains made by the Sunbelt have actually reduced some of its attractiveness to business. By the end of the decade, Bernard L. Weinstein of the University of Texas at Dallas and the Southern Growth Policies Board predicted in 1981, "The South will no longer be able to market itself on the basis of cheap labor, inexpensive housing, and lower living costs." In mid 1982 the *New York Times*, whose February 1976 series was influential in building up the Sunbelt image, published a six-part litany of Sunbelt problems. *Newsweek* ran a long article about the "Dark Side of the Sun Belt," and *U.S. News* reported that "Job Hunting in the Sun Belt [had become] a Fool's Errand for Many."[30]

Indeed the Sunbelt boom cannot last forever at the frenzied pace set since the close of World War II. But those who would dismiss the region's real advantages are acting rashly. Most of the recent negative accounts of Sunbelt life compare the region with its own halcyon days, not with the Frostbelt. The editor of the Southern Growth Policies Board's Commission on the Future of the South report explained that "these detriments are not expected to end growth but, rather, to slow down its momentum."[31] David C. Perry, coeditor of *The Rise of the Sunbelt Cities*, was probably premature when he remarked recently that "the bloom is off the rose." The climate, despite the record-setting heat of the summer of 1980 and the bone-chilling (by Sunbelt standards) cold of January 1982, will remain a drawing card as anyone who has spent a winter in Milwaukee will attest. As one former Chicago resident said of her move to Sunbelt California, "It always seems like one beautiful August."[32] The housing stock is newer, and the people really are friendlier along the southern rim. The beaches are still sandy, and the lifestyle is still more relaxed. The major tourist attractions—Disney World and Disneyland, Busch Gardens, Stone Mountain, Bourbon Street, the Las Vegas strip, the Grand Ole Opry, and, of course, the Alamo—are not going to move.

In March 1982 Professor Hekman surveyed the managers of 204 new or recently expanded firms in three states and asked them to rank the factors in the site choices. State and local industrial climate ranked first. He predicted that the regional cost and attitude advantages would persist and that "the trend in the near-to-immediate future would appear to be for a continuation of high investment in the Sunbelt." Hekman noted that many observers "have voiced concern, that the movement of industry to the Southeast will of itself eliminate the very advantages that brought it there, for example, by driving up wages and producing congested urban areas." But he dismissed such concerns by saying, "There is little or no evidence for this so far."[33]

The Sunbelt can now build on its own history. Federal spending for defense and other purposes combined with a hospitable business climate and an attractive quality of life to create the boom, but now it has a momentum of its own. "Economic growth in the Sunbelt," Weinstein declared, "has become self-sustaining as a result of growing markets and broadening industrial base."[34] To be sure, growth will be spotty and will have its ups and downs with the national economy. Growth will not be uniform throughout the region, and it never has been. Real differences will continue to exist between the Southeast and the Southwest, and Texoma will continue to be a blend of the two. But all indications are that for the rest of the century the factors that fashioned the Sunbelt phenomenon after World War II will continue to give the region relative advantages over the Frostbelt.

What have been the political consequences of the historic rise of the Sunbelt? At the national level, one obvious consequence is the region's gain in the House of Representatives and thereby in the electoral college. As a result of the 1980 census, the Sunbelt gained eleven seats in Congress while the industrial Northeast and Midwest lost seventeen. Such a transfer of power does not portend well for Northeast-Midwest efforts to redirect federal spending. Every man elected to the presidency since 1964 has come from the Sunbelt (in 1964 and 1980, both major candidates came from that region) and few have shown much sympathy for the Frostbelt as a region. The power shift is discouraging news for the Democratic party and American liberalism. More conservative than the rest of the nation since the days of Reconstruction, the South, including Texas and Oklahoma, has become ever more Republican. This conversion is due only in part to the influx of the type of people most likely to vote Republican, namely white middle- and upper-class suburbanites tired of northern state and city social programs. It is also the result of a significant crossover of longtime southern Democrats unhappy about their party's stands on civil rights, welfare, and defense. The West too is more conservative than the Northeast and Midwest, or at least it has been for the past decade or more. Southern California and Arizona are hotbeds of right-wing Republicanism, and in the past few years New Mexico has shown tendencies in that direction. But whether conservatives remain in the Democratic party as "boll weevils" or transfer their allegiance to the Reagan-controlled Republicans, they will certainly oppose liberal spending and endorse greater funding for the military installations located along the nation's southern rim. Similarly, at the state level, Republican strength should hold firm in the far Southwest and grow in the states from New Mexico eastward, though the process of conversion should continue to be much slower than at the national level.[35]

The essays that follow, however, concentrate not on national or state politics but on the impact of postwar growth upon the political developments within each metropolitan area. Certainly each city has had its own unique characteristics and personalities that have shaped many local issues, but some important common features stand out when the cities are examined as a whole.

During the late 1940s, both political and economic power in the cities under consideration rested substantially in the hands of cliques of central city–oriented businessmen. They effectively dominated or circumvented the politicians in city hall and were generally unthreatened by the politically impotent minority groups within the city. Government officials in outlying areas were sometimes troublesome, but suburbanization in the Sunbelt had not advanced to the point that these people could seriously challenge the existing political order. The elites did not always get their way, but they were undoubtedly the driving force in community decision making. In the archetypical city of Dallas, the chief executive officers of the main firms formed the Citizens Council, which planned and carried out an agenda for the entire populace. In Houston it was the 8-F Crowd; in Oklahoma City it was the Chamber of Commerce; in Atlanta it was the group that Floyd Hunter dubbed "the power structure." In New Orleans and Tampa the business elites had to contend with entrenched political machines, but they managed to reach accommodations that acquiesced in the machines' control of patronage in exchange for an agreement that the machines would not disrupt business activities.

In some cities this old guard got too complacent with politics as usual, and young entrepreneurs and professionals in the old-fashioned good-government tradition organized to get politics back on track. The reformers, however, did not question the assumption that downtown business interests should set the agenda for the metropolis. They merely sought honest and efficient politics to carry it out. On the crucial subject of economic growth, they often proved to be "more royal than the king." Their cries for industrial development were often those of men on the make rather than those who had it made. The goal of such groups as the Phoenix Charter Government Committee (Barry Goldwater's first political base), the San Antonio Good Government League, and Oklahoma City's Association for Responsible Government was not to challenge rule by business clique but to improve the policy-making process by broadening the elite circle to include themselves.

Whereas these businessmen-reformer-politician alliances did not fundamentally change power structure rule, real and effective challenges did emerge in most of these twelve metropolitan areas. In none of these metropolises do the downtown commercial-banking-professional elites retain the preeminent position they once occupied, although they remain much more powerful in some communities than in others. The two main causes of this political transformation have been the fragmentation of the metropolitan areas into dozens of autonomous governmental units and the rising influence of minority and neighborhood politics. In these ways the Sunbelt cities are becoming more like their many Frostbelt counterparts, which have long faced ethnic politics and suburban strangulation.

The first of these serious challenges—suburban political influence—occurs when the central city is unable to capture peripheral growth within its corporate limits. Sometimes preexisting governments such as counties or formerly rural towns assert authority. In other instances, suburbanites create new governmental units to serve their needs. This fragmentation effectively prevents one group of central city leaders from controlling the destiny of the entire metropolis. The presence of a host of governments (municipalities, counties, special districts, metropolitan councils of governments, and similar agencies) diffuses power throughout the metropolitan areas. Sometimes the cost of government is increased, and always public planning is complicated and public responsibility is obscured. The visions of the downtown promoters are no longer those of the organic city.

As a rule, however, Sunbelt cities have not been as plagued by the multiplicity of governmental units as have the cities of the Northeast. With some exceptions, notably Atlanta and Miami, these central cities tend to contain a relatively high percentage of total SMSA population. In Houston, San Antonio, Albuquerque, and Phoenix, annexation has been so successful that the core cities actually have larger populations than the outlying areas. In Oklahoma City, San Diego, and New Orleans the principal municipalities approach half of the metropolitan total (Table 1.2). From the viewpoint of central city power forces, annexation best solves the problems of suburbanization because it increases the city's tax base by including fringe construction within the city's boundaries and because it truncates potential political opposition that often flows from suburban autonomy. When annexation has failed for legal or political reasons, some Sunbelt cities have worked out fairly effective intergovernmental arrangements capable of handling many common problems. Miami and Dade County have a unique sharing arrangement. The Lakewood Plan allows Los Angeles County to influence its munici- palities through the sale of service packages on a contract basis. The predecessor agency to the present Atlanta Regional Commission was the nation's first publicly supported, areawide planning agency. Even when such cooperative arrangements move toward solving im- portant service-delivery and planning problems, they reflect a shar- ing of power that was once virtually unknown to the elites of many Sunbelt cities.

The second serious assault on old-line business leadership has come mainly from within the central cities themselves. Minority politics and neighborhood power are fairly new to the Sunbelt, al- though aspects of these struggles have their roots in the nineteenth century. Prior to World War II, the electorates of these cities were ethnically homogeneous even if their populations were not. In fact, blacks and/or Hispanics have long constituted significant segments of the populations of all of the cities studied here except Oklahoma City (Table 1.4). Generally speaking, the larger the size of the minor- ity population the harder the dominant whites worked to keep it ex- cluded. Georgia and Texas utilized the white primary to prevent blacks from casting ballots in the Democratic primaries, the only races that really mattered in the solid South. Direct and indirect, legal and illegal pressures kept black and Mexican-American voters away from the polls. Many cities diluted minority voting strength through at-large elections in which votes from the segregated neigh- borhoods were overwhelmed in the citywide totals that actually chose the mayors and councils. The end of such restrictions has af- fected politics in all the Sunbelt cities and has literally reshaped it in some. The court-ordered end of the white primary in the late 1940s was the beginning. Early civil-rights legislation helped some more. But the significant changes came with the Voting Rights Act of 1965 and its 1975 amendments that protected Spanish-speaking voters. Sometimes under political pressure and other times under legal compulsion, the Sunbelt cities have ended or limited at-large voting, so minority candidates now often win election to city councils and other governing boards. Southern cities are probably still years away from a situation like that in Los Angeles where a black mayor can rule without race being the pervasive issue, but in the Negro major- ity municipalities of New Orleans and Atlanta blacks have been elected. Hispanics serve as mayors in San Antonio and Miami. In the latter whites play only a minor role in the power struggles between Cubans, blacks, and Puerto Ricans.

TABLE 1.4. Black and Hispanic Percentages of the Populations of Major Metropolitan Areas in the Sunbelt: SMSAs, Central Cities, and Outlying Areas, 1940–1980[a]

Metropolitan Area	% Black					% Hispanic[b]	
	1940	1950	1960	1970	1980	1970	1980
Southeast							
Atlanta							
SMSA	29.3	24.6	22.8	22.3	24.6	1.0	1.2
City of Atlanta	34.6	36.6	38.3	51.3	66.6	1.0	1.4
Outlying area	17.8	13.0	8.5	6.2	13.5	1.0	1.1
Miami							
SMSA	17.7	13.1	14.7	15.0	17.2	23.6	35.7
City of Miami	21.4	16.2	22.4	22.7	25.1	45.4	55.9
Outlying area	9.4	10.0	11.2	12.2	15.1	15.8	30.3
Tampa–St. Petersburg							
SMSA	18.2	13.9	11.5	10.2	9.3	5.4	5.1
City of Tampa	21.5	21.9	16.8	20.0	23.5	14.5	13.3
City of St. Petersburg	19.7	14.4	13.3	14.8	17.2	1.1	1.8
Outlying area	7.0	8.3	5.8	4.4	3.9	3.0	3.7
New Orleans							
SMSA	29.0	29.1	30.8	31.0	32.6	4.2	4.1
City of New Orleans	30.1	31.9	37.2	45.0	55.3	4.4	3.4
Outlying area	16.4	15.4	14.1	12.3	12.6	4.0	4.6
Texoma							
Dallas–Fort Worth							
SMSA	14.8	12.6	13.0	14.2	14.1	5.7	8.4
City of Dallas	17.1	13.1	19.0	24.9	29.4	7.5	12.3
City of Fort Worth	14.2	13.2	15.8	19.9	22.8	7.9	12.6
Outlying area	9.8	10.9	4.9	3.8	3.9	3.5	5.3
Houston							
SMSA	19.8	18.5	19.8	19.3	18.2	9.9	14.6
City of Houston	22.4	20.9	22.9	25.7	27.6	11.3	17.6
Outlying area	11.6	11.6	10.3	8.8	6.7	7.7	11.0
San Antonio							
SMSA	6.5	6.5	6.6	6.9	6.8	43.8	44.9
City of San Antonio	7.6	7.0	7.1	7.6	7.3	51.4	53.7
Outlying area	2.5	4.2	3.7	4.5	5.3	20.1	20.8
Oklahoma City[c]							
SMSA	8.9	8.0	8.0	8.5	9.0	1.7	2.2
City of							
Oklahoma City	9.5	8.6	11.6	13.7	14.6	2.0	2.8
Outlying area	1.7	6.1	1.9	1.6	3.8	1.4	1.7

TABLE 1.4 (continued)

Metropolitan Area	1940	1950	% Black 1960	1970	1980	% Hispanic[b] 1970	1980
Southwest							
Los Angeles–Long Beach[d]							
SMSA	2.6	5.0	6.9	10.8	12.6	17.0	27.6
City of Los Angeles	4.2	8.7	13.5	17.9	17.0	17.1	27.5
City of Long Beach	0.4	1.7	2.8	5.3	11.3	6.0	14.0
Outlying area	0.9	2.0	3.1	6.2	9.6	17.9	28.9
San Diego[e]							
SMSA	1.7	3.1	3.8	4.6	5.6	11.0	14.8
City of San Diego	2.0	4.5	6.0	7.6	8.9	10.7	14.9
Outlying area	0.3	1.0	1.1	1.4	2.7	11.4	14.7
Phoenix							
SMSA	5.2	4.3	4.0	3.4	3.2	13.3	13.2
City of Phoenix	6.5	4.9	4.8	4.8	4.8	12.7	14.8
Outlying area	3.6	4.1	2.2	1.3	1.4	14.1	11.4
Albuquerque[f]							
SMSA	1.2	1.1	0.9	2.1	2.2	39.2	36.1
City of Albuquerque	1.5	1.3	0.9	2.2	2.5	34.9	33.8
Outlying area	0.9	0.8	1.1	1.8	1.4	42.8	42.5

[a]For boundary explanation see Table 1.2 and chapter 1, note 11.

[b]Hispanic data for SMSAs are unavailable for years prior to 1970. The 1970 figures are for Spanish-speaking people, but the 1980 ones are for people with Spanish origins (self-defined in each case), and thus the two columns are not exactly parallel.

[c]According to the 1980 U.S. Census category, the Oklahoma City population includes American Indians, Eskimos, and Aleuts in the following percentages: SMSA, 3.0; central city, 2.6; and outlying area, 3.3. Virtually all of these figures represent American Indians.

[d]According to the 1980 U.S. Census category, the Los Angeles–Long Beach population includes Asians and Pacific Islanders (primarily Japanese, Chinese, and Filipinos) in the following percentages: SMSA, 5.8; city of Los Angeles, 6.6; city of Long Beach, 5.4; and outlying area, 5.3.

[e]According to the 1980 U.S. Census category, the San Diego population includes Asians and Pacific Islanders (primarily Japanese, Chinese, and Filipinos) in the following percentages: SMSA, 4.8; central city, 6.5; and outlying area, 3.3.

[f]According to the 1980 U.S. Census category, the Albuquerque population includes American Indians, Eskimos, and Aleuts in the following percentages: SMSA, 4.6; central city, 2.2; and outlying area, 11.0. Virtually all of these figures represent American Indians.

Not all neighborhood politics are ethnic or racial in nature. City residents, often in alliance with planning professionals, have worked to preserve in-town communities from highways, high rises, and high density office and commercial development. Fear of such encroachment led neighborhood groups in San Diego to resist a series of redevelopment ideas. In Atlanta they stopped construction on two major limited-access highways even after right-of-way acquisition had begun. In New Orleans they blocked a river-front expressway. Controlled-growth advocates with neighborhood bases in Albuquerque elected a one-term mayor. Neighborhoods of all races and ethnic groups have often functioned as veto groups for the grand ideas of the downtown elite.

Taken as a whole, these two big challenges have caused varying degrees of change in metropolitan politics. Three broad categories of impact are evident. In Atlanta, Miami, New Orleans, and San Antonio, suburbs or minorities (or combinations thereof) have been relatively effective in challenging the business elite for political control of the metropolitan destiny. The dichotomy between economic and political power in these places means that decision making must be shared. In the second group—Los Angeles, Houston, Tampa, Dallas, San Diego, and Albuquerque—challengers have arisen and have won some significant victories and concessions, but the forces of neighborhood and fringe have not yet upset the power establishments. The movements for change have had the least impact in Oklahoma City, Fort Worth, and Phoenix. In these areas, downtown Chamber of Commerce leaders still call most of the shots. Once in a while suburban officials and minority group spokesmen will fire telling blasts, but the elite's armor remains intact.

In the long run, the newer cities of the Sunbelt will age and will probably come more to resemble their older northern counterparts in many aspects of growth and politics. But during the period from 1945 to 1981, the historical development of the Sunbelt cities has been significantly different from that of the sluggish metropolitan areas of most of the Frostbelt. Sunbelt cities have served as the spearheads of a significant transformation of American regionalism. Fred Hofheinz, former mayor of Houston, stated it best: "People have been saying for years that the South and Southwest are frontiers of the new industrial America, where people can still reach the American dream. This is the new Detroit, the new New York. This is where the action is."[36]

NOTES

1. Large SMSAs exceeding 40 percent growth (when adjusted for boundary change) are Austin, Houston, and McAllen, Texas; Daytona, Ft. Lauderdale, Tampa, Orlando, and West Palm Beach, Florida; Phoenix and Tucson, Arizona; Las Vegas, Nevada; and Oxnard and Santa Rosa, California. Santa Rosa would be in a loosely defined Sunbelt but is not within the definition used here.

2. Kevin Phillips, *The Emerging Republican Majority* (New Rochelle, N.Y.: Arlington House, 1969); *New York Times*, 8–12 February 1976; Gurney Breckenfield, "Business Loves the Sunbelt (and Vice-Versa)," *Fortune* 95 (June 1977): 133ff.; "The Second War between the States," *Business Week*, 17 May 1976, 82ff.; Horace Sutton, "Sunbelt vs. Frostbelt: A Second Civil War?" *Saturday Review* 5 (15 April 1978): 28–37; "A New Milestone in the Shift ot the Sunbelt," *Nation's Business* 65 (May 1977): 69.

3. Clyde E. Browning and Wil Gesler, "Sun Belt-Snow Belt: A Case of Sloppy Regionalizing," *Professional Geographer* 31 (February 1979): 66, 74 (italics added).

4. Kirkpatrick Sale, *Power Shift: The Rise of the Southern Rim and Its Challenge to the Eastern Establishment* (New York: Random House, 1975), 11.

5. Breckenfield, "Business Loves the Sunbelt," 134–135; "Sunbelt: Contrasts in Growth," *Sales and Marketing Management* 121 (24 July 1978): A62; Bernard L. Weinstein and Robert E. Firestine, *Regional Growth and Decline in the United States: The Rise of the Sunbelt and the Decline of the Northeast* (New York: Praeger, 1978), 1; Jeanne C. Biggar, "The Sunning of America: Migration to the Sunbelt," *Population Bulletin* 34 (March 1979): 1–42; Thomas R. Dye, *Politics in States and Communities*, 4th ed. (Englewood Cliffs, N.J.: Prentice-Hall, Inc., 1981), 13; David C. Perry and Alfred J. Watkins, "People, Profit, and the Rise of the Sunbelt Cities," in David C. Perry and Alfred J. Watkins, eds., *The Rise of the Sunbelt Cities*, vol. 14, Urban Affairs Annual Reviews (Beverly Hills, Calif.: Sage Publishing Co., 1977), 277–305 (Memphis in the Sunbelt); Alfred J. Watkins, "Intermetropolitan Migration and the Rise of the Sunbelt," *Social Science Quarterly* 59 (December 1978): 553–661 (Memphis in the Northeast, i.e., Frostbelt).

6. Carl Abbott, "The American Sunbelt: Idea and Region," *Journal of the West* 18 (July 1979): 5–18; Carl Abbott, *The New Urban America: Growth and Politics in Sunbelt Cities* (Chapel Hill: The University of North Carolina Press, 1981), 33. Other historians have recently begun to pay attention to the Sunbelt phenomenon. See James C. Cobb, *The Selling of the South: The Southern Crusade for Industrial Development, 1936–1980* (Baton Rouge: Louisiana State University Press, 1982), especially chap. 7, "The Emergence of the Sunbelt South"; Charles N. Glaab and A. Theodore Brown, *A History of Urban America*, 3d ed. (New York: Macmillan Publishing Co., 1983), 346–350; David R. Goldfield, *Cotton Fields and Skyscrapers: Southern City and Region, 1607–1980* (Baton Rouge: Louisiana State University Press, 1982).

7. Sam Allis, "Regions," *Wall Street Journal*, 14 April 1981; Joel Garreau, *The Nine Nations of North America* (Boston: Houghton-Mifflin Co., 1981), 132, 141; "The Sun Belt Today," *Changing Times* (September 1981): 25–29. See also special Sunbelt issues of *Dissent* (Fall 1980) and *Texas Business Review* (March–April, 1980). Nicholas Lemann, "Searching for the Sunbelt," *Harper's* 264 (February 1982): 14–19 discusses how journalists have treated the Sunbelt.

8. Bob Gottlieb, "Place in the Sunbelt—Phoenix Growth Machine," *Nation*, 29 December 1979, 680–683; "A Sunbelt City Plays Catch-Up," *Business Week*, 6 March 1978, 69–70.

9. John S. Reed, "The Heart of Dixie: An Essay in Folk Geography," *Social Forces* 54 (June 1976): 925–939.

10. Bradley R. Rice, "Searching for the Sunbelt," *American Demographics* 3 (March 1981): 22–23. Cities with three or more listings not mentioned in the text included Phoenix (9); Tulsa (8); Austin, New Orleans (7); Jackson, San Antonio, Albuquerque (6); Birmingham, Ft. Worth (5); Los Angeles area (4); and El Paso, Memphis (3).

11. The 1940 and 1950 figures in this paragraph and in Tables 1.2 and 1.3 use the metropolitan definition in effect in 1950. For 1960, 1970, and 1980, the figures are for the populations within the boundaries of that year, unadjusted for the addition of more counties at later dates. The editors believe that the expansion of the metropolitan definitions by the periodic addition of counties to certain SMSAs is itself a measure of the expanding influence of the urban area, a fact that should be reflected in percentage increases. These figures will differ in some cases from those found in official census releases that standardize boundaries and from those used by some of the authors in this volume. In mid-1983 the Census Bureau redefined some metropolitan areas and redesignated them as MSA rather than SMSA. This book uses the pre-1983 definitions.

12. Rudolf Herberle, "The Impact of the War on Population Redistribution in the South," *Institute of Research and Training in the Social Sciences*, vol. 7, *Papers* (1945), 5–6.

13. Philip J. Funigiello, *The Challenge to Urban Liberalism: Federal-City Relations during World War II* (Knoxville: University of Tennessee Press, 1978), 12–13.

14. Neal R. Peirce, *The Pacific States of America: People, Politics and Power in the Five Pacific Basin States* (New York: W. W. Norton, 1972), 176.

15. Richard S. Morris, *Bum Rap on America's Cities* (Englewood Cliffs, N.J.: Prentice-Hall Inc., 1980), 147–148.

16. *Atlanta Constitution*, 11 May 1981, quoting Employment Research Associates.

17. Joel Havemann, Rochelle L. Stanfield, and Neal R. Peirce, "Federal Spending: The North's Loss Is the Sunbelt's Gain," *National Journal*, 26 June 1976, 878–891; "The Second War," *Business Week*; Sutton, "Sunbelt vs. Frostbelt."

18. Nick Taylor, "The Second Civil War," *Business Atlanta* 10 (November 1981): 38–42; *New York Times*, 2 November 1976. See Robert Jay

Dilger, *The Sunbelt/Snowbelt Controversy: The War over Federal Funds* (New York: New York University Press, 1982).

19. Joel Havemann and Rochelle L. Stanfield, "Neutral Federal Policies Are Reducing Frostbelt-Sunbelt Spending Imbalances," *National Journal*, 7 February 1981, 233–236. On the issue of Frostbelt concerns over Reagan's policies see *Atlanta Constitution*, 11 May 1981; *Atlanta Journal-Constitution*, 14 June, 26 July 1981; *Milwaukee Journal*, 14 January 1981; "The North Fights Back," *U.S. News and World Report*, 15 June 1981, 27. One government study commission recommended that federal policy should encourage migration to the Sunbelt and allow northern cities to decline. See "Burning Up the Snowbelt," *Time*, 12 January 1981, 19.

20. "No Welcome Mat for Unions in the Sunbelt," *Business Week*, 17 May 1976, 108–111; Alfred J. Watkins, "Good Business Climates, the Second War between the States," *Dissent* 27 (Fall 1980): 476–485; Breckenfield, "Business Loves the Sunbelt."

21. Breckenfield, "Business Loves the Sunbelt"; Jon S. Hekman, "What Are Businesses Looking For? A Survey of Industrial Firms in the South," *Economic Review* (Federal Reserve Bank of Atlanta) 67 (June 1982): 6–19.

22. James S. Fisher and Dean M. Hanink, "Business Climate: Behind the Geographic Shift of American Manufacturing," *Economic Review* (Federal Reserve Bank of Atlanta) 67 (June 1982): 20–31.

23. Jacqueline Mazza and Bill Hogan, *The State of the Region 1981: Economic Trends in the Northeast and Midwest* (Washington, D.C.: Northeast-Midwest Institute, [1980?]), 25.

24. Ibid.

25. Ibid., 15–17; "Studies Diverge on the Sunbelt's Economic Lure," *Nation's Cities* 16 (June 1978): 19; John Hekman and Alan Smith, "Behind the Sunbelt's Growth: Industrial Decentralization," *Economic Review* (Federal Reserve Bank of Atlanta) 67 (March 1982): 4–13.

26. Biggar, "The Sunning of America," 26.

27. Philip L. Rones, "Moving to the Sun: Regional Job Growth, 1968–1978," *Monthly Labor Review* 103 (March 1980): 17.

28. "Southward Ho for Jobs," *Time*, 11 May 1981, 23. Black workers have been among those attracted to Houston. See James H. Johnson and Walter C. Farrell, Jr., "Implications of the Black Move to the South," *Black Enterprise* 12 (January 1982): 21.

29. Rones, "Moving to the Sun," 18; Biggar, "The Sunning of America," 26.

30. "Worries on the Rise in the Sun Belt, Too," *U.S. News and World Report*, 15 June 1981, 31; *New York Times*, 5–10 July 1982; "Dark Side of the Sun Belt," *Newsweek*, 19 July 1982, 46–50; "Job Hunting in the Sun Belt: A Fool's Errand for Many," *U.S. News and World Report*, 19 April 1982, 103–104.

31. Pat Watters, "Southern Growth," *Atlanta* 21 (March 1982): 56.

32. "Worries on the Rise," *U.S. News and World Report*, 30 (quoting Perry); *New York Times*, 11 February 1976.

33. Hekman, "What Are Businesses Looking For?" 19.

34. Weinstein and Firestine, *Regional Growth and Decline*, 28.

35. For some examples see Alan Ehrenhalt, "Growth, Diversity Re-shape Sun Belt's Politics," *Congressional Quarterly Weekly Report*, 23 January 1982, 107–113. Reapportionment did not help the Republicans in 1982. Of the seventeen House seats shifted, the Democrats made a net gain of three.

36. *New York Times*, 9 February 1976.

2

ATLANTA
IF DIXIE WERE ATLANTA

by Bradley R. Rice

I have never been able to sing "Dixie." I cannot sing "Dixie" because to me Dixie means all the segregation, discrimination, exploitation, brutality, and lynchings endured for centuries by black people. . . . If Dixie were Atlanta or Atlanta were Dixie, I could sing "Dixie." Not that Atlanta is what it ought to be or what it could and must be, but because Atlanta has come a long way. . . . I know from my wide travels that Atlanta is not the typical South. It is better.—Benjamin E. Mays, retired president of Morehouse College and the Atlanta School Board

From its beginning in 1842 as the spot from which the state-financed railroad to Chattanooga would be built, Atlanta has entertained visions of greatness. In 1847 boosters coined the name Atlanta (feminine of Atlantic) to overcome the provincial sound of the earlier names: Terminus and Marthasville.

Since those early days, boosterism in Atlanta has gone through four stages. The first goal was to become the leading city of the state—to capture vitality and growth from the port city of Savannah and transfer it to the Piedmont railroad town. Sherman's destruction of Atlanta in 1864 was only a minor setback to this objective. The Yankee general himself returned to the city some fifteen years later, observed the phoenix-like resurgence, and declared, "The same reason which caused me to destroy Atlanta will make it a great city in the future." In 1868 Atlanta became the state capital, and before the turn of the century it ranked as Georgia's largest city.[1]

Not satisfied with being the state's preeminent community, Atlanta's second goal was to become the metropolis of the South. The city of 75,000 celebrated its considerable progress toward this end in the great Cotton States and International Exposition of 1895. With much hullabaloo and considerable exaggeration, the exposition hailed the creed of the New South and proclaimed Atlanta as the capital of the emerging section. Boosters sought to solidify and advance their regional city status with the ambitious Forward Atlanta campaign sponsored by the Chamber of Commerce in the mid 1920s.

Shortly after World War II, Atlanta celebrated its centennial as an incorporated municipality and entered its third stage of boosterism. Business leaders were no longer content for Atlanta to remain a mere regional city. They wanted Atlanta to become a metropolitan entity of national impact, and by the end of the 1960s Atlanta clearly had arrived as a national city complete with big-league sports. The visionaries of never-ending growth then looked to the future and dubbed Atlanta "the world's next great city." If boosters are as dedicated to this fourth goal as they were to the previous three, the prediction may become more than Chamber of Commerce puffery.

These changing economic stages forced political adaptation. For twenty-five years a business elite dominated Atlanta politics with policies of economic expansion and racial moderation, but since about 1970 the influence of this power structure has been on the decline. The elite has had to share control of metropolitan destiny with assertive central-city blacks and dozens of growing suburban jurisdictions.

Atlanta's economy, like that of other Sunbelt cities, received a significant boost from the Second World War. Founded in 1867, normally sleepy Fort McPherson on the southwest edge of town geared up as it had in two previous wars. Soon other installations ringed the city. In anticipation of wartime needs the army erected large brick warehouses and elaborate railroad switchyards on a 1,500-acre tract in Clayton County fifteen miles southeast of downtown. The enormous supply depot, now called Fort Gillem, opened just before the attack on Pearl Harbor. Meanwhile along Peachtree Road in the northeastern suburban fringe, the government utilized the site of a World War I camp to establish a naval air station and an army hospital. The army airfield, located next to the municipal airport since 1929, served as an important stopover point for military aircraft.

An estimated one hundred Atlanta firms dedicated their total output to the war effort, and dozens of others benefited less directly. Atlanta-born Coca-Cola and its bottlers, for example, distributed five billion Cokes to thirsty servicemen around the world. By far the most important single war industry in the area was the Bell bomber plant, located northwest of the city near the little Cobb County town of Marietta. By 1944 patronage on the Marietta interurban line had quadrupled to handle the nearly thirty thousand workers in the huge factory. By V-J Day the plant had produced seven hundred B-29s.

MAP 2.1. The Atlanta SMSA

General Motors had since 1928 operated a large assembly plant near the federal penitentiary in southeast Atlanta, and Ford had also maintained an Atlanta plant for a short while before the war; but the city's economy received a major boost shortly after the war when both auto giants decided to locate new manufacturing facilities in the Atlanta area. The GM plant was built in the Doraville area on the far northeast and the Ford installation was placed in Hapeville on the south side near the airport. By the late 1940s Ford employed over 2,300 workers and produced 350 cars per day in its Hapeville plant.

Although these and other production facilities provided about 53,000 jobs, manufacturing represented only 19 percent of the metropolitan work force in 1950. The community's greatest potential for growth lay in other sectors. Atlanta was, in the words of former governor Ellis Arnall, "the financial and wholesale and transportation capital of the South." The city's leading businessmen resolved to build upon that base. In 1944 they commissioned a major study of intrametropolitan transportation needs, and the resulting Lochner report served as the blueprint for street improvements and expressways for the next generation. Atlanta began major freeway construction well before massive federal aid became available in the late 1950s under the interstate highway program.

Intercity transportation facilities also benefited from postwar improvements. The railroads upgraded both passenger depots, Terminal Station and Union Station. At the end of the decade, 108 passenger and 164 freight trains served Atlanta each day. At the municipal airport the city utilized war surplus facilities and materials to erect a modern and efficient passenger terminal for only $270,000.[2]

Although Atlanta business and political leaders were pleased with the rapid economic growth of the area during and after World War II, they were disturbed by the fact that most of the population growth in the 1940s, as in the prewar decades, had occurred outside the corporate limits of the city. During the war decade the city added 29,000 residents for a 9.6 percent increase, but outside Atlanta the metro region gained about 200,000, resulting in an overall metro growth rate of 52 percent.

Until the 1930s Atlanta's municipal boundaries had grown in a fairly orderly manner with consistent annexation. Despite the existence of Decatur to the east and the tri-cities of College Park, East Point, and Hapeville to the south, Atlanta was not hemmed in by suburban municipalities. Most of the metropolitan growth was in unincorporated territory, especially in the affluent north Fulton County area broadly known as Buckhead. Atlanta thus appeared to have a wide field for annexation in its own Fulton County and in DeKalb County to the east, where the city had acquired about eight square miles in the 1920s. In fact, however, between 1930 and 1950 the city added less than three square miles for a total of thirty-seven.

Growing concern over the problems of tax inequity and service inefficiency led Atlanta, Fulton County, and the Atlanta Chamber of Commerce in 1938 to commission a comprehensive study of metropolitan governance. The report, conducted by Thomas H. Reed of the National Municipal League, concluded that the ideal situation would be "a new consolidated city and county . . . embracing all the *real* Atlanta and a reasonable margin for future growth." Recognizing, however, that such a plan was probably politically unacceptable, Reed made a series of more modest administrative suggestions. The Atlanta Chamber of Commerce backed Reed's "one government" recommendation, but a special study commission in 1940 declared that extensive annexation and some service consolidation was a more feasible alternative.

The leading advocate of annexation was Atlanta's mayor William B. Hartsfield. Although his motives were partially based on administrative efficiency and fiscal exigency, they were also political and racial in nature. He recognized that blacks would soon become a potent political force, and he wanted to capture as many white suburban voters within the city as possible. Throughout the 1940s he pushed hard to get the state legislature to authorize an annexation referendum in fashionable Buckhead; but in 1947 when the election finally came, the voters soundly rejected the proposal to join Atlanta. Some residents of Buckhead and surrounding areas preferred the low taxes and minimal services they received from Fulton County. Organized opposition, however, was centered in the Buckhead Fifty Club, which maintained that full city-county consolidation was the "only sane and sensible" plan.

Hartsfield's next move was to encourage the election of a proannexation slate to the Georgia General Assembly, but only one of his so-called Four Horsemen of Annexation won. Consequently by 1948 the forces supporting the expansion of Atlanta's city limits were at an impasse. On the one hand, authoritative study groups had dismissed city-county consolidation as wise but politically impossible; on the other hand, political forces outside the city had effectively killed all serious annexation moves. The Chamber of Commerce, then engaged in a Keep Atlanta Ahead promotion, feared that the debate between annexation and consolidation might ironically serve to block all expansion.

The chamber decided to seek a solution through a blue-ribbon commission behind whose proposals the power structure could unite. The state legislature created the desired Local Government Commission, but compromises with the DeKalb County delegation severely limited its scope. To make sure that their county was not "swallowed up" by Atlanta, the DeKalb salons not only excluded their county from the commission's jurisdiction but also obtained half the positions on it. In the long run, this compromise was enormously important. Population growth was so great in unincorporated DeKalb that within twenty-five years the county government was providing municipal-type services to about as many people as resided in Atlanta proper.

Throughout 1949 the Local Government Commission conducted staff investigations and held public hearings. Its report, officially known as the *Plan of Improvement*, rejected the one-government idea and advocated passive annexation accompanied by a reshuffling of service responsibilities between Atlanta and Fulton County. Publicly, Mayor Hartsfield praised the report as "very much like what I've been advocating for years," but privately he was upset by the provisions that would transfer the health department and a few other services to the county. Although the authors of the report carefully avoided use of the politically sensitive word "annexation," the plan in fact called for adding about eighty-two square miles and 100,000 residents to Atlanta. Such a move would triple the city's physical size and increase its population by one-fourth.

The state legislature scheduled an advisory referendum on the *Plan of Improvement* in conjunction with the Democratic primary in June 1950, and the Chamber of Commerce launched a massive campaign for its passage. Most of the civic organizations in town backed the plan, and it received the endorsement of the influential bipartisan Atlanta Negro Voters League. "Not in my memory," Chamber of Commerce president Richard Rich declared six months after the election, "has there ever been a matter involving votes where so many groups and individuals in the community worked to-gether." Sociologist Floyd Hunter in his classic study *Community Power Structure* reported that top leaders regarded the plan as one of their highest priorities of 1950. The opposition, on the other hand, was comparatively quiet and unorganized. Some homeowners feared increased taxes and Fulton County officials were loath to lose juris-diction over so much territory, but they failed to mount an effective counterattack. The plan carried overwhelmingly with a 90 percent approval within the city and 62 percent in the areas to be annexed. This decisive vote effectively silenced the opposition, and with only minor changes the plan received the necessary legislative and con-stitutional amendments for implementation.[3]

Aware that the city would never capture the entire urbanized area by annexation, the Chamber of Commerce also worked to im-plement metropolitanwide planning along the lines called for in the 1938 Reed Report. In 1947 the chamber secured legislative autho-rization for the establishment of the Metropolitan Planning Com-mission (MPC), which Fulton County, DeKalb County, and the city of Atlanta would finance jointly. Beginning operations in 1949, this body was the nation's "first official metropolitan planning organiza-tion supported from the beginning entirely by public funds."[4]

Thus as Atlanta entered the new decade, the future seemed bright for both the city and the metropolitan area. On 1 January 1952 the *Plan of Improvement* went into effect. Atlanta jumped from thirty-seven to 118 square miles and from about 330,000 to 430,000 in population.

The 1950s brought great growth to the metropolitan area, and much of the expansion continued to be fueled by government expen-diture both for military and domestic projects. Following the war, the huge bomber plant in Marietta closed, but within a few years the site became the locus for a big suburban growth spurt that brought the population of Cobb County to 114,000. The army airfield moved there from the Atlanta airport and became Dobbins Air Force Base. The naval air station later transferred to a small corner of the Dob-bins facility, leaving its old quarters for general aviation use. Most important, however, the Lockheed Corporation moved into the old Bell factory and began producing B-47s. Four years later the plant started turning out the reliable C-130 Hercules transport. By 1959 Lockheed's payroll had reached 15,000 and would eventually climb to 30,000 in the late 1960s during production of the massive but troubled C-5A. (A new boom is predicted to accompany C-5B production in the mid 1980s.)

Meanwhile in the south suburbs, the Atlanta Army Depot went through a Korean War expansion that fueled a burst of development in Clayton County, more than doubling its population in the 1950s to over 46,000. Three small new municipalities incorporated near the facility and the existing town of Forest Park grew from 2,653 in 1950 to 14,201 ten years later.

In 1950 the U.S. Army Corps of Engineers broke ground for Buford Dam on the Chattahoochee River north of Atlanta. The U.S. House Appropriations Committee voted to cut off the project's funds the next year, but intense lobbying by Mayor Hartsfield and others won a funding renewal. The reservoir was essential, Hartsfield implored. It would become the "future water supply upon which the very life or death of our community depends." The corps completed the dam in 1957, and 37,000-acre Lake Lanier began to fill.[5]

According to official estimates, the population of metropolitan Atlanta reached one million on Saturday morning, 10 October 1959. The Chamber of Commerce marked the milestone with a special day of speeches, bands, and general celebration. The mayor declared, "We roll out the red carpet for every damn Yankee who comes in here with two strong hands and some money. We break our necks to sell him." Since the beginning of World War II the city had more than doubled its metropolitan population and had attracted more than 2,800 new firms. Regional leadership was assured. On the occasion of the million population commemoration, *Newsweek* wrote, "The Georgia capital is the nerve center of the New South."[6]

By 1960 Atlanta was ready to become the city of national importance its boosters envisioned. Ivan Allen, Jr., who as Chamber of Commerce president would lead a new Forward Atlanta promotion and who as mayor would guide the city through a delicate racial transition, explained the transition: "In 1959 we were known for Coca-Cola, Georgia Tech, dogwoods, the Atlanta Crackers [baseball team], and easy southern living; by 1969 we were known for gleaming skyscrapers, expressways, the Atlanta Braves, and . . . traffic jams." The city had moved, in Allen's words, "from being a somewhat sluggish regional distribution center to a position as one of the dozen or so truly 'national cities.'"[7] The regional rivals were left far behind. Neither metropolitan Memphis nor New Orleans had reached a million population by 1960. Birmingham, which had trailed Atlanta by only 35,000 in 1940, found that the gap was an overwhelming 400,000 only twenty years later.

Major-league sports and skyscrapers may not be the most important indexes of economic growth, but they are the visible badges of urban maturity that Atlanta lacked and coveted. Atlanta was tired of being a minor-league town. Mayor Allen decided that if Atlanta had a big-league stadium, big-league sports would follow, so he set out on a crash program to build one. With vague but enthusiastic encouragement from Kansas City A's owner Charlie Finley and with the financial endorsement of Mills Lane, Jr.'s C & S Bank, Allen decided to locate the stadium on an urban renewal tract just south of downtown and the capitol where three interstate highways would soon meet in a giant interchange. The stadium authority paid a bonus for quick work, and in the spring of 1965, a scant fifty-one weeks after the ground breaking, the facility was complete. The $18 million price tag and the 3 percent interest seem bargain basement in retrospect. Litigation delayed Atlanta's theft of the Milwaukee Braves for a year, but major-league sports arrived officially with the Braves' home opener on 12 April 1966.

In the meantime, the city profited from the war between the established National and the nascent American Football leagues. The stadium authority was on the verge of an agreement with the newer league when Pete Rozelle came to town and sewed up an NFL deal with Rankin Smith of Life of Georgia. The Falcons also began play in 1966, and they set a season ticket record for an expansion team. Two years later the National Basketball Association Hawks arrived from St. Louis, and Atlanta had scored a big-league hat trick with three major-league franchises acquired within about three years. Studies indicated that by the end of the decade major-league sports were worth as much as $60 million a year to the area's economy. In ensuing years the National Hockey League and the North American Soccer League would come and then go, unable to generate continuing fan support for those distinctly nonsouthern sports.

Most of Atlanta's population growth and much of its economic expansion during the 1960s and 1970s occurred in the suburbs, but impressive central business district (CBD) development, an easy camera scan from the stadium, was probably more important to the city's image. The twenty-six story Fulton National Bank Building, completed in 1956, was the only skyscraper built from the depression to 1960. But in the following decade the city ranked eighth na-

tionally in downtown construction with thirty buildings from fifteen to twenty-nine floors and four more with over thirty. Eleven of
the city's dozen tallest buildings in 1970 had been erected in the previous ten years. Most important among these many projects was the
carefully planned and coordinated Peachtree Center development,
which literally pulled downtown north along Peachtree Street from
its traditional center at Five Points. Patterned somewhat after Rockefeller Center, Peachtree Center began in 1960 with the twenty-two-
story merchandise mart. In announcing the project, developer John
Portman said, "It will be just about the only true merchandising mart
in the country, outside of Chicago. This whole thing has all sorts of
side benefits. After exhibits come down, sales forces, branches, assembly plants and warehouses will follow."[8] The mart was an unqualified success. It doubled in size in 1968, and by the end of the
decade it drew a quarter of a million buyers a year. In 1979 a giant
apparel mart opened next door. Peachtree Center's fifteenth major
project, a mammoth 1,800-room Marriott Hotel, began in July 1981.[9]

Another important and unusual downtown project was the
Omni International megastructure. The complex, erected on air
rights above railroad switching yards, involved a mixture of private
and public capital. The private development included offices, shops,
bistros, and a hotel built around a huge enclosed ice-skating rink.
Adjacent are the publicly owned 18,000-seat Omni Coliseum and
the gigantic World Congress Center. Other downtown projects of
note in the 1970s and early 1980s included new skyscrapers to house
the corporate headquarters for Coca-Cola, Georgia Power, Southern
Bell, and Georgia Pacific. A new federal building and twin state office towers also opened recently.

Although downtown construction was most visible and spectacular, Atlanta was also a national leader in office park construction. Most of the major new construction was along the extensive
interstate expressway system, technically completed in 1969 but
seemingly always under construction. Executive Park, the first major complex beyond the CBD, opened in 1965. Perimeter Center,
with 510 acres of coordinated offices, hotels, and shopping, is the nation's largest such park. Other major projects include Corporate
Square and Technology Park. As a result of this development, almost
exclusively on the north side, downtown's share of metro office
space dropped to about 44 percent in 1977.[10]

Most of the money for the office-hotel boom came from out-of-
town sources. In 1970 a local mortgage corporation estimated that
80 to 90 percent of the area's commercial construction financing
came from outside of the South. (The figure was only 40 percent for

residential construction.) Atlanta developer Tom Cousins was among the nation's early leaders in joint venture financing whereby insurance companies, real estate investment trusts, and other lenders receive an equity interest in return for favorable terms. Cousins called it "sharecropping in real estate." European and Arab investors have also moved in to purchase such landmarks as the First National Bank Building, the Life of Georgia Tower, and the Hilton–Atlanta Center office-hotel complex. According to a recent exposé in *Atlanta* magazine, "Atlanta has become a city owned largely by absentee landlords."[11]

Atlanta's most important asset, literally its raison d'être, is transportation. Railroads continue to be important, but the remarkable postwar growth is in air transport and trucking.

In 1961 the Atlanta passenger terminal moved out of its glorified Quonset hut into a modern new facility that would be outmoded and abandoned itself in less than twenty years. The new terminal (Hartsfield International Airport built in 1980) is located literally in the middle of the airport so that planes can taxi to their gates quicker. Between 1960 and 1969 the Atlanta airport moved from tenth to third busiest in the nation, and by 1980 only Chicago's O'Hare handled more passenger boardings and only eight airports exceeded Atlanta's in air freight tonnage. Delta, the nation's most consistently profitable airline, is headquartered at Hartsfield International Airport, and Eastern and Republic maintain major facilities there. In April 1981 airlines and related businesses employed 29,673 people at the airport with an annual payroll of $892 million.

Trucks and warehouses may be less glamorous than jets and airports, but they are also crucial to the city's development. In 1970 metro Atlanta ranked twenty-first in population but was thirteenth in truck registration. About 350 regulated motor carriers served Atlanta in 1980, and nearly seventy of them maintained major terminal facilities. "The big industries, the big manufacturers," said the president of the Georgia Motor Trucking Association, "think of Atlanta as one big warehouse." A special Chamber of Commerce report declared that excellent rail, air, and highway connections combined to cinch "Atlanta's position as the main southeastern notch in the Sunbelt."[12]

The highways and airways (and even occasionally the railways on Amtrak's "Crescent") help make Atlanta a leading convention center. In 1965 the city had venerable hotels, an aging auditorium, a lackluster promotion effort, 175,000 convention visitors, and a number twenty-three ranking in convention business. Ten years later it hosted over six-hundred thousand conventioneers and trailed only

New York and Chicago. The change began in 1965 when the downtown Marriott Hotel opened and the city broke ground for its new bond issue–financed civic center, featuring a large auditorium and an exhibit hall. Two years later the Hyatt Regency in Peachtree Center unveiled its much-copied multistory atrium-lobby. By 1976 the Hilton, the Sheraton, and the Peachtree Plaza, then the world's tallest hotel, were in business. Atlanta could thus boast about nine thousand rooms within the CBD and nearly twenty thousand more in the metro area. With the opening in that year of the state-financed World Congress Center, Atlanta was equipped to handle the very largest conventions and trade shows. The Congress Center's 351,639-square-foot main floor is the nation's largest single-level exhibition space. The facility, soon to be enlarged, has numerous meeting rooms and a two-thousand-seat auditorium. The economic impact of this industry is enormous. The Convention and Visitors Bureau estimated that in 1978 the big convention hotels and facilities directly employed eighteen thousand people. A Georgia State University accounting professor expected a million 1980 delegates to spend a quarter of a billion dollars with a 2.25 multiplier effect. He estimated the resultant tax revenue at $19.3 million—more than enough to cover the operating deficits of the publicly owned facilities. When major attractions such as Six Flags over Georgia and Stone Mountain Park are included, it is no wonder that a Chamber of Commerce report declared that the "convention/tourist/hospitality" industry may be Atlanta's largest with 75,300 employees in 5,820 businesses in 1979.[13]

Despite all this success, Underground Atlanta, one of the city's more nationally recognized convention-tourist projects, has all but died. The ground floors of blocks of nineteenth-century buildings near the state capitol had long been neglected following the erection of viaducts over the railroad "gulch." Seeking an ambience less tawdry than New Orleans's Bourbon Street but more exciting than St. Louis's Gaslight Square, entrepreneurs turned the area into an entertainment center featuring seventeen bars, twenty-eight shops, and twenty eateries at its height in 1974. An estimated one thousand people worked there to serve 4.5 million visitors annually. But the euphoria did not last. When Underground opened in 1969 the two largest suburban counties were dry, so parched revelers had to visit Atlanta. Cobb and DeKalb counties, however, soon had their own bars, and suburbanites could drink closer to home. Perceptions of downtown crime also deterred locals, so the Underground merchants had to cater more and more to conventioneers. The coup de grace was disruptive MARTA subway construction that kept the area in turmoil. The completion of the subway failed to bring about the anticipated rejuvenation.[14]

Federal employment, as well as federal grants, helped fuel Atlanta's 1960s to 1970s boom. In addition to the well-known military bases, federal penitentiary, and Center for Disease Control, Atlanta is Washington's principal regional headquarters city, with forty thousand federal employees and a 1970 payroll of $305 million. The *Atlanta Journal-Constitution* declared, "Atlanta has the largest concentration of federal agencies outside of Washington, D.C. of any city in the country." Of course, state government employment has been important to Atlanta since 1868, when it snatched the capital from Milledgeville. Total government employment in the SMSA reached 160,200 in 1980. Only the retail and services sectors exceeded that number.[15]

Two state institutions of higher education helped spur the 1960s and 1970s expansion. Georgia Institute of Technology, famous for its "Ramblin' Wreck" football teams, turns out highly sought engineering graduates for local and national firms. Its research activities are crucial to attracting high technology firms to the area, especially to the four-hundred-acre Technology Park, which Tech founded. One of the park's corporate tenants, Scientific Atlanta, which had its genesis in 1951 with Georgia Tech faculty, has since grown to be a world leader in satellite communications equipment. Tech has also aided the city's growth-promotion efforts by doing economic impact studies and preparing industrial site analyses.

Georgia State University serves the less technological aspects of the metropolis's business needs. Located in the heart of downtown near Five Points, the institution began as a night business school and operated under various auspices and appellations until it acquired its present name in 1969. In 1961 the school had 3,447 students enrolled almost exclusively in business courses. By 1970 enrollment had reached almost thirteen thousand, and the university offered twenty degrees in 150 fields, including ten doctoral programs. President Noah Langdale declared, "We are the first truly urban university in the South."[16] The present headcount exceeds twenty thousand. Other major and minor institutions dot the area, including Emory University, heavily endowed with Coca-Cola money, and the predominantly black Atlanta University Center. Both Morehouse College, within the Atlanta University complex, and Emory have medical schools.

The reasons for Atlanta's impressive development since World War II, and especially since 1960, are difficult to isolate. Certainly one reason is the economic balance among government, transportation, wholesaling, manufacturing, and other sectors. "The fact that Atlanta does not lead in any major employment sector," a 1970 comparison of forty-one southern SMSAs declared, "reveals a broad diversification of economic activity. This would seem to be a favorable point since diversification serves as insurance in the event of a decline or lag in any given sector of the economy."[17]

Quality-of-life factors have also attracted businesses. The north Georgia climate is mild with especially beautiful autumns and springs. At 1,050 feet, Atlanta is the highest major metropolis east of the Mississippi and thus is cooler and less humid than most southern cities. The rolling hills of mixed hardwood and pine forests provide the setting for some of the nation's most pleasant and impressive residential neighborhoods. Few of the new subdivisions are located on the sterile, flat, treeless tracts often seen in rapidly growing areas.

Cultural opportunities abound throughout the metropolis, but the focus of the city's high culture is the impressive Memorial Arts Center erected in honor of a large group of arts patrons who died in a 1962 airplane crash in Paris. The center houses the symphony, the Alliance Theater, the Atlanta College of Art, and the High Museum of Art, soon to be expanded thanks to the continued philanthropy of Robert Woodruff of Coca-Cola.

Two recent studies have tried to quantify the quality of life in Atlanta. A 1976 survey asked industrialists in Atlanta, Chicago, and Detroit to name the biggest advantage of their current location. The Atlanta sample cited transportation (29 percent) and recreational-cultural opportunities (23 percent) most often. Chicago and Detroit businessmen, on the other hand, mentioned the recreation-culture factor only 5 and 1 percent of the time, respectively. The study also asked the respondents to rate the overall quality of life in their community as compared with other metropolitan areas in the United States. In Atlanta an overwhelming 95 percent said life in their locale was better. In contrast, only 48 percent in Chicago and 8 percent in Detroit so rated their cities. In 1981 Rand McNally and Company published the *Places Rated Almanac*, which ranked 277 SMSAs on the basis of numerous factors. In that study Atlanta came out number one as "the best all-around place in America."[18] The city has made the most of this ranking in its recent promotional material.

A third advantage has been the general resurgence of the South. Atlanta so solidified its regional leadership position in the 1950s that the local power structure stopped worrying about staying ahead of Memphis, Nashville, and Birmingham. In fact, as Opie Shelton, executive vice-president of the Chamber of Commerce, put it, "We found that it was to our advantage to do all we could to help the Jacksonvilles and Tampas. We found out that while Atlanta was trying to be a regional city, it had become one of a handful of national cities."[19] As the leading regional headquarters city for insurance companies, trade associations, distributors, and the federal government, Atlanta naturally benefited from Dixie's general growth.

In the early 1960s the business leadership decided to launch a major effort to exploit Atlanta's advantages of diversification, quality of life, and regional dominance. Throughout the 1950s the Chamber of Commerce had failed to take the initiative. As of 1960, a chamber president later recalled, "The chamber was hopelessly underfinanced . . . the professional staff . . . was small and lacked direction. Consequently Atlanta's goals for the future were vague and ultra conservative for a major city."[20]

In 1960, Ivan Allen, Jr., chamber president and soon to be mayor, proposed a six-point program that provided the direction and goals that had been missing. Allen resolved to (1) keep the public schools open in the face of integration, (2) complete the expressway system, (3) support urban renewal and public housing, (4) erect a civic center and stadium, (5) press for large-scale rapid transit, and (6) launch a Forward Atlanta promotion program.[21]

The chamber ran advertisements in national business publications and established *Atlanta*, its own slick promotional magazine. It prepared elaborate site analyses for prospective industries and visited New York and other cities to extol Atlanta's virtues. C & S Bank allowed the chamber to use its helicopter to whisk visiting executives around town. From 1960 to 1976 the chamber spent in excess of $5 million on its promotional efforts. By 1973 the chamber billed Atlanta as "the world's next great city." The following year, the Organization of American States met in Atlanta, the first time that it had ever met in the United States outside of Washington, D.C. The international city label continues to be a bit optimistic, but for a city with a world trade club, simultaneous translation facilities in the World Congress Center, and nonstop flights to London, Amsterdam, Brussels, Frankfurt, Mexico City, and the Caribbean, it is not entirely hyperbole.

As Atlanta has grown from regional city to national metropolis, its politics have also gone through two stages. From World War II to 1970 the white business power structure dominated. Since that time political and economic power have become separate entities, and the old forces increasingly have had to share political influence with blacks, neighborhood groups, and the suburbs.

During the 1940s and 1950s Atlantans did not recognize much difference between business and politics. An economic elite, described pseudonymously in Floyd Hunter's *Community Power Structure*, dominated civic affairs.[22] The biggest challenges to its domination were suburbanization and racial unrest, but these factors seemed to be fairly well under control. The adoption of the *Plan of Improvement* and the establishment of the Metropolitan Planning Commission appeared to solve the suburban problem. Whites with a sense of noblesse oblige forged a coalition with blacks, who were grateful for what passed as racial moderation. The working-class whites were the powerless group.

For over two decades Mayor William B. Hartsfield headed this coalition. Born in 1890, Hartsfield became an alderman in 1923 and a state legislator ten years later. Except for an eighteen-month hiatus in 1941–42, Bill Hartsfield served as mayor from 1937 until his retirement in January 1962. His biggest assets were his hard-driving nature, his political sense, and his lifelong friendship with Robert Woodruff, president and chairman of the board of Coca-Cola. His principal liabilities were his temper and his lack of long-term vision, except perhaps in his beloved field of aviation. Ralph McGill, Pulitzer Prize–winning editor of the *Atlanta Constitution*, called Hartsfield a "conservative progressive." One Chamber of Commerce president said, "At times Bill acts as if he actually owned the town. And that's why he is one of the most effective mayors in the whole country." A 1947 article in *Fortune* magazine confirmed this local pride when it named Hartsfield one of America's nine best mayors.[23]

The black-white electoral coalition began in 1946 soon after the United States Supreme Court struck down the white primary system that had so effectively disfranchised Georgia blacks. In 1945 Atlanta's three thousand registered black voters constituted about 4 percent of the city's total, but over the next year Atlanta University professor Clarence Bacote and others mounted an incredibly effective drive that added eighteen thousand more blacks to the rolls. This raised the total to 27.2 percent of the electorate by June 1946, and despite annexation the total remained between 25 and 30 percent through 1961. Not only did the blacks register, they voted. The percent of black turnout consistently exceeded that of the whites.[24]

In 1948 Hartsfield appointed the city's first black policemen, and this move proved crucial to his capturing the black vote in 1949. Shortly after the mayor's reelection, Bacote wrote him, "I hope that your administration continues along the progressive lines that it has taken in the past, and, if it does, you can be assured of Negro support as long as you desire to remain a public servant."[25] Political scientist Jack Walker described how the coalition functioned:

> The majorities for Hartsfield in 1953 and 1957 and the majority for [Ivan] Allen in 1961 all came from the same parts of the city. These two men gained their strength from the predominantly Negro precincts which are clustered around the center and the west side of the city, and from the predominantly white precincts on the north side. . . . This line of political division within the white community follows in general a line of economic and social differences. To the north of the line are the upper- and upper-middle-class white neighborhoods, and to the south of the line are the middle- and working-class white neighborhoods.

The Atlanta Negro Voters League, under the leadership of attorney A. T. Walden and Republican J. W. Dobbs, kept the black vote well organized and disciplined. Walker's precinct analysis showed that Hartsfield regularly got over 90 percent of the vote in black areas. Allen received an astounding 99 percent in many predominantly black precincts.[26]

All of the Atlanta officeholders at the time ran in citywide elections, although aldermen did have to reside within the wards they represented. Consequently, blacks were unable, save in one instance, to win office themselves. The only black to get elected in this period was Rufus E. Clement, president of Atlanta University, who won a school board seat in 1953.

Moderate, affluent whites were able to retain the loyalties of black voters through such actions as their support of Clement. Hartsfield regularly consulted with a so-called kitchen cabinet of black advisors, including Walden and Urban League director Grace Hamilton, and he made some important symbolic gestures. In Memphis, local officials had forced the races to visit the national Freedom Train on different days, but Hartsfield allowed Atlantans to view the patriotic documents on a desegregated basis. One of his mayoral opponents had, as county commissioner, been responsible for the use of separate windows for black and white voter registration, and the mayor scored this action. When the NAACP held its national convention in Atlanta in 1951, Hartsfield gave a warm welcoming speech. He ordered city functionaries to address blacks as Mr. and Mrs., and he gradually had the "white" and "colored" signs removed from airport restrooms. He carefully cooperated with black ministers to stage the incident that led to peaceful desegregation of city buses. Then in October 1959, the mayor coined the phrase that would be the slogan of Atlanta's progressive racial image during the 1960s. "We're too busy to hate," he told a *Newsweek* writer. "Our aim in life is to make no business, no industry, no educational or social organization ashamed of the date line 'Atlanta.'"[27]

But as of 1960 Atlanta was still a rigidly segregated city. In his heart the mayor still believed in Jim Crow. As police chief Herbert Jenkins candidly remembered, "He was just as liberal as necessary to get the black vote."[28] The black policemen had to stay in nonwhite neighborhoods. Blacks could shop at Rich's and other stores but could not go to the restroom, have lunch, or try on the clothes they wanted to buy. Hotels and restaurants were off limits. The schools were completely separate and not very equal. And, of course, the economic gap between black and white was enormous.

In the closing years of the Hartsfield administration, pressure built up in the black community for a full assault on Jim Crow. The targets were the schools and the downtown businesses, and the weapons were the courts and the streets, respectively. If it were to retain the electoral support of the blacks, the white power structure would have to respond.

The first order of business was to integrate the schools. In 1958 the NAACP filed suit against Atlanta's dual system, and it was clear that a desegregation order would soon follow. The governor and most state politicians vowed never to surrender. The issue was whether angrily to resist or gracefully, if reluctantly, to obey the law. Hartsfield and the white business leaders, prompted by liberal ministers, Ralph McGill, and a coalition of reform groups, chose the latter course. As early as 1957 the mayor had told a civic club, "We do not want the hatred and bitterness of Montgomery or Little Rock."[29]

When the time arrived in September 1961 for the entry of ten black students into four previously all-white high schools, the administration was ready. Expecting to witness repeats of recent violence and hysteria in New Orleans, over two hundred reporters from around the country converged on the city. The flabbergasted newsmen found that Hartsfield had set up a press room in city hall, scheduled a bus tour of the nicer black neighborhoods, and arranged a racially mixed cocktail party at the fashionable Biltmore Hotel. A citizens coalition had prepared an informative background booklet, and the Chamber of Commerce had purchased full-page newspaper ads urging calm. Chief Jenkins carefully screened and trained the policemen who would be on hand to see that no nasty incidents occurred. The mayor proclaimed, "We're going to ride herd on these damn rabble rousers." The result was peaceful, if token, integration

for blacks and a giant public relations coup for Atlanta. President
Kennedy lauded Atlanta in a press conference and *Newsweek*, the
New York Times, *Look*, *Life*, and even *Good Housekeeping* praised
the city.[30]

Meanwhile, segregation in downtown business establishments
was becoming an issue. Here the pressure came not from the established black elite but from younger, more militant leaders—primarily students from the Atlanta University colleges. Their ringing
manifesto declared, "We cannot tolerate . . . the discriminatory conditions under which the Negro is living today in Atlanta, Georgia—
supposedly one of the most progressive cities in the South."[31]

The Student Nonviolent Coordinating Committee (SNCC) and
the Southern Christian Leadership Conference (SCLC) led the
movement. They targeted Rich's, the largest department store in the
South, and demonstrations began in the fall of 1960. Police arrested
Martin Luther King, Jr., and over 150 students, most of whom refused bond in order to dramatize their appeal. The mayor held back
from major involvement, so this crisis thrust Ivan Allen, Jr., the
Chamber of Commerce president and a Rich's board member, to the
fore. In early 1961 he called the owners of twenty-five major businesses and the old-line black leaders to a series of secret meetings at
the influential, and officially segregated, Commerce Club. The
young blacks had, for the first time, forced the whites to negotiate
rather than dictate.

The businessmen agreed to end segregation in their stores and
to drop charges against the demonstrators. Allen later conceded that
"the main thing guiding them was business pragmatism." The businesses insisted that the implementation of the agreement be put off
until after the tense beginning of school in the fall. The student mil-
itants, who had been excluded from the high-level talks that their
actions had inspired, chafed at the delay; but the old leaders and the
young Dr. King kept them in check. Many establishments, not party
to the compromise, remained staunchly segregated, but in late 1961,
three years before the federal public accommodations act, black
shoppers could at least go downtown without facing Jim Crow at
every turn.[32]

This development, along with the peaceful school desegregation, was in sharp contrast with the situation in most of the rest of
the South, so the praise of Atlanta accelerated. In his valedictory address to the city council, 3 January 1962, Bill Hartsfield boasted, "Atlanta's mature and friendly approach to the problems of racial
change has earned for us the respect of the nation."[33]

In the midst of the implementation of the school order and the

business agreement, Ivan Allen, Jr., was elected mayor. Like Hartsfield, he relied on the counsel of strategist Helen Bullard and the
votes of blacks and affluent whites. He received virtually all the
black vote and almost half the white vote to defeat restaurant owner
and arch-segregationist Lester Maddox, who had also run against
Hartsfield in 1957. Unlike Hartsfield, a middle-class lawyer who
politicked his way into the elite, Allen was born there—son of a former Chamber of Commerce president who owned a large office supply company. Allen explained in his memoirs, "We had shared the
same problems, interests, and ambitions our entire lives. [We were]
the business-civic leadership of the city: the 'power structure.'"[34]

The black-white coalition extended beyond the balloting for
mayor and city council. In twenty-one local, state, and national elections from 1960 to 1977, black-supported candidates captured an
average of 93 percent of the black votes and a substantial minority of
the affluent white ballots. In four other southern cities (Dallas,
Houston, Memphis, and New Orleans) the opposite pattern appeared, in which the black-backed candidates did better with lower
socioeconomic whites (unless the politician himself was black, in
which case the Atlanta style prevailed in all five). Charles Weltner, a
moderate white Democrat, unseated an old segregationist in the
1962 congressional primary and managed to reverse the traditional
Republicanism of the black community in the general election.
Even though his district was only 29 percent black, Weltner was one
of only two southerners to vote for the Civil Rights Act of 1964.
With Weltner and Lyndon Johnson leading the 1964 ticket, Atlanta
blacks became permanent Democrats. Even on local bond and liquor-
by-the-drink referenda, blacks and upper-income whites voted alike
in opposition to the other whites. "If there is anything the coalition
fears most," two political scientists explained, "it is the seizure
of the city government by what are called the 'red neck,' 'wool hat'
elements."[35] As long as this fear remained, the uneasy alliance
persisted.

Whether purely from economic pragmatism or from the sincere
liberalism that Allen claimed he gradually acquired, the mayor tried
to make sure that the power structure deserved its black support. Allen made mistakes, notably in blocking off a street to discourage
neighborhood integration, and, as usual, Atlanta lagged far behind
what needed to be done to conquer institutional racism. But the city
stayed way ahead of the rest of Dixie. As the Democratic administration's favorite southern mayor, Allen was able to extract considerable federal funding for Model Cities, urban renewal, and public
housing programs. He and his allies among the more liberal busi-

ness- and churchmen convinced their hesitant colleagues that the city should host a banquet to honor Martin Luther King, Jr., for receiving the Nobel Peace Prize. Three years later Allen personally attended the King family after the assassination. Atlanta escaped major rioting in the tense years between 1965 and 1968, and Allen strode confidently, if ineffectually, into the midst of one minor outbreak (one dead, twenty injured) that did occur near the stadium. By 1969 he had raised the proportion of black city employees to 39 percent, although all the department heads and most of the supervisors were still white. Blacks constituted 20 to 30 percent of most juries. Meanwhile, Birmingham dropped out of the Southern League rather than let blacks play baseball with whites; but Allen threw out the ball at the first integrated Crackers game, and soon brought in the Braves with such black stars as Hank Aaron and Eddie Mathews. What probably endeared Allen to the black community more than anything else was the fact that he was the most prominent white southerner to testify in favor of Kennedy's civil rights bill.[36]

Despite the progress, much of the praise for Atlanta as "the city too busy to hate" was, in the words of the Urban League's Whitney Young, like "rewarding a child for not having a tantrum."[37] Black political power was limited to choosing sympathetic, or less hostile, whites. Black economic power, greater in Atlanta than in any other southern metropolis, was still relatively inconsequential. But political dominance was on the way.[38]

A black Atlantan entered the reapportioned state senate in 1963, and two years later one obtained a city council seat. In 1969, when the electorate was 41 percent black, black voters broke with the now less monolithic white economic elite to insure the election of Sam Massell, a maverick Jewish real estate man. Maynard Jackson, a thirty-one-year-old black lawyer, became vice-mayor; and black representation on the city council went from one to five out of eighteen. One-third of the school board was black, including retired Morehouse College president Benjamin Mays, who was elected board president. Massell rewarded blacks with two department heads, and he significantly increased minority hiring; but he angered many with his racially motivated calls for annexation and by his insensitive handling of a garbage collectors' strike.

Black political power arrived with the 1970s. Former King aide Andrew Young went to Congress in 1972, and the next year blacks also captured city hall. Maynard Jackson came within three thousand votes of winning without a runoff over incumbent Massell, black state legislator LeRoy Johnson, and former congressman Charles Weltner. The old downtown powers, for the first time, did not have a candidate of their own in the race. In the runoff, Massell tried to rally white voters with racist appeals but instead provoked a larger black turnout and alienated white liberals. Jackson carried 95 percent of the black vote and 17.5 percent of the white for a combined figure of almost 60 percent. This was the first election under a new city charter that abandoned the old at-large vote/ward residency system in favor of twelve district and six at-large councilmen. The charter strengthened the power of the mayor and created the position of city council president, which white liberal Wyche Fowler won. He got about 30 percent of the black vote to defeat civil-rights activist Hosea William, whom many regarded as too radical. The incoming council included nine members of each race, and blacks carried a majority on the school board.

Four years later the mayor won a landslide reelection while the racial balance on the council remained the same. Significantly, through Jackson's administration the council was not racially polarized on most issues. Neighborhood loyalties and political ideologies seemed to outrank race as determinants of council voting.

Jackson, like Martin Luther King, Jr., is the son of an influential Baptist minister and a graduate of Morehouse College. After earning his law degree cum laude at North Carolina Central University, he briefly worked for the National Labor Relations Board and then joined a firm in Atlanta. Brash, articulate, and physically imposing, Jackson ran a quixotic race against Senator Herman Talmadge in 1968 but managed to carry Atlanta. Some of the older black leaders, such as the publisher of the conservative Republican *Atlanta Daily World*, resented the pushy newcomer, but his vote-getting power, demonstrated against Talmadge and again in the 1969 vice-mayor race, established him as the city's leading black politician. Especially important to Jackson was the support of Jesse Hill, the millionaire president of Atlanta Life Insurance Company and in 1978 the first black president of the Atlanta Chamber of Commerce. Although Jackson had the support of most of the black power structure, he was painfully aware that he did not fit in with Ivan Allen's crowd. "I, of course," the new mayor pointed out, "have never played golf with those guys, have never been invited to their homes, didn't grow up with them, didn't go to school with them."[39]

Much of the white business community resented Jackson's nondeferential, some would say abrasive, style. They charged him with reverse discrimination in his contracting and hiring practices, but the mayor rejoined that he was only giving minorities the just due that previous administrations (despite their progressive images) had denied them. He declared, "The easily definable symbols of rac-

ism—like access to public accommodations—are behind us."
Charles Weltner, today a state supreme court justice, explained,
"There is a vast mutual distrust between City Hall and the Chamber
of Commerce. They used to be two hearts beating as one for many
years but no more." When Jackson took over, less than 1 percent of
the municipal contracts went to minority firms, but by 1981 black
companies were handling about one-fourth of the city's business.
His administration insisted on and obtained significant minority
participation in building the giant new mid-field airport terminal
and saw the project completed on time and within budget. Crime
continued to plague the core city, but charges of police brutality virtually disappeared under Jackson's two black commissioners of Public Safety.

By the end of his term, Jackson could reasonably declare that
"Atlanta has the best race relations of any city in the country," even
if he had failed in his promise to "pull off the marriage between the
white economic power and the black masses." To put things in perspective, journalist Michael Hinkelman concluded, "Atlanta has allowed itself to become racially integrated—both politically and economically—to a degree unprecedented in other American cities,
which is less a piece of praise for Atlanta than it is a criticism of
other cities."[40]

The 1981 city elections divided along clear racial lines. For the
first time, as a result of continued white flight and of the new charter, blacks won a majority of the city council seats. By law Jackson
could not serve a third consecutive term, and in the race for a successor former congressman and United Nations ambassador Andrew
Young defeated a white long-time state legislator with a solid moderate record. Precinct returns indicated that about 90 percent of the
voters of each race cast their ballots for the candidate of their own
color.

Biracial politics, however, is not dead in Atlanta. The fifth congressional district, white by a bare majority when it sent Andy
Young to Washington, replaced Young with Wyche Fowler, the liberal white city council president, even though the district had become majority black. Reapportionment, necessitated by the 1980
census and shaped by Voting Rights Act–inspired litigation, created
a revised district with a black majority of over 65 percent. Popular
black legislator Julian Bond declined to run in 1982 for personal, political, and financial reasons, and Fowler won reelection with over
80 percent of the vote against two weak black opponents—a Republican and an independent. Young's overtures to the business community and Fowler's popularity with blacks indicate that while race

may be the dominant factor in Atlanta politics, it is not the only consideration. The three congressmen who represent suburban Atlanta include an unabashed John Birch Democrat, a Jack Kemp–type Republican, and a moderate Jewish Democrat who seems to get more conservative every year. All three won comfortable reelection in 1982.[41]

Both the rise of black political power and the decline of the old power structure's influence are to a large extent products of metropolitan growth and the consequent political fragmentation. The 1952 *Plan of Improvement* was only a temporary solution. The Atlanta Regional Commission (ARC), successor agency to the MPC, has an important voice in regional issues, notably transportation, water, and sewerage, but it lacks significant power.

Regional transportation planning was one of the first issues that taught the downtown elite that it could no longer dictate policy. So-called veto groups could stall or alter their grand designs. White middle-class neighborhoods that had experienced some gentrification stopped major expressways to the north and east. The demands of inner-city blacks and the racial fears of white suburbanites in Cobb and, to a lesser extent, in Clayton and Gwinnett counties forced major changes in the mass-transit plans conceived in the early 1960s under the direction of Richard Rich. Only DeKalb and Fulton counties voted full participation in the Metropolitan Atlanta Rapid Transit Authority (MARTA), which runs the buses and the partially completed subway–rapid rail system.[42]

Since 1950, suburban Atlanta population has increased about 1.25 million while city population peaked at around 500,000 in 1970 and has since declined to about 425,000. In 1980 the city had 68,000 fewer whites and 162,000 more blacks than it had in 1950. The suburbs meanwhile gained 1.1 million whites and only 170,000 blacks (all but 10,000 of whom came after 1970 as they began to move into the southern portions of Fulton and DeKalb counties). A blend of low black income, suburban zoning practices, outright discrimination, and black affinity for the city kept most nonwhites out of the suburbs.

Georgia has some of the smallest and politically most potent counties in the nation. The Atlanta SMSA has more counties (fifteen) than any other in the country. With a few exceptions, suburban municipalities are relatively unimportant because the commissioners of DeKalb, Cobb, Fulton, Gwinnett, and Clayton counties (in descending order of non-Atlanta 1980 population) provide a full range of police and fire protection, parks, planning, and other municipal functions. Each county and three small cities have their own school systems. These governmental units are jealous of their own prerogatives, and they are all, especially Cobb, sometimes motivated by anti-Atlanta sentiment. Much of the resentment is racial. In 1961 a Clayton County newspaper editor minced no words:

> Atlanta officials have said that acceptance of desegregation would be good for industry and business growth. We'll see, as time goes on, how wrong they are. It will have nothing whatever to do with location of plants or growth of business. You can mark these words well. See for yourself. The [United States Supreme] Court is actually bringing about a Congo on the Chattahoochee.[43]

A Cobb County legislator responded to a 1977 suggestion that Atlanta adopt metropolitan tax sharing along the lines of Minneapolis–St. Paul by saying, "That's the latest Atlanta proposal to milk the suburbs. We have to mount the white steed, get out my suit of armor and go down to the [Chattahoochee] river to do battle with those devils."[44] Whether such intrametropolitan rivalry will stymie the area's growth remains to be seen. "The challenge of the 1980s," according to Research Atlanta, an independent, nonprofit think tank, "is to develop ways of applying the region's strengths to the region's problems by overcoming weaknesses inherent in economic, social, and political fragmentation."[45]

NOTES

1. Benjamin E. Mays, *Born to Rebel, an Autobiography* (New York: Charles Scribner's Sons, 1971), 275; William S. Ellis, "Atlanta, Pacesetter City of the South," *National Geographic* 135 (February 1969): 249 (quoting Sherman). The standard account of Atlanta history prior to World War II is the encyclopedic Franklin Garrett, *Atlanta and Environs* (Athens: University of Georgia Press, 1969), 2 vols., originally published in 3 vols. in 1954. For a breezier account see Norman Shavin and Bruce Galphin, *Atlanta: Triumph of a People, an Illustrated History* (Atlanta: Capricorn Corp., 1982).

2. Paul W. Miller, *Atlanta: Capital of the South*, American Guide Series (New York: Oliver Durrell, Inc., 1949), viii (quote), passim; O. E. Carson, *The Trolley Titans: A Mobile History of Atlanta* (Glendale, Calif.: Interurban Press, 1981), 121; Diane Thomas, "Meanwhile, outside the Lockheed Gates," *Atlanta* 12 (June 1972): 64–70.

3. Bradley R. Rice, "The Battle of Buckhead: The Plan of Improvement and Atlanta's Last Big Annexation," *Atlanta Historical Journal* 25 (Winter 1981): 5–22.

4. *Regional Development Plan* (Atlanta: Atlanta Regional Commission, 1976), 6.

5. Harold D. Martin, *William Berry Hartsfield: Mayor of Atlanta* (Athens: University of Georgia Press, 1978), 87 (quote), 86, 111, 120; William A. Emerson, Jr., "Where the Paper Clips Jump . . ." *Newsweek*, 19 October 1959; 94–96; Thomas, "Lockheed Gates," 68.

6. Emerson, "Where the Paper Clips Jump," 94.

7. Ivan Allen with Paul Hemphill, *Mayor: Notes on the Sixties* (New York: Simon & Schuster, 1971), 145–146. The discussion of economic growth draws from Allen, *Mayor*; Ellis, "Pacesetter City"; "Amazing Atlanta," *Atlanta Journal-Constitution*, 18 January 1970, special section; a general survey of *Atlanta* magazine and the *Atlanta Economic Review*; and various Chamber of Commerce publications.

8. Emerson, "Where the Paper Clips Jump," 95.

9. *Atlanta Journal-Constitution*, 19 July 1981.

10. Truman A. Hartshorn, *Metropolis in Georgia: Atlanta's Rise as a Major Transaction Center*, in vol. 1, book 4, Association of American Geographers Comparative Metropolitan Analysis Project (Cambridge, Mass.: Ballinger Publishing Co., 1976), 187–189; Alexander S. Wright III, "The Office Market: Central Atlanta vs. Suburbs," in Andrew M. Hamer, ed., *Urban Atlanta: Redefining the Role of the City*, Research Monograph no. 84 (Atlanta: College of Business Administration, Georgia State University, 1980), 91–96.

11. *Atlanta Journal-Constitution*, 18 January 1970; Neil Shister, "Who Owns Atlanta?" *Atlanta* 20 (January 1981): 51.

12. *Atlanta Journal-Constitution*, 18 January 1970 (first quote); Atlanta Chamber of Commerce, *Atlanta on the Move* (1980) (second quote); Judith Schonbak, "Turmoil on the Southside," *Business Atlanta* 10 (September 1981): 39–46; John Bennett and Ian M. Howard, "The Exciting Story of Georgia's Booming Air Industry," *Atlanta Economic Review* 19 (August 1969): 5; Martin, *Hartsfield*, 138.

13. Atlanta Chamber of Commerce, *Meeting in Atlanta* (1978), E-3; Vincent J. Giovinazzo, "Measuring Convention Impact," in Hamer, ed., *Urban Atlanta*, 97–109; James W. Hurst, "Conventions and the City's Economy," in Edwin N. Gorsuch and Dudley S. Hinds, eds., *The Future of Atlanta's Central City*, Research Monograph no. 73 (Atlanta: College of Business Administration, Georgia State University, 1977), 27–32; Bruce Galphin, "Atlanta: The Convention City," *Atlanta* 16 (January 1977): 49–51ff.; Bruce Galphin, "Atlanta's $35 Million Salesman," *Atlanta* 14 (January 1975): 60–61ff.

14. *Atlanta Journal-Constitution*, 14 June 1981.

15. Ibid., 18 January 1970 (quote); Research Atlanta, *Decade of Decision* (1980), 81.

16. *Atlanta Journal-Constitution*, 18 January 1970 (quote); 25 October 1981; "Scientific-Atlanta: Soaring Growth in Telecommunications," *Dun's Review* 113 (April 1979): 20.

17. J. Carroll Simms and Margaret L. Andersen, "Needs of the Metropolitan Area from a Regional Standpoint," *Atlanta Economic Review* 20 (June 1970): 38.

18. Lewis Mandell, "Quality of Life Factors in Business Location Decisions," *Atlanta Economic Review* 27 (January–February 1977): 4–7; Richard Boyer and David Savageau, *Places Rated Almanac* (Chicago: Rand McNally & Co., 1981), 371.

19. "The Big Name Hunt," *Atlanta* 16 (July 1976): 57ff.

20. Ibid.

21. Allen, *Mayor*, 33–34.

22. Floyd Hunter, *Community Power Structure: A Study of Decision Makers* (Chapel Hill: University of North Carolina Press, 1953); idem, *Community Power Succession: Atlanta's Policy-Makers Revisited* (Chapel Hill: University of North Carolina Press, 1980). Hunter used actual names in the later study.

23. Ralph McGill, "You'd Think He Owns Atlanta," *Saturday Evening Post*, 31 October 1953, 96, 29; "New Strength in City Hall," *Fortune* 56 (November 1957): 156.

24. Jack Walker, "Negro Voting in Atlanta: 1954–1961," *Phylon* 24 (Winter 1963): 379–387; Clarence A. Bacote, "The Negro in Atlanta Politics," *Phylon* 16 (Winter 1955): 335–350.

25. Bacote to Hartsfield, 19 January 1950, Clarence A. Bacote Papers, Atlanta University.

26. Walker, "Negro Voting," 381–382.

27. Emerson, "Where the Paper Clips Jump," 95–96; see Walker, "Negro Voting" and Martin, *Hartsfield*, passim.

28. *Atlanta Journal-Constitution*, 18 January 1981.

29. Martin, *Hartsfield*, 129.

30. Virginia Hein, "The Image of 'A City Too Busy to Hate,' Atlanta in the 1960s," *Phylon* 33 (Fall 1972): 207; Alton Hornsby, "A City Too Busy to Hate," in Elizabeth Jacoway and David R. Colburn, *Southern Businessmen and Desegregation* (Baton Rouge: Louisiana State University Press, 1982), 120–136.

31. Mays, *Born to Rebel*, 287.

32. Allen, *Mayor*, 137.

33. George J. Lankevich, comp. and ed., *Atlanta: A Chronological and Documentary History* (Dobbs Ferry, N.Y.: Oceana Publications, Inc., 1978), 128.

34. Allen, *Mayor*, 31; see Bradley R. Rice, "Lester Maddox and the Liberal Mayors," *Proceedings and Papers of the Georgia Association of Historians, 1983* (forthcoming).

35. M. Kent Jennings and Harmon Zeigler, "Class, Party, and Race in Four Types of Elections: The Case of Atlanta," *Journal of Politics* 28 (May 1966): 406 (quote); Richard Murray and Arnold Vedlitz, "Racial Voting Patterns in the South: An Analysis of Major Elections from 1960 to 1977 in Five Cities," *The Annals of the American Academy* 439 (September 1978):

29–39; Joseph H. Dimon IV, "Charles L. Weltner and Civil Rights," *Atlanta Historical Journal* 24 (Fall 1980): 7–20.

36. Allen, *Mayor*, passim.

37. Hein, "Image," 210.

38. The following discussion draws from Alton Hornsby, Jr., "The Negro in Atlanta Politics, 1961–1973," *Atlanta Historical Bulletin* 21 (Spring 1977): 7–33; Duncan R. Jamieson, "Maynard Jackson's 1973 Election as Mayor of Atlanta," *Midwest Quarterly* 18 (1976): 7–26; Mack H. Jones, "Black Political Empowerment in Atlanta: Myth and Reality," *The Annals of the American Academy* 439 (September 1978): 90–117; Stephen Burman, "The Illusion of Progress: Race and Politics in Atlanta, Georgia," *Ethnic and Racial Studies* 2 (October 1979): 441–454; Bruce Galphin, "Politics Are Black and White and Spread All Over," *Atlanta* 15 (October 1975): 10ff.; and *Atlanta Constitution* clippings, October 1981.

39. "Can Atlanta Succeed Where America Has Failed?" *Atlanta* 15 (June 1975): 40–41ff., an interview with Jackson. In 1981 contractor Herman Russell became the second black chamber president. For a description of the old black elite and their white counterparts see Seymour Freedgood, "Life in Buckhead," *Fortune* 64 (September 1961): 109ff.

40. Michael Hinkelman, "A Tale of Two Cities," *Atlanta* 21 (September 1981): 60, 99.

41. *Atlanta Constitution*, October 1981, November 1982, passim.

42. Richard Hébert, "Atlanta: A City Too Busy," in *Highways to Nowhere: The Politics of City Transportation* (Indianapolis: The Bobbs-Merril Co., Inc., 1972), 97–139; Sid Davis, "MARTA—A Reassessment," in Hamer, ed., *Urban Atlanta*, 187–195.

43. Jack Troy, *Forest Park Free Press*, 6 September 1961.

44. Joe Mack Wilson, *Atlanta Constitution*, 9 January 1977.

45. Research Atlanta, *Decade of Decision*, 12.

3
MIAMI

by Raymond A. Mohl

During the past few years, the city of Miami has exploded into the national consciousness. The outbreak of violence and rioting in Miami's Liberty City ghetto in May 1980 shocked Americans who believed that substantial progress had been made in race relations since the last rage of black violence in the 1960s. Similarly, the massive influx of over 125,000 new Cuban refugees, along with a smaller but continuous immigration of poverty-stricken Haitians, focused attention on Miami and south Florida. Meanwhile, in 1980 Miamians discovered themselves in the midst of a nationally publicized crime wave. Miami entered the 1980s with an unenviable reputation as the nation's drug and murder capital.

Despite the impact of these diverse and unsettling events, Miami's economy surged ahead in the late 1970s. Florida tourism continued to expand, and Miami emerged as a dynamic center of international banking and commerce. The city's central business district, formerly in decline, began to take on a new look and a new vitality. New skyscrapers and building projects in various stages of construction gave the city the apppearance of a boom town. In addition, the population of the Miami metropolitan area continued to increase substantially, surpassing 1.6 million in 1980. The diversity of the population and the increasing proportions of Cuban and other Latin American and Caribbean immigrants made Miami a new melting pot as well as a new boom town. Local politics took on a new flavor, as first blacks and then Hispanics began exerting power at the polls. Ethnic politics added a new dimension to already existing political tensions stemming from the introduction of metropolitan government in the 1950s—an innovative system in which Dade County divided governmental responsibilities with Miami and twenty-six other municipalities.

All the elements of a new Florida boom have come together in metropolitan Miami—tourism, new immigration, banking and business prosperity, and feverish real estate and building development. "Miami seems to have grown young again," one writer has noted. "Rather then nodding off with the old folk, Miami goes roaring into the 80s. . . . Miami boils and bubbles, making history faster than even South Florida ever saw before. This is an urban frontier, full of the risk and turbulence and opportunity that all true frontiers offer."[1] Unique in a variety of ways, Miami by the early 1980s nevertheless shared with other Sunbelt cities the dynamism and vitality characteristic of those rapidly growing and changing metropolitan centers.

Miami traces its origins as a city to the 1890s, when urban boosters and land speculators turned their attention to the new Florida frontier. Florida's chief urban builder and promoter was Henry M. Flagler, a partner in John D. Rockefeller's Standard Oil Company. Having made a fortune in oil, Flagler in the 1880s shifted his interests to Florida, building hotels and the Florida East Coast Railroad along the state's Atlantic Coast. A tiny village of two hundred people when Flagler's railroad arrived in 1896, Miami grew rapidly toward city status as a result of his investments and promotions. Flagler erected a huge tourist hotel, laid out streets, built a rail terminal, and provided for an electric plant, a sewage system, and a waterworks. He helped establish public schools and churches, donated land at the town's center for municipal buildings, built docks and wharfs, and dredged the Miami River and harbor to accommodate ocean-going ships. By 1913, when Flagler died, Miami had become a thriving town of 11,000 permanent citizens and 125,000 annual tourists.[2]

Until Flagler touched the place with his railroad and his millions, Miami had few prospects. But by building on its essential natural resources—sunshine, seashore, and subtropical climate—Miami, and indeed all of south Florida, became by the 1920s a thriving center of tourism.[3] First by railroad, then by automobile, vacationing northerners came in ever-increasing numbers. In addition, like earlier frontier areas in the American West, south Florida attracted land speculators and developers. Some of these promoters were fabulously successful: for example, Carl G. Fisher, who literally built Miami Beach, and Coral Gables developer George E. Merrick. By the mid 1920s, Miami, along with the surrounding area, was in the midst of a full-scale real estate boom. By 1923, according to a historical study of the Miami real estate market by Frank B. Sessa, Dade County had sprouted some 275 residential subdivisions, and real estate and construction had begun to rival tourism as major factors in the local economy.[4]

This south Florida land boom collapsed in 1926 as a result of speculation, overbuilding, land frauds, bank failures, a major hurricane, and resultant bad publicity. Nevertheless, during the 1920s Miami's population rose from 29,571 to 110,637. In addition, annexations expanded the city's territory from two square miles in 1900 to eight and one-half square miles in 1920 to forty-three square miles in 1925. The land boom of the 1920s also stimulated suburban development outside Miami's city limits. Beginning in 1925, when Miami made its last annexation, numerous new municipalities incorporated on the suburban fringe, including Coral Gables, Miami Springs, South Miami, North Miami, Opa-locka, Hialeah, and Golden Beach.[5]

The patterns of tourism, real estate development, and population growth continued through the 1930s, despite the Great Depression. A recent study of Miami Beach demonstrated that by the mid thirties, new building and construction, tourism, tax collections, and city budgets all surpassed predepression highs. Indeed, by the end of the thirties, Miami Beach was in the midst of a great surge of new hotel building, and the metropolitan area was entertaining some two million vacationers annually.[6]

The area's resident population also grew at a tremendous rate during the thirties. For example, Miami Beach's permanent population soared from about 6,500 in 1930 to over 28,000 in 1940. Similarly, Miami continued its upward population growth, rising from 110,637 in 1930 to 172,172 in 1940. Dade County's population as a whole rose by 87.3 percent during the depression decade. Small suburban municipalities continued to incorporate, particularly developments on the northern fringe of Miami—Miami Shores, North Miami Beach, Biscayne Park, Surfside, El Portal, and Indian Creek Village. Unincorporated places grew as well, and by the end of the 1930s, more than 15 percent of the county's population lived outside any municipality. In short, between 1920 and 1940, Miami was one of the fastest growing metropolitan areas in the United States.[7]

The transition from peace to war in the 1940s had a particularly significant impact on Miami and south Florida generally. The subtropical climate and year-round flying weather encouraged the federal government to construct dozens of airfields in Florida, primarily for training purposes. Beginning in 1942, the Army Air Corps virtually took over Miami Beach, leasing more than a hundred tourist hotels to provide housing for men stationed there. The army and navy established training and rehabilitation facilities in Miami, Miami Beach, Opa-locka, Homestead, and Coral Gables. The navy, for instance, took over all of Miami's port facilities and established a

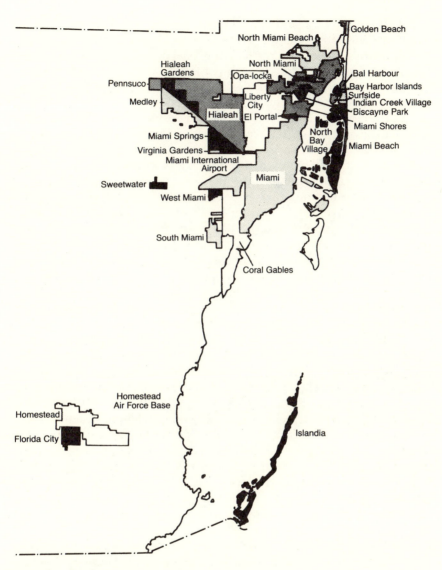

MAP 3.1. Miami and Its Suburbs

naval air station in Opa-locka. A major military air base was located in Homestead, in the southern section of Dade County. The enormous military payroll pumped up the local economy throughout the war, providing tourist hotels with year-round rather than the normal seasonal business and stimulating the retail and service trades. Moreover, thousands of civilian workers came to the area to build and maintain military installations and service the military establishment. Thus, while the war dampened tourism, new war-related activities more than compensated the local economy. Hotel managers, who at first opposed the military occupation of beachfront hotels, soon viewed the military presence as an economic lifesaver. As one Miami businessman noted in 1943, "without the army this town would have been bankrupt by now." By stimulating the economy in new directions, the war had a positive impact on the Miami region.[8]

The postwar era was one of dynamic growth in the Miami metropolitan area. The Dade County population, for instance, continued to increase in the late 1940s, rising to 495,000 in 1950, an increase of almost 85 percent over 1940. The pattern of urban deconcentration, evident as early as the 1930s, intensified. The greatest growth during the forties took place in the suburban fringe, which registered an increase of about 152 percent over 1940, and in the unincorporated areas, where the ten-year growth amounted to 164 percent (see Table 3.1). As early as 1945, the *Miami Herald* noted a brisk trade in vacant land in Miami, Coral Gables, Miami Beach, and smaller waterfront municipalities such as Surfside and Golden Beach. Coral Gables was reported on the verge of "widespread new development" in 1945, and by 1950 it had more than doubled its 1940 population.[9] In several suburban municipalities, particularly Hialeah, Opa-locka, and North Miami, population rocketed upward, reflecting the surge of real estate development and housing construction in the Miami area. Nine new municipalities incorporated in the forties, all but one in the postwar period.[10]

Explosive population growth and accompanying housing shortages stimulated a new building and construction boom in Miami and its suburban fringe. Between 1945 and 1950, in-migration of new residents touched off a tremendous building program, mostly in new residential construction but also in commercial and factory buildings. Employing over 10 percent of the 1950 Dade County labor force, construction had become "one of the most important economic activities in the region."[11] The building boom typified the multifaceted growth of the Miami area. Reviewing the Miami labor

market in 1948, the Florida Industrial Commission noted the changing economic character of the Florida metropolis:

> A magnet of population influx, Miami is the fastest growing
> metropolitan district in the southern United States. Unlike
> many big industrial cities, it has grown primarily not by ac-
> quisition of new industries, but by a steadily increasing popu-
> lation that has lasted through booms and depressions. Starting
> as a winter resort area, it has grown in trade, finance, service
> and manufacturing. Although the winter resort business is still
> growing, other industrial activities have given an increasing
> degree of year-round stability to the area. . . . Miami's unique
> climate and geographical position at the crossroads of two con-
> tinents are natural factors contributing to further development
> in industry.[12]

In the postwar period, therefore, Miami and its suburban fringe began to take on economic characteristics similar to those of nonresort
urban centers.

By 1950, the Miami metropolitan area consisted of the central
city of Miami, twenty-five suburban municipalities (a twenty-sixth
municipality—Islandia—was added in 1961), and a growing unincorporated fringe that totaled almost one-fourth of total metropolitan population. Like other Sunbelt areas, metropolitan Miami
has grown throughout the entire postwar period. As Table 3.1 reveals, however, the central city has grown much more slowly than
the suburban fringe. Actually, Miami's population growth has been
slowing since the 1930s, and during the 1970–1980 decennial period
the central city grew by only 3.6 percent. Similarly, Miami's share
of the total SMSA population has been declining since the 1930s.
In 1980, the city of Miami comprised only 21.3 percent of Dade
County's population, compared to 64.3 percent in 1940. At the same
time, Miami's suburban communities and unincorporated areas
have acquired new population at a remarkable rate, particularly during the 1940s and 1950s. Since 1960, the suburban municipalities
have experienced slower rates of growth—35.9 percent in the 1960s
and 21 percent in the 1970s. The most rapidly growing portion of
the Miami SMSA since 1940 has been the unincorporated section,
which more than doubled and tripled in population during the 1940s
and 1950s. Growth has been more modest since 1960, but the rate of
growth has nevertheless hovered around the 50 percent mark for the
past two decades. As a result of this startling increase of population,

TABLE 3.1. Population Distribution in the Miami SMSA, Central City, and Suburban Fringe, 1940–1980

	1940 Population	% of Total SMSA	1950 Population	% of Total SMSA	% of Increase	1960 Population	% of Total SMSA
Miami	172,172	64.3	249,276	50.3	44.8	291,688	31.2
Suburban municipalities	54,016	20.2	135,949	27.5	151.7	291,142	31.1
Unincorporated areas	41,551	15.5	109,859	22.2	164.4	352,217	37.7
Total Dade County	267,739	100.0	495,084	100.0	84.9	935,047	100.0

SOURCE: U.S. Bureau of the Census.

by 1980 almost one-half of the entire SMSA population resided in the unincorporated portion of Dade County.

This pattern of urban deconcentration and suburban dispersal has affected central cities in the Northeast and Midwest throughout the twentieth century. Decentralization of city population became especially discernible after about 1900, when the annexation movements of the late nineteenth century came to a halt. By contrast, many of the newer Sunbelt cities of the South and West have been pushing out their municipal boundaries, thus recapturing population through annexation.[13] A somewhat different pattern was followed by Miami. Miami's residents did not spill out into surrounding suburbs as they did in the North right after the war. Rather, massive in-migration of new residents provided most of the population filling up Miami's suburban and unincorporated fringe.

The failure of annexation explains the contemporary municipal structure of the Miami SMSA. Until the mid twenties, Miami expanded its boundaries rapidly, encompassing some forty-three square miles of land by 1925. However, Miami's last annexation took place in 1925 during the height of the great real estate boom. During that period of expansion and speculative development, Miami incurred a high level of bonded indebtedness for roads, bridges, schools, utilities, drainage facilities, and other services. The advent of the Great Depression brought financial disaster to Miami's municipal finances. By the early thirties, debt service was costing the city 31 percent of its total budget, and in July 1932 the city defaulted on interest payments. Unable to carry through its ambitious

% of In- crease	1970 Popula- tion	% of Total SMSA	% of In- crease	1980 Popula- tion	% of Total SMSA	% of In- crease
17.0	334,859	26.4	14.8	346,931	21.3	3.6
114.2	395,640	31.2	35.9	478,702	29.5	21.0
220.6	537,293	42.4	52.5	800,346	49.2	48.9
88.9	1,267,792	100.0	35.6	1,625,979	100.0	28.3

program of urban development, Miami deannexed territory in 1931, reducing the city's size from forty-three to thirty-four square miles of land. Services were cut back and programs of municipal development abandoned. Property assessments rose somewhat in the late thirties, providing additional city income and permitting a reduction of Miami's bonded indebtedness, but the city's financial position remained relatively weak.[14]

Miami officials demonstrated little interest in annexing new land after the twenties. The financial burdens of additional service areas were simply too steep. Indeed, Miami's city government faced severe problems in sustaining growing operations within its own boundaries. Even as late as the 1950s, according to University of Miami economist Reinhold Wolff, Miami's city government was weak and unable to cope with growing urban needs. Under the circumstances, therefore, Miami's status began to wither. Not surprisingly, some commercial and industrial establishments also abandoned the central city for outlying areas with their cheaper land and lower taxes. Suburban municipalities promoted this sort of economic decentralization. Hialeah, for example, made a substantial annexation of undeveloped land in 1960, hoping to attract new industrial growth to the city. As Wolff noted, the region's "interest in annexation has been based solely on whether or not it would mean a direct gain in net tax revenues."[15]

The changing distribution of population in the Miami SMSA, then, reveals much about the emerging metropolitan structure. Examining the population patterns in adjacent SMSAs adds further in-

TABLE 3.2. Population Growth of Three South Florida SMSAs, 1930–1980

	1930 Population	1940 Population	% of Increase	1950 Population	% of Increase
Miami SMSA (Dade County)	142,955	267,739	87.3	495,084	84.9
Fort Lauderdale– Hollywood SMSA (Broward County)	20,094	39,794	98.0	83,933	110.9
West Palm Beach SMSA (Palm Beach County)	51,781	79,989	54.5	114,688	43.4

SOURCE: U.S. Bureau of the Census.

sight. Since 1960, Dade County population growth has been slow-ing, but two nearby Florida SMSAs have been growing rapidly. As Table 3.2 suggests, the Fort Lauderdale–Hollywood SMSA (Broward County), located just north of Dade County, has registered higher rates of population increase since 1930. With a population of just over one million in 1980, Broward County grew more than twice as rapidly as Dade in the last decade. The West Palm Beach SMSA (Palm Beach County) has acquired new population at a faster rate than Dade since 1950. The West Palm Beach area population stood at just over 573,000 in 1980, and like Broward its growth rate more than doubled that of the Miami SMSA between 1970 and 1980.[16]

The rapid growth of these three contiguous Florida SMSAs sug-gests the emergence, as the *New York Times* noted in 1973, of a new southeastern megalopolis. Taken together, the three SMSAs experi-enced a growth rate of 115.8 percent during the 1950s and 49.4 per-cent during the 1960s. In the decade between 1970 and 1980, popu-lation growth in this highly urbanized region amounted to 43.6 percent—about the same as the 43.4 percent population growth rate recorded for the state of Florida as a whole during the same decade. The population of this new megalopolis is crowded into a relatively narrow strip of land along the Atlantic coastline stretching about one hundred miles from north of West Palm Beach to south of Miami and Coral Gables. Much of the land in this populated strip has been subdivided, developed, and built upon. Most new develop-ment in the three-county area is located on the western fringes of the built-up territory, where new subdivisions encroach upon the Everglades and endanger the region's fragile ecosystem.[17]

1960 Population	% of Increase	1970 Population	% of Increase	1980 Population	% of Increase
935,047	88.9	1,267,792	35.6	1,625,979	28.3
333,946	297.9	620,100	85.7	1,014,043	63.5
228,106	98.9	348,993	53.0	573,125	64.2

Throughout these three SMSAs, urban and suburban sprawl has eliminated any geographical separation or physical differentiation among the numerous municipalities. As one scholar has noted, "A neighborhood in the city of Miami often looks little different from that in the surrounding municipalities. . . . One municipality melts into the other, or into the unincorporated areas without visible landmarks or traces of differentiation in street patterns, architectural features or type of land uses." Journalist Tad Szulc suggested a similar lack of differentiation in 1974: "Driving along the coastal highway in Florida, say from South Miami to Palm Beach, I never had the sensation of advancing from one place to another, though I crossed three counties. It was one continuous, homogenized, semi-urban landscape." Thus, the Miami SMSA is only a part of a larger urbanized region sprawling over three counties and a total of ninety-two separate municipalities strung out along the Atlantic shoreline.[18]

Despite the seeming uniformity of building style, street layout, and physical appearance, differences exist in patterns of population distribution, particularly with regard to race and ethnicity. Blacks were among the early residents of Miami, particularly Bahamian blacks who worked as masons and carpenters in the local construction industry. Substantial numbers of blacks also made their living as farm workers in Dade County's important agricultural industry, while others were employed as service workers in the local tourist hotels and restaurants.[19] During the Florida boom of the twenties and the quick recovery from the depression in the thirties, new white residents were attracted to the area in higher proportions than blacks. Thus, by 1940 the black population of the Miami metro-

politan area totaled 49,518, but the percentage of blacks had fallen to
18.5 percent from 31 percent in 1920. Between 1940 and 1980, the
black population of the Miami SMSA increased roughly in proportion to total population growth. In 1980, blacks constituted 17.2 percent of total SMSA population (see Table 1.4).

The composition of Miami's black population has been altered
somewhat by the presence of substantial numbers of black immigrants. As noted, Bahamian blacks settled in Miami early in the
twentieth century, and a constant infusion of new arrivals from the
islands has helped to maintain a definable Bahamian presence in the
city. Although relatively few Cuban blacks came to Florida in the
Cuban migrations of the 1960s and 1970s, perhaps 20 percent—or
about 25,000—of the Cubans arriving in the Mariel boatlift of 1980
were blacks. In addition, some 50,000 to 60,000 Haitian refugees
have come to Miami in recent years, and an estimated 25,000 to
30,000 Jamaicans live in the Miami metropolitan area. Thus, the
black population of the Miami SMSA is much more diverse than in
most metropolitan areas.[20]

Most black people in the Miami SMSA are concentrated in ten
segregated communities. Miami's earliest black residents settled in
the city's Coconut Grove section, located a few miles southwest of
the central business district (CBD). A second and larger black neighborhood emerged in the heart of Miami and just west of the CBD.
Until the 1960s, this so-called Overtown district remained the
largest single cluster of black settlement in Miami. As a result of
scattered public housing programs in the late thirties and early forties, black population began to decentralize. For example, in 1937
work began in northwest Miami on a large-scale, low-rent public
housing project called Liberty Square. It became the nucleus of the
present-day Liberty City ghetto. Emerging about the same time was
Brownsville, a second northwest Miami black community separated
from Liberty City by a white residential area. As a consequence of
white flight from the intermediary zone during the 1950s, Liberty
City and Brownsville became a single continuous black settlement
by the 1960s. By 1980, the Liberty City–Brownsville community
had expanded far beyond the city boundaries of Miami into the unincorporated area, and its population had grown to about 160,000.[21]

Not all Miami blacks live in the inner-core neighborhoods. A
number of smaller black communities developed on the urban periphery, some as far as thirty miles from downtown Miami. On the
city's northwest fringe some fifteen miles from the CBD, several
large postwar housing and apartment developments for blacks went
up in Opa-locka. By the 1970s, blacks began moving into Carol City,

a formerly all-white community near Opa-locka. Eighteen miles southwest of Miami, a private developer created a black subdivision, Richmond Heights—a community of single-family homes built in the 1950s that attracted primarily black professionals and middle-class people. Still further south on the agricultural fringes of the Miami SMSA, black communities grew in the unincorporated towns of Perrine and Goulds and in the incorporated municipalities of Homestead and Florida City. Moreover, the urban renewal and ex-pressway building of the 1950s and 1960s destroyed much of the older inner-city black district and resulted in a substantial resi-dential relocation to other areas.[22] Thus, the black population of the Miami SMSA is not concentrated in the central city, but has de-centralized and spread to almost a dozen distinct communities.

Although geographically fragmented, the black population of the Miami SMSA has been and remains quite isolated from whites. Surveying the residential neighborhoods of metropolitan Miami in 1938, appraisers of the federal Home Owners Loan Corporation found the black sections of the city to be totally segregated. A 1956 study of 185 cities by sociologist Donald O. Cowgill listed Miami as the nation's most segregated city in 1940 and the second most segre-gated in 1950. As black neighborhoods expanded in the postwar years, some temporary integration occurred on the frontiers of the ghetto. Writing in 1951, investigators from the University of Miami noted: "Generally, Negro areas are inhabited throughout by non-whites, although occasionally a few white families may be found in such districts, especially near the periphery, as conversely Negro families are scattered in white neighborhoods."[23] The process of resi-dential transformation was full of tension and conflict, and it was often accompanied by white protest meetings, harassment of blacks, cross burnings, and even shootings and bombings. In one such inci-dent, the decision in 1951 to build a black housing project in a white neighborhood on the edge of Liberty City touched off a wave of dyna-mitings at the building site and throughout the Miami area.[24]

Community by community, racial segregation has become in-tense. Successive censuses, for example, reveal minuscule propor-tions of blacks in Miami Beach, Hialeah, Miami Springs, North Miami, and the smaller waterfront and oceanside municipalities. By contrast Opa-locka went from just over one-third black in 1960 to nearly two-thirds in 1980.[25]

Not surprisingly, some 58 percent of Dade County's blacks now live in the unincorporated areas of the SMSA. As some scholars have noted, the process of municipal incorporation has become a way of maintaining exclusively white suburbs. At the same time, already established cities are not interested in annexing outlying black neighborhoods; generally, low property appraisals translate into small tax revenues, while overcrowded black neighborhoods draw heavily on municipal services and facilities. Consequently, the city of Miami has never expressed any interest in annexing the large segment of Liberty City lying outside its municipal boundaries. The city's disinterest leaves servicing to the county government. Similarly, Hialeah to the west has aggressively pursued a policy of annexing undeveloped industrial land, but has ignored Liberty City along its eastern boundary. As a result, black community organizations in Liberty City have sought to incorporate a new, fifteen-square-mile municipality. Black supporters of the plan view this so-called New City as a means of acquiring local political power and a community-controlled police force—an important issue in the wake of the 1980 Liberty City riots.[26] Thus, since 1940 the black population of the Miami SMSA has increased roughly in proportion to total population, but growth has been accompanied by dispersal from central city neighborhoods and concentration in unincorporated areas.

As in a number of other Sunbelt cities, Miami's blacks share their minority status with a large and rapidly increasing Hispanic population. Even before World War II, a sizable middle-class Cuban community existed in Miami. In the immediate postwar years, Miami experienced a noticeable influx of working-class Puerto Ricans. Careful estimates placed the Spanish-speaking population of the Miami SMSA at about 20,000 in 1950 and at least 50,000 in 1960.[27] A massive exodus of Cuban exiles began in the wake of the Cuban Revolution in 1959 and continued sporadically over the next two decades. Between 1959 and 1980, over 800,000 Cubans left their homeland for the United States. Despite government efforts to relocate Cuban exiles throughout the United States, most eventually settled in the Miami area. By the early 1970s, Miami had become the world's second largest Cuban city, smaller only than Havana.[28]

The full dimensions of the Hispanic presence in the Miami SMSA have been revealed in the 1970 and 1980 census reports. In 1970, when the Hispanic category was first recorded, almost 300,000 Hispanics made their homes in the Miami metropolitan area. By 1960, the Spanish-speaking population had almost doubled to just over 581,000, and the percentage of Hispanics had increased from 23.6 percent to 35.7 percent of total SMSA population (see Table 1.4). These statistics do not include the recent wave of 125,000 Cuban refugees who arrived between April and December 1980 during the boatlift from Cuba's Mariel harbor. Thus, by the end of 1980, the Hispanic total for the Miami SMSA soared to at least 700,000, or about 40 percent of the entire metropolitan population.[29]

Cubans make up the great majority of the Hispanics in the Miami SMSA, but as many as 100,000 to 150,000 are non-Cuban Latins. In 1979, the *New York Times* reported that Miami's Cubans shared their new land with an estimated 25,000 Puerto Ricans, 25,000 Colombians, 20,000 Venezuelans, 10,000 Peruvians, 6,000 Chileans, 6,000 Mexicans, and smaller concentrations of other Central and South American peoples. Recent revolutions in Nicaragua and El Salvador have brought an estimated 20,000 to 30,000 new exiles. In addition, the U.S. Border Patrol in Miami has admitted that "tens of thousands" of illegal aliens, mostly Latin Americans, have entered the south Florida area, often using fraudulent visas and posing as tourists. Thus, the Hispanic population of the Miami SMSA, although mostly Cuban, is actually quite diverse in terms of national origins.[30]

Cubans are highly centralized residentially in Miami's "Little Havana," a vast 800-block area spreading south and west from the CBD. Most of this area is located within the city of Miami, but it overlaps into the neighboring municipality of Coral Gables. By 1970, about 160,000 Latins, almost all Cubans, had settled in the Little Havana section. Ten years later, Little Havana's population surpassed 200,000.

Bisected by Southwest 8th Street and 27th Avenue, Little Havana was once a declining section of empty lots, run-down businesses, and older, single-family homes. The enormous influx of Cubans, attracted by low rents, cheap properties, and accessibility to downtown Miami, began to concentrate in this section. As in earlier immigrant cities, owners converted their single-family dwellings into multiple units and residential densities soared. New apartments went up on cleared land, Cubans established businesses and a vibrant cultural and institutional life, and the section grew by absorbing new arrivals from the island as well as Cubans who had first settled in other parts of the United States. Through a process of "population invasion," Cubans quickly replaced non-Latin whites and the boundaries of Little Havana expanded to accommodate the burgeoning Cuban influx.[31]

The growth of Little Havana revolutionized the demographic structure of the Miami SMSA in two decades. Hispanics, for instance, made up 45.4 percent of the city of Miami's population in 1970 and 55.9 percent in 1980. The spread of Cuban settlement into Coral Gables pushed that city's Hispanic proportion from 17.2 percent in 1970 to 29.6 percent in 1980. Hialeah provides the most startling example of the diffusion of Hispanic population out of Little Havana. Virtually an all-white city in 1960, Hialeah had become three-quarters Hispanic by 1980. Its tally of 108,000 Hispanic residents was second only to Miami's 194,000. Most of Dade County's other large municipalities also experienced a substantial surge in Hispanic population, although none exceeded 25 percent. By 1980, Cubans and other Latins were pouring into some of the smaller municipalities as well, particularly to the south and west of the CBD. For example, on the western fringes of the metropolitan area, according to the 1980 census, 81 percent of Sweetwater's population was Hispanic. Nearby, in the small city of West Miami, Hispanics made up 62 percent of the population. In addition, over 200,000 Hispanics now reside outside of any city and constitute 26 percent of the county's unincorporated area population. As a result of the dramatic growth of these Cuban settlements and those of other Latins, non-Hispanic white people had become a minority in the SMSA population by 1980—a twenty-year demographic revolution without precedent in American history.[32]

From the city's origins, Miami's economic health depended upon tourism. By 1940, the Miami metropolitan area was serving about two million vacationers each year. At the outbreak of World War II, one observer wrote, the tourist dollar was "the lifeblood that feeds the economic organism." The war cut tourism drastically, although war-related activities helped to sustain the economy. The postwar era witnessed a great hotel-building boom, with most new construction in Miami Beach and other oceanfront communities to the north. In 1942 Miami Beach had 291 hotels; by 1955, the number had increased to 382. Tourists continued to come to the Miami area in ever larger numbers—5.5 million in 1960, over 6 million in 1970, and 12.6 million in 1980.[33] But, while total tourist volume rose, the proportion of SMSA workers employed in tourism gradually declined. In 1940, for example, about 35 percent of all Dade County workers earned their living in hotel, restaurant, and other service occupations. The proportion of tourist-related workers declined to about 20 percent of the labor force in 1960, and to about 10 percent in 1979.[34]

Nevertheless, tourism remains the largest single economic force in the Miami SMSA. The tourist industry has promoted the area in recent years as a center for foreign vacationers. "The British are coming," some 327,000 of them in 1980, the *Wall Street Journal* reported in an article on Miami Beach. They were joined by 67,000 Germans, 38,000 Spaniards, 22,000 French, and thousands of other

Europeans. However, the European tourist influx pales before the two million annual visitors from Central and South America and from the Caribbean. These newcomers have pumped up the local retail trade, purchasing designer clothing, jewelry, appliances, electronic equipment, and other consumer items. Indeed, according to local tourist officials, the 12.6 million tourists who visited Miami in 1980 spent $9.1 billion in local hotels, restaurants, and retail establishments.[35] New high-rise hotels are going up in downtown Miami to accommodate the influx, while industry officials are seeking to tap the Japanese tourist market. In addition, Miami is the nation's leading cruise ship port, with more than 1.6 million passengers in 1980.[36] Thus, through boom and recession, tourism remains a mainstay of the Miami economy. However, the nature of the industry has changed, and increasing proportions of European and Latin American tourists have added to Miami's international character.

Air travel facilitated the postwar tourist boom. In the years since 1945, commercial aviation has provided another major impetus to Miami's economic growth. As a result of military aviation activities in south Florida during World War II, Miamians entered the postwar era with a new consciousness of the importance of air travel. Several major airlines, including Pan Am, Eastern, and National, originated in Miami in the prewar period. In 1945, the Dade County Port Authority formed to administer the city's airports and seaport, and Pan Am's terminal facilities were purchased for a public airport (now the site of Miami International). City and county officials sought authorization for new routes and began promoting Miami as the gateway for international air travel, particularly to Latin America.[37] Several airlines located their aircraft overhaul, repair, and maintenance facilities at Miami's airport. With over seven thousand workers, Eastern Airlines was the largest single employer in the Miami SMSA in 1960, and by 1980 Eastern employment had doubled. Miami passenger traffic and international air freight skyrocketed in the 1970s. Miami International is the ninth busiest airport in the world in passengers and the sixth largest in air cargo tonnage. Moreover, among U.S. airports, Miami stands second only to New York's Kennedy Airport in international passengers and cargo. An estimated 160,800 workers, or about one-fifth of the Miami labor force, are directly or indirectly employed in airport and aviation activities.[38]

The growing influx of tourists has combined with the rapidly rising population of permanent residents to support a vigorous construction industry in the Miami SMSA. In 1940 and again in 1950, about 10 percent of the Dade County labor force worked in the building trades. The postwar era began with a ten-year boom in new hotel building. At the same time, the demand for new apartments and single-family homes remained high, sustained by metropolitan population increases of over 80 percent in both the 1940s and 1950s (see Table 3.1). In 1954, when new homes were going up at the rate of eleven thousand per year, Miami led all metropolitan areas in new home construction per one thousand population.[39] Between 1960 and 1980, the building industry thrived on real estate subdivision and development on the suburban periphery and on high-rise condominium construction in Miami Beach and on the fringes of the CBD. Interestingly, by the early seventies, Cuban-owned construction companies were putting up at least 35 percent of all Dade County's new buildings.[40] As the 1980s began, seventy major construction and development projects were under way in downtown Miami, including dozens of new skyscrapers, hotels, office buildings, and condominiums—a virtual Miami "renaissance," according to some observers. Some $2.2 billion in private and government funds have been invested in this downtown construction. Thus, throughout the entire postwar period, the construction industry has been an integral part of the local economy.[41]

Although heavily dependent upon tourism and tourist-related activities, the Miami economy has developed an increasingly important manufacturing sector since World War II. Miami was the least industrialized metropolitan area in the United States in 1940, when only about 3.3 percent of the labor force held factory jobs. By 1950, manufacturing employment had risen to 9.4 percent. At the end of the fifties, factory work had expanded still further, employing some 38,000 people—about 13 percent of the labor force. "Tourism," one study suggested in 1962, "appears to be gradually giving way to manufacturing in relative importance." This prophecy has never been completely fulfilled, but manufacturing employment continued to rise steadily after 1960, reaching an estimated 118,000 in 1980, or about 18 percent of total employment.[42]

In the early postwar period, most of Miami's manufacturing took place in relatively small plants and centered on consumer goods: food products, bread baking, meat packing, bottled beverages, home furnishings, fishing and sports equipment, and clothing. In addition, local factories provided other products for area needs: concrete and lumber products, fabricated metal and aluminum goods, printing and publishing, and boat building. By the 1970s, however, Miami manufacturers were expanding beyond local and regional markets and beginning to tap national and international markets. New industries included plastics, electronic equipment, aircraft parts, and medical technology.[43] An extensive garment industry emerged, often using refugees and illegal aliens who labor under conditions reminiscent of old-time sweatshops.[44] Most of the Miami SMSA's manufacturing firms—some 4,700 of them in 1980—are small, but taken together they have helped to create a more balanced economy no longer exclusively dominated by tourism.[45]

Over the course of the postwar era, the location of manufacturing has shifted. At first, most manufacturing was located in the city of Miami, either in the CBD or along a north-south strip running parallel to the two rail lines entering the city. By the 1950s, many industries had relocated to Hialeah, North Miami, and the northwest unincorporated area. More space, cheaper land, lower taxes, the availability of working-class population, county zoning policies, and other inducements drew industry outward. Designation of large sections in the western unincorporated area for industrial development, as well as the growth of industrial parks near Miami International Airport and major expressways, has tended to decentralize Dade County manufacturing.[46]

While industry has decentralized in Dade County, international trade and banking has concentrated in Miami and Coral Gables. Local officials and businessmen began promoting Miami's place in international and especially Latin American trade soon after World War II, but not until the 1970s did Miami become a true center of international trade and banking. The dramatic emergence of Miami in a new world role stems from a combination of geographic location, excellent air and sea links to Latin America, aggressive business leadership, and the growth of a bilingual culture. The Port of Miami provides a base for no less than eighty-five steamship companies, most of them operating freighters to Central and South America. During 1979, ships and planes carried more than $5 billion in goods from Miami to Caribbean and Latin American countries.[47]

At least three other developments of the 1970s contributed to Miami's emergence as an international trade center. First, U.S. multinational corporations began to locate their Latin American headquarters in the Miami area, particularly in Coral Gables. Some fifty-five regional offices had been established in Coral Gables by 1977, and by 1980 the number had increased to an even one hundred. The multinationals betting on the Miami area's future prospects included Exxon, Gulf Oil, Texaco, Dow Chemical, International Harvester, ITT, DuPont, Alcoa, General Electric, Goodyear, Uniroyal, Lockheed, American Express, and others. At the same time, numerous Latin American and Caribbean governments and corporations have set up shop in Miami and Coral Gables to facilitate trade and business with North America.[48] Second, under the provisions of the federal Edge Act, twenty-four large U.S. banks established branches in Miami by 1981 in order to engage in international banking and finance. Similarly, after favorable state legislation in 1978, forty-three foreign bank agencies opened offices in Miami by early 1981. These banks, along with about two dozen major local banks with aggressive international departments, have revolutionized trade, finance, and banking in Miami in a very short time. The city now stands second only to New York as an international banking center. Miami, one financial writer noted in 1980, had become banking's new "frontier town."[49]

The third significant business development was the establishment of the Miami free trade zone, a large area west of Miami's airport accommodating almost two hundred companies involved in international trade. In addition, a free zone industrial park to be located in Homestead is planned for 1982. The largest of several such free trade zones in the United States, the Miami zone provides a place for export-import companies to store, process, manufacture, assemble, display, or reexport goods from abroad without first paying tariffs. Local businessmen expect this free trade zone to handle $2 billion worth of goods per year.[50] Enormous changes, therefore, have taken place in metropolitan Miami's business pattern during the past ten years. Miami is finally fulfilling the dreams of early postwar businessmen who envisioned their city as the gateway to Latin America. As Joel Garreau has suggested in his recent book, *The Nine Nations of North America* (1981), Miami experienced a sweeping "geographic reorientation" during the past decade—one that made Miami the economic and cultural capital of the entire Caribbean basin.[51]

While Miamians have been developing new overseas business and banking connections, foreigners have been investing in Florida on a vast and unprecedented scale. According to economist Mira Wilkins, author of *Foreign Enterprise in Florida* (1979), Miami "has proven to be a magnet for non-U.S. investments in land and real estate, construction, manufacturing, retail and wholesale trade, transportation services, insurance, and banking."[52] The full extent of this foreign financial involvement in the Miami SMSA is unknown, but it undoubtedly represents a huge investment. One hint as to how huge comes from Charles Kimball, a south Florida real estate analyst, who found that 1980 property sales involving Netherlands Antilles corporations alone totaled a staggering $1 billion in Dade County and another $900 million in Broward and Palm Beach counties. Foreign investors also use corporations registered in such offshore tax havens as Panama, the Bahamas, and the Cayman Islands. This tremendous investment has pumped up the south Florida economy and partially insulated Miami from the economic woes of the rest of the nation, but it has also tended to make the city dependent upon the continued flow of foreign capital.[53]

A substantial portion of the money flowing into south Florida—no one knows exactly how much—is illegal drug money. From its earliest days as a tourist playground, Miami and Miami Beach attracted gamblers, bookies, and gangsters. Racketeering became even more widespread in the postwar era, and in 1955 the *Miami Herald* called the city the nation's leading gangster haven. When mobsters began buying up swank Miami Beach hotels in the 1960s, *Newsweek* labeled the place "Mob Town, U.S.A."[54]

In the 1970s, a new kind of crime wave swept metropolitan Miami: illegal drug smuggling, mostly organized by gangs of Cuban and Colombian "cocaine cowboys." Like many legitimate products, smuggled cocaine, marijuana, and other illegal drugs come to Miami by sea and air from Latin America and the Caribbean. Like legitimate business profits, much of the drug money, properly laundered, finds its way into Miami banks, real estate, and business operations. "Illegal money is a major factor in the current boom in south Florida," says real estate man Kimball. Almost half of all Miami real estate sales to offshore corporations or foreign investors, Kimball contends, are paid for with laundered "narcobucks." At least four Miami banks, law enforcement authorities say, are actually owned by drug smugglers. Federal officials estimate that at least $28 billion worth of illegal drugs come into the United States through south Florida each year. Miami in the 1980s is the undisputed drug capital of the world. Joel Garreau argues that drug smuggling has become south Florida's number one industry, surpassing even tourism. Illicit drug dealing, another writer claims, "may be Florida's biggest retail business." True or not, even as staid a source as the *New York Times* agreed in 1980 that the multibillion dollar transfusion of drug money protected Miami's economy from recession.[55]

In many ways, therefore, the economy of metropolitan Miami has been dramatically transformed in only a few short years. It would be difficult to dispute the contention that the remarkable progress of the Cuban refugees after 1960 had a lot to do with Miami's changing economy. "There's no doubt about it," *Miami Herald* editor Jim Hampton wrote in 1980. "Refugees have been the economic salvation of Dade County. They've given it a rich cultural milieu. They've been instrumental in turning an unremarkable Southern tinseltown into an international city of unlimited potential."[56] With its downtown in decline, its image as a tourist playground losing its glitter, and its population dispersing to the suburbs, Miami was rejuvenated by the Cuban influx of the 1960s and early 1970s. In essence, an entire professional and middle-class population was uprooted from Cuba and set down in Miami. After a short period of adjustment, the Cubans pursued the American dream with a vengeance. By 1980, they had established some 18,000 businesses in the Miami area: restaurants; banks; construction companies; service stations; wholesale and retail outlets; clothing, shoe, and cigar factories; auto dealerships; and fishing fleets. Over a period of two decades, their economic success has been nothing short of spectacular. Moreover, they made Miami into a Latin American city, one in which the Spanish language and Latin culture exist side by side with English and the native Anglo culture. This Latin ambience has attracted businessmen and tourists from Central and South America, and Miami Cubans have aggressively promoted international trade and commerce.[57] "It is an article of faith in Miami," one writer noted in 1980, "that without the impetus provided by the Cuban-exile community the city today would be just another Sun Belt spa well past its prime."[58]

Metropolitan Miami's demographic and economic changes have been matched by significant innovations in urban government. In July 1957, a countywide metropolitan government began functioning in Dade County—the first such "Metro" government in the United States. Although buffeted by localist opponents for almost twenty-five years, Miami's Metro government has gradually expanded its power and functions at the expense of the county's fragmented municipalities.

The idea of a consolidated urban government for Dade County grew out of the conditions of the 1930s and 1940s. With the collapse of the Florida land boom in the twenties and the depression of the thirties, Miami's central city status weakened. Financially in trouble, the city could not afford to expand its boundaries or extend municipal services. Meanwhile, the vast population growth of Dade County's unincorporated area brought consequent demands for the services enjoyed by city residents—demands that were increasingly provided by the existing county government. Thus, as early as the 1930s, local power was beginning to drift from city to county.[59]

This trend was accelerated during World War II and immediately thereafter, when a number of functional consolidations took place. In 1943, for instance, a countywide public health department was created. In 1945 the Dade County Port Authority was established, and state legislation consolidated ten separate Dade County school districts into a single countywide school system. A few years later, in 1949, the city of Miami transferred Jackson Memorial Hospital, the area's major public health care facility, to Dade County. Nevertheless, because of the fragmented municipal structure of the county, most government functions and services, if provided at all, were administered by the separate cities in the metropolitan area.[60]

The functional consolidations of the 1940s created an awareness among local political reformers that county government might serve as the vehicle for a consolidated metropolitan government. The growing sentiment for such a government led to three major efforts to merge various municipalities with Dade County. In 1945, a plan proposed by Miami mayor Leonard K. Thompson to merge Miami and its suburban municipalities into a single countywide metropolitan government died in the Florida legislature. In another consolidation effort in 1948, Dade County voters rejected a plan to merge Dade County with Miami and four small municipalities. A referendum in 1953 on a proposal to abolish the city of Miami and transfer its functions to the county failed by a very small margin. Political battle lines hardened during each of these consolidation efforts, with suburban opponents seeking to maintain local power and control and supporters asserting the efficiency and economy of a consolidated metropolitan government.[61]

The closeness of the 1953 referendum encouraged advocates of consolidation to push ahead. Supported by the Miami press, civic groups, and the Miami Chamber of Commerce, the Miami city commission created a twenty-member Metropolitan Miami Municipal Board (3M Board) to study the feasibility of consolidation. The 3M Board, in turn, hired a Chicago consulting firm, the Public Administration Service (PAS), to research and report on the issue. The PAS report, published in 1954 as *The Government of Metropolitan Miami,* essentially recommended a two-tiered metropolitan government—a federated structure in which existing municipalities retained certain local services and a new metropolitan government took over designated areawide functions such as planning, mass transit, recreation, water and sewage, health and welfare, and so on. The 3M Board accepted the PAS recommendations, then successfully guided a Dade County home-rule provision through the state legislature and a statewide referendum. The legislature also established a Metropolitan Charter Board to draft a new Dade County charter. In May 1957, by a narrow margin, county voters ratified the plan.[62]

The new county charter built upon the recommendations of the PAS report. It established the two-tiered governmental system that conferred broad powers on the new countywide metropolitan government and left a number of local functions to the individual municipalities. The powers of Dade's Metro government included mass transit and expressway building, health and welfare programs, parks and recreation, housing and urban renewal, air pollution control, beach erosion control, flood and drainage control, industrial promotion, regulation of water supply and sewage and solid waste disposal, libraries, uniform building codes, assessing and collecting taxes, comprehensive development plans, provision of all services in the unincorporated areas, and the setting of minimum standards for all governmental units in the county. The individual municipalities retained fire and police protection, regulation of taxes and alcoholic beverage sale, and the ability to exceed minimum county standards in zoning. No new municipalities could be created nor could existing municipalities make new annexations without county approval. The new Metro government was headed by a nine-member, nonpartisan board of commissioners elected at large for four-year terms. One of the commissioners served as a figurehead mayor, but the chief administrator was a county manager, who served at the pleasure of the commission.[63]

In some ways, Dade County's new Metro government represented a compromise between the "consolidationists" and the "localists." Consolidationists promoted abolition of the separate municipalities and the creation of a single supergovernment. Good government reformers who supported Metro included Miami business and professional leaders, civic groups like the League of Women Voters, the *Miami Herald* and the *Miami News*, and the Dade County delegation to the state legislature. Given the earlier failures to achieve consolidation, Metro advocates pushed the federated, two-tiered approach as the only realistic means of getting an areawide government for the Miami metropolitan region. They focused on the inadequacies of the existing municipal structure and emphasized the efficiency, tax savings, and better service that a metropolitan government would bring. Although not the single, centralized supergovernment many consolidationists wanted, Dade's new Metro government possessed broad and sweeping powers that cut across municipal boundaries and permitted a unified approach to areawide problems.[64]

The localists, by contrast, sought to retain power at the municipal level, opposed the Metro idea, and fought to destroy it once it became a reality. Political scientist Edward Sofen, in his book *The Miami Metropolitan Experiment*, identified the localists as the officials and employees of the individual municipalities (who feared loss of power and even their jobs), the Dade County League of Municipalities, several suburban newspapers, and various business and citizens groups in the smaller cities. Defeated in the crucial 1957 referendum, the localists immediately began a sustained attack on the new Metro government. The attack took several forms. Many of the municipalities refused to cooperate with the new county government, and political sniping became the order of the day. The localists also resorted to the courts, and by 1961 they had filed some six hundred law suits challenging Metro authority. Miami Beach, for instance, took its case for retaining a separate traffic court all the way to the U.S. Supreme Court, but lost. As a result of its hostility to the new governmental system, Miami Beach, along with the neighboring municipalities of Surfside, Golden Beach, Bal Harbour, and North Bay Village, tried to secede from Dade County in 1960, but without success. Miami Beach, which had adequate tax revenues and excellent municipal services, "resisted Metro to the bitter end," Sofen noted.[65]

Localists also fought Metro by trying to dilute or undermine its power through amendments to the Dade County charter. One such proposed amendment in 1958 would have restored autonomy to the municipalities, effectively nullifying metropolitan government. This autonomy amendment lost decidedly in a countywide referendum, but the localists did not give up. Another serious anti-Metro challenge occurred in 1961, when a proposed amendment would have introduced thirty-seven changes in the Metro charter, including abolition of the council-manager form of government and termination of Metro control of such countywide functions as water supply, sewage, transportation, and planning. Dade County voters also rejected this amendment, but in later years passed others curbing the county manager's broad powers. Even some Metro advocates eventually became unhappy with what they had created, and in the 1960s good government reformers began circulating petitions for a charter amendment to eliminate the council-manager plan in favor of the strong mayor system. In a 1972 referendum this strong mayor plan met defeat, but in 1981 a charter revision commission revived the idea.[66]

Political controversy has surrounded Miami's Metro government from the very beginning. Metro's first two county managers were forced out of office, one for pursuing consolidation too aggressively, and the other for being too conciliatory toward the municipalities. The expected tax savings promised by Metro advocates never materialized, and increased property tax assessments to pay for expanded services alienated many Dade County voters. Taxation,

planning, land use, and development policies stirred great controversy.[67] As one recent study noted: "Miami Metro provides an example of how metropolitan government can breed extended conflict,
even where it is successfully implemented. From the outset Miami
has been a case study of how not to reform, and many of the political
wounds remain open today."

But while political conflict between Metro and the municipalities continued, Metro consolidated its powers and functions and
began to make itself indispensable. By the end of the 1970s, according to another recent analysis, "Metro now enjoys general acceptance, or at least tolerance, both in the cities and in the unincorporated area." Proposed changes in the Metro charter are no longer
"challenges to the supremacy of countywide government," but rather
"adaptations to the times." Metro had not only endured, but to many
observers it had proved its worth as a form of urban government.[68]

A lack of strong political leaders has further complicated Miami's politics. With the exception of the 1930s, when a short-lived
political machine emerged, political leadership in south Florida has
been fragmented. As a result, no strong political loyalties have developed among Miami metropolitan area residents. A long tradition of
one-party politics and the recency of arrival of most Miamians have
also contributed to this weak political structure. Moreover, the at-
large system of electing the Metro commission has tended to isolate
Metro government from the people. Indeed, as the racial and ethnic
character of Dade County's population changes, the Metro commission is perceived as less and less representative, more and more distant. By the mid 1970s, one study of Miami reported that local political issues were "shifting from Metro versus the cities to Metro
versus the people." Thus, politics in the Miami SMSA is increasingly
being organized around racial and ethnic issues, as blacks and Hispanics begin to assert their political strength.[69]

Despite a sizable demographic base in Dade County, blacks remained politically impotent until the 1970s. Prior to the creation of
Metro in 1957, local political power lay primarily in the hands of the
Miami city commission. In the early 1920s, the five members of the
city commission were the city's leading bankers. In succeeding decades, bankers, realtors, and others from the city's white business and
professional elite continued to dominate elected offices. Blacks were
effectively frozen out of political office at first by the white primary
system and after 1945 by the low registration of black voters and the
at-large system of electing members of the Miami city commission.
By the 1960s, however, as a result of the civil-rights movement and

voter registration drives in the black community, black Miamians began to participate more actively in city politics.[70]

One early sign of the new black political power came in 1959 with the creation of a black political "machine" by community organizer Charles Hadley. Hadley's organization, called Operation Big Vote, delivered large blocs of votes to favored candidates, black or white. This sort of clientage politics began to wither in the late 1960s. In 1967 Athalie Range, a black businesswoman and civic leader, was elected to the Miami city commission. The following year, black voters elected a Metro commissioner and sent a black representative to the state legislature, the first black elected to that body since Reconstruction. These black positions on the Miami city commission, on the Metro commission, and in the state legislature have remained traditionally "safe" black seats since the late 1960s.[71] By the 1980s, Miami's black voters had elected three additional state legislators and a Dade County school board member, while blacks had been appointed to such prominent positions as Miami city manager, Miami city attorney, and Dade County school superintendent. In Opa-locka, where they gained a substantial majority during the 1970s, blacks hold two seats on the five-member city commission, as well as the positions of mayor, city manager, and police chief.[72]

Despite these individual achievements, most Miami area blacks are unhappy with what they consider an unresponsive political system. With only 16 percent of the registered voters in 1980, blacks in Dade County have never had sufficient political strength to obtain redress of their major grievances—police brutality, bad housing, unemployment, inadequate schools and recreation facilities, and poor municipal services in the ghetto. These complaints have helped to trigger the "New City" incorporation movement.[73]

The growing power of the Cuban and Hispanic vote has also undermined the strength of Miami's blacks at the polls. When the Cubans first came to Miami in the 1960s, they came as exiles rather than refugees. Almost universally, they hoped to depose Fidel Castro and return to their homeland. Thus, for many years Castro and Cuba were more important to Miami's newcomers than local political issues. Because they planned to return, few became naturalized citizens. But by the 1970s, the hope of return had fizzled for most. As the Cuban exiles increasingly came to view their new home as permanent, they put down roots and became citizens and voters. By the end of the 1970s, Hispanic political strength in south Florida had become formidable, particularly in Miami and Hialeah.[74]

The power of the Latin vote has been increasingly apparent in

Miami since the mid 1970s. By 1981, more than 36 percent of the city's registered voters were Hispanic, as were three of the five members of the city commission, including Puerto Rican Maurice Ferre, who serves as mayor. In the 1981 city elections, Ferre barely survived a challenge by Cuban-born Manolo Reboso, and local political observers predict a growing Hispanic political presence in Miami during the 1980s. Hispanic voters have also become a powerful force in Hialeah and in a few of the smaller municipalities such as Sweetwater. In 1981, Hialeah voters ousted an Anglo mayor, electing a Cuban in his place. In Sweetwater, Cubans hold the mayoralty and several city council seats. Even in Miami Beach, where the 1980 Hispanic population was 22 percent and rising, local politics is becoming Cubanized.[75]

The Hispanic voting bloc is even stronger than numbers suggest because the Cubans turn out on election day in larger proportions than Anglos or blacks, and because they tend to vote along ethnic lines against white or black candidates. However, Cuban politics in Miami is also very fragmented, with numerous factions and groups organized around old-country or anti-Castro issues. This political fragmentation has carried over into local political contests and, to a certain extent, has weakened the Hispanic voting bloc.[76]

Hispanics have been less successful in running for county and state offices. However, a Cuban was appointed to the Dade County school board in 1980, and voters elected a Cuban to the Metro commission for the first time in October 1982. Until 1982 no Hispanic had been elected to the state legislature from Dade County, mainly because of multimember legislative districting, which works against geographically concentrated voting blocs. However, legislative reapportionment in 1982 resulted in the election of three Hispanic state legislators.[77] With 18 percent of the registered vote in Dade County in 1981, Hispanics have become a significant political force. Primarily because of their political conservatism, their strong anticommunism, and their support of the Nixon-Ford-Reagan anti-Castro policy, most of the Hispanic voters have supported Republican candidates. These voters helped to give Ronald Reagan a huge majority in Dade County during the 1980 presidential election. Thus, a new kind of ethnic politics has emerged in the Miami metropolitan area—a political picture that will continue to change as more Cubans and other Hispanics become citizens and voters and as Dade County becomes a Republican stronghold.[78]

While a new kind of ethnic urban politics was emerging in Miami, an old pattern of intergovernmental conflict continued between Dade County and the state of Florida. The Florida state legislature has traditionally been dominated and controlled by rural and conservative north Florida politicians. As late as the 1960s, when the state government was still run by the so-called Pork Chop Gang, Florida had "one of the most archaic and unrepresentative" state governments in the nation. Tied to special interests and easily swayed by powerful legislative lobbies, the "pork choppers" ignored the special problems of urban south Florida and particularly disliked the liberal, black, and Jewish constituencies of the Miami metropolitan area. The distribution of tax revenues typified the discriminatory treatment Miami received at the hands of the state legislature. In 1958, for instance, some $36 million worth of tourist-related taxes (sales taxes, alcoholic beverage taxes, race track receipts) were taken out of Dade County by the state. Only about $1 million of this amount was returned to Dade in grants to local agencies.[79]

Reapportionment of legislative districts in the 1960s rectified the rural-urban imbalance somewhat, but rural north Florida politicians have retained power in the legislature through their control of key legislative posts. Florida's current governor, Robert Graham, began his career as a Dade County politician and won his present post in 1978 on the strength of Florida's urban Democratic vote, but he has been ineffective in dealing with the legislature. Legislators from Miami, Tampa, Jacksonville, and other urban areas have recently joined together in an urban coalition to secure better funding for schools, roads, and other urban concerns, but with little success. "Urban needs get clubbed in Tallahassee," a *Miami News* columnist noted as the 1981 legislative session drew to a close. The message was not new, but one that Miamians had received regularly from successive legislatures in the postwar era.[80]

Miami's relationship with the federal government has been more positive. In the depression years of the 1930s, the federal government began bypassing the state legislatures and dealing directly with city governments on such issues as welfare and public housing. During World War II, of course, the federal presence in Miami intensified with the establishment of air and naval bases. In the postwar period, a number of important federally funded programs were implemented in Miami, including major expressway construction, urban renewal, public housing, Model Cities, community development block grants, and the like. Metro has created its own Department of Housing and Urban Development—"Little HUD," it is called—to administer the various federal housing and social programs. In addition, the federal government created an extensive refugee assistance program. By 1973, more than $1 billion had been spent to assist Cuban resettlement in the United States. Federal funds have also provided most of the support for the construction of Dade County's new and still unfinished rapid transit system—a planned fifty-mile overhead metrorail linked to a smaller downtown people-mover system. More recently, some additional federal funds have been delivered to Dade County for the newest refugee crisis and for postriot reconstruction in Liberty City. However, the Reagan administration's penchant for budget cutting will reduce federal spending in Miami and other cities. In an age of diminishing federal activity, Miamians will have to learn to expect less of their municipal government or pay more in local taxes.[81]

In the course of the postwar period, the Miami metropolitan area has experienced rapid growth and change—patterns that have intensified as Miami emerges in the 1980s as the booming metropolis of the southeastern Sunbelt. But growth and change have not come without accompanying social and political tensions. The issues of race, ethnicity, and immigration, for instance, bear with particular intensity on the city. For Miami's blacks the city has become a symbol of despair, but paradoxically, for Cuban, Haitian, and other refugees Miami is a symbol of hope. Other conflicts focus on environmental issues. Continued development, most experts agree, threatens the subtropical paradise. The fragile south Florida ecosystem cannot take much more concrete and asphalt before the Everglades dry up and the underground water supply disappears. Meanwhile, Miami suffers the social problems common to most big cities—high crime rates, an aging and overcrowded housing stock in the central city and older suburbs, and inadequate governmental funding. Thus, Florida's new boom town has some rather severe problems that need attention and resolution.

The issue of race hit home in the Liberty City riot of May 1980. Touched off by a not-guilty verdict for several Metro police officers charged in the beating death of Arthur McDuffie, a black insurance man, the Miami riot of May 17–19 resulted in eighteen deaths and at least $200 million worth of property damage. It differed from the ghetto riots of the 1960s in the intensity of antiwhite violence.[82]

To many observers, the Liberty City riot reflected the desperation and despair of Miami's black community. One careful study of the riot identified the underlying causes as the small proportion of black policemen, the low frequency of black store ownership in the ghetto, and the discriminatory at-large electoral system for city and county political offices. These conditions, the study suggested, gave blacks a sense of economic and political powerlessness. Others pointed to the high rates of poverty and unemployment among blacks in Miami, or to widespread slum housing conditions. It was "the political economy of racism," one scholar contended, that made Liberty City and other black neighborhoods "ripe for rebellion." Moreover, most blacks were fully aware of the lack of change since an earlier Miami ghetto riot in 1968. As T. Willard Fair, director of Miami's National Urban League branch, noted in 1980, "The black community has made no significant progress here in the past ten years and may even be regressing." In the wake of the rioting, federal and state officials promised to help rebuild the burned-out areas and promote black capitalism in the ghetto. But as the *Miami Herald* noted a year after the riot, little has been accomplished.[83]

Some analysts attribute the slow economic progress of Miami's blacks to competition with the Cuban refugees in the 1960s and 1970s. Although penniless on arrival in Miami, the Cubans had education, skills, and a strong work ethic. In addition, they faced less racial prejudice. They moved quickly into the low-paying service-type jobs traditionally held by blacks, particularly in tourist hotels and restaurants. They also found work in construction, in the Miami garment industry, and in other blue-collar jobs where they competed with black workers. "The economic penetration of the refugees is now universal," *Ebony* magazine reported in 1963. "The Cubans are slowly taking over the business of Dade County," Miami's black newspaper, the *Miami Times*, complained in 1966.[84]

Cuban entrepreneurial success often came at the expense of black-owned businesses. For example, blacks owned 25 percent of all the gas stations in Dade County in 1960. By 1979 black ownership of service stations had dropped to 9 percent, but Hispanic-owned stations accounted for 48 percent of the total. In addition, say black spokesmen, the federal government has discriminated in funding minority economic development. Between 1968 and 1979, the Small Business Administration distributed about $100 million to Miami area businesses. Hispanics received 47 percent of the total over the twelve-year period, Anglos 46.5 percent, and blacks 6.4 percent. Moreover, the refugee resettlement program included special education classes, housing assistance, and medical and welfare benefits for Cuban newcomers. Black resentment built up over such special treatment and the rapid economic rise of the Cubans. Black emotions flared in the Liberty City riots, and they intensified with the new influx of Cubans in the so-called freedom flotilla.[85]

Few cities have had to cope with the immigration and refugee problems that have faced Miami in recent years. The massive flow of Cuban and Haitian refugees—some 160,000 in 1980 alone—amounted to a population increase of 10 percent for the Miami SMSA in less than a single year. Indecisiveness on the part of the

Carter administration and the lack of a clearly stated U.S. immigration policy added to the dimensions of the refugee crisis. Unlike earlier waves of Cuban refugees, the Marielitos were poorer, less educated, and less skilled. Those with relatives in the Miami area were quickly resettled, but most were not so fortunate. Severe problems of housing, employment, education, and social services created new tensions in the city. Particularly disturbing was the large number of criminals among the new refugees; some 23,000 of them had served time in Cuban jails, and at least 5,000 were hard-core criminals. Within a year, ninety Marielitos had been murdered in Miami, mostly by fellow refugees. Miami crime and homicide statistics soared, surpassing all other American cities in 1981. The impact of the 1980 Cuban refugee migration on metropolitan Miami will be felt for years to come.[86]

The continuing migration of Haitian refugees to south Florida has produced another source of tension. Some 50,000 to 60,000 illegal Haitian refugees arrived in south Florida between 1979 and 1981. Arriving on Florida beaches in leaky, rotting boats, the Haitians have received a less than enthusiastic welcome. Haitian supporters suggest a double standard in American immigration policy—one that welcomes refugees from Cuban communism but rejects black immigrants from Haiti seeking economic opportunity. Critics contend that there are limits to the number of refugees that can be accepted. The *Miami Herald*, for instance, editorialized that "South Florida cannot absorb all the upward-striving Caribbean residents who long for the political freedom and economic opportunity of the United States." Nevertheless, most of the Haitians are here to stay, and a fifty-square-block "Little Haiti" has emerged in the Edison–Little River section of Miami. In the absence of American aid for Haitian economic development, the Miami area will continue to serve as a magnet for the poverty-stricken people of Haiti.[87]

The refugee crisis of 1980 stimulated ethnic and racial tension in Miami. These tensions overflowed in a bitter controversy over bilingualism. Reflecting the demographic changes in the Miami metropolitan area, the Metro commission officially made Dade County bilingual in 1973. As a result, most Metro agencies hired Hispanics to serve Spanish-speaking residents; official documents appeared in English and Spanish, and informational signs became bilingual. But not all Miamians supported bilingualism. As early as 1975, Miami Anglos vehemently protested a bilingual school program that required English-speaking elementary school children to study Spanish.[88]

The issue heated up considerably in 1980 when an Anglo group named Citizens of Dade United began circulating a petition to force a referendum on a proposed antibilingualism ordinance. The key section of the ordinance proposed that "the expenditure of county funds for the purpose of utilizing any language other than English, or promoting any culture other than that of the United States, is prohibited. All county government meetings, hearings, and publications shall be in the English language only." Various Hispanic groups fought the proposed ordinance and the newspapers editorialized against it. In a "pre-emptive move," the three Latins on the Miami city commission voted to make Miami officially bilingual. Nevertheless, in what the *Miami Herald* described as an "ethnic-line vote," Dade County voters approved the antibilingualism ordinance by a large majority. Observers noted that the bilingualism issue reflected a new sort of ethnic polarization in Miami, one perhaps worsened by the enormous influx of new Cubans earlier in the year. As the bilingualism controversy suggests, ethnic emotions have boiled over into the political arena, where they are likely to remain for some time to come.[89]

The issue of development has also generated much political conflict in recent years. The controversy has two arenas—business-oriented building and development in Miami's downtown, and residential subdivision and industrial expansion on the outer fringes of the metropolitan area. Downtown development has been a hot political issue in Miami city politics since the late 1950s. An ambitious plan for a "Magic City Center" in 1961 and another redevelopment plan proposed by internationally famous city planner Constantinos Doxiadis in 1967 stimulated much local controversy and never came to fruition.[90] However, in the 1970s, as Miami emerged as an important center of international trade and finance, an unplanned downtown building boom began to reshape the central business district. The Miami city commission sought to maintain control over this new surge of development through its zoning ordinances and a quasi-official Downtown Development Authority. Critics lamented the lack of any overall downtown plan and the hodgepodge of building and architecture. The *Miami Herald* regularly blasted the city commission, labeling downtown Miami "a disaster of urban architectural planning." In addition, the *Herald* and the *Miami News* have criticized both city commission zoning concessions to developers and the politics involved in plans for bay-front park development, a downtown sports complex, and an amusement park on a Biscayne Bay island.[91]

Similarly, development on the urban periphery has touched off hot political debate. On the southwestern edge of the SMSA and along the undeveloped bayfront below Miami and Coral Gables, residential developers are anxious to subdivide and build. On the northwestern fringe, developers are seeking approval for industrial expansion. Since 1975, when Dade County's Metro commission adopted a Comprehensive Development Master Plan, development on the outskirts of the urbanized area has been closely controlled and restricted. Metro planners oppose leapfrog development and back a careful program of growth management and infill development. They contend that a sufficient amount of vacant land is available within the urbanized area to accommodate as many as 800,000 additional people in Dade County over the next twenty years. The biennial review of the master plan by the Metro commission provides a periodic opportunity for pro- and antidevelopment forces to test their political muscle. To date, the Metro commission has adhered closely to the master plan, despite pressure from the developers.[92]

What makes the planning and development issue so crucial in Miami is the fragile nature of the south Florida ecosystem. Continued development on the urban fringe, even within the limits established by the Metro master plan, threatens the Everglades to the west. As agricultural land, mangrove swamps, and other wetlands give way to drainage and development, water is drawn from the underground aquifer and the local water supply is threatened by saltwater intrusion and wastewater pollution. For some time, a coalition of scientists, environmentalists, and other concerned citizens has been challenging the developers and seeking tougher controls on growth. Some ecologists even suggest that growth must be halted in its tracks if the Florida environment is to survive.[93] In the 1980s, when the federal government is rolling back regulations of all kinds, it is unlikely that growth and expansion can be checked in the Miami metropolitan area. Thus, development will continue to be controversial in local politics—perhaps ultimately becoming the most serious issue of all.

The Miami metropolitan area, then, has been a dynamic and changing urban region since World War II. Beginning as a tourist and retirement haven, Miami has emerged as an exciting center of international trade and finance. Its downtown is booming and development is mushrooming all across the urban periphery. The arrival of Cuban and other Caribbean refugees has permanently altered the ethnic composition and the political realities of the area. The new immigrants have made Miami as much a Latin American as an American city. The unique experiment in metropolitan government has helped to overcome a fragmented municipal structure. There is a darker side—drug smuggling, crime, racism, rioting, environmental danger—but it, too, suggests something of the dynamic forces of change at work in the Miami metropolitan area. As the *Miami Herald* noted in 1980, "Nowhere in America is the cutting edge of 20th century change more evident than in Miami."[94] Miami has become a contemporary urban laboratory unlike any other for testing the twenty-first century.

NOTES

1. Al Burt, "Miami Today: The Best of Times?" *Miami Herald Tropic*, 28 September 1980.

2. Sidney Walter Martin, *Florida's Flagler* (Athens: University of Georgia Press, 1949), 150–168; Nathan D. Shappee, "Flagler's Undertakings in Miami in 1897," *Tequesta* 19 (1959): 3–13.

3. Victor Rainbolt, *The Town That Climate Built* (Miami: Parker Art Printing Association, 1924).

4. T. H. Weigall, *Boom in Paradise* (New York: Alfred H. King, 1932); Frank B. Sessa, "Real Estate Expansion and Boom in Miami and Its Environs during the 1920s" (Ph.D. dissertation, University of Pittsburgh, 1950).

5. Frank B. Sessa, "Miami in 1926," *Tequesta* 16 (1956): 15–36; Millicent Todd Bingham, "Miami: A Study in Urban Geography," *Tequesta* 9 (1948): 97; R. D. McKenzie, *The Metropolitan Community* (New York: McGraw-Hill, 1933), 338; *The Government of Metropolitan Miami* (Chicago: Public Administration Service, 1954), 5–9.

6. Vernon M. Leslie, "The Great Depression in Miami Beach" (M.A. thesis, Florida Atlantic University, 1980); Reinhold P. Wolff, *Miami Metro: The Road to Urban Unity* (Coral Gables: University of Miami Press, 1960), 6; Federal Writers' Project, *Florida: A Guide to the Southernmost State* (New York: Oxford University Press, 1939), 214.

7. *Government of Metropolitan Miami*, 8–17; Wolff, *Miami Metro*, 42–45, 72; Reinhold P. Wolff, *Miami: Economic Pattern of a Resort Area* (Coral Gables: University of Miami Press, 1945), 11.

8. *New York Times*, 2 August 1942, 20 June 1943; *Miami Daily News*, 14 February 1943; Sidney M. Shalett, "Play-Grounds to Parade-Grounds," *New York Times Magazine*, 2 August 1942, 10–11, 24; "Miami Beach Goes to War," *Life*, 28 December 1942, 65–66.

9. *Miami Herald*, 6 January, 11 February 1945.

10. *Government of Metropolitan Miami*, 9–11, 16.

11. Vance V. Wilson, "Preliminary Economic Base Study" (Miami Planning Department, May 1954, mimeo), 6.

12. Florida Industrial Commission, "Miami Labor Market Review, September 1947–September 1948," Bureau of Employment Security Records, Record Group 183, Box 63, National Archives, Washington, D.C.

13. On annexation, see Kenneth T. Jackson, "Metropolitan Govern-

ment versus Political Autonomy: Politics on the Crabgrass Frontier," in Kenneth T. Jackson and Stanley K. Schultz, eds., *Cities in American History* (New York: Alfred A. Knopf, 1972), 442–462; Jon C. Teaford, *City and Suburb: The Political Fragmentation of Metropolitan America, 1850–1970* (Baltimore: Johns Hopkins University Press, 1979); Carl Abbott, *The New Urban America: Growth and Politics in Sunbelt Cities* (Chapel Hill: University of North Carolina Press, 1981), 50–51.

14. Wolff, *Miami Metro,* 41–54.

15. *Miami Herald,* 26 October 1960; Wolff, *Miami Metro,* 44, 53, 65–66.

16. *Miami Herald,* 17 March, 4 April 1974, 23 July 1975, 8 February, 14 June 1976, 27 May 1981; Philip Weidling and August Burghard, *Checkered Sunshine: The Story of Fort Lauderdale, 1793–1955* (Gainesville, Fla.: Wake-Brook House, 1974), 242–257; Robert Johnson, "Palm Beach County: Florida's Land of Contrast," *Florida Trend* 18 (February 1976): 46–56.

17. *New York Times,* 22 April 1973.

18. Wolff, *Miami Metro,* 75; Tad Szulc, *Innocents at Home: America in the 1970s* (New York: Viking Press, 1974), 180.

19. Charles Garofalo, "Black-White Occupational Distribution in Miami during World War I," *Prologue* 5 (Summer 1973): 98–101; Paul S. George, "Colored Town: Miami's Black Community, 1896–1930," *Florida Historical Quarterly* 56 (April 1978): 432–447.

20. "Cuban and Haitian Refugees, Miami SMSA, 1980" (Metropolitan Dade County Planning Department, January 1981, mimeo); *New York Times,* 14 May 1980; *Wall Street Journal,* 5 May 1980; *Miami News,* 31 July, 5 September 1981; *Palm Beach Post,* 6 September 1981.

21. Elizabeth L. Virrick, "New Housing for Negroes in Dade County," in Nathan Glazer and Davis McEntire, eds., *Studies in Housing and Minority Groups* (Berkeley: University of California Press, 1960), 135–143; Harold M. Rose, "Metropolitan Miami's Changing Negro Population, 1950–1960," *Economic Geography* 40 (July 1964): 221–238; David B. Longbrake and Woodrow W. Nichols, Jr., *Sunshine and Shadows in Metropolitan Miami* (Cambridge, Mass.: Ballinger Publishing Company, 1976), 47–49; Anthony Ramirez, "Simmering Streets," *Wall Street Journal,* 30 March 1981.

22. Ronald Abler, ed., *A Comparative Atlas of America's Great Cities* (Minneapolis: University of Minnesota Press, 1976), 241, 243; Reinhold P. Wolff and David Gillogly, *Negro Housing in the Miami Area: Effects of the Postwar Housing Boom* (Coral Gables: University of Miami, 1951); *Miami Herald,* 11–18 December 1955; *Miami Times,* 16 March 1957, 16 January, 23 April, 11 June, 19 November 1965, 18 February, 15 April, 14 October 1966; *Psycho-Social Dynamics in Miami* (Coral Gables: University of Miami, 1969), 531–554.

23. "Security Area Descriptions, Metropolitan Miami, Florida," 24 September 1938, Records of the Federal Home Loan Bank System, Record Group 195, National Archives, Washington, D.C.; Donald O. Cowgill,

"Trends in Residential Segregation of Non-whites in American Cities, 1940–1950," *American Sociological Review* 21 (February 1956): 43–47; Wolff and Gillogly, *Negro Housing*, 17.

24. *Miami Times*, 29 September, 1 December 1951; Stetson Kennedy, "Miami: Anteroom to Fascism," *Nation*, 22 December 1951, 546–547; Charles Abrams, *Forbidden Neighbors: A Study of Prejudice in Housing* (New York: Harper, 1955), 120–136.

25. *Miami Herald*, 17 March 1981.

26. *Miami News*, 10, 15 April, 21, 22, 25 September 1981; *Miami Herald*, 20 April, 16 May, 1, 7, 15 July, 24, 26 September 1981; *Miami Times*, 16 April, 24 September, 1 October 1981.

27. William W. Jenna, Jr., *Metropolitan Miami: A Demographic Overview* (Coral Gables: University of Miami Press, 1972), 97; Bryan O. Walsh, "Cubans in Miami," *America*, 26 February 1966, 286; "Housing Plan, Miami Metropolitan Area" (Metropolitan Dade County Planning Department, March 1978, mimeo), 6.

28. Sergio Díaz-Briquets and Lisandro Pérez, "Cuba: The Demography of Revolution," *Population Bulletin* 36 (April 1981): 25–26. See also Raymond A. Mohl, "Cubans in Miami: A Preliminary Bibliography," *Immigration History Newsletter*, forthcoming.

29. Díaz-Briquets and Pérez, "Cuba," 26, 34–36. On the Cuban refugees in Miami, see also *The Cuban Immigration, 1959–1966, and Its Impact on Miami–Dade County, Florida* (Coral Gables: University of Miami, 1967).

30. *Miami Herald*, 7 September 1975, 26 September 1980, 25 January, 7 May 1981; *New York Times*, 5 March 1979; *Miami News*, 19, 28 March, 6, 14 April 1981.

31. B. E. Aguirre et al., "The Residential Patterning of Latin American and Other Ethnic Populations in Metropolitan Miami," *Latin American Research Review* 15 (1980): 35–63; Morton D. Winsberg, "Housing Segregation of a Predominantly Middle Class Population: Residential Patterns Developed by the Cuban Immigration into Miami, 1950–1974," *American Journal of Economics and Sociology* 38 (October 1979): 403–418; "Havana, Fla.," *Newsweek*, 1 September 1969, 59; Susan Jacoby, "Miami Si, Cuba, No," *New York Times Magazine*, 29 September 1974, 28, 103–110, 114, 123; "Miami: New Hispanic Power Base in U.S.," *U.S. News and World Report*, 19 February 1979, 66–69.

32. Abler, ed., *Comparative Atlas*, 242–245; Roberto Fabricio, "Miami Goes Latin and Likes It," *Florida Trend* 18 (April 1976): 140–146; *Miami Herald*, 30 August 1981; "Population Counts for Dade County" (Metropolitan Dade County Planning Department, April 1981, mimeo).

33. Wolff, *Miami*, 39; "Miami Beach Hotels: 12 Years of Building and Still SRO," *Business Week*, 15 January 1955, 28–29; "Stampede to the Sun," *Business Week*, 9 March 1963, 108–112; *Miami Herald*, 21 January 1973; *Miami News*, 25 April 1981.

34. Wolff, *Miami*, 154; Jenna, *Metropolitan Miami*, 34; "The Dilemma

of Miami-Dade," *Florida Trend* 15 (December 1972): 30; *Miami News*, 17 March 1981.

35. Wolff, *Miami Metro*, 5; Jenna, *Metropolitan Miami*, 34; Susan Harrigan, "Paul Revere Rides into Miami Beach," *Wall Street Journal*, 17 June 1980; *Miami News*, 25 April 1981; Mimi Whitefield, "North to Florida," *Miami Herald, Business Monday*, 10 August 1981.

36. Larry Birger, "Major Hotel Construction Bejewels the Gold Coast," *Miami Herald, Business Monday*, 8 December 1980; Dan Millott, "The Cruise Capital of the World," *Florida Trend* 19 (April 1977): 144–146; *Miami News*, 17 March 1981.

37. *Miami Herald*, 4, 7, 11, 12 January, 5 April 1945; Edward Sofen, *The Miami Metropolitan Experiment*, 2d ed. (New York: Anchor Books, 1966), 22–23; Aurora E. Davis, "The Development of the Major Commercial Airlines in Dade County, Florida: 1945–1970," *Tequesta* 32 (1972): 3–16.

38. Davis, "Major Commercial Airlines," 3, 10; Wolff, *Miami Metro*, 15–16; *Miami News*, 24 April 1981; Mimi Whitefield, "Middlemen Guide Billions in Freight through S. Florida," *Miami Herald, Business Monday*, 6 October 1980; Martin Merzer, "Airports: S. Florida's Money Machines," *Miami Herald, Business Monday*, 18 May 1981.

39. Wolff, *Miami*, 101; Wolff, *Miami Metro*, 12–13; "Why Florida Grows So Fast," *U.S. News and World Report*, 13 April 1956, 71; "Southeast—Where the Action Is," *Florida Trend* 14 (April 1972): 200–201.

40. "How the Immigrants Made It in Miami," *Business Week*, 1 May 1971, 88; "Success with a Spanish Accent," *Nation's Business*, 60 (March 1972): 78.

41. *Miami News*, 19 March, 5 May, 24 July 1981; Robert Dodge, "Superbuilders Redraw South Florida's Skyline," *Miami Herald, Business Monday*, 18 August 1980; Fred Tasker, "South Florida Review," *Southeast Real Estate News* 9 (March 1981): 1, 20–25, 31; Roy Kenzie, "Miami: A City Seeks an Image," *Urban Design International* 2 (March–April 1981): 12–17; William G. Conway, "Miami," *Progressive Architecture* 61 (August 1980): 49–59.

42. Wolff, *Miami*, 154; "Growth of Manufacturing in Metropolitan Dade County," *Miami Economic Research* 12 (October 1959): 2; *Metropolitan Miami* (Miami: Urban Development Services, 1962), 31; Robert Johnson, "Recession Sick Southeast Seeks New Medicine," *Florida Trend* 18 (April 1976): 67; "Region's Focus Turns toward Development," *Miami Magazine* (September 1977): 33.

43. Wolff, *Miami*, 85–94; Wolff, *Miami Metro*, 13–15; Jenna, *Metropolitan Miami*, 43–51; Gene Burnett, "Medical Technology Quietly Becomes a South Florida Growth Industry," *Florida Trend* 19 (April 1977): 149–158; Michael Silver, "Electronics: The Circuits Connect Here," *Miami Herald, Business Monday*, 11 August 1980.

44. James Risen, "Sweatshops Pervasive in Miami," *Miami Herald, Business Monday*, 18 May 1981; Bernard Swartz, "Sweatshops in Fashion,"

Miami Magazine 32 (August 1981): 40–43, 92; *Miami News*, 21–23, 28 May 1981; *Miami Herald*, 25 May 1981.

45. "Region's Focus," *Miami Magazine*, 33.

46. Wolff, *Miami Metro*, 45–49; Jenna, *Metropolitan Miami*, 43–53; "Industrial Parks Plentiful," *Miami Magazine* (September 1977): 48.

47. Joel Garreau, *The Nine Nations of North America* (Boston: Houghton Mifflin, 1981), 167–206; Robert Stickler, "Florida: Marketplace in the Heart of the Americas," *Miami Herald, Business Monday*, 26 January 1981; *Miami News*, 31 August 1981.

48. *Miami Herald*, 21 January 1973; David A. Heenan, "Global Cities of Tomorrow," *Harvard Business Review* 55 (May–June 1977): 79–92; Robert Stickler, "Multinationals Find the Gateway in Coral Gables," *Miami Herald, Business Monday*, 22 September 1980; Joe Hice, "Coral Gables: Trade Center for the Americas," *Florida Trend* 23 (February 1981): 54–59.

49. *New York Times*, 10 December 1980; *Miami News*, 1 May 1981; Erik Calonius, "Banking's Frontier Town," *Florida Trend* 22 (March 1980): 62–66; Emmanuel N. Roussakis, "The Edges Come to Miami," *Bankers Magazine* 164 (May–June 1981): 82–91; *Miami Business Journal*, 10 May 1982.

50. *Miami Herald*, 14 October 1980, 26 January, 3 September 1981; *Miami News*, 3 September 1981; Annetta Miller, "Miami Free Trade Zone," *Florida Trend* 23 (November 1980): 60–64.

51. Garreau, *Nine Nations*, 172; Mimi Whitefield, "Miami: International City," *Miami Herald, Business Monday*, 14 September 1981.

52. Mira Wilkins, *Foreign Enterprise in Florida: The Impact of Non-U.S. Direct Investment* (Miami: University Presses of Florida, 1979), 104.

53. Larry Birger, "Billion-Dollar Money Funnel into S. Florida," *Miami Herald, Business Monday*, 4 August 1980; Phyllis Berman, "Miami: Saved Again," *Forbes*, 1 November 1977, 37–41; Jeffrey Tucker and Wayne Falbey, "Foreigners Find Florida Safer Than Their Banks," *Florida Trend* 21 (March 1979): 26–33; Erik Calonius, "Offshore Money Floods Miami," *Florida Trend* 22 (April 1980): 38–47.

54. *Miami Herald*, 9–14 February 1945, 4 May 1955; Henning Heldt, "Miami: Heaven or Honky-Tonk?" in Robert S. Allen, ed., *Our Fair City* (New York: Vanguard Press, 1947), 88–91; "Miami: Mob Town, U.S.A," *Newsweek*, 13 February 1967; 38–39.

55. "Miami: Latin Crossroads," *Newsweek*, 11 February 1980, 41; Garreau, *Nine Nations*, 169, 176, 183–196; "Miami's 'Narcobucks,'" *Newsweek*, 9 June 1980, 44; Stanley Penn, "The Pot Trade," *Wall Street Journal*, 22 July 1980; Hank Messick, "The Drug Enforcement Farce," *New Florida* 1 (August 1981): 48–53; "The Sun Belt Today," *Changing Times* 35 (September 1981): 28; *New York Times*, 1 April 1980.

56. *Miami Herald*, 11 May 1980.

57. "To Miami, Refugees Spell Prosperity," *Business Week*, 3 November 1962, 92–94; "La Saquesera: Miami's Little Havana," *Time*, 14 October 1974, 24; "Miami: Headquarters Town for Latin Business," *Business Week*,

7 August 1978, 40–41; Anthony Ramirez, "Making It," *Wall Street Journal*, 5 May 1980; David Wilkening, "Pluck and Luck in Little Havana," *Florida Trend* 23 (December 1980): 46–48; "Hispanics Make Their Move," *U.S. News and World Report*, 24 August 1981, 60.

58. Herbert Burkholz, "The Latinization of Miami," *New York Times Magazine*, 21 September 1980, 46.

59. Wolff, *Miami Metro*, 35–39.

60. Sofen, *Miami Metropolitan Experiment*, 16–26; Wolff, *Miami Metro*, 103–126; James F. Horan and G. Thomas Taylor, Jr., *Experiments in Metropolitan Government* (New York: Praeger Publishers, 1977), 91–92.

61. *Miami Herald*, 4, 6, 11, 16 March, 5 April 1945, 14 March, 1, 8, 11 June, 2 July 1953; Sofen, *Miami Metropolitan Experiment*, 27–35.

62. Sofen, *Miami Metropolitan Experiment*, 36–73; Wolff, *Miami Metro*, 126–131; *Government of Metropolitan Miami*, 87–111.

63. Aileen Lotz, "Metropolitan Dade County," in *Regional Governance: Promise and Performance*, Case Studies, vol. 2 (Washington, D.C.: Commission on Intergovernmental Relations, 1973), 6–16; Horan and Taylor, *Metropolitan Government*, 94–98; John C. Bollens and Henry J. Schmandt, *The Metropolis* (New York: Harper and Row, 1965), 459–463.

64. Sofen, *Miami Metropolitan Experiment*, 8, 74–91; O. W. Campbell, "Progress Report on Metropolitan Miami," *Public Management* 41 (April 1959): 85–89; Harry T. Toulmin, "Metro and the Voters," *Planning* (1959): 63–69.

65. Sofen, *Miami Metropolitan Experiment*, 8, 173–174; "Reprieve for Metro," *Economist*, 28 October 1961, 336–338; Joseph Metzger, "Metro and Its Judicial History," *University of Miami Law Review* 15 (Spring 1961): 283–293; *Miami Herald*, 27 October 1960.

66. Sofen, *Miami Metropolitan Experiment*, 115–127, 176–197; Thomas J. Wood, "Basic Revisions in Dade Charter," *National Civic Review* 53 (January 1964): 39–41; Bollens and Schmandt, *Metropolis*, 463–469; Horan and Taylor, *Metropolitan Government*, 99.

67. Sofen, *Miami Metropolitan Experiment*, 243–252; "Another Crisis for Metro," *Business Week*, 18 February 1961, 102; "Blow at Miami's Metro," *Business Week*, 1 September 1962, 92; Thomas J. Wood, "Dade Commission Dismisses a Manager," *National Civic Review* 53 (October 1964): 498–499.

68. Horan and Taylor, *Metropolitan Government*, 99, 104; Juanita Greene, "Dade Metro: Turbulent History, Uncertain Future," *Planning* 45 (February 1979): 16.

69. Heldt, "Miami," 91–93; V. O. Key, *Southern Politics* (New York: Alfred A. Knopf, 1949), 82–105; Edward Sofen, "Problems of Metropolitan Leadership: The Miami Experience," *Midwest Journal of Political Science* 5 (February 1961): 18–38; Longbrake and Nichols, *Sunshine and Shadows*, 20.

70. Wolff, *Miami Metro*, 32–35; Thomas J. Wood, "Dade County: Unbossed, Erratically Led," *Annals of the American Academy of Political and Social Science* 353 (May 1964): 67–68.

71. *Miami Times*, 17, 24 November, 8 December 1967, 8 November 1968; *Miami Herald*, 1, 11, 17 November 1981, 12 September 1982; *Miami News*, 19 February, 19 September 1981.

72. *Miami Times*, 6 December 1980, 19 March, 9 April 1981; *Miami News*, 2, 5 February, 6 March, 11 May 1981; *Miami Herald*, 17 March, 23 May 1981.

73. U.S. Commission on Civil Rights, *Confronting Racial Isolation in Miami* (Washington, D.C., 1982); *Miami Times*, 1, 15, 22 September, 10 November 1967, 28 August 1980, 16 April, 3 September 1981; *Miami Herald*, 12 April, 23 August 1981.

74. William C. Baggs, "The Other Miami—City of Intrigue," *New York Times Magazine*, 13 March 1960, 25, 84–87; "Miami, Haven for Terror," *Nation*, 19 March 1977, 326–331; Neal R. Peirce, *The Megastates of America* (New York: Norton, 1972), 484–485; "Miami's Cubans—Getting a Taste for Politics," *U.S. News and World Report*, 5 April 1976, 29.

75. *Miami Herald*, 7 October 1979, 8 February, 6 April, 5, 13 May, 19 June, 13, 26 July, 29 August, 4, 11 November 1981; *Miami News*, 11 May, 23 June 1981; *Miami Times*, 12 February 1981; *El Sol de Hialeah*, 20, 27 August 1981.

76. *New York Times*, 18 November 1973; *Miami Herald*, 5 May, 29 August 1981; *Miami News*, 24, 25, 26 April 1981; *Diario Las Americas* (Miami), 25, 26 April 1981; *La Nación* (Miami), 31 July, 7 August 1981.

77. *Miami Herald*, 29 May 1980, 6 April, 2 June, 20 July, 22, 29 August, 5 September 1981; *Miami News*, 28 April, 18 August, 2, 3 September 1981.

78. *Miami Herald*, 5 November 1980; Paul S. Salter and Robert C. Mings, "The Projected Impact of Cuban Settlement on Voting Patterns in Metropolitan Miami, Florida," *Professional Geographer* 24 (May 1972): 123–131; Benigno E. Aguirre, "Ethnic Newspapers and Politics: *Diario Las Americas* and the Watergate Affair," *Ethnic Groups* 2 (1979): 155–165; Dan Millott, "Cuban Thrust to the GOP," *New Florida* 1 (September 1981): 70–71.

79. Peirce, *Megastates*, 467; "The Partition of Florida," *National Civic Review* 48 (June 1959): 284–285; William C. Havard and Loren P. Beth, *The Politics of Mis-Representation: Rural-Urban Conflict in the Florida Legislature* (Baton Rouge: Louisiana State University Press, 1962); "The Cost of Local Government in Metropolitan Dade County," *Miami Economic Research* 12 (July 1959): 6.

80. James Nathan Miller, "How Florida Threw Out the Pork Chop Gang," *National Civic Review* 60 (July 1971): 366–371; David R. Colburn and Richard K. Scher, *Florida's Gubernatorial Politics in the Twentieth Century* (Tallahassee: University Presses of Florida, 1980), 87–90; Dan Millott, "The Duel for Dade County," *Florida Trend* 20 (February 1978): 37–40; *Miami News*, 27 May 1981.

81. *Hearings before the National Commission on Urban Problems*, vol. 3 (Washington, D.C., 1967), 332–373; E. Randolph Preston and Preston E. Beck, "The Metro-Dade Story: A Place in the Sun for Rapid Transit," *Railway Age*, 12 March 1979, 36–42; *Miami Herald*, 20 February 1978,

12 April, 8 June 1981; *Miami News*, 21 February, 10 March, 7 April 1981; *New York Times*, 18 October 1981; *Psycho-Social Dynamics in Miami*, 334–357.

82. *Miami Herald*, 18–21, 25 May 1980, 12 April, 17 May 1981; *Miami Times*, 22 May 1980; *New York Times*, 25 May 1980; "Three Days of Black Rage in Miami," *Newsweek*, 2 June 1980, 34–39; "Fire and Fury in Miami," *Time*, 2 June 1980, 10–15.

83. *Miami Herald*, 12 April, 17 May 1981; *Miami Times*, 29 May, 5, 12, 26 June 1980; Manning Marable, "The Fire This Time: The Miami Rebellion, May, 1980," *The Black Scholar* 11 (July–August 1980): 7, 9; Burkholz, "Latinization of Miami," 84–88.

84. "Miami: No Place Like It," *Time*, 12 November 1965, 36; "Havana-in-Exile," *Economist*, 3 August 1968, 33–34; Neil Maxwell, "New Influx of Cubans Faces Cool Reception from Many Miamians," *Wall Street Journal*, 12 October 1965; Allan Morrison, "Miami's Cuban Refugee Crisis," *Ebony* 18 (June 1963): 96–104; *Miami Times*, 15 July 1966.

85. *Miami Herald*, 17 May 1981; Marable, "Fire This Time," 8–9; Susan Harrigan and Charles W. Stevens, "Roots of a Riot," *Wall Street Journal*, 22 May 1980; Anthony Ramirez, "Cubans and Blacks in Miami," *Wall Street Journal*, 29 May 1980.

86. *Miami Herald*, 11 May, 1, 15 June, 26 July, 28 August, 18 September, 30 October, 14 December 1980, 26, 31 May, 4 June, 31 July 1981; *Miami News*, 18 April 1981; "Coping with Cuba's Exodus," *Newsweek*, 12 May 1980, 60–63; "Carter and the Cuban Influx," *Newsweek*, 26 May 1980, 22–28; Robert L. Bach, "The New Cuban Immigrants: Their Background and Prospects," *Monthly Labor Review* 103 (October 1980): 39–46.

87. Kristine Rosenthal, "In the Shadow of Miami," *Working Papers Magazine* 9 (September–October 1982): 18–26; Kevin Krajick, "Refugees Adrift: Barred from America's Shores," *Saturday Review*, 27 October 1979, 17–20; Patrice Gaines-Carter, "Boat People Come Ashore," *Black Enterprise* (November 1979): 21–22; *New York Times*, 14 May 1980; *Miami Herald*, 20 April, 11 May 1980, 17 May, 17, 28 June, 2, 16 August 1981; *Miami News*, 1, 19 May 1981; "A New Immigration Policy," *Newsweek*, 3 August 1981, 25–26.

88. *New York Times*, 18 April 1973; "Backlash in Miami," *Newsweek*, 17 March 1975, 29–32.

89. *Miami Herald*, 3 August, 30 September, 7, 26 October, 5 November 1980, 20 February, 13 July 1981; *Diario Las Americas*, 25 July, 10 August, 23 October, 7 November 1980. See also Raymond A. Mohl, "Miami Metro, Charter Revision, and the Politics of the 1980s," *Florida Environmental and Urban Issues* 10 (October 1982): 9–13, 21–23.

90. Arthur E. Darlow, "Miami to Upgrade Its Downtown," *American City* 74 (August 1959): 123–127; *Magic City Center Plan for Action* (Metropolitan Dade County Planning Department, 1960); *Miami Herald*, 8 October 1961; *New York Times*, 17 December 1967.

91. Sam Jacobs, "Miami: Manhattan of the South," *Planning* 45 (February 1979): 10–13; John Sugg, "Downtown Miami: Feuding over Its Fu-

ture," *Florida Trend* 24 (May 1981): 34–37; Kenzie, "Miami," 12–17; *Miami Herald*, 5 October 1980, 25 January, 11, 26 February, 18, 19, 29 March, 23, 28 May, 10, 24, 25 June, 13 September 1981; *Miami News*, 18, 20, 30 March 1981.

92. *Comprehensive Development Master Plan* (Metropolitan Dade County Planning Department, 1979); *Miami Herald*, 17 October 1980, 17 March, 26 April, 23 May, 2, 7, 14, 30 June, 5 July 1981; *Miami News*, 15 May 1981.

93. "Water: A Growing South Florida Problem," *Florida Trend* 17 (October 1974): 22–34; Al Burt, "What the Environmentalists Are Afraid to Say," *Miami Herald Tropic*, 6 September 1981, 18; *Miami News*, 3 March, 5 May, 5 September 1981; *Miami Herald*, 29 July, 2 August 1981; *Palm Beach Post*, 12 October 1980; Luther J. Carter, *The Florida Experience: Land and Water Policy in a Growth State* (Baltimore: Johns Hopkins University Press, 1974), 138–186.

94. *Miami Herald*, 3 November 1980.

4

NEW ORLEANS

SUNBELT IN THE SWAMP

by Arnold R. Hirsch

New Orleans never fits in. Beginning as the most European city in the United States, it became the greatest urban center in a region devoted to agriculture, and is today included—more by geographical accident than anything else—in America's booming Sunbelt. New Orleans has always gone its own way, at its own inimitable pace, with seemingly little regard for the way things are done elsewhere. What else could be expected of a town, located on the fringes of the Bible Belt, that revels in its sensuality and betrays either apathy or a perverse kind of civic pride when confronted with evidence of persistent corruption? This, it must be added, has become more difficult of late, but the legacy of the past has had its impact. New Orleanians defy easy categorization.

The same is true when trying to gauge New Orleans's place in the Sunbelt. Geography provides the simplest and most basic definition of the Sunbelt and, by any reasonable standard, New Orleans is part of it. Yet if the term "Sunbelt" implies more—demographic and economic growth in youthful cities with new technologies, low wages, and improving race relations—then New Orleans is misplaced. At first glance there seems little reason to include the Crescent City in any meaningful comparison with Houston and Dallas, its immediate neighbors, let alone the more distant cities of California, Florida, or the Southwest. Its metropolitan area has grown at a rate considerably slower than most of its Sunbelt counterparts, and the city itself—in terms of population growth—has been stagnating. While the Sunbelt is supposed to be youthful, flexible, and exuberant, New Orleans is older, more staid, and more conservative. The Mardi Gras city celebrates the past with the same enthusiasm newer towns devote to building the future. New Orleans does possess a docile, low-wage labor force, but it is so poorly educated and inefficient that the business community considers it a deterrent, rather than an attraction, for industry.[1] And in an age when racial moderation is the watchword, this most heterogeneous corner of the American South finds residential segregation increasing, its public school system largely black and ineffective, its black and white communities polarized over the issues of crime and police brutality, and the poverty of its nonwhite citizens chronic and debilitating. As late as 1978, one local journalist characterized the city as "the municipal equivalent of a banana republic, a tropical paradise where the friendly natives unload the freighters by day and pull down the tourists' beds for the evening."[2]

But this dark portrait of the Crescent City is one-sided and incomplete. Even though the city has lost population recently, the suburban ring has grown steadily, and the region is rapidly industrializing. The metropolitan economy also has its bright spots, and the brightest are those most clearly associated with Sunbelt development—energy and tourism. Oil and natural gas production, along with the secondary industries they support, are rising dramatically. Together with tourism and the Port of New Orleans, petroleum dominates an economy local boosters claim is "booming."[3] These sectors of strength are also reshaping the city. The central business district is undergoing a revival in which real estate development and construction figure prominently. Oil money is finding its way into office towers, and new high-rise hotels cater to increasing numbers of tourists.

The federal government has played its part, too. Within the last generation, interstate highway development has engendered physical growth accompanied by urban sprawl. And government spending sustains much of the industry that remains in the city's dwindling manufacturing base. Most notably, NASA funds have poured into the Michoud Assembly Facility where fuel tanks for the space shuttle are under construction. More significant than any direct allocation of federal dollars, however, has been federal energy policy. The deregulation of oil and natural gas prices in the late 1970s has led to a great expansion in oil and gas exploration and mushrooming industrial investments in southern Louisiana.

There are other ways in which New Orleans displays some similarity to more typical Sunbelt cities. Despite the persistence and severity of its racial problems, New Orleans has made great strides in minimizing discrimination since World War II. The most spectacular gains were made in politics. By 1970, the city had in Moon Landrieu a mayor who was firmly committed to bringing blacks into full participation in government. By 1978, Ernest N. Morial reigned as the city's first black chief executive. The color line, as it was traditionally defined in the South, had been shattered irreparably. The

MAP 4.1. The New Orleans SMSA

election of these mayors was symptomatic of other changes as well. By the 1960s, the city's conservative social elite found itself surrounded by new, eager, and aggressive forces. Social preeminence, political clout, and economic power, long held in virtual monopoly by the city's traditional leadership, were rapidly becoming discrete entities. If the old elite still occupied an enviable position, theirs was no longer singular power.

New Orleans's relationship to the Sunbelt thus displays a dual nature. It is unquestionably in it, and at least partly *of* it, but it remains a city of the past as well as the future. It is a place where, thanks to the legacy left by Huey Long, one could still make a nickel telephone call in the late 1970s. It is, moreover, a city that looks at its neighbor, Houston—that symbol of Sunbelt growth and prosperity—with eyes both envious and scornful. New Orleans, it seems, is at war with itself. Prosperity and ever-wider cultural exchanges are having their impact, and as New Orleans is integrated into the national and international market it has to change. The hold of tradition is broken, but the extent of the transformation is not clear. New Orleans has co-opted and absorbed outside influences before. A new amalgam is in the making.

Over the past forty years, the region's growth has clearly revealed New Orleans's dual nature. Southern Louisiana paralleled other Sunbelt territory in that it was the most rapidly expanding area in a growing southern state. The entire New Orleans SMSA (Orleans Parish, which is coextensive with the city, Jefferson Parish, St. Bernard Parish, and St. Tammany Parish) has grown substantially. A look at the city itself, however, reveals an urban center that would be disturbingly familiar to residents of Detroit or Cleveland. The Crescent City lost population between 1960 and 1980, developed black majority by the latter year, and found itself surrounded by a ring of white suburbs.

There is no ambiguity about the regional growth of southern Louisiana. Between 1940 and 1980 the state grew by 77.8 percent (Table 4.1). The northern, more rural part of Louisiana, however, grew by only 34.1 percent. The New Orleans area and the southeastern portion of the state, in contrast, were booming. The twenty-two southern parishes lying east of the Atchafalaya River grew by 114 percent between 1940 and 1980. By 1980, the population of metropolitan New Orleans exceeded that of the entire northern half of the state. Even more important, the southeastern subregion grew to include nearly 53 percent of all the people living in Louisiana. In short, at least since World War II, the population of Louisiana has been flowing steadily to the south and east.

Despite such impressive figures, however, New Orleans's growth was leisurely when measured against its Sunbelt competition. In 1940 both New Orleans and its metropolitan area led the Old South in population. But by 1980, the city ranked only fifth and the SMSA had dropped to sixth place. Despite this relative decline, the suburban parishes ringing New Orleans showed remarkable expansion. Combined, the suburban parishes of Jefferson, St. Bernard, and St. Tammany grew 673.7 percent between 1940 and 1980 as their total population increased from 81,331 to 629,243 (in a total metropolitan population of 1,186,725).

Even more significant than the simple rates of population growth, however, was the character of that change. Here, more than anywhere else, New Orleans most closely parallels the older cities of the Frostbelt. As central-city New Orleans lost population, it became increasingly nonwhite. Indeed, between 1960 and 1980 the white population declined by 155,627 while the nonwhite population grew by 85,854. Whites became a minority, representing but 42.5 percent of the city's 557,482 inhabitants. In contrast, New Orleans's suburbs not only remained overwhelmingly white throughout the 1940 to 1980 period, but they became increasingly so with time, from 78.7 percent in 1940 to 87 percent in 1970. The latest

TABLE 4.1. Population of Louisiana by Region, 1940 and 1980

	1940 Population	% of 1940 Population	1980 Population	% of 1980 Population	% Increase 1940– 1980
Louisiana (All 64 parishes)	2,363,880	100.0	4,203,972	100.0	77.8
Southeast Louisiana (22 parishes)	1,034,576	43.8	2,218,522	52.8	114.0
New Orleans area (5 parishes)	588,186	24.9	1,212,774	28.8	106.2
Outside New Orleans area (17 parishes)	446,390	18.9	1,005,748	23.9	125.3
Southwest Louisiana (13 parishes)	445,251	18.8	800,368	19.0	79.8
North Louisiana (29 parishes)	884,053	37.4	1,185,082	28.2	34.1

SOURCE: U.S. Census.

data reveal a slight moderation of this trend as the 1980 white suburban percentage declined to 85.4. The result is that eight out of every ten blacks in the New Orleans SMSA live within the city proper, while seven out of every ten whites reside in the growing suburbs. Significantly, the outlying districts contained barely 14 percent of the area's population as recently as 1940. By 1980, an absolute majority, 53 percent, lived in the suburbs.

This city-suburban, black-white cleavage is the most striking feature in the recent ecological development of the New Orleans metropolitan area. Extensive suburban growth came late to New Orleans. The most important reason for this was topography. New Orleans is simply not a very hospitable site for a city. Much of it is below sea level, and the city itself—like a giant saucer—lies wedged in between the Mississippi River and Lake Pontchartrain. Its low-lying center is crisscrossed by ridges left by ancient distributary streams that were once part of the Mississippi. For nearly two hundred years,

New Orleanians built only on natural levees and high ground. This situation remained unchanged until the early twentieth century, when the city used heavy-duty pumps to drain its waterlogged mid-section. The Great Depression and World War II temporarily halted further development, but the technology existed to attack the marshes that still lay within and beyond the city's borders.[4]

Before that could be done, however, engineers had to make such land accessible. Vacant land, even if drained, was of little value until some form of transportation linked it to the city. Before World War II, Governor Huey Long made the greatest strides in this area, particularly with the construction of the area's first bridge across the Mississippi. Depression, war, and the availability of vacant land within the city, however, inhibited outward expansion through the early 1950s (map 4.2).[5]

The coming of Interstate 10 and other suburban improvements opened fresh areas to the automobile and inaugurated a new era. Growth, especially in east Jefferson Parish, was rapid, massive, and uncontrolled. According to the parish's assistant planning director, the "subdividers just came in here and placed their divisions where they wanted, and the streets where they wanted," thus leaving to local officials the task of coping with the problems caused by such haphazard development. The decentralization of shopping, entertainment, and industry followed quickly. West of the city, the Lakeside Shopping Center symbolized the maturation of Jefferson Parish. Similarly, the Plaza, an enormous closed mall that placed eleven acres and more than one hundred stores under a single roof, marked the arrival of eastern New Orleans in 1974. Fat City, an eighty-five-square-block area adjacent to Lakeside, also offers more than fifty bars, restaurants, and other establishments in tawdry emulation of the French Quarter. And significant industrial decentralization has occurred not only in Jefferson Parish (where Elmwood Park has lured many of its 550 businesses and 22,000 jobs from the central city), but also in St. Tammany parish, where the interstate facilitated the growth of suburban Slidell and the placement of NASA facilities in neighboring Hancock County, Mississippi.[6]

Although swamps have been drained and concrete ribbons now lie over subsiding bogs, crossing the Mississippi River remains an intractable problem. The river has hampered expansion of the metropolitan area on the west bank in both Orleans and Jefferson parishes. Aside from the Huey P. Long Bridge in Jefferson Parish, the only other span is the Greater New Orleans Bridge, which connects the city's central business district (CBD) to the Algiers community. Opened in 1958, the GNO bridge provided the impetus for an initial spurt of west bank growth. Indeed, in the mid 1950s, while the GNO bridge was still under construction, residential development accelerated rapidly in Algiers. West bank growth was such that the GNO bridge soon became the scene of traffic jams severe enough to discourage the faint-hearted. Fratricidal squabbling between Orleans and Jefferson parishes sidetracked efforts to get a third bridge approved until the late 1970s. It was 1981 before work began on a new span parallel to the GNO. By then, west Jefferson Parish and the upper reaches of Plaquemines Parish were already feeling the impact of new development.[7]

Despite this substantial activity—and the subsequent racial cleavage of the metropolitan area—the expansion of New Orleans is more a meander than a genuine sprawl. Good land for development remains in short supply, and the river, lake, and swamps that earlier delayed growth still exert some restraining influence. Persistent flooding has tortured both east Jefferson Parish and some west bank areas, leading officials to propose slowing or limiting expansion until there is proper drainage. Developers have so far lobbied successfully against formal restrictions, but there is greater caution evident since the heavy rains of May 1978 and April 1980.[8] Similarly, shoddy construction by early developers and subsidence problems have plagued eastern New Orleans. The result is that the New Orleans metropolitan area remains geographically compact when compared to such truly sprawling metropolises as Los Angeles or Houston. An automobile ride from the farthest reaches of east Jefferson Parish to downtown New Orleans still takes only about twenty minutes on Interstate 10—an insignificant jaunt in California or Texas.

The overall configuration of the New Orleans region thus differs considerably from that of its Sunbelt counterparts. The newer cities of the South and West grew to maturity in the automobile age. They are spatially dispersed and lack traditionally defined downtowns. New Orleans differs from them on each of these counts. It is an old city that has only grudgingly accommodated the horseless carriage. Citizens' groups, for example, defeated proposals for both a Riverfront Expressway and an Uptown River Bridge in the 1960s; and a nineteenth-century streetcar still serves uptown commuters as well as providing a romantic, nostalgic, and authentic tourist attraction. The city also has a clearly distinguishable and vital downtown that functions as the heart and soul of the metropolitan area. In short, the Crescent City belies the "no town" label that recent historians have so accurately fastened to the newer Sunbelt complexes.[9]

There are many reasons for the strength of New Orleans's

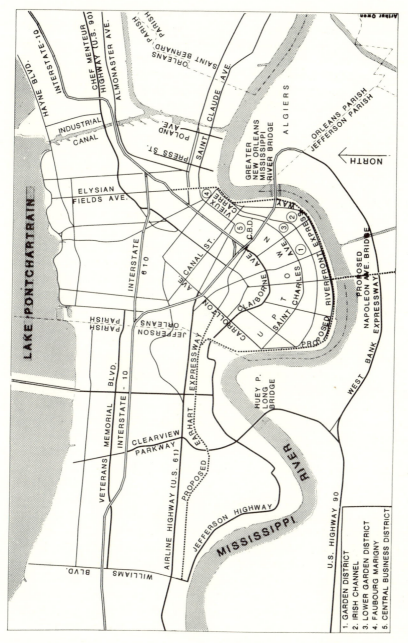

MAP 4.2. The City of New Orleans

downtown. Unquestionably the French Quarter (Vieux Carré) is primary among them. Including the entire area of the original city as it was established in 1718, the Vieux Carré became by the 1920s a refuge for bohemians where rents were cheap and "respectable" New Orleanians feared to tread. Private efforts to resuscitate the Quarter and preserve its unique character began as early as World War I and the city lent official, if ineffective, support to such efforts in the 1920s. In 1936, the state amended its constitution to permit the creation of a Vieux Carré Commission that would regulate the development of the area. The next year, a municipal ordinance set up the commission and mandated the preservation of the Vieux Carré's "quaint and distinctive character." Even the federal government became involved. WPA funds and personnel reconditioned the area around Jackson Square, the very heart of the district and site of some of the nation's greatest architectural treasures. Not only did tourism and land values increase, but city dwellers once again—in sharp contrast to the trend in other cities—went downtown for an evening's entertainment. By the 1970s, the Quarter's lure was so strong that publicly financed renovations and private projects (particularly high-rise hotels) surrounded and altered the district, obscuring the "European city" that charmed natives and tourists alike.[10]

There was more than the French Quarter, however, holding the old central city together. In such a historically and culturally rich city, social barriers, reinforced by time, restricted access to some inner-city neighborhoods and maintained them in spite of the eventual exodus of white, middle-class population from the city as a whole. The French Quarter, which is still a residential district in addition to its myriad other functions, is one such area. The Garden District, the home of stately antebellum mansions, is another. Tradition helped sustain it as a desirable locale, and it simply refused to deteriorate under pressures that overwhelmed well-to-do areas in other cities. By the 1970s, the strength of the Vieux Carré and the Garden District was flowing into neighboring communities. Renovators bought aged properties in Faubourg Marigny, the Irish Channel, and the Lower Garden District, evicted their poor tenants, and restored both homes and neighborhoods. While this process of gentrification created problems of its own, it was evidence of the persistent vitality of the city's core.[11]

The parsimonious nature of the suburbs that surrounded New Orleans also assured the continued use of the city's institutions and downtown. Jefferson Parish, specifically, has earned a reputation as the "most parasitic suburb in the United States." Despite its status as the state's wealthiest parish, Jefferson's refusal to tax itself has produced schools of questionable quality. Its parks, drainage, and transportation are inadequate; and the parish has no auditorium or zoo. These suburbanites rely, simply, on New Orleans for those services that they prefer not to pay for themselves. While this upsets many New Orleanians, it also means that the city continues to function as the vital center of its region.[12]

Finally, a changing economy and an evolving business leadership contributed to the revitalization of the CBD. There is no question that the flight of the middle class and the appearance of suburban shopping centers and industrial parks damaged downtown New Orleans. The CBD's share of metropolitan retail sales, for example, plunged from 42 percent in 1948 to 24 percent in 1963. In the eyes of one local reporter, "What had been a first-class shopping area took on a dowdy look. Dirt and litter accumulated, crime increased, and shoppers stayed away in droves." Further uptown, the construction of the GNO bridge and the obsolescence of an old warehouse district contributed to the decay of the CBD. Since the mid 1960s, however, and especially during the administrations of Moon Landrieu (1970–1978) and the current mayor, Dutch Morial, high-rise hotels have proliferated along Canal Street and office towers have appeared along Poydras between the river and the new Louisiana Superdome. The surge in construction was so strong that 3.5 million square feet of office space went into the CBD between 1970 and 1979; as of July 1981, a dozen office buildings were either under construction or "in the pipeline." The center does hold in New Orleans. Orleans Parish daily receives over 100,000 workers (representing 28.4 percent of the jobs in the city) who commute from neighboring parishes, while Jefferson (61,195), St. Tammany (19,946), and St. Bernard (11,745) "export" commuters, most of whom, presumably, toil in New Orleans.[13]

The downtown construction boom, however, was only symptomatic of the desire displayed by New Orleans's economic and political leadership to save the central city. The best evidence of CBD revival could be found not in bricks and mortar, but in the creation of the Downtown Development District (DDD). A special taxing district created by the state legislature and approved by city voters in a 1975 referendum, the DDD grew out of the cooperative efforts of the local Chamber of Commerce and Mayor Landrieu. The DDD, which supports itself by levying a special property tax on CBD sites, initially concerned itself with supplementing city services, subsidizing its own police force, shuttle buses, cultural events, and sanitation pickups. With the authorization of a $6.5 million bond issue, however, the DDD began to plan capital projects. It has already given financial support to the Historic Faubourg St. Mary Corporation, which is renovating properties in the heart of the city's skid row. By beginning its own projects, the DDD hopes to spark additional development. What the DDD represents, then, is a fair degree of innovation and a great deal of determination not only to preserve the CBD, but to enhance it. As Landrieu told a Senate committee in 1979, "I didn't believe the neighborhoods could be strong if we couldn't keep the generator working. . . . I didn't want to see the downtown die."[14]

The ecology of the New Orleans region is but a reflection of deeper realities, the spatial expression of the area's economic and social structure. The black-majority core of the central city, the ring of white suburbs, the compactness of the settled area, and the revivification of downtown districts reveal, again, New Orleans's ambiguous status as a Sunbelt city.

As was the case in population growth, the New Orleans economy displayed contradictory tendencies in the generation following World War II. Expansion in the local economy was evident, particularly during the boom years of 1962 to 1966 when NASA poured enormous sums of money into the Michoud Assembly Facility. But, overall, the dominant tendency of New Orleans's postwar economy was toward stagnation. The Crescent City was consistently outperformed by Houston, Dallas, and Atlanta, and such growth as did occur was not sufficient to absorb the increasing numbers of New Orleanians entering the labor force. Consequently, unemployment increased virtually every year between 1966 and the late 1970s. In 1977, unemployment averaged 8.9 percent in Orleans Parish; by 1978, well over 33,000 individuals were out of work in the New Orleans SMSA—more than at any time since World War II.[15]

Signs of change did appear, however, in the second half of the 1970s. Between 1970 and 1979, the Louisiana economy generated over 365,000 new jobs, two-thirds of that growth coming after 1974. In key sectors such as mining (including petroleum), manufacturing, and construction, workers' incomes doubled and tripled between 1974 and 1979. In all cases the gains were concentrated in the southern half of the state. The chief beneficiaries were those parishes along the Gulf Coast or those astride the Mississippi. Three-quarters of the new opportunities (268,471 jobs), for example, opened in just eleven of the state's sixty-four parishes, and seven of those were located on the coast or along the river.[16]

Did metropolitan New Orleans share in the southern Louisiana bonanza? There is no doubt that the energy crisis, the subsequent flow of money into the Sunbelt, New Orleans's emergence as an international tourist attraction, and CBD development contributed to a boom of sorts. Even economist James R. Bobo, whose influential and grimly pessimistic *The New Orleans Economy: Pro Bono Publico?* shocked placid New Orleanians in 1975, believed by 1981 that conditions had improved since his study appeared and that "events . . . have dumped prosperity into New Orleans' lap." Problems remained, however, and Bobo struck at the heart of the issue when he warned that the city still needed to "establish a social equilibrium to be certain that economic success is available to everyone."[17]

In *The New Orleans Economy* Bobo described the dual economy that functions in New Orleans. In addition to the conventional, or mainstream, economy, there is an underground economy. This underground system is characterized not only by high unemployment but excessive subemployment as well.[18] Perhaps half the New Orleans labor force has been subemployed since the late 1960s. There is considerable economic despair in New Orleans, and it is concentrated within the city proper and among poorly educated blacks. In 1969, 16.4 percent of all families in the New Orleans SMSA fell below the federally defined poverty line. This nearly doubled the average figure for SMSAs, and greatly outdistanced Atlanta's 9.1 percent, Houston's 9.8 percent, and Dallas's 8.6 percent. In terms of race, 38.2 percent of all black families in the New Orleans metropolitan area fell below the poverty line; only 8 percent of the nonblack families occupied a similar position.[19] The real issue, as Bobo perceived, is whether advances in the conventional economy will reach those who—for reasons of race, education, or poverty—are not in the mainstream.

The local economy's strongest sectors are among those associated with Sunbelt prosperity—oil and tourism. The Crescent City was particularly well situated to take advantage of the Arab oil embargo of 1973 and the federal deregulation of oil prices in early 1979. As Mayor Victor H. Schiro (1961–1970) once so colorfully put it: "We in New Orleans are sitting on some of the greatest assets in the world." The major breakthrough in mineral-rich Louisiana came in offshore drilling in the Gulf of Mexico. The Kerr-McGee Corporation brought in the first offshore well in 1947. Thirty years later, oil companies had sunk over 14,000 wells off the Louisiana coast, and the 1979 change in federal policy made certain that efforts would be redoubled. At the end of 1980, 442 rigs were active in the Gulf—the largest number since the mid 1950s.[20] Also significant, a consortium of oil companies opened the Louisiana Offshore Oil Port (LOOP) in 1981 to capture the imports brought in aboard giant supertankers, and new land-based discoveries have produced "frantic" drilling along the Tuscaloosa Trend in southern Louisiana. It is clear that the health of the local economy is, and will remain, closely tied to that of the oil industry generally.[21]

The success of the oil industry has led to intensive development throughout southern Louisiana. An industrial corridor, which has New Orleans as its focal point, has emerged and extends from Baton Rouge to the Gulf of Mexico. Aluminum and synthetic rubber companies first located there during World War II. Soon, however, the petrochemical industry took over, attracted by the region's deepwater port and plentiful supplies of oil, natural gas, sulfur, and salt. Mayor deLesseps S. ("Chep") Morrison (1946–1961) worked hard in the postwar years to build this industrial base, and succeeded in getting Kaiser Aluminum to locate a massive plant near the city. Others, such as Shell Oil and American Cyanimid, soon followed. It was also during the Morrison years that the federal government lent a helping hand with the construction of the Mississippi River–Gulf Outlet (MRGO). Authorized by Congress in 1956 and built by the Army Corps of Engineers (at a cost of $100 million), the MRGO cut forty miles off the trip from New Orleans to the Gulf and expanded the capacity of the city's port. This, in turn, attracted additional industry to the region—particularly to the upriver parishes of St. Charles, St. James, and St. John the Baptist (now known collectively with Orleans, Jefferson, St. Bernard, and Plaquemines parishes as the River Region)—and the lower Mississippi Valley became, for local boosters, the "American Ruhr."[22]

By 1980, the Economic Development Council (EDC) of the local Chamber of Commerce estimated that one out of every four jobs in the seven-parish area was related to oil. The extraction, refining, and production of petroleum and related chemical products *directly* employed 34,775 people in 1980 (an increase of 45.5 percent over 1970). Wages on the oil rigs and in the eleven refineries and thirty chemical plants of the region averaged a hefty $23,400; those employed by the oil industry earned an annual $814 million payroll. The "sickly sweet smell of hydrocarbons" that wafted over the petrochemical corridor was, according to oilmen, the "smell of money."[23]

New Orleans was a prime beneficiary of this activity. Thirty-five major oil firms rented nearly 30 percent of the CBD's office space in 1980, and the major tenants who sparked the construction boom were Amoco, Exxon, Mobil, Chevron, Getty, Gulf, Texaco, and Shell. Such corporations provided 9,230 jobs (representing one out of every seven in the CBD) in their regional or exploration headquarters. Even residential areas felt the oil boom. One "colony" of oil executives moved "virtually intact" from Houston's West Side to New Orleans's West Bank.[24]

Tourism was the second pillar of Sunbelt prosperity to help support the postwar New Orleans economy. Like oil, its most striking developments are recent. As late as 1970, New Orleans had fewer than four thousand first-class hotel rooms and hosted fewer than two hundred national meetings. Ten years later, the Crescent City entertained over eight hundred major meetings and attracted six million visitors annually. Over twenty thousand first-class hotel rooms were available in the area, ten thousand of them within a one-square-mile area in the CBD. Mayor Landrieu, particularly, courted the tourist trade through his support of the Louisiana Superdome, his promotion of the Greater New Orleans Tourist and Convention Commission, and his efforts to revive the city's core. Large hotel chains, subsequently, found New Orleans attractive. A 1,200-room Marriott Hotel opened on Canal Street in 1972 to start the boom. The Hyatt Regency followed in 1976, and the Hilton opened a year later. By the late 1970s, tourism generated at least 20 percent of the jobs held in New Orleans. And the boom is not over yet. The 1,200-room New Orleans Sheraton is now going up on Canal Street, and construction will begin shortly on a half-dozen other hotels. Tourism has become a billion-dollar industry.[25]

Along with tourism and oil (and the real estate speculation and construction they spark), there is another more traditional support for the New Orleans economy—the port. The most recent study of the port estimated that "more than half of the . . . goods and services produced in the area are in some way dependent on ocean-going commerce." The port, second busiest in the country, has been the region's most important economic asset. Now the oil industry is challenging it for supremacy, but, in fact, it is nearly impossible to disentangle the two. The LOOP, for example, has ties to both the oil industry and the port. The petrochemical plants it will support and attract will use oil for production and the port for distribution. Even now the largest indirect revenue source for the port is the sale of refined petroleum goods.[26]

But the port has had, and continues to have, its problems. Many of its facilities became obsolete or fell into disrepair after World War II. The completion of the St. Lawrence Seaway made Chicago a deepwater port in the 1950s and threatened New Orleans's position in the nation's agricultural heartland. More recently, technological changes—particularly the widespread use of container vessels that demand special port facilities—have created problems for the ill-equipped commercial center. The Port of New Orleans adapted haltingly to such changes, developing a thirty-year plan for port expansion and modernization only in 1970. Moreover, competition from other ports on the Gulf is intense and growing, so New Orleans's relative standing in the region is not what it was a decade earlier. Currently, there is some hope for the development of New Orleans as a major coal port. Much depends, however, on the provision of federal money to dredge the mouth of the Mississippi River so that it can accommodate the huge oceangoing colliers that would carry the solid "black gold" to Europe and Asia.[27]

The question remains: How much of this recent economic activity has reached the submerged half of the New Orleans population? The oil industry's impact has been relatively minor. Most of the nonexecutive jobs associated with the industry are not located in the city, but are upriver or along the coast. Of the $6.5 billion in industrial investments made in the eight-parish New Orleans area (the River Region plus St. Tammany) between 1956 and 1979, half (49.8 percent) has gone into St. Charles, St. James, and St. John the Baptist parishes. More important, this trend accelerated from 1975 to 1979 when 86 percent of such investments went into these three parishes. These capital- and energy-intensive industries demand skilled workers only. Moreover, the CBD oil firm employee is a white-collar worker averaging $24,000 per year. Some oil money undoubtedly trickles down to the poor through the consumer and service demands made by such well-paid employees, but oil industry jobs are not direct opportunities likely to benefit inner-city blacks.[28]

Similarly, changes in the port do not produce grounds for optimism. Indeed, the modern container ship is a labor-saving innovation that is reducing the number of jobs available for unskilled workers. Between 1971 and 1976, the port actually showed a net *loss* of forty-seven transportation jobs.[29]

Some greater measure of hope is offered by tourism, but it too is a mixed blessing. More than half the jobs associated with the tourist industry were lower-echelon service positions. The average salary in the tourist industry was only $5,743 at the end of the 1970s, and many of the positions are only part-time. Local boosters applaud the creation of such opportunities for unskilled, city-based workers, noting that some employment is better than none—and they are not wrong to do so. Tourism was largely responsible for reducing unemployment in New Orleans from 8.5 percent in 1976 to 6.4 percent in 1979; the sector employed some 46,000 people in the latter year.[30] It remains to be seen, however, whether the tourist industry provides the impoverished with a channel to the economic mainstream, or whether it leads to a dead sea of economic subsistence.

The one sector that might make a real difference to New Orleans's underground economy is manufacturing. But despite NASA and petroleum, it is the one area in which the Crescent City's performance has been weakest. Never really an industrial city, New Orleans has been losing manufacturing jobs since the early 1950s. In 1953, the New Orleans SMSA had 57,300 manufacturing jobs representing 18.5 percent of its work force. By 1978, despite the growth of the labor force, the number of manufacturing positions declined to 49,895. Only 12.1 percent of the SMSA's workers were engaged in manufacturing in 1978, and only 10.2 percent of those in Orleans Parish were so employed.[31]

The only exceptions to this overall downward trend were those areas supported by federal assistance. The space program provided the most direct involvement through NASA's Michoud Assembly Facility. Built during World War II, the plant became a white elephant after the Korean War. Impressed by the facility's access to a deepwater port, the favorable climate, and political considerations, the government brought the space age to New Orleans in 1962. Between 1963 and 1966 the reopened plant employed, on an average, over 10,000 workers and was the largest industrial employer in Louisiana. It provided only transient relief, however, and ultimately had a destabilizing effect on the local economy. The space program did not spur great development or cause a massive in-migration to New Orleans as it did in more dynamic Houston. It simply absorbed workers from the large pool of resident unemployed. Also unlike the Manned Spacecraft Center in Houston, the Michoud plant was simply a production facility. It had a narrower skill-mix than the Houston site, which had both scientific and managerial responsibilities. The result is that program cutbacks in the late 1960s hit New Orleans hard. The Michoud plant remained in operation in the 1980s, turning out fuel tanks for the space shuttle; but the 1,500 to 3,000 workers employed there constituted only a fraction of those used during the mid 1960s.[32]

Indirectly, the federal government has bolstered industrial employment in New Orleans through its encouragement of the oil industry. The support services demanded by oil companies, particularly shipbuilding and repair, remain a vital part of the local economy. And the recent boom created thousands of immediate openings for skilled carpenters, welders, metalworkers, and shipfitters. But the poorly educated New Orleans labor pool lacks the ready tools for such employment and some firms are turning to modular construction and computerized steel cutting to save on labor costs. In any event, the manufacturing support provided by the space program and shipbuilding has not been sufficient to offset losses in the food-processing, paper products, and apparel industries. The city lost another 6,685 industrial jobs between 1976 and 1978 alone.[33]

Still, the important fact about New Orleans's recent development is not simply that it is losing manufacturing jobs as it turns toward a more service-oriented economy. After all, it is only reflecting—in fact exceeding—national trends in that regard. The important fact is that New Orleans is changing at all. It is a crucial development in a city that once wore its timelessness as a badge of honor.

The city's long past, however, continues to restrain economic development. Some of the impediments are physical. The lock at the Industrial Canal, for example, cannot meet the demands of modern commerce and will remain a bottleneck for years to come. Other obstructions are legal. State laws prohibit Louisiana banks from expanding across parish lines, thus restricting asset growth and keeping lending limits uncompetitively low. Moreover, resurgent nativism led the 1980 state legislature to restrict foreign banking so severely that foreign capital is finding the atmosphere more congenial in Houston, Miami, Dallas, and Atlanta. Similarly, the city's financial problems have acted as a drag on economic growth. The state's constitution prohibits local governments from levying income or severance taxes, and greatly restricts the income derived from property taxes. The city, consequently, finds itself in a state of perpetual financial crisis. Three-quarters of its 1981 operating revenues came from a horribly regressive sales tax with supplements from the state and now shaky federal sources. New Orleans cannot adequately fund existing services on such a shoestring, let alone add the infrastructure to undeveloped land that would attract new industry.[34]

Even more confining are the attitudes of many New Orleanians. This is evident even in those areas in which the city does well. In 1954, the Chamber of Commerce publicly opposed Mayor Morrison when he tried to establish a Tourist Commission. The chamber already had its own convention bureau, President Lawrence A. Molony pointed out, and the city's hotels were doing well. "I do not believe we should ever be satisfied with a 'good enough' attitude," an annoyed Morrison replied, "particularly where tourist dollars are concerned." Indeed, as a Morrison advisor commented, the answer was "more hotels," not the calculated rejection of new business. Despite being "threatened and sabotaged" by Roosevelt Hotel owner Seymour Weiss and the local hotel association, Morrison successfully pushed for the construction of the Royal Orleans Hotel in the French Quarter in 1960. Before this the venerable Monteleone was the only first-class hotel in the Vieux Carré. The city, however, did not aggressively pursue tourism until the Landrieu era.[35]

In like fashion, New Orleans remains a regional headquarters for the oil industry while national bases are tied to Houston. True, the Texas oil industry is older than Louisiana's, and Houston enjoys a geographical advantage compared to the Crescent City. Oil executives, however, maintain that Houston "aggressively courted the oil industry" and that the "conservative character" of New Orleans was a factor "equal in importance" to the others. As John G. Phillips, chairman of the Louisiana Land and Exploration Company, explains: "New Orleans remains an older, more traditional, less risk-oriented economy, while Houston's economy and leadership are more risk-oriented." New Orleans's financial conservatism made Texas more attractive to the high rollers in the oil business.[36]

These attitudes reflect the nature of the city's traditional elite. It would be a mistake, however, to assume that such suspicion of change is peculiar to the elite or that it has been destructive in every case. New Orleans, for example, avoided much of the damage inflicted on central cities by urban renewal through its inability to overcome opposition to the program. Mayor Morrison tried on several occasions to take advantage of the federal largess. But neighborhood hostility combined with rural doubts to secure state laws in 1954 that prevented the implementation of urban renewal programs. Until 1968, when the legislature reversed itself, Louisiana was the only state in the union lacking the enabling legislation needed to obtain renewal funds. Then, when large-scale development rapidly claimed more than one-third of the CBD during Moon Landrieu's first term, preservationists seeking to maintain the city's architectural heritage forced a moratorium on demolition in 1974.[37]

The long and bitter controversy over the proposed Riverfront Expressway provided perhaps the best example of productive nonaction. First proposed by New York's Robert Moses in 1946, the Riverfront Expressway was the darling of central-city business interests who finally tried to build it in the 1960s. Improved automobile access to the CBD, they argued, was necessary to combat postwar suburban growth. Preservationists feared the impact of the highway on the Vieux Carré and fought the downtown establishment by mounting an articulate, nationwide campaign. Luckily for the opposition, environmental concerns had become fashionable in Washington, and they succeeded in halting the project in 1969. From the preservationists' perspective it was a defeat for those with "old New Orleans names" and "Kansas City minds" who had prostrated themselves before a "brazen god of dollars." Expressway proponents, on the other hand, lamented the lack of a "unity of purpose between the [city's] business and professional leaders."[38] Ironically, the attraction of a French Quarter unspoiled by Moses' elevated highway was crucial to the 1970s revival of the CBD.

Despite the preservationists' rhetorical linkage of old New Orleans names with mindless boosterism, the victory of the expressway opponents depended on the significant financial and social standing of their own leadership. Moreover, if downtown businesses craved a concrete fix for their ills, it is not true that the city's traditional elite was simply a gaggle of Babbitts. The Chamber of Commerce's rejection of Morrison's Tourist Commission and the cautious policies followed by New Orleans financiers are testimony to the contrary. It is, in fact, the old elite (those families that have dominated New Orleans's business and society since the end of the Civil War) that has been the city's most successful preservationists—only it has been working on social, rather than physical, structures.

A pronounced distaste for crass materialism is clearly evident in the old elite's disdain for its Sunbelt neighbors—particularly Houston. The New Orleans aristocracy views the glittering prosperity of such rivals as merely the success of the grasping nouveaux riches. The Crescent City's elite is preoccupied with social rituals, such as Mardi Gras, which reinforce and emphasize its status. The parading organizations (krewes), whose balls and processions are the focal points of the Carnival season, remain exclusive. Rex, among the older groups, has only recently admitted Jews, nonnatives, and politicians. Other organizations remain more restrictive. On a daily basis, the elite retreats behind the social parapets of the Boston, Louisiana, and Pickwick clubs, where it dines in splendid isolation. What remains distinctive about New Orleans, according to the *Times-Picayune*, is a "state of mind." It is a town where, in contrast to its more businesslike competitors, it is perfectly proper to "keep a luncheon club member at the rummy table while a client waits at the office."[39]

Such practices express the nature of the city's traditional leadership. It is native born, with family roots sunk generations deep in local soil. In no other American city does birth, as opposed to achievement, count for so much. Such values and the social intimacy of the group mean that newcomers, no matter how successful, have great difficulty circulating in the city's highest circles. This, of course, has had serious economic consequences for the city. It has stifled the rise of new leadership and sustained the "good enough" attitude so frustrating to Mayor Morrison. It has also discouraged new business and industry from locating there. In the generation after World War II, it meant that New Orleans, bound by complacency, stagnated while other Sunbelt cities developed rapidly.[40]

The city's economic surge, however, is a clear indication that things are now changing. It is also evident that much of the impetus for change has come from outside the old aristocracy. Developers, like Joseph Canizaro of Biloxi, Mississippi, are altering the face of the CBD, and if New Orleans banks are unwilling or unable to finance such projects, they will find capital elsewhere. Significantly, this prodding from outsiders has led the local banking community to become more aggressive itself. Even the New Orleans Chamber of Commerce is trying to project a new image. It now calls itself The Chamber/New Orleans and the River Region, and has established an Economic Development Council (with an annual $500,000 budget) to vigorously promote the area.[41]

Nowhere, however, is New Orleans's recent willingness to engage in the entrepreneurial game more apparent than in its construction of the Louisiana Superdome and its unashamed promotion of a 1984 World's Fair. The Dome was a gargantuan or, more accurately, a "Texan" undertaking. Large enough to hold Houston's Astrodome comfortably inside (one of its sources of local appeal), the Dome's final cost exceeded original estimates by nearly 500 percent. The financial wizardry that brought the Dome into existence was the work of Dallas native Jimmy Jones, the enterprising president of the First National Bank of Commerce in New Orleans. Despite the refusal of the city's largest bank (the Whitney) to purchase the Superdome's bonds, Jones successfully managed the issue, finding, among others, the Citizens and Southern National Bank of Atlanta eager to help. Jones's efforts were matched by the political artistry of Governor John McKeithen and Mayor Moon Landrieu, both of whom worked tirelessly on the Dome's behalf. When opened in 1975, the giant stadium triggered a land boom that transformed "old faded Poydras Street . . . [in]to a glittering promenade of sky-scrapers and high-rise hotels." The Superdome was a "staggering symbol of the city's rush to Americanization," the *New York Times* declared; it represented the end of New Orleans's insularity and was a monument to "big-time sports, big-time tourism, and big-time business."[42]

Nothing confirmed the breakdown of New Orleans's insularity more strikingly than its determined efforts to get a World's Fair. The Landrieu administration first advanced the idea for the fair in 1974, and organizers claim that it will bring eleven million visitors to the city between May and November 1984. Boosters also emphasize expected long-range benefits. The Louisiana Pavilion will be housed in a new $90 million Exhibition Hall that will combine with the existing Rivergate complex and Superdome to give New Orleans convention and trade show facilities matched by few competitors. Developers are also planning permanent family-oriented entertainment centers to broaden the city's appeal to tourists, and backers similarly expect that the fair will lead to the redevelopment of the city's riverfront. As with the Dome, however, critics are quick to attach a "doggle" to the "boon" predicted by the fair's supporters. Mayor Morial has expressed reservations about the fair's disruptive impact, the cost of delivering services to millions of visitors, and the need for New Orleans to derive more residual benefits from the event. Unlike earlier fairs, the improved site in New Orleans will revert to private, and not municipal, ownership. The mayor, consequently, is trying to extract financial aid from the state as a quid pro quo for the city's cooperation.[43]

Equally important was the very process through which the fair was approved. All such undertakings require both national and international sanction. When it appeared that financial backing for the fair was in doubt, Secretary of Commerce Malcolm Baldridge gave the city three days to raise $16 million. Thanks to the spirited lobbying of Governor David Treen and the furious action of the local business community (moving at a pace that would have made a Texan proud), corporate contributions rolled in. Although the staid Whitney Bank again withheld support, contributions of $1 million or more came from each of twelve oil and three utility companies. Local hotels and real estate developers were also conspicuous among the backers. The pledged support was sufficient to rescue the fair.[44]

The leadership of mayors and the governor in promoting the Superdome and the World's Fair illustrates the remarkable change in local politics since World War II. The political arena, once the preserve of white, male Democrats, has grown to include elements that had been excluded from the political process since the late nineteenth century—and some that had never been in it before. Activist mayors deLesseps S. ("Chep") Morrison, Moon Landrieu, and Ernest ("Dutch") Morial used their political leverage to spur economic growth and social change. Significantly, neither Landrieu nor Morial had ties to the social elite. Landrieu's parents ran a grocery store in front of his modest home. Morial is a light-skinned black. And when promoters needed help to bail out the World's Fair, a Republican governor from suburban Metairie provided critical support. Dave Treen is the state's first chief executive elected from metropolitan New Orleans and the first Republican governor since Reconstruction.[45]

Chep Morrison began the process of opening up New Orleans

politics when he took on the city's Regular Democratic Organization (RDO)—one of the few big-city machines in the South. Members of the New Orleans machine were known as the "Old Regulars" or the "Choctaws." The Choctaw Club was a Democratic organization created in 1896 to wrest control of the city away from a coalition of reformers, Republicans, and blacks who had dominated municipal elections that year. Riding the rising tide of racism, the Choctaws eliminated the black vote in the Louisiana constitution of 1898 and thereby cut the electoral heart out of their opposition. They seized control of the city's government in 1900 and—with the exception of a single mayoral term (1921–1925)—remained in control through World War II. As New Orleans entered the postwar era, its chief executive, Robert Maestri, presided over a machine that functioned much as it had a generation before. The Choctaws were meticulously organized on the ward and precinct level, held together by the glue of patronage, and expert in the techniques of electoral legerdemain practiced by most big-city machines. Maestri himself was a caricature of the stereotypical boss. Unlettered, if not unintelligent, Maestri was a man of few words and these, when uttered, often proved embarrassing. Still, he was an unqualified success in private business, and his depression-era leadership demonstrated concern, skill, and effective action. He tended more to his machine than his city in later years, however, and in 1946 he faced a reelection campaign in which charges of corruption and spoils politics proved his undoing.[46]

Chep Morrison, a young colonel fresh out of the U.S. Army, was the beneficiary of popular dissatisfaction with the Old Regulars. Running an exquisitely crafted campaign, Morrison took advantage of an electorate expanded by a registration drive conducted by the League of Women Voters, the backing of a host of reform, veterans', and women's groups, and the overconfidence and disunity of the Old Regulars to score a stunning upset. Once in office, Morrison became a progressive mayor convinced that visible accomplishments and physical achievements were the keys to political success. The man whose election was to officially end machine rule in Louisiana then set out to build his own machine.[47]

The young colonel had defeated the Old Regulars, but he had not broken them. Fifteen years of bitter political warfare ensued. It was a war that eventually did destroy the RDO and, in the process, restructured the political relationship between New Orleans and the state of Louisiana. Morrison created his own organization, the Crescent City Democratic Association (CCDA). The young mayor copied the ward and precinct structure of the RDO, co-opted those of its leaders who could be swayed by patronage and favors, and employed tactics against the Old Regulars that rendered the CCDA indistinguishable from its adversary. "Chep had a bigger machine than Maestri," Congressman F. Edward Hebert recalled, "and I think he was more ruthless than Maestri. Chep was cold-blooded as hell." The Choctaws discredited themselves when they struck back by supporting Governor Earl Long's legislative attacks on the city and its mayor in 1948. Morrison rallied New Orleans against the "mudslinging hatchet men" who were trying to "damage" the city. The mayor won reelection and the Old Regulars' fall from grace was irreversible. Earl Long, sensing the demographic trends, further undermined the Old Regulars by supporting a home rule charter for New Orleans.[48]

The Old Regulars faded slowly, never able to defeat Morrison. When Morrison resigned in 1961, RDO strongman James E. Comiskey finished third in the first mayoral primary of 1962. Morrison's successor, Vic Schiro, bargained feverishly for RDO support before his successful runoff confrontation with Adrian Duplantier, but that was the last time the Choctaws played so prominent a role in citywide politics. By the 1970s, the power brokers of the old machine, the popularly elected assessors, still held their own seats almost as family heirlooms, but their influence had diminished greatly. Dutch Morial, for example, was elected mayor despite the old-timers' virtually unanimous opposition. All that was left of the machine was its skeleton, the numerous and fragmented elective offices and political subdivisions that now impeded the smooth functioning of government.[49]

Chep Morrison was thus a transitional figure in New Orleans politics. Never more than a vehicle for his personal ambitions, the CCDA was a one-man organization. It may have emulated the Old Regulars' organization in structure, but it was a framework imposed from above, rather than one that grew from the grass roots. All power remained in Morrison's hands. He hoarded it, used it for his own purposes (primarily in three unsuccessful gubernatorial races), and left the CCDA a hollow shell when he resigned as mayor in 1961. The organization dissolved almost immediately into feuding factions, and Morrison himself cynically cultivated Old Regular leaders in his 1963 gubernatorial campaign. Morrison's failures were every bit as significant as his successes. In the end, he destroyed all the citywide political organizations in New Orleans—including his own.[50]

The second step in opening up politics in New Orleans involved the reenfranchisement of blacks. Locked out of the system since the

1896 mayoralty, the Supreme Court encouraged black voting and registration by outlawing white primaries in the 1940s and attacking the separate but equal doctrine in the 1950s. The Court's opinions on desegregation, however, also inspired new White Citizens' Councils to purge black voters from the registration lists. Through the early 1960s, consequently, blacks made only minor gains. Black voters represented only 13 percent of the Orleans Parish electorate in 1952, and twelve years later 35,736 registrants still accounted for only 18 percent. The real breakthrough came with the Voting Rights Act of 1965. Between the presidential elections of 1964 and 1968, the number of black voters increased by 76.8 percent, totaling 63,165 (28 percent of all New Orleans's voters) in 1968. When Dutch Morial became mayor in 1978, 100,243 blacks, representing 43.7 percent of the city's electorate, were registered.[51]

The combined impact of federal action and demographic shifts, however, is best illustrated in the campaigns and administrations of Moon Landrieu and Dutch Morial. The crucial second Democratic primary in 1969 was especially revealing. That contest matched Landrieu against Jimmy Fitzmorris, a candidate who had the backing of all the traditional political organizations. Landrieu waged an aggressive campaign, openly deriding New Orleans's status as a second-rate city and promising explicitly not only to bring blacks into the highest levels of government, but to secure an ordinance barring discrimination in public accommodations. While Fitzmorris followed conventional political wisdom and temporized on such controversial issues, Landrieu demanded the destruction of the old political structure for the good of the city.[52] Landrieu subsequently won the support of all the city's major newspapers (both white and black), as well as that of the black political action groups that had developed in the wake of the Voting Rights Act. The results were unprecedented. Fitzmorris won a majority of the white vote, but Landrieu fashioned a coalition of blacks and well-to-do, business-oriented whites to score a stunning victory. His defeat in the white community was more than offset by a virtual sweep of black precincts; he won over 90 percent of the black vote. Both the *States-Item* and the *Louisiana Weekly* agreed that Landrieu "probably altered New Orleans politics forever."[53]

Dutch Morial rode the same coalition to power in 1977, becoming the first black mayor in the city's history. Although he did better with blacks (winning 97 percent of their vote) and less well with whites than Landrieu did (Morial won about 20 percent of the white vote, half of Landrieu's 1969 total), the combination of forces that propelled Landrieu into city hall held together for Morial as well.

Joseph DiRosa, Morial's opponent, analyzed his defeat and pointed a finger, not at the overwhelming black vote, which was expected, but squarely at one of the city's more fashionable districts and the home of Tulane University. "The Uptown white vote killed us," was DiRosa's terse assessment.[54]

The combination of business-oriented whites and the black community—both advocates of economic growth—was a natural one, and the Landrieu and Morial administrations responded to their constituencies. Reflecting on his eight years as mayor, Landrieu said that his pioneering work in changing racial attitudes in New Orleans was his "single greatest accomplishment." "When Moon came in," one city official explained, "the only blacks you saw at City Hall were pushing brooms." Breaking a pattern of discrimination that found black job finalists routinely ignored, Landrieu increased black civil service employment from 1,833 positions (19 percent of all such jobs) in 1970 to 4,304 (43 percent) in 1978. During his administration city employment rose by 21.8 percent; black city employment rose by 168.2 percent. Nor were these simply lower-echelon jobs. His chief administrative officer, Terrence Duvernay, was the first black ever appointed to that lofty position. Blacks also served as department heads, and even obtained political fringes such as the service contracts awarded by the Superdome.[55]

As for business, Landrieu characterized himself as a "development-minded mayor." He energetically pursued federal aid and obtained funds that New Orleans had never tapped before. His renovation of the French Market, construction of pedestrian malls around Jackson Square, and the creation of the aptly named Moonwalk overlooking the Mississippi River in the French Quarter—along with his sponsorship of the Superdome and new CBD construction—were all actions designed not only to bolster tourism, but to break the long era of economic stagnation that had haunted the city. At the end of his administration, Landrieu thought that the New Orleans business community had become much more progressive and that it now saw "City Hall not as an enemy but as a friend, catalyst, a supportive device for the downtown area."[56]

If Landrieu got New Orleans off dead center, however, the more difficult, long-term task was left for Dutch Morial. Tourism was something of a quick fix. It demanded a low-skill labor force for its low-paying jobs, required small investments on the part of a financially strapped city, and seemed to be "a relatively painless and pollution-free" solution for pressing economic problems. It did nothing, however, to improve the quality of New Orleans's schools or its labor force and, far from attracting industry, it drove manufacturing concerns out of the city (witness the appropriation of much of the CBD's old warehouse district as the site for the 1984 World's Fair). More than anything else, Morial wanted to alter permanently and substantially the local economy, retaining and attracting the kind of industry that would provide the solid economic base the city had always lacked. Significantly, he remained dubious of "six-month wonder federal programs that end abruptly and leave people in despair." He turned, instead, to private business and espoused the gospel of "economic growth . . . [as] urban salvation." His support for the development of the Almonaster-Michoud Industrial Corridor in eastern New Orleans, an attempt at public-private sector cooperation that would provide the type of jobs New Orleans has traditionally failed to attract, was evidence of his commitment. Those who were concerned about the impact a black mayor would have on business were quickly reassured.[57]

The full impact of the Landrieu and Morial administrations remains to be seen. It is clear, however, that the city's recent economic growth owes much to the political transformation that preceded it. Moreover, both were predicated on the enfranchisement of black voters. The black hands that pulled New Orleans's voting levers for the first time after 1965 hoisted progressive business into the saddle.

Those black hands also led to the further diversification of local politics. Republicanism initially reappeared in Louisiana after World War II in presidential contests as the Democratic party's identification with the civil-rights revolution weakened its grip on the state. David Treen, whose three unsuccessful congressional races kept the fledgling Republicans alive in the 1960s, represented many of those who felt betrayed by the Democrats. Treen had been the chairman of Louisiana's States' Rights party and had appeared at segregation rallies with arch-racists Leander Perez and Willie Rainach. Similarly, it was another States' Righter, Ben Toledano, who made the first serious Republican bid for the New Orleans mayoralty by challenging Moon Landrieu in the general election of 1970. The initial impetus for the Toledano effort was Landrieu's startling sweep of the black vote in his primary contest with Jimmy Fitzmorris. Toledano charged that Landrieu's success with the "bloc vote" made "race an issue," and he attacked Landrieu's public accommodations ordinance. Though defeated, Toledano won 41 percent of the vote—the best showing made by a Republican in a New Orleans mayoralty race since Reconstruction.[58]

But there was more to the Republican movement than racism. Indeed, its leaders soon made their appeals more on conservative ideological grounds than on the basis of race. Treen himself openly wished that he could erase his earlier segregationist leanings from the record. The real strength of the Republican party in Louisiana lies in those same demographic patterns that gave newly enfranchiséd blacks the upper hand in the central city. Louisiana Republicanism is a metropolitan phenomenon, with its greatest strength in the burgeoning suburbs. It is there that appeals to social and economic conservatives, devoid of explicit racist content, find their most appreciative audience. Democrats protected Congressman Hale Boggs by gerrymandering suburban east Jefferson Parish out of his district, but that action turned the suburbs over to the Republicans and Treen, who was elected to Congress four times—the last time without opposition. Similarly, the other suburban New Orleans congressional district, Democratic for 102 years, elected Republican Bob Livingston to office in 1977.[59]

Louisiana Democrats, accustomed to assuming office after winning their party's nomination, passed an Open Primary Law in 1975 to undercut the growing Republican party. By forcing all candidates, regardless of party, into a single open primary, Democrats hoped to end the Republicans' free ride into the general election while eliminating their own expensive multiple primaries. The law backfired and actually accelerated the development of the Republican party. Previously, registering as a Republican had prohibited one from voting in the all-important Democratic primary. It was the equivalent of disfranchisement in what was a one-party system. The open primary removed the penalty for registering as a Republican and thus encouraged changes in party affiliation. Moreover, the open primary made it easy for conservative Democrats to vote for Republican candidates without switching political allegiance. Disciplined Republicans, consequently, have run a single candidate in such elections against an array of Democrats. Concentrating their resources, the Republicans have had good success not only in getting their candidates into runoffs, but in winning such contests. That was Treen's route to the governor's mansion in 1979, and it was also how, in 1980, Bryan Wagner became the first Republican to sit on the New Orleans City Council since Reconstruction. Louisiana Republicanism, which began as a quadrennial exercise in presidential politics, had successfully reached down to the ward level in well-to-do Uptown New Orleans.[60]

Republican prospects are promising. The GOP is hard at work broadening its base, trying, particularly, to overcome its past and attract black adherents (the party's still small statewide registration was 92 percent white in 1978). Reynard Rochon, Mayor Morial's chief administrative officer, and Henry Dejoie, one of the publishers of the *Louisiana Weekly*, are among a small but growing number of prominent black converts attracted to Republicanism for ideological or tactical reasons. Republicans have also pioneered the latest political techniques. Bob Livingston's first successful congressional campaign demonstrated that a well-financed, sophisticated media blitz can more than make up for the hordes of "sidewalk inspectors" used by the RDO in an earlier era.[61]

The opening up of the political process in New Orleans has not been without cost. While the new-found diversity of metropolitan politics is a welcome development, it has also led to fragmentation and polarization—especially where racial issues are concerned. Black New Orleanians have only recently tasted the fruits of electoral victory. The first real breakthrough came in 1967 when Dutch Morial was elected to the state House of Representatives and two other blacks won election to the Orleans Parish Democratic Committee. The New Orleans City Council remained all white, however, until its members appointed the Reverend A. L. Davis to fill a vacancy in 1974. By 1981, the mayor and three of the city's seven councilmen were black, but the process of gaining representation was sometimes an embittering one.[62]

The battle over reapportionment in the 1970s, perhaps more than anything else, helped cast New Orleans politics in racial terms. The city council's initial plan was an obvious gerrymander designed to save the seats of the seven white incumbents. The Justice Department rejected it under the review procedures mandated by the Voting Rights Act of 1965. The council produced a second plan in 1973 that "guaranteed" the election of only a single black councilman. New Orleans blacks sued and, after years of litigation, the Supreme Court approved the second council plan in 1976. Believing 1970 census figures entitled them to three of the council's seven seats, blacks had to wait until 1981 before Lambert Boissiere won that third seat in a racially divisive campaign against a white Republican.[63]

The disruption of the racial status quo in New Orleans politics, followed by the polarization of blacks and whites, was a pattern followed by race relations generally in the postwar era. Progress was most rapid when economic incentive and outside influence came together. The refusal to guarantee accommodations for black delegates cost New Orleans an American Legion convention in 1963 and prompted four hotels (each operated by a national chain) to drop their restrictive policies. Local institutions resisted such change, however, and in 1969 the Roosevelt Hotel was the scene of a nationally publicized incident involving black representatives from the American Federation of Teachers. Protests over continued discrimination were punctuated with threatened cancellations of already scheduled meetings. Shortly after the Roosevelt incident, Moon Landrieu steered his antidiscrimination ordinance through the city council. Since the ordinance included establishments not covered by existing federal law, Landrieu boasted that New Orleans's chief competitors for the tourist and convention dollar—Dallas, Houston, Miami, and Atlanta—lacked similar safeguards. The city's establishment backed Landrieu's efforts and recommended passage of the new measure in "the name of justice and economic progress."[64]

In other areas, however, it is less clear how much "change" has really occurred. During the Morrison and Schiro years, there were a number of firsts for black New Orleanians. During Morrison's tenure, the police force was integrated on a token basis, the city complied with court-ordered desegregation of its transit system, and blacks gained symbolic recognition as the mayor sought their votes and bestowed a number of material benefits upon black neighborhoods. Morrison, however, accepted segregation (indeed, he championed it during his second gubernatorial campaign) both privately and as a political fact of life. The playgrounds, parks, and street lights he provided for blacks were all offered in the hope that truly equal facilities would permit the races to remain truly separate. He sought to improve conditions for blacks only "within the framework of existing state laws and customs."[65]

Similarly, change and continuity characterized race relations during the Schiro administration (1961–1970). The NAACP quickly tested the Civil Rights Act of 1964 in local establishments, but discrimination neither immediately nor completely disappeared. Only when segregation threatened New Orleans's tourist trade and the city's attempt to win a National Football League franchise were the most glaring problems eliminated. Even an institution such as Charity Hospital, which pledged total desegregation, kept its blood supply racially labeled until mid 1965 and then had trouble getting its staff to accept the new policy. When the courts ordered the desegregation of New Orleans's parks and recreational facilities, the Schiro administration "closed 17 . . . swimming pools, converted the City Park swimming pool into a seal pool and monkey house, and discontinued the use of the Olympic-sized swimming pool in Audubon Park." Despite such blatant racism, Schiro considered himself an egalitarian leader whose greatest accomplishment was the preservation of peace between the races "while other cities were being torn asunder by civil violence."[66]

If Schiro thought his actions had saved the city from racial violence, he was mistaken. As with so much else in New Orleans, the sixties did not happen until the seventies. While there were no massive disorders paralleling the northern ghetto uprisings, there were repeated deadly confrontations between armed blacks and the New Orleans Police Department. The first major incident came in 1970 when more than one hundred police engaged in a gun battle with a group of Black Panthers who had ensconced themselves in a house near the city's Desire housing project. After an initial confrontation and the arrest of more than a dozen blacks, police returned to the area and shot four others, one fatally, in a disputed series of events. The alienation between the black and white communities reached its apex in January 1973 when Mark Essex, a young black, climbed atop the Howard Johnson's motel at the edge of the French Quarter and laid siege to the city, killing nine people, five of them police officers, before he was slain. Chillingly, black spectators shouted encouragement to the rooftop sniper as his shots rang through the CBD. Such bitterness betrayed the chronic and unresolved tension between blacks and police. Charges of brutality against the police abound in the records of the local NAACP, and show no signs of abating. In early 1983 three white officers were convicted of beating alleged witnesses to the murder of a fellow policeman in Algiers.[67]

The tensions generated by such incidents are indicative of other persistent racial problems. Housing patterns, for example, reflect increasing polarization as well. New Orleans was not only more segregated in 1970 than it was earlier, but it lost its favorable standing among American cities in this regard. According to segregation indexes, New Orleans was less segregated than the average American city in 1960. Ten years later, it was more so. The overall segregation index for cities was declining, but New Orleans was heading in the opposite direction.[68]

The best example of New Orleans's ability to resist change even while seeming to succumb to it is its public school system. In 1947, Superintendent Lionel J. Bourgeois frankly admitted that many "Negro children are deprived of an equal opportunity for education with children in more favored circumstances." On the eve of desegregation, in 1959, white schools were only 73 percent full, while black schools operated at 114 percent of their capacity and endured double shifts and combined classes. The previous year, nearly 11,000 black children were bused past empty seats in their neighborhood schools in order to maintain segregation.[69]

The cataclysm came in 1960. The governor and the state legislature bitterly resisted desegregation and spent countless hours trying to outmaneuver federal court orders in the name of preserving the

"Southern way of life." The local White Citizens' Council took to the streets and parents boycotted the involved schools. The families of those attending the integrated programs faced unmerciful harassment. Chep Morrison, fearful of the political consequences of direct involvement, did little to ease tensions. The chaos lasted for a year, until the less ambitious Vic Schiro instructed police to clamp down on the more disorderly protesters.[70]

What came of the struggle born of such intense emotions? When the U.S. District Court declared New Orleans's schools a unitary system in 1975, the city's public schools served 94,088 students—75,400 of them black. Almost 60 percent of New Orleans's white school-age children attended the more than one hundred private and parochial schools in the city while others fed the swelling tide of suburban migration. Moreover, the performance of the public schools was hardly encouraging. A recent survey revealed that the poor quality of education in New Orleans was second only to the state's lack of a right-to-work law in discouraging firms from locating in the city. The state has since passed a right-to-work law; the educational system is unchanged.[71]

The public schools are not the only things that remain unchanged in New Orleans. Less exclusive Mardi Gras krewes, which measure status in dollars rather than pedigrees, have recently arisen to entertain tourists and accommodate newcomers. But the New Orleans elite, and those who aspire to it, still finds its time, money, and attention devoted to Carnival. If recent arrivals find it difficult to work during the social season, they learn, in a year or two, not to worry about it. The local economy may be growing, but the economic structure of the community has not changed. Black successes in politics have not been matched by comparable social or economic gains. Much of the black community still exists on the margins of society, and remains so insecure as to feel threatened by the Vietnamese refugees who entered New Orleans in the late 1970s. Competition for jobs, increased pressure on inadequate government resources, and suspicion of preferential treatment for the Vietnamese in housing (where blacks were finding supplies dwindling due to gentrification) combined to further alienate New Orleans's black majority. Despite the influx of petrodollars, the boom in tourism, and the CBD's gleaming new face, New Orleans still marches to its own drummer. The beat is faster than it was a few years ago, but it is still New Orleans's own.[72]

As for New Orleans's place in the Sunbelt, it remains ambiguous. Demographically and ecologically it is a misfit, resembling more the older industrial cities of the Northeast and Midwest. Yet there is no doubt that the sources of Sunbelt growth and change are infiltrating the bayous of southern Louisiana. Regional, national, and international currents regularly lap at the Crescent City and there is tangible evidence of a new worldliness. Such activity, however, is posing as many problems as it is solving. Economic growth holds some promise for the social health of the area, but it has also brought a growing number of increasingly dangerous industrial accidents and more pollution to the already carcinogen-laden Mississippi River. It has also raised the question as to what degree traditional New Orleans must be destroyed as a trade-off for new jobs and economic opportunity. It would, however, be a mistake to underestimate the resiliency and assimilative power of New Orleans's culture. If the Crescent City is being swept up belatedly in the rise of the Sunbelt, it will never be mistaken for Houston.

NOTES

1. "A Sunbelt City Plays Catch-Up," *Business Week*, 6 March 1978, 69–70.

2. James K. Glassman, "New Orleans: I Have Seen the Future and It's Houston," *Atlantic* 242 (July 1978): 10ff.

3. *Times-Picayune* (New Orleans), 25 January 1981.

4. Ibid., 28 September 1980; Peirce F. Lewis, *New Orleans: The Making of an Urban Landscape* (Cambridge, Mass.: Ballinger Publishing Co., 1976), 75.

5. Lewis, *New Orleans*, 76; H. W. Gilmore, "The Old New Orleans and the New: A Case for Ecology," *American Sociological Review* 9 (August 1944): 385–394.

6. East Jefferson Parish is that portion of the parish situated on the east bank of the Mississippi River. The bend in the river as it courses through southern Louisiana actually bisects the parish into northern and southern portions, but the segments take their names from the riverbanks. The geographically northern sector is thus "east Jefferson Parish." *Times-Picayune*, 12 January 1975, 2, 6 June 1980, 15, 19 March 1981; Lewis, *New Orleans*, 76–79; Lynne Brock, George Gurtner, and Joe Manguno, "Jefferson Parish," *New Orleans* 11 (July 1977): 8ff.; Ken Kolb, "St. Tammany Parish: The Boomlet across the Lake," *New Orleans* 11 (July 1977): 35; Economic Development Council of the Chamber/New Orleans and the River Region, "East New Orleans Area."

7. City of New Orleans, *Annual Report of the Mayor, 1956–1958*; *Times-Picayune*, 12 January 1975, 28 March 1981; Economic Development Council of the Chamber/New Orleans and the River Region, "West Bank Area."

8. *Times-Picayune*, 10 May 1978.

9. Blaine Brownell and David R. Goldfield, *Urban America: From Downtown to No Town* (Boston: Houghton Mifflin, 1979), 397.

10. Lewis, *New Orleans*, 88–90; Bureau of Governmental Research, *Plan and Program for the Preservation of the Vieux Carré* (New Orleans: Bureau of Governmental Research, 1968); *Times-Picayune*, 25 January 1981.

11. Gilmore, "The Old New Orleans and the New," 385–394; Helen Rosenberg, "Areas of Relocation of Displaced Lower Garden District and Irish Channel Residents" (M.A. thesis, University of New Orleans, 1977); League of Women Voters, *Housing Displacement in New Orleans* (New Orleans: League of Women Voters, n.d.); Jason Berry, "The Upgrading of New Orleans," *Nation*, 23 September 1978, 270–275; Shirley Laska and Daphne Spain, "Inner City Renovation: What Can We Expect?" *Louisiana Business Survey* 9 (October 1978): 4–7; *Times-Picayune*, 30 October 1977; *States-Item*, 25 October 1977.

12. Neal R. Peirce, *The Deep South States of America* (New York: W. W. Norton & Co., Inc., 1974), 113–114; Brock, Gurtner, and Manguno, "Jefferson Parish," 8ff.; Iris Kelso, "Lawrence of Jefferson," *New Orleans* 11 (July 1977): 19–24.

13. Lewis, *New Orleans*, 86; *Times-Picayune*, 18, 20 January 1981, 12 July 1981; Mayor's Office of Policy Planning, *New Orleans Economic Development Strategy* (New Orleans: Mayor's Office of Policy Planning, 1979), 26.

14. *Times-Picayune*, 18, 25 January 1981; *Figaro*, 5 May 1980; U.S. Congress, Senate, Committee on Banking, Housing, and Urban Affairs, *Hearings before the Committee on Banking, Housing, and Urban Affairs*, 96th Cong., 1st sess., 6 September 1979, 59.

15. James R. Bobo, *The New Orleans Economy: Pro Bono Publico?* (New Orleans: University of New Orleans, 1975).

16. *Times-Picayune*, 25 January 1981, 8 February 1981, 9 May 1981, 12, 21 July 1981.

17. Ibid., 25 January 1981.

18. The "subemployed" include those who are underemployed, part-time workers seeking full-time jobs, and those who should be part of the labor force but have dropped out of it. None of these people are captured by unemployment figures.

19. Bobo, *New Orleans Economy*, 32, 62, passim.

20. *Times-Picayune*, 21, 26 July 1981; John Alan Simon and Ira Harkey III, "Oil: Louisiana's Liquid Asset," *New Orleans* 12 (July 1978): 9ff.

21. Robyn Leary, "LOOP Pulls It All Together," *New Orleans* 15 (March 1981): 17ff.; Edward McCabe, "Tuscaloosa Trend: Pay Dirt for Oildom," *New Orleans* 14 (July 1981): 50ff.; *Times-Picayune*, 28 December 1980.

22. "Baton Rouge to the Gulf," *Fortune* 63 (January 1961): 105–113; Edward F. Haas, *DeLesseps S. Morrison and the Image of Reform: New Orleans Politics, 1946–1961* (Baton Rouge: Louisiana State University Press, 1974), 156–157; Gary Bolding, "The New Orleans Seaway Movement,"

Louisiana History 10 (Winter 1969): 49–60; see also the *Annual Report of the Mayor,* 1952–1959.

23. *Times-Picayune,* 25 January 1981, 14 June 1981; *New York Times,* 25 March 1979.

24. *Times-Picayune,* 25 January 1981, 14 June 1981.

25. Mayor's Office of Policy Planning, *New Orleans Economic Development Strategy,* 26; *Times-Picayune,* 25 January 1981, 8 August 1981; William D. Crawford and E. C. Nebel III, *Application of the Travel Economic Impact Model to New Orleans* (New Orleans: University of New Orleans, 1977), 19–20, passim.

26. John A. Reinecke and Caroline Fisher, "The Economic Impact of the Port of New Orleans," *Louisiana Business Survey* 12 (January 1981): 4–7; Mayor's Office of Policy Planning, *New Orleans Economic Development Strategy,* 24.

27. Lewis, *New Orleans,* 67–75; *Times-Picayune,* 20 January 1981, 6, 7 December 1980, 27 January 1981, 21 April 1981, 17 June 1981; Mayor's Office of Policy Planning, *New Orleans Economic Development Strategy,* 24–25; *Figaro,* 3 November 1980; *Gambit,* 30 May 1981.

28. Economic Development Council of the Chamber/New Orleans and the River Region, "Industrial Investments, 1956–1979" (n.d.).

29. Mayor's Office of Policy Planning, *New Orleans Economic Development Strategy,* 24.

30. Ibid., 26; *Times-Picayune,* January 25, 1981.

31. Bobo, *New Orleans Economy,* 8–9; Economic Development Council of the Chamber/New Orleans and the River Region, "General Information: Business Mix—New Orleans Region, 1978" (n.d., mimeo); *Figaro,* 28 April 1980; *Times-Picayune,* 2 November 1980, 25 January 1981, 29 March 1981.

32. Ronald M. Konkel, "Space Employment and Economic Growth in Houston and New Orleans, 1961–1966" (M.A. thesis, Tulane University, 1968); John Gillan, Jr., "Shuttling Off to Michoud," *New Orleans* 11 (August 1977): 14ff.; *New York Times,* 4 August 1962; *Times-Picayune,* 2 November 1980; Bobo, *New Orleans Economy,* 9.

33. Mayor's Office of Policy Planning, *New Orleans Economic Development Strategy,* 29, 31–34; *Times-Picayune,* 29 March 1981.

34. *Figaro,* 28 July 1980; *Times-Picayune,* 21 June 1980, 11, 14 January 1981, 29 March 1981; Mayor's Office of Policy Planning, *New Orleans Economic Development Strategy,* 36–37, 41–43.

35. DeLesseps S. Morrison (DSM) to Lawrence A. Molony, 20 October 1954; Scott Wilson to Chep, 8 October 1954, 30 March 1959, all in the Scott Wilson Papers, Special Collections, Tulane University; Errol Laborde, "Tourism: The Marketing of New Orleans," *New Orleans* 15 (January 1981): 68ff.

36. Simon and Harkey, "Oil," 10.

37. William Forman, Jr., "The Conflict over Federal Urban Renewal Enabling Legislation," *Louisiana Studies* 8 (Fall 1969): 251–267; J. R. Andre,

"Urban Renewal and Housing in New Orleans, 1949–1962" (M.A. thesis, Louisiana State University, 1963); Haas, *DeLesseps S. Morrison*, 173–174; Berry, "The Upgrading of New Orleans," 272; *New York Times*, 21 April 1974, 12 May 1974.

38. Richard O. Baumbach, Jr., and William E. Borah, *The Second Battle of New Orleans: A History of the Vieux Carré Riverfront-Expressway Controversy* (University: University of Alabama Press, 1981), 51, 60, 147, 154, passim.

39. Morton Inger, *Politics and Reality in an American City* (New York: Center for Urban Education, 1969), 76–90; Charles Y. W. Chai, "Who Rules New Orleans?" *Louisiana Business Survey* 2 (October 1971): 2–7; Glassman, "New Orleans," 10, 14–15; Peirce, *Deep South States of America*, 102–103.

40. Glassman, "New Orleans," 10ff.; Chai, "Who Rules New Orleans?" 2–7; Inger, *Politics and Reality*, 76–90.

41. "A Sunbelt City Plays Catch-Up," *Business Week*, 69–70; *New York Times*, 25 March 1979; Errol Laborde, "Economic Perspectives," *New Orleans* 15 (January 1981): 14ff.

42. Peirce, *Deep South States of America*, 102–103; Lewis, *New Orleans*, 94–95; *New York Times*, 2 August 1975; Joey Morgan, "Superdome—Past, Present, and Future," *New Orleans* 7 (January 1973): 71ff.

43. *Times-Picayune*, 17 January, 22 April, 2 June, 27 September 1981; *Figaro*, 7 April, 14 April 1980.

44. *Times-Picayune*, 4, 9, 10, 12, 22–24 April 1981, 9, 15–16 May 1981.

45. Ibid., 12 March 1980.

46. George M. Reynolds, *Machine Politics in New Orleans, 1897–1926* (New York: AMS Press, 1968); John R. Kemp, ed., *Martin Behrman of New Orleans: Memoirs of a City Boss* (Baton Rouge: Louisiana State University Press, 1977); Iris Kelso and Rosemary James, "When the Caucus Ruled the World," *New Orleans* 5 (May 1971): 21ff.; Edward Haas, "New Orleans on the Half-Shell: The Maestri Era, 1936–1946," *Louisiana History* 13 (Summer 1972): 283–310; David Lloyd Sigler, "Downfall of a Political Machine: The New Orleans Mayoralty Election of 1946" (B.A. honors thesis, Tulane Univerisy, 1968), 36.

47. Haas, *DeLesseps S. Morrison*, 26–66; F. Edward Hebert with John McMillan, *Last of the Titans: The Life and Times of Congressman F. Edward Hebert of Louisiana* (Lafayette, La.: Center for Louisiana Studies, 1976), 230–231, 235; Scott Wilson to Harold, 22 April 1946, in the Wilson Papers.

48. Herman Deutsch, "New Orleans Politics—The Greatest Free Show on Earth," in Hodding Carter, ed., *The Past as Prelude: New Orleans, 1718–1968* (New Orleans: Pelican Press, 1968), 332–334; Joseph B. Parker, "Machine and Reform Politics in New Orleans: The Morrison Era" (Ph.D. dissertation, Tulane University, 1970); Michael Kurtz, "DeLesseps S. Morrison: Political Reformer," *Louisiana History* 17 (Winter 1976): 19–39; "The

Demagogue and the Liberal: A Study of the Political Rivalry between Earl Long and DeLesseps S. Morrison" (Ph.D. dissertation, Tulane University, 1971), 45, 47, 55–74, passim; Haas, *DeLesseps S. Morrison*, 119–153.

49. *Times-Picayune*, 27–29 January 1962, 3–5 March 1962, 15 November 1977, 30 March 1978; *States-Item*, 12 October 1961; Eric Wayne Doerries, "James E. Comiskey, the Irish Third Ward Boss: A Study of a Unique and Dying Brand of Politics" (B.A. honors thesis, Tulane University, 1973); William E. Rittenberg and Gordon A. Saussy, "The Politicalization of Public Administration in New Orleans," *Louisiana Business Survey* 12 (July 1981): 1–4.

50. Parker, "Machine and Reform Politics," 97, 108–110, 167, 179–180, passim; William C. Havard, "From Bossism to Cosmopolitanism: Changes in the Relationship of Urban Leadership to State Politics," *Annals* 353 (May 1964): 84–94.

51. David W. Fredericks, "The Role of the Negro Minister in Politics in New Orleans" (Ph.D. dissertation, Tulane University, 1967), 30–32; Allen Rosenzweig, "The Influence of Class and Race on Political Behavior in New Orleans, 1960–1967" (M.A. thesis, University of Oklahoma, 1967), 108–127; Addison C. Carey, Jr., "Black Political Participation in New Orleans" (Ph.D. dissertation, Tulane University, 1971), 52–53, 56; Neil R. McMillen, *The Citizens' Council: Organized Resistance to the Reconstruction, 1954–1964* (Urbana: University of Illinois Press, 1971), 222–223, 227; State of Louisiana, *Report of the Secretary of State*, 1953, 1969, 1979.

52. *Louisiana Weekly*, 13, 20, 27 January 1962, 10, 17 February 1962, 9, 23 October 1965, 6, 20 November 1965; *Times-Picayune*, 6 November 1965.

53. *States-Item*, 9, 12, 13, 15 December 1969; *Louisiana Weekly*, 8 November, 20 December 1969; *Times-Picayune*, 10 November, 12, 14, 15 December 1969; Furnell Chatman, "Black Politics: A Concept in Search of a Definition," *New Orleans* 5 (August 1971): 29ff.; Rosenzweig, "Influence of Class and Race," 140–150.

54. *Times-Picayune*, 12–14 November 1977.

55. Ibid., 2 October 1977, 12 March, 19 April 1978, 31 July 1979.

56. U.S. Congress, *Hearings before the Committee on Banking, Housing, and Urban Affairs*, 46, 58, passim; *Times-Picayune* 12, 17 March 1978.

57. *Times-Picayune*, 2 May 1978; *Wall Street Journal*, 1 May 1979; Iris Kelso, "Rising to the Mayor's Office," *New Orleans* 12 (November 1977): 18ff.; Bonnie Warren Crone, "Mayor Morial: New Verse or Same Old Song at City Hall?" *New Orleans* 12 (May 1978): 13ff.

58. Numan V. Bartley and Hugh D. Graham, *Southern Politics and the Second Reconstruction* (Baltimore: Johns Hopkins University Press, 1975), 87, 92, 102–103, 156–157; Deutsch, New Orleans Politics," 340; Rosenzweig, "Influence of Class and Race," 36–39; *Times-Picayune*, 17 July 1978, 16 December 1969, 4, 8 April 1980.

59. Jack Bass and Walter DeVries, *The Transformation of Southern Politics* (New York: Basic Books, 1976), 180–181; *Times-Picayune*, 18 No-

vember 1979, 28 August 1977; Richard Engstrom, "The Hale Boggs Gerrymander: Congressional Redistricting, 1969," *Louisiana History* 21 (Winter 1980): 59–66.

60. *Times-Picayune*, 5 April 1970, 25 January 1976, 23 August 1977, 23, 25, 28 February , 27 May 1978, 10, 17, 18 April, 21 May 1980.

61. Ibid., 23 January, 22 August 1981, 17, 28 August 1977; *Figaro*, 5 May 1980; *Gambit*, 11 July 1981.

62. Chatman, "Black Politics," 29ff.; *Times-Picayune*, 12 January 1975.

63. *States-Item*, 1 April 1976; *Times-Picayune*, 31 March, 1 April 1976, 9 November 1977, 2 October 1981.

64. Speech at a Union Convention, 15 June 1965, at the Fountainbleau Motor Hotel, New Orleans, Louisiana, in the John P. Nelson Papers, Amistad Research Center (ARC); *New York Times*, 11 September 1963; Community Relations Council of Greater New Orleans, Statement Delivered to the City Council of New Orleans, 14 January 1965, in the NAACP Field Director's Papers, ARC; *Times-Picayune*, 12 December 1969; Buddy Diliberto, "Saints—More Than Just Football," *New Orleans* 7 (January 1973): 63ff.

65. Haas, *DeLesseps S. Morrison*, 67–81; DSM to Arthur J. Chapital, Sr., and Ernest N. Morial, 18 April 1960, in the New Orleans Branch NAACP Papers, University of New Orleans (UNO).

66. "A Brief Report of the Activities of the New Orleans Branch NAACP Youth Council in 1964," n.d., in NAACP Papers; *Louisiana Weekly*, 6 November 1965; "Report of the Activities of the New Orleans Youth Council for the Period April 1–May 3, 1965 Inclusive," in NAACP Papers; George Gurtner, "The Hurricane Mayor Still Answers His Phone," *New Orleans* 12 (October 1977): 22–23; Horace C. Bynum to Most Reverend John P. Cody, S.T.D., 25 June 1965, in NAACP Papers.

67. "Desire under the Guns," *Newsweek*, 28 September 1970, 28ff.; Edward Haas, "The Southern Metropolis, 1940–1976," in Blaine Brownell and David R. Goldfield, eds., *The City in Southern History* (Port Washington, N.Y.: Kennikat Press, 1977), 184; Peter Hernon, *A Terrible Thunder: The Story of the New Orleans Sniper* (Garden City, N.Y.: Doubleday & Co., Inc., 1978), 156, passim; *Times-Picayune*, 8–10 January 1973, 10 July 1981, March 1983, passim; *Louisiana Weekly*, 13 December 1980; Arthur J. Chapital, Sr., to Civil Rights Division, U.S. Department of Justice, 13 September 1961, and Arthur J. Chapital to Provosty Dayries, 14 May 1958, in NAACP Papers; see also the file on alleged police brutality in the A. P. Tureaud Papers, ARC.

68. T. L. Van Valey, W. C. Roof, and J. E. Wilcox, "Trends in Residential Segregation, 1960–1970," *American Journal of Sociology* 82 (January 1977): 826–844; Lewis, *New Orleans*, 98; J. Lambert Molyneaux and Anthony V. Margavio, "Population Change in New Orleans from 1940 to 1960," *Louisiana Studies* 9 (1970): 228–242.

69. Mary Lee Muller, "The Orleans Parish School Board and Negro Education, 1940–1960" (M.A. thesis, University of New Orleans, 1975), 6,

22, 27–28; Lionel J. Bourgeois to A. P. Tureaud, 30 September 1947, in NAACP Papers; William R. Adams, "A Study of Some Tangible Inequalities in the New Orleans Public Schools," n.d., in Tureaud Papers.

70. Inger, *Politics and Reality*, passim; Edward L. Pinney and Robert S. Friedman, *Political Leadership and the School Desegregation Crisis in New Orleans* (New York: McGraw-Hill, 1963); Louisiana State Advisory Committee, *The New Orleans School Crisis: Report to the United States Commission on Civil Rights* (New Orleans: Louisiana State Advisory Committee, 1961); Mary Lee Muller, "New Orleans Public School Desegregation," *Louisiana History* 17 (Winter 1976): 69–88; Haas, *DeLesseps S. Morrison*, 252–282; McMillen, *The Citizens' Council*, 267, 286–292.

71. *Times-Picayune*, 25 January 1976; Mayor's Office of Policy Planning, *New Orleans Economic Development Strategy*, 12–15; Lynne Brock, "Public Education under Siege," *New Orleans* 11 (August 1977): 18ff.

72. Martha C. Ward and Zachary Gussow, "The Vietnamese in New Orleans: A Preliminary Report," in John Cooke, ed., *Perspectives on Ethnicity in New Orleans* (New Orleans: The Committee on Ethnicity in New Orleans, 1979), 37–41; Alma H. Young, "Vietnamese-Black Interaction in New Orleans: A Preliminary Assessment," in John Cooke, ed., *Perspectives on Ethnicity in New Orleans* (New Orleans: The Committee on Ethnicity in New Orleans, 1980), 53–62.

5

TAMPA
FROM HELL HOLE TO THE GOOD LIFE

by Gary R. Mormino

Tampa Bay is too romantic and lovely a place for one to attempt describing it. I wish some perfumed, cigar smoking, novel writer, city man monkey was here, he could not describe it, he would die of a fit of reality. Tampa is a perfect Arcadia. . . . Florida could be made a heaven on earth. . . . The more I see of T. Bay the more I like it, it is a romantic and truly picturesque place . . . Tampa, Tampa what a beautiful heavenly and luscourious [sic] spot thou are . . .—Bartholomew M. Lynch, 1836

Tampa is Stevedore and Realtor. New Atlanta. Incorrigible Waterfront. Thrall of Phosphate. Grandson of Cigars. Organized Crime. Old, old Money. . . .—St. Petersburg Times, *1982*

The specter of disaster in 1980 and 1981 should have muted the growing ballyhoo of all but the most unflagging regional boosters: Witness the collapse of the Skyway Bridge, the sinking of the Coast Guard vessel *Blackthorn* at the mouth of Tampa Bay, the renewed infestation of medflies, race riots in Miami and Orlando, the influx of 150,000 Cuban and Haitian refugees, and the spiraling menace of imported drugs. A feature article in a national magazine lamented, "The sad fact is that Florida is going down the tube."[1] Yet Florida in general and Tampa in particular could hardly contain tourists and new residents, eager to share in the new-found prosperity of the dynamic Sunbelt. It was not always so. In fact, Tampa languished for nearly four hundred years before developing the rudiments of an urban life.

"Here is a noble harbor," rhapsodized Hernando de Soto in 1539. A majestic physical setting awaited permanent settlers: a perfect natural harbor astride Florida's southwest coast; a lavishing of fresh springs; a rich and varied hinterland of black mucky soil, ghostly swamps, and meandering rivers as yet unstraightened by the Army

Corps of Engineers; and a moderate climate that would tantalize future Chambers of Commerce.

The establishment of Fort Brooke in 1824 inaugurated permanent settlement, but once the Seminole Indian threat was removed the government deactivated the fort. Tampa became a frontier trading camp. In 1880, census takers reported a scant 720 inhabitants, a loss of seventy-six people from the previous decade. "Tampa once reached is found to be a sleepy, Southern town," noted an observer in 1882.[2]

Events in the 1880s awakened Tampa to modernity. In 1883 the entrepreneur Henry Bradley Plant selected Tampa as a terminus for his rail line. To underpin his investment, Plant also constructed the lavish Tampa Bay Hotel, a Moorish palace that today functions as a main building of the University of Tampa. By 1894 Dr. L. L. Weedon reported that twenty thousand tourists visited Tampa annually. "Everybody is coming to Florida this winter," gushed the *Tampa Morning Tribune* in 1896, adding that "the Queen City of the Gulf Coast is the most progressive city south of the Mason-Dixon Line." To promote industry, the Board of Trade took out a thirty-eight-dollar ad in New York newspapers.[3]

Tobacco fueled Tampa's drive toward the twentieth century, as American and European smokers struck matches to the millions of cigars rolled annually at the city's two hundred factories by 1900. In 1885 a Spanish *patron*, Don Vicente Martinez Ybor, chose Tampa as the prime site for his cigar-making operation. The region's humidity, transportation facilities, and cheap land met the needs of his product. This decision recast Tampa's slumbering economy into the cigar capital of the world.[4]

Ybor's arrival also permanently altered the area's ethnic composition. The inception of Ybor City in 1886 (soon incorporated into Tampa) lured thousands of "Latins" (Cubans, Spaniards, and Italians). By 1900, three-quarters of Tampa's 15,839 inhabitants claimed Latin status or Afro-American background. Nearby West Tampa, absorbed into the main city in 1924, was even more ethnic.[5]

"The cigar industry is to this city what the iron industry is to Pittsburgh," editorialized the *Tampa Morning Tribune* in 1896, half optimistic and half pessimistic about the health of a one-industry town.[6] The city hosted other businesses, of course, but these endeavors were small scale. Although fabulous deposits of phosphate were discovered at Bone Valley just east of Tampa in 1888, export of this fertilizer proceeded slowly until Congress deepened the Port of Tampa after World War I. Tampans also exported cattle and guns to Cuba, the beginning of a long and quixotic relationship that blossomed after Tampa served as the chief port of embarkation during the Spanish-American War.[7]

The great Florida land boom of the 1920s swept Tampa into a building frenzy—highlighted by the construction of Davis Islands at the mouth of the bay—but the city plunged deeply into the land bust and Great Depression of the following decade. The 1930s represented a great watershed for Tampa. The depression devasted an industry whose sales depended on its quality: hand-rolled cigars. As Americans switched to cheaper and more popular cigarettes, cigar-making collapsed, never to recover fully. In 1927 the city's 159 cigar factories and their 13,000 employees produced 504 million cigars; by 1945 there were only 5,500 cigarworkers—many of them unskilled workers brought in to man the new machines.[8] Indicative of this new Tampa was the labor climate: In 1920 the AFL claimed Tampa had the highest per capita labor union membership of any comparably sized city in America; by 1945 the local union movement was negligible.[9] Moreover, a series of shattering strikes between 1899 and 1931 antagonized Latin-Anglo relationships well into the twentieth century. Cigars, which had given Tampa an international identity and an ethnic ambience unique in the South, would no longer determine the city's destiny.[10]

On the eve of World War II Tampa groped for a new identity and a new direction. Established businesses resisted change, and Tampa's mercantile climate attracted few outside investors. Conservative commercial leaders dominated the local economy. "They liked the community the way it was," recalled a local banker. "They resisted any change they could not control."[11] For example, in 1930 Pan American Airway Systems agreed to move its operations to Tampa if the city would construct a new airport. Local businessmen and politicians squabbled away their chance and Miami obtained the company.[12]

The threat of war changed this situation. On 14 July 1939, officials announced plans for the construction of MacDill Field at the lower end of the interbay peninsula then known as Catfish Point. The county agreed to donate 3,500 acres while they army purchased an additional 2,295 more. The million-dollar complex helped maintain the nation's B-17 and B-29 fleets. To facilitate transportation between this base and the air corps's Drew Field, the government also constructed Dale Mabry Highway, destined to become a major north-south artery.[13]

The impact of thousands of soldiers in Tampa during the war years cannot be overestimated. At the height of the conflict, the army stationed 25,000 men at MacDill Field. Most were seeing Flor-

MAP 5.1. The Tampa–St. Petersburg SMSA

ida for the first time, and many left with plans to return to the Sunshine State someday. The wartime economy also lured thousands of civilians to the Tampa Bay area. Employment at the Tampa shipyards reached 16,000, and the facility constructed nearly one hundred ships. The shipyard payroll exceeded $750,000 a week. War had regenerated the city.[14]

Defense spending provided much-needed relief to a battered urban economy, but Tampa groped for more permanent cures for its malaise. In its search for a new postwar identity, Tampa had to confront and overcome its own sleazy image. During the 1930s the American Civil Liberties Union had branded Tampa as one of the eleven major centers of repression in the United States, a residue of the city's antilabor, antiradical heritage. "Hell Hole of the Gulf Coast," headlined a leading men's magazine in 1950, a nickname that stuck for many years, along with "Little Chicago" and "Sin City of the South." "Practically every tourist of any sense by-passes Tampa now because they think of Tampa as a grimy factory town or a shotgun-killing city," moaned the *Tampa Tribune*.[15]

Tampa's image—the product of its Latin heritage, nativist excesses, and changing moral climate—reached its nadir in 1950 during the Kefauver hearings. The root of the problem involved bolita, Tampa's numbers game based on the old Cuban lottery. Bolita had long been a prevalent sport in the city's Latin quarter, but the institution changed in the 1940s. After the repeal of prohibition and the crackdown on prostitution (at the request of MacDill Field officials), interest shifted to bolita as a principal source of revenue and

the stakes became higher. What was once a relatively harmless pas-
time became a condor in search of victims.[16]

Everyone knew that bolita needed political protection, but what
distressed so many Tampans was that by 1947 it was the politicians
who needed bolita, not vice versa. "Who else but gamblers can afford
to finance elections today?" shrugged a frustrated resident in 1947.[17]
In that election, Danny Alvarez, Mayor Curtis Hixon's liaison between organized crime and city hall, estimated that he collected
$100,000 from "our friends." He recalled that $40,000 went directly
to purchase votes and official acquiescence. Ironically, Hixon was
viewed by voters as the reform candidate, and his excesses were not
discovered until years later.[18] Sam Davis, president of Tampa Ship
Repair, recounted a vivid recollection of this sordid system: "Nobody but the racketeers would get out and vote . . . They stuffed ballot boxes, stole ballot boxes, 'crooked the count' at the polls . . . An
honest man wouldn't run for office because he knew he didn't have a
chance. An honest citizen wouldn't vote because he knew he had no
representation."[19]

Tampa politics had never been graced with purity: In 1935 only
the state police guarding voting booths prevented a civil war; *Tribune* editor James Clendinen arrived that same year and quickly pronounced Tampa "one of the rottenest towns in the country."[20] Not
much had changed by 1945. What made the postwar milieu so dis-
tasteful was the openness of fraud and the national exposure that the
Kefauver investigation generated in December 1950.[21] These hearings uncovered enough dirt to scandalize even the most cynical
Tampans: testimony of cash payments to Sheriff Hugh Culbreath,
whom the gamblers called "Melon Head"; missing records from police files; hundreds of protected bolita spots; and seventeen unsolved
gangland slayings.[22]

The national smear prompted Tampa citizens to clean up their
city in order to make the "Suncoast" more attractive to investors,
tourists, and migrants. Over the next two decades, politicians waged
bitter war over the image of Tampa and the city's direction. The
focal point of the controversy was the mayor's office, institutionally
the strongest in the state.

A traditionalistic social class colored Tampa's political environment from the Civil War until World War II. Rooted in the Old
South's deference to elites and nurtured by the New South's embrace of the marketplace, politics in Tampa revolved around the
strength of several old families and entrenched downtown business
interests. Political parties exercised little control (still true today)

and in such an environment groups not actively involved in governing, such as Afro-Americans, were not expected to participate, let
alone vote.[23] Cubans, Spaniards, and Italians displayed little interest
in politics until the New Deal, in part because of their old-world
backgrounds, in part because of the implacable opposition shown by
the Anglo community. In 1930, for instance, only 24 percent of
Tampa's foreign-born population was naturalized, easily the lowest
percentage of any large city in the United States.[24] But the politics of
the old order was threatened in the 1950s by a number of factors: the
migration to Tampa of tens of thousands of new inhabitants, the
civic maturation of second- and third-generation Latins, and the
emergence of a remarkable figure, Nick Chillura Nuccio.

The son of Sicilian immigrants, Nuccio became the first Latin
successfully to wrestle power from the predominant Waspish power
structure. Nuccio's career, except for a few years as a postal clerk,
was devoted to the pursuit of power, first as a city alderman in 1929,
then as a county commissioner in the 1930s, and finally as mayor
from 1956 to 1959 and again from 1963 to 1967. His first taste of
clout came as county commissioner, a powerful patronage post in
Hillsborough County because the county is responsible for human
services and welfare. "There were more than 2,000 W.P.A. jobs in my
district during the Depression," he recollects today.[25] "Nick was
a twenty-four hour a day politician," reminisced Roland Manteiga,
editor of the influential *La Gaceta*, the nation's only trilingual paper
(Spanish, Italian, and English). "Nick ate, drank, and slept politics—
not in the bad sense, but as a man who wanted to be known for doing things and helping people. Nick functioned like an employment
agency. He kept long hours in his office and in his home just to accommodate job seekers."[26]

In an area without Irish protégés, Nuccio successfully learned
the art of boss politics. "You know a lot of people were born here and
never learned to speak English," explained restaurateur Angel Me-
nendez. "Nick was always glad to run downtown and pay the old
people's taxes or pay a bill for them."[27] But Nuccio's strength lay in
the shrinking Latin neighborhoods, always loyal but ever diminishing in a growing city. Nuccio appealed to the Latins—in Spanish,
Italian, and broken English—as one of them and as an example. "I
can pave the way by my conduct and my performance for all Latin
people," he promised in 1956.[28] Outside of Ybor City and West
Tampa, detractors often caricatured Nuccio as an anachronism, a re-
lic of corrupt ward politics and a stigma from the city's dark days.
Since Tampa and Florida voted solidly Democratic (in 1982 Demo-

crats still outnumbered Republicans 3 to 1), urban elections increasingly revolved around personality and the future direction of the city.[29]

In 1955 Nuccio challenged the popular incumbent, Mayor Curtis Hixon, a former druggist with a store near Ybor City who is credited with first hiring Latins on the police and fire departments. Hixon, a fiscal conservative, profited heavily by a 1954 extension of the city limits that added 91,000 persons—mostly WASPs who knew little of Nick Nuccio except his Latin surname. Also aided by a vicious Drew Pearson story that linked Nuccio to the Mafia, Hixon easily defeated Nuccio by 9,000 votes. The loss, however, failed to dampen Nuccio's indomitable spirit, and when Hixon died the following year, he made a second run for the chief executive's post.[30]

Nuccio again met formidable opposition, chiefly from the influential *Tampa Tribune*. "He was an alderman during the most violent and corrupt period of Tampa's history," bemoaned the *Tribune*. Despite his difficulties with the press, Nuccio scored a major upset, defeating the tainted and weak interim mayor J. L. Young by a mere 125 votes. Nuccio scored heavily in the Latin precincts, 3,021 to Young's 440 in West Tampa and Ybor City. The campaign "made everyone in the city with a Latin name no matter where he lived, realize he was Latin and had a stake in the election," remembered one elderly participant. The *Tribune* offered the winner an embittered challenge: "History has bestowed upon Mr. Nuccio the long-coveted opportunity to show that he can rise above the level of ward politician and make a mayor of which the whole city can be proud."[31]

One of the keys to Nuccio's triumph was the emerging black vote. Blacks played no role in Tampa politics until after World War II due to the restrictive white municipal primary. In 1950, 7,387 blacks registered to vote; however, that figure quickly dropped to 3,630 in 1954 as blacks became disillusioned and threatened by local politics. Blacks failed to support Nuccio's candidacy in the 1955 election, but the years 1955 to 1956 proved to be critical for the relationship of the two. In 1956, a celebrated Tampan, General Sumter Lowry, ran unsuccessfully for governor on a white supremacy ticket and finished second in Hillsborough County in a four-way race: Leroy Collins, the eventual winner, won the county with 32,206 votes while Lowry received 14,337. Sensing the importance of the black vote, Nuccio appealed to black voters in the mayoral campaign of 1956, and they responded with a resounding mandate. "He was the first public official who would come regularly to our meetings in our community—

he was calling blacks 'mister' when most politicians were still saying 'boy' or 'nigger,'" remembered C. Blythe Andrews, publisher of Tampa's black newspaper, *Florida's Sentinel Bulletin*.[32]

Nuccio served as mayor until 1959 when the *Tribune*-backed candidate Julian Lane defeated him 37,823 to 32,910. Lane represented everything Nuccio could not. A football captain at the University of Florida, a baseball hero at Hillsborough High (Nuccio had dropped out of school in the eighth grade), and a self-made dairy farmer, Lane won the election by appealing to the city's middle- and upper-class neighborhoods. The indomitable Nuccio returned to challenge Lane in 1963. Ironically, Lane was hurt by the white backlash vote because of his attempts to peacefully integrate downtown facilities. Nuccio, moreover, ran a polished campaign, fully utilizing the nascent medium of television. On election day, nature proved as decisive as electronics. High winds and showers kept many Anglo voters at home, but not the faithful Latins. Nuccio defeated Lane 35,902 to 33,992. In one West Tampa precinct, Nuccio won 1,565 to 309.[33]

Tampans remember the Nuccio years as periods of dynamic urban growth and commercial prosperity. Like other modern political bosses, Nuccio accommodated himself to the business community, successfully luring state and federal monies to clear slums and launch major construction projects. "Nick Nuccio was interested in public projects with high visibility," recalled a veteran reporter.[34] Yet stylistically he never left his roots. He preferred the ambience of Ybor City to the corporate lunchroom; every morning at five A.M. he frequented Cuervo's Cafe, ready to meet the public on its ground.

The man who conquered Nick Nuccio and became the transitional figure in modern Tampa politics was Dick Greco, Jr. Greco became a force in Tampa and Florida politics because of an irresistible combination of personal and professional qualities. Like his adversary, he was also of Latin heritage. Greco solidly defeated Nuccio in the 1967 mayor's race, 34,011 to 25,169. Four years later Greco won by an even wider margin. In the first of these two races, the *Tampa Tribune* convinced voters that "the main issue is, as it always was, spoils system policies vs. the promise of modern public administration."[35]

At thirty-four Greco became the youngest mayor of any major city in the United States. Trilingual, he could play dominoes at Centro Español or talk business with Chester Ferguson of the Lykes' Corporation. Well tailored, handsome, and articulate, he was identified as the ambassador for the new Tampa. Significantly, Greco appealed to the voters who harbored few labor ties and no awareness of or interest in past politics. His timing proved keen, for fewer than half of Tampa's 250,000 citizens in 1968 were Florida natives.[36]

Greco used a businesslike approach to modernize city hall. He recruited aides with public administration degrees and appointed the first black to a city hall job. But Greco also brought a youthful, "New Frontier" image to the job. "I used the media a lot," Greco reflected. "I did three radio programs a week; I even did one in Spanish . . . [including] a recap of the week, 'What's going on at City Hall.'" Greco heralded the promise of Tampa across the state, and in 1973 he chaired the finance committee of the National League of Cities. He also headed Democratic Mayors for Nixon in 1972. "Dick Greco," remembered James Clendinen, "was one of the best political personalities we've had from the standpoint of communications with the people. He was great at public relations; not so great at administration. He gave the city a good image."[37]

Greco's success at the local level was in part related to events in the state and nation. Lyndon Johnson's Great Society earmarked federal funds at theretofore unimaginable levels for cities. Even more extraordinary was the new-found urban clout exercised on the state level. Into the 1960s, Florida retained one of the country's most malapportioned legislatures. According to 1960 census figures, 12 percent of the voters elected a majority in each house; the five most populous counties contained over half the population but merited only 14 percent of the senators. In the words of *Tribune* editor James Clendinen, "pork choppers . . . more interested in pork than principle" ruled the state.[38] The United States Supreme Court's mandate in *Reynolds* v. *Sims* changed that—but only after a grueling fight. Tampa quickly capitalized on its growing urban power base. No Tampan had ever served as Speaker of the State House of Representatives until 1973. Another Tampan held the position in 1982. In the upper house, Louis de la Parte became president of the Senate in 1974.[39] Dick Greco and his successors now found it worthwhile to make the long trek to Tallahassee, for lobbying became as necessary for city government as computers and public relations.

Greco exemplified the new mood of city hall: Tampa would be governed by businessmen; what was good for business was good for Tampa. When Dick Greco left office, it came as no surprise that he accepted a high-level position with the Edward DeBartolo Corporation to serve as a liaison between business and government and to oversee the expansion of shopping malls across the state. His successors, William Poe (1974–1979) and Robert Martinez (1979–) both fit the business-professional image cast by Greco.[40] By the 1960s

Tampa's economic growth was lockset; Tampa had come to represent the essence of American business, another New South city too busy to hate.

Tampa's kinetic energy, the product of local, regional, and national forces, manifested itself in a fantastic variety of economic forms. The most important factors in the postwar Tampa economy included massive federal appropriations for defense and urban renewal; the development of a diversified industrial base; the maintenance of a strong agribusiness sector; the emergence of the area as an important transportation and distribution center; the continuing real estate and construction booms; the maturation and promotion of a tourist/leisure society; and the urban renaissance of downtown Tampa.

Businessmen may have directed the financial fortunes and reordered the image of postwar Tampa, but the federal government provided the initial stimulus and the subsequent stream of subsidies for the metropolitan-military complex. V-J Day did not halt government spending. Instead Tampa continued to be an integral part of the national defense system. MacDill Field expanded operations and is today the permanent home of the Raid Deployment Joint Task Force. During fiscal year 1980, over 15,000 people were affiliated with the base, drawing salaries totaling $115 million. MacDill also awarded contracts totaling $106 million in 1980. The presence of the base has attracted over 100,000 retired army personnel to the area, a figure that doubles every winter when northern pensioners arrive for the season.[41]

Following World War II, Drew Field had become an international airport that by 1947 was recording 13,000 takeoffs and landings a year. The army gave its 2,000-acre training base, Henderson Field in northeast Tampa, to Hillsborough County. In addition to Henderson Field, the government also ceded Fort Hesterly Armory to the city, providing residents with their largest auditorium. The shipyards on Hooker's Point went to private industry to supply the burgeoning maritime economy.

In 1956, after an extensive lobbying effort by a group of influential businessmen (the Committee of 100) and local political leaders, the state and federal government appropriated nearly $10 million to begin construction of the University of South Florida on the site of the abandoned Henderson Field. The university became the first of a series of urban campuses to serve the mushrooming downstate population. By 1980 the university enrolled 25,000 students and had become an important cultural and economic force on the Suncoast.[42]

In addition to massive defense-oriented expenditures, Uncle

Sam stimulated metropolitan Tampa Bay's growth with federal appropriations for highways, two interstate expressways, harbor dredging, sewers, a new international airport, and urban renewal. Tampa became the first city in Florida to tap federal funds for urban renewal. The results stand as a testimony to good intentions, flawed execution, and broken promises. Bluntly, city fathers gutted Tampa's historic jewel, Ybor City, the one authentic cultural artifact that might have become Florida's French Quarter. As Florida drifted into a postwar period of architectural blandness and neon tackiness, Ybor City stood out as a genuine—if tattered—historic district. In truth, time had changed the sprawling Spanish, Cuban, and Italian enclave. Factories lay abandoned and blacks quickly moved in to replace Latins as the dominant residential group, but thousands of cigarworkers remained in Ybor City, defiantly determined to spend their final days near their beloved Latin clubs.[43]

In 1965 Mayor Nick Nuccio announced the redevelopment of Ybor City, predicting, "Seven years from now you will be boastful about it." The chairman of Tampa's Urban Renewal Commission prophesied that the new Ybor City would become "a tourist attraction second to none in the U.S." Instead, Ybor City became an urban wasteland as homes, businesses, and factories gave way to desolation. Officials misled the people, the Great Society trimmed its sails, and bureaucrats pointed fingers at one another. Today, fifty-one vacant acres sit where once there were to be retirement villages and Spanish walled cities.[44]

One episode of tragicomedy epitomized the debacle. In 1967, Tampa industrialist Jim Walter proposed to transform Ybor City into a "Walled City," a Latin mecca that would lure free-spending tourists with the theme of a Spanish oasis and "bloodless bullfighting." After arm twisting a recalcitrant legislature to legalize such "sport," an exhibition was staged to demonstrate the gaiety of the spectacle. Unfortunately the bull raged berserk and was shot by state police before he could gore hysterical spectators. The Walled City died along with the bull.[45]

The betrayal of Ybor City is even more puzzling when viewed from an international perspective. Latin Americans, especially Cubans, had displayed a fondness for Ybor City throughout the 1940s and 1950s.[46] And yet Tampa received relatively few (25,000) of the 400,000 Cuban refugees after Castro's takeover. At precisely the moment they were tearing down Cuban homes in Tampa, émigrés searched for housing in Miami. To add insult to imports, the embargo on Cuban tobacco spelled near-disaster to an already ailing cigar industry.

Most Tampans shed few tears over the sterilization of Ybor City, for city fathers had long since replaced cigar factories with newer industries. Never again would a one-industry economy victimize Tampa. Lured by omnipresent sunshine, aggressive promotion, a low tax base, and ample industrial parklands, over eight hundred new businesses have relocated in Tampa since World War II. Tampa's emergence as a dominant economic center has come quite suddenly. In 1948, Rupert Vance compared southern cities in regard to their metropolitan function (wholesale sales, branch offices, retail sales, value added by manufacture) and Tampa ranked below El Paso, Little Rock, and Jacksonville and only slightly above Shreveport and Corpus Christi. Vance decribed Tampa as possessing only a "residual metropolitan function."[47] Diversity characterizes the new industrial profile: from brewing to canning to steel, from shrimp processing to shipbuilding to meat packing.[48] The 1980 Ranally City Rankings label Tampa as a major regional business center—still below the national class as held by Miami—but in the same category as Charlotte, Birmingham, Louisville, and Tulsa.[49]

Once Tampa enjoyed a reputation as a strong union town, but labor leaders have found the new industries particularly difficult targets to organize. In 1944, Florida became the first state to pass a right-to-work law. In 1976, only 12 percent of the Tampa work force wore the union label. Charles Cowl, director of the area AFL-CIO, moans that "Florida is the best place in the world to live in but the worst in which to make a living."[50] Statistics show that wages in the area run well below national averages; in 1979, Tampa Bay families earned an average $16,515, constituting the lowest median family income among the thirty-seven major urban areas.[51]

Unions have also been singularly unsuccessful in organizing Florida's elusive migrant labor population. Agribusiness continues to loom as a powerful force in the Tampa area: Hillsborough County ranked in 1981 as the forty-fourth most important agricultural county in the nation with its 3,400 farmers producing $200 million in crops. In 1980 Hillsborough County farmers harvested ten million boxes of citrus and supported 80,000 cattle on 248,000 grazing acres. Meat packing, egg production, dairy products, and nursery/greenhouse stock are also important activities.[52]

Even though agribusiness remains important, Tampa, like much of the Sunbelt, has seen much of its valuable farmland devoured by the insatiable demand for urban real estate. The percentage of farmers in Hillsborough County declined from 12 percent of the population in 1940 to barely 1 percent in 1970.[53]

The enormous demand for housing has created a major growth

industry in the construction and real estate sector. The housing boom has thrust four Florida cities, including Tampa, into the ten hottest real estate markets of the 1980s. In 1979, the Tampa–St. Petersburg area had the fifth largest sales volume in the nation. Fully 16 percent of new Floridians during the period 1970 to 1976 relocated in Hillsborough or Pinellas County, areas especially appealing to residents of the frosty north-central states.[54] With air conditioning, the summer months could be as appealing as the near-perfect winters.

Air conditioning not only allowed Floridians to escape the oppressive summer humidity, but changed architectural motifs, cultural mores, and economic patterns. From the construction of the ubiquitous concrete-block, ranchstyle house, to the family retreat from the once-fashionable front porch to the environmentally controlled television room, to the transformation of tourism from a six-month to a year-round business, air conditioning wrought a revolution in lifestyles. Statistics dramatically illustrate the suddenness of the phenomemon: In 1960, only one Tampa Bay household in six was cooled by this new technology; by 1980, only one household in seven did *not* possess air conditioning; indeed, central cooling predominated in more than half the homes.[55]

Responding to shrewd local promotion, millions of tourists have visited Tampa, energizing whole segments of the business community. The central focus of Tampa's tourist industry for the past two decades has been Busch Gardens. Originally offering a low-key, free-admission adjunct to brewery tours, the park rapidly expanded as Anheuser-Busch officials realized that tourists were more interested in rides and bird shows than in the intricacies of producing the "King of Beers." In 1959 when the park opened, only 70,000 tourists a year were visiting Tampa. Within a dozen years, Busch Gardens, billed as the "Dark Continent" (the name dismayed Afro-Americans), had become the state's leading attraction and was drawing a million and a half visitors annually. In 1971 Walt Disney World opened near Orlando, and Tampa's attraction soon lost its number-one ranking to the new giant. But even as number two, the Dark Continent flourished with its share of the millions Mickey Mouse and his friends drew to Florida. In 1980 Busch Gardens generated about one visitor for each dollar of its three-million-dollar advertising budget. That is more tourists than came to the entire state in 1945.[56]

Rooted in tradition that began in 1918 when St. Petersburg became the world's first city to hire a press agent, urban boosterism is serious business on the Suncoast. Hillsborough and Pinellas counties now spend close to $4 million a year to persuade tourists to migrate southward.[57]

Since practically everyone is from somewhere else—only 27 percent of the 1980 residents of the bay area were born in Florida—and since growth and progress erased most of the remnants of the past, the citizens of metropolitan Tampa lacked a common identity. What finally generated both local pride and national identity, both sociologists and businessmen agree, was big-league sports. The Tampa Bay Rowdies survived the fledgling North American Soccer League, but the crucial break was the formation of the National Football League Buccaneers, which confirmed the image businessmen wished to project of Tampa as a "major-league city."

Since the 1920s, Tampa had served as a springtime baseball training center, but distance and demographics combined to keep the city out of the big leagues.[58] City boosters failed to capitalize on college sports when their 1947 Cigar bowl flopped and when the University of Tampa gave up its football program in the early 1970s. In 1965 promoters formed the Tampa Sports Authority and built a stadium within two years. Finally, the demographics and timing were right. The population of the southwest Florida counties of Hillsborough, Pinellas, Manatee, Pasco, and Sarasota—all within easy driving distance—had skyrocketed to nearly two and a half million people, and investors were able to secure the long-sought NFL franchise.[59]

As evidence of Tampa's arrival as a Sunbelt power, the NFL selected Tampa as the 1984 Superbowl site. Consider the prerequisites (a minimum 65,000-seat stadium, 20,000 hotel rooms, and a quality airport) and the payoff (a minimum 50,000 visitors spending $160 a day for four days, four hours of prime-time television coverage, the gathering of 1,500 newspaper and video journalists, and an overall windfall of perhaps $50 million not counting future investment deals).[60] Visitors to the athletic-social promenade will be whisked to the city by expressways, the many airlines serving the region, or perhaps by yacht—all underscoring the fact that Tampa serves as a major transportation hub of Florida.

Most visible to tourists and visitors in the 1980s is Tampa International Airport, recently voted in a poll by the National Airline Passengers' Association as the best facility in the United States. Constructed in the 1970s, in 1981 TIA ranked as the twenty-second busiest national terminal, serving eight million passengers on fifteen major and five regional airlines.[61]

Tampa Bay also houses six operating port facilities and in 1980 ranked third in foreign export tonnage, including thirty-two million tons of phosphate valued at $1 billion. Nationally it stands as the seventh busiest port, just behind Philadelphia. The port authority has recently embarked upon major construction projects, New York Yankee owner and Tampa newcomer George Steinbrenner spearheaded the $23 million development of a new drydock, and a new fishport just opened on the causeway. Annually, the port generates 36,000 jobs.[62]

One of the most dramatic recent events in Tampa's socioeconomic history has been the urban redevelopment of the city's core. Downtown Tampa in the 1950s faced a grim future. The rapidly decaying central business district was straddled by warehouses, rail tracks, skid-row streets, and one-acre blocks, abandoned in the urban exodus to suburban malls and strip developments. Spearheaded by Mayor Nuccio and the Committee of 100, the city purchased from the Atlantic Coastline Railroad twenty-one acres of prime riverfront land in the late 1950s. Utilizing federal grants, the city constructed a convention center (soon outdated), parking garages, and a library. Still downtown languished. Between 1961 and 1979, nearly seven thousand hotel rooms were constructed in the county, but the central business district's share amounted to only 866 rooms.[63]

The 1970s, however, brought a turnaround as new money stimulated the development of downtown Tampa. The 1980s are undergoing an urban renaissance in which scarcely a week passes without the unveiling of still another skyscraper or financial tower to alter the skyline. In total, more than $800 million is being spent on fifty-five major projects including the Tampa City Center—a thirty-nine-story office building that will house corporate headquarters and the Hyatt Regency Hotel, a proposed Franklin Street Mall, the forty-two-story Executive Center, the thirty-story Tampa Financial Center, and an ambitious art center. "Downtown Tampa is reemerging as the hub of business, commercial and financial activity," exulted Tampa Electric Company president H. L. Culbreath.[64]

And people are actually returning to the urban frontier. A variety of penthouses and condominiums are slated for construction, but the most exciting and synergic idea focuses on a heretofore barren two-hundred-acre island, located just south of the confluence of the river and bay. Dredged from baybottom muck in 1905, Seddon Island had served mainly as a phosphate-loading terminal until sold for $3 million in 1979. Beneficial Corporation recently unveiled a billion-dollar plan (believed to be one of the largest private construction projects in history) to fill the island with four thousand dwelling units, a 550-room hotel, retail offices, and cobblestone streets.

The architect behind the project, J. Robert Hillier, feels that the newly rechristened Harbour Island will be "a clean slate upon which will be drawn a formula for urban living of the future."[65]

Unlike many of Florida's feverish developmental centers, Tampa retains a distinctive mixture of older communities along with its newer suburbs. Turn-of-the-century neighborhoods such as Tampa Heights, Seminole Heights, and Hyde Park exude a sense of historic time, place, and character. These neighborhoods have also benefited from Tampa's bullish profile. Hyde Park, for example, had deterio-rated badly by the 1960s, in part because of an ill-planned Crosstown Expressway. But the community has undergone a rejuvenation of its handsome bungalows and Victorian homes. In 1980, the Amlea Cor-poration of Canada gained the city's permission to begin a contro-versial $53 million residential-retail center for the area, a devel-opment fought by many residents because of its impact upon the neighborhood.[66]

Success has come yet swiftly for Tampa, but critics quickly point out that even a Superbowl loses its appeal when fish kills be-come commonplace, traffic threatens to paralyze commuters, and overdevelopment floods overtaxed sewers. Even the bay itself, noted a *Sports Illustrated* writer, is filth. "It's a mess," lamented a marine ecologist. "There will never be an oyster in Tampa Bay again."[67] The summer of 1981 added an eerie footnote to the area's tale of watery disaster: For the first time, the health department declared that no river in the county was safe for swimming.[68]

When Juan Ponce de Leon sailed into Tampa Bay in 1513, he dis-covered a complex wetlands system whose mangroves and sea grasses manicured the 212-mile shoreline. Recent studies confirm that 44 percent of the bay's original 25,000 acres of mangroves and marshes have been destroyed; only four natural sections of wetlands remain undisturbed in 1982. The four-hundred-square-mile Tampa Bay offers one of the largest estuaries anywhere. More than one and a half million people live in the three counties bordering its shores. Development has tested the resilience of this magnificent eco-system: A 1970 oil spill dumped 10,000 gallons on the waters; fifty-five sewage treatment plants pump seventy-two million gallons of effluent into the bay each day, wreaking havoc upon the commercial and recreational fisheries; in 1957 developers nearly persuaded offi-cials to drain Old Tampa Bay, a project that environmentalists pre-dict would have been disastrous. Novelists, doomsayers, and plan-ners all predict that a killer hurricane would bring retribution upon the west coast's condominiums and barrier island developments.[69]

Largely oblivious to the area's oysters and mangroves, countless

Tampans agonize over the daily struggle to get to work on the endless miles of asphalt and concrete. Back in 1947, the *Tampa Daily
Times* found the erection of a stoplight on the fast-moving Dale
Mabry Boulevard newsworthy.[70] Today, neither traffic lights nor the
jeremiad of urban planners can eliminate the record traffic jams confronting the hapless commuter on Dale Mabry. "They are turning
Tampa into the customary nothing," complains a character from
John D. MacDonald's *Bright Orange for the Shroud.* "It used to
be memorable as one of the grubbiest and most infuriating traffic
mazes south of Chelsea . . . Now they are ramming the monster
highways through it, and one day soon it will become merely a mo-
mentary dinginess."[71]

The rediscovery of downtown Tampa augurs immediate and
long-range problems. The 1980 working population of the downtown averaged 24,000 people. By 1990, experts estimate that perhaps
100,000 tourists, shoppers, and workers will descend upon the district daily. Tampa mayor Robert Martinez put it bluntly: "We just
don't have the ability to move traffic on a four-lane capacity." Nor
does Tampa possess anything resembling mass transit facilities to
relieve the besieged highway arteries, nor does Tampa harbor hope of
developing such a system. In 1980, less than 2 percent of the residents
of the bay area utilized mass transit to get to work; only suburbanites
of Los Angeles traveled less frequently in public transportation.[72]

The environmental and transportation ills reflect an obvious
trend: Growth has outstripped the capacity of bay-area planners to
predict and supply services. During the decade from 1970 to 1980,
the Tampa–St. Petersburg SMSA (comprising Hillsborough, Pinellas, and Pasco counties) increased by 40 percent, to 728,409, making
it the twenty-fourth fastest growing metropolitan unit and sixth
fastest among SMSAs with populations of more than 300,000. Three
of the top seventeen units anchor Florida's west coast: Fort Myers,
Sarasota, and Bradenton.[73] If demography is destiny, the future of
Florida points toward massive metropolitanization.

Hillsborough County has mirrored the unabashed growth of
Florida since World War II. In 1945, the county contained only
207,844 people, increasing to 397,788 in 1960, to 490,265 in 1970,
and 646,960 in 1980. Demographers predict a million residents by
the year 2000. The growth, called by an embattled county commissioner "barely contained chaos," has occurred almost exclusively
in the unincorporated areas, which accounted for 83 percent of the
population increase of the 1970s.[74]

Hillsborough County, unlike Miami's Dade County, contains
only three incorporated cities: Tampa, Plant City, and Temple Ter-

race. The unrestrained and ill-planned growth in the unincorporated areas poses major problems for the future. The unincorporated hamlet of Brandon, for instance, located just east of Tampa, totaled only 1,655 persons in 1960, but by 1980 the bedroom suburb had mushroomed to almost 70,000. Brandon, which already supports the largest high school in the state, expects future growth with the completion of an interstate bypass. New industries locate in these unincorporated areas. Between 1958 and 1967, Tampa attracted a meek 3 percent increase in manufacturing employment compared to the county's growth of 280 percent.[75]

Tampa remains a small city (81.5 square miles) within a large county, Hillsborough (1,038 square miles). The city annexed large sections of the county in the 1950s—in 1945, almost 50,000 people lived within ten miles of city hall and yet resided outside the city limits—but future consolidations seem unpromising. Consequently, Tampa will never boast a large population. In 1940 the city counted 108,391 persons, a population that expanded to 124,681 in 1950, further increasing to 274,970 in 1960. However, the last two decades have seen scant population growth; indeed, the city declined 2 percent in 1980, falling from 277,714 in 1970 to 271,523 (the fifty-third largest city in the United States). In terms of settlement, Tampa stands as one of the least densely populated cities: For example, its 3,287 persons per square mile in 1970 was only one-fifth that of San Francisco.[76]

Demographically, growth has changed the composition and character of the Suncoast. Most dramatically, the region that once identified itself with youthful exuberance has noticeably grayed at the edges. Florida claims the highest percentage (17.3 percent) of elderly persons, but the mixture varies widely in the Tampa Bay area. The median age of Hillsborough County residents stood at 30.4 in 1980, compared to Pinellas County's 45.8 and Pasco County's 52.8. In Pasco County, fully 19 percent of the total household income emanates from the mailbox economy provided by Social Security, as compared with 13 percent of the incomes in Pinellas and only 6 percent in Hillsborough counties.[77]

Racially, Tampa has changed perceptibly since the days the city was known as "Little Havana." Tampa's Cubans and Spaniards constitute an old population, compared to Miami's Hispanics, and in 1980 10 percent of the residents claimed Spanish/Hispanic origin. The group's upward mobility is evidenced by the fact that only 56 percent of the county's Hispanics reside in the city, the others having migrated to the suburbs. The continued success of Latin politicians is a testimony to the group's successes.[78]

Not so successful is Tampa's black community. In 1980, Afro-Americans constituted 23.5 percent of Tampa's residents. That 74 percent of the county's blacks reside in Tampa speaks to their inability to achieve physical and economic mobility. In 1969, a race riot gripped the city and since then conditions have not improved markedly. In 1980, only New Orleans and Milwaukee had higher poverty rates for blacks than Tampa (35.1 percent). More optimistically, in 1983 Tampa sent to Tallahassee its first black legislator since Reconstruction and elected its first black city council member.[79]

Tampa Bay is a collection of dynamic and recklessly growing communities, held together by vigorous and administrative climate—business and natural—and brought together by the fortunes—cathartic and athletic—of its football team. For a city that was once known as the "Hell Hole of the Gulf Coast," the journey to metropolitan status has been dizzying. Demographers predict that Tampa should reach a population of 400,000 by the year 2000, and the metropolitan region should spiral to three and a half million persons.[80]

Growth then remains the manifest challenge to Tampans. Assimilating the endless stream of new migrants into an embattled environment will tax future generations. Efforts to clean up wastewater, air pollution, and jammed expressways will supersede questions of urban promotion and Superbowls. "Tampa has made its recovery, and, in fact, has surprised itself with the extent to which it has gone beyond revitalization," reflected the *Tribune* recently. "But if that expansion isn't guided by elected officials and by the self-motivation of developers, today's good life will be tomorrow's bad dream."[81] Recently Mayor Robert Martinez boasted, "They [the rest of the nation] know who we are."[82] Now Tampans must determine just how well they know themselves.

NOTES

1. Robert Boyle, "There's Trouble in Paradise," *Sports Illustrated*, 4 February 1981, 81.

2. Kirk Munroe, "A Gulf Coast City," *Christian Union*, 19 January 1882.

3. *Tampa Morning Tribune*, 9 November 1894, 25 November 1896 (hereafter cited as *Morning Tribune*); Tampa Board of Trade, *Minutes*, 1885.

4. L. Glenn Westfall, "Don Vicente Martinez Ybor, the Man and His Empire," (Ph.D. dissertation, University of Florida, 1977); Durwood Long, "The Making of Modern Tampa," *Florida Historical Quarterly* 69 (April 1971): 333–345.

5. Joan Marie Steffy, "The Cuban Immigration of Tampa, Florida, 1886–1898" (M.A. thesis, University of South Florida, 1975); Louis A. Perez, "Cubans in Tampa: From Exiles to Immigrants, 1892–1901," *Florida Historical Quarterly* 57 (October 1978): 129–141; Gary Mormino, "Tampa and the New Urban South," *Florida Historical Quarterly* 60 (January 1982): 331–356; U.S. Bureau of the Census, *Compendium of the Eleventh Census: 1890*, Table 20.

6. *Morning Tribune*, 30 July 1896.

7. William John Schnellings, "Tampa, Florida: Its Role in the Spanish-American War, 1898" (M.A. thesis, University of Miami, 1954).

8. James W. Covington, "The Story of Davis Islands, 1924–26," *The Sunland Tribune* 4 (1978): 16–30; "3000 Jobless Cigarworkers Create Problems for Tampa," *Morning Tribune*, 1 May 1947; *Florida Trend* 2 (June 1959): 2; *Tampa Tribune*, 23 September 1951, 30 October 1955 (hereafter cited as *Tribune*).

9. *Morning Tribune*, 9 September 1951; Durwood Long, "The Open-Closed Shop Battle in Tampa's Cigar Industry, 1919–21," *Florida Historical Quarterly* 67 (October 1968): 101–121.

10. Durwood Long, "Labor Relations in the Tampa Cigar Industry, 1885–1911," *Labor History* 8 (Fall 1971): 551–559; George E. Pozzetta, "Italians and the Tampa General Strike of 1910," in George E. Pozzetta, ed., *Pane E Lavoro: The Italian Working Class* (Toronto: Multicultural History Society of Ontario, 1980), 29–47.

11. Quoted in *Tribune*, 23 November 1969. See also *Florida Trend*, a prominent business periodical since the 1950s.

12. Karl Grismer, *Tampa* (St. Petersburg, Fla.: St. Petersburg Printing Co., 1950), 274.

13. Grismer, *Tampa*, 277–281; *Tribune*, 28 June 1981; "Our Readers Recall Tampa during WWII," *Tribune*, 18 October 1979; "We Get the Big Air Base," *Morning Tribune*, 14 July 1939.

14. Ben Rogers, "Florida in World War II: Tourists and Citrus," *Florida Historical Quarterly* 29 (July 1960): 34–41; *Morning Tribune*, 4 May 1947.

15. *Tribune*, 3 July 1961; Virginus Dabney, *Below the Potomac* (Port Washington, N.Y.: Kennikat Press, 1942), 128; Robert Ingalls, "The Tampa Flogging Case, Urban Vigilantism," *Florida Historical Quarterly* 56 (July 1977): 13–28.

16. Interview with Tony Pizzo, 23 April 1980; "Tony Pizzo's Ybor City," *Tampa Bay History* 1 (Spring/Summer 1980): 62–63; *Tribune*, 7 May 1978.

17. Quoted in J. A. Murray, "Gambling Interests Rated Number One Power in Tampa's Politics," *Morning Tribune*, 5, 6 October 1947.

18. "Political Careers Rested on Votes—Tied to Gamblers," *Tribune*, 8 May 1978; "Pay Off List Blew Lid," *Tribune*, 9 May 1978.

19. Quoted in *Tampa* 1 (April 1969): 12.

20. Interview with James A. Clendinen, 22 August 1980. All interviews on deposit at the University of South Florida Oral History Project.

21. *Morning Tribune*, 30 December 1950.

22. Estes Kefauver, *Crime in America* (Garden City, N.Y.: Doubleday, Inc., 1951), see especially pp. 69–74.

23. See Daniel Elazar, *American Federalism: A View from the States* (New York: Crowell, 1966).

24. U.S. Bureau of the Census, *Fifteenth Census of U.S.: 1930*, Population, Table 21.

25. Interview with Nick Nuccio, 10 June 1979; *Tribune*, 2 October 1955, 15 August 1959.

26. "Nuccio, Another Time," *Tribune*, 19 May 1971, Florida Accent section.

27. Ibid.

28. Ibid.

29. *Tribune*, 2 October 1955; interview with Nick Nuccio, 10 June 1979; *Tribune* , 22, 26 September 1956.

30. *Morning Tribune*, 3 March 1956; *Tampa Times*, 21 May 1956, 13 December 1955.

31. *Tribune*, 22, 28 September 1956.

32. Chas. Parrish, "Minority Politics in a Southern City, 1950–60, Tampa" (M.A. thesis, University of Florida, 1960), 39; *Tribune*, 9 May 1971; Hugh Price, *The Negro and Southern Politics: A Chapter of Florida History* (New York: New York University Press, 1957).

33. Interview with Victoriano Mantiega, editor of *La Gaceta*, 14 June 1981; *Tampa Times*, 23 September 1959, 5 September 1967.

34. Interview with James Clendinen, 22 August 1980.

35. *Tribune*, 27 September 1967, 23 September 1971.

36. Interview with Dick Greco, Jr., 14 September 1980; *Tampa* 1 (March 1969): 9–10; *Tampa Bay* 1 (September 1975): 11; Rory O'Connor, "The Rise and Fall of Dick Greco," *Tampa Magazine* 2 (October 1982): 32–40.

37. Interview with James Clendinen, 22 August 1980.

38. Manning Dauer, Jr., "Florida: The Different State," in William Havard, ed., *The Changing Politics of the South* (Baton Rouge: Louisiana State University Press, 1972), 92–165; Neal Peirce, *The Megastates of America* (New York, 1974), 462; William Havard, *The Politics of Mis-Representation: Rural-Urban Conflict in the Florida Legislature* (Baton Rouge: Louisiana State University Press, 1962); interview with Jamers Clendinen, 22 August 1980.

39. *The Florida Handbook, 1981–82* (Tallahassee, Fla.: Peninsular Publishing Co., 1981), 212–213.

40. Martinez, when elected in 1979, was one of only two Hispanic mayors in the United States.

41. Roger Lotchin, "The City and the Sword: San Francisco and the Rise of the Metropolitan-Military Complex, 1919–1941," *Journal of American History* 65 (March 1979): 996–1020; *Morning Tribune*, 4 May 1947; Grismer, *Tampa*, 267; *St. Petersburg Times*, 19 August 1981.

42. "University of South Florida Clippings," MS, University of South Florida Library.

43. "Riot and Red Tape Snarled Ybor Revival," *Tribune*, 14 May 1979; "HCC's 51 Acres to Remain Barren," *Tribune*, 15 May 1979; "Broken Promises, Broken Hearts," *Tribune*, 13 May 1979; "Blacks Gain, Lose in Ybor," *Tribune*, 16 May 1979.

44. *Tribune*, 2 June 1965.

45. Ibid., 13 May 1979.

46. "Cubans Tell of Tampa's Attractions," *Tribune*, 29 November 1951; *Tribune*, 28 January 1951; "Cuba Pledges Funds to Roof Cuban Club," *Morning Tribune*, 21 May 1954. According to the 1980 census, nearly 36,000 Tampans claim Spanish-Cuban origin. Officers of the Círculo Cubano estimate 25,000 Cuban refugees came to Tampa in 1959–1960. See *Tribune*, 16 September 1977; *Population and Housing Estimates, 1970–80* (Tampa, 1980).

47. Rupert Vance and Sara Evans, "Metropolitan Dominance and Integration," in Rupert Vance, ed., *The Urban South* (Chapel Hill: University of North Carolina Press, 1954), 114–127.

48. *Nation's Business* (September 1976): 58–60; "Tampa: Industry's Youngest Giant," *Tampa* 1 (June 1969): 8; *Florida Trend* (July 1974): 75; *Nation's Business* (September 1976): 53.

49. "Ranally City Rankings," *Commercial Atlas and Marketing Guide* (New York, 1981).

50. Quoted in *Nation's Business* (September 1976): 60.

51. Clayton Reed, "The New Immigrants: Young Workers Are Moving Here, but It's Not for the Money," St. Petersburg *Times* (*The Floridian*), 22 October 1978; Research Department, *St. Petersburg Times*, 1980 Census.

52. *Tribune*, 11, 12, 21 December 1959, 28 June 1981; D. A. Strick, "The Man and the Meat," *Tampa* 1 (June 1969): 15.

53. *The Urbanization of Florida's Population: An Historical Perspective of County Growth, 1830–1970* (Gainesville, Fla.: Bureau of Economic and Business Research, 1979), Table 4.

54. *St. Petersburg Times*, 27 January 1980; "Florida Is Hot—In More Ways Than One," *St. Petersburg Times*, 14 September 1980.

55. *St. Petersburg Times*, 20 August 1978; Ray Arsenault, "The End of the Long Hot Summer: The Air Conditioner and Southern Culture" (paper presented at the annual meeting of the American Studies Association, Memphis, April 1982 [forthcoming in the *Journal of Southern History*]); Research Department, *St. Petersburg Times*, 1980 Census.

56. Interview with Rod Caborn, Marketing Department, Busch Gardens, 16 July 1981; *Tribune*, 7 July 1961; Paul S. George, "Passage to the New Eden: Tourism in Miami from Flagler through Everest G. Sewell," *Florida Historical Quarterly* 59 (April 1981): 440–464; *Orlando Sentinel*, 22 November 1970; *Tribune*, 6 June 1970; *Tribune*, 4 November 1965; *Florida Trend* (June 1981): 61.

57. Kathleen Begley, "Selling the Suncoast with Image," *Tampa Magazine* 1 (February 1981): 44–45; William Rivers, "Florida: The State with the Two-Way Stretch," *Harper's*, 210 (February 1955): 33–34; *St. Petersburg Times*, 27 January 1980.

58. J. Roy Stockton, "Spring Training in Florida," *Florida Historical Quarterly* 39 (January 1961): 221–231.

59. *Tampa Daily Times*, 1 January 1947. *Population: A Comprehensive Analysis for the Tampa Bay Region* (Tampa, 1973), 4–5.

60. *Tribune*, 4 June 1981; *St. Petersburg Times*, 4 June 1981.

61. Raymond Moley, "The Tampa Gateway," *Newsweek*, 11 April 1955, 120; *Florida Trend* (September 1960): 15; *Tribune*, 9 July 1980, 5 August 1959.

62. *Tampa Port 1981 Handbook* (Jacksonville: Howard Publishers, 1981); *Tribune*, 28 June 1981, 31 July 1957; *St. Petersburg Times*, 16 October 1978; "Special Report," *Florida Trend* (September 1967): 23; "Pink Gold," *Florida Trend* (November 1969): 8.

63. John Rupertus, "Franklin Street: A History of Tampa Downtown, 1890–1980" (M.A. thesis, University of South Florida, 1980), 97.

64. "A Salute to Industry," *Tribune*, 19 July 1981; *Tribune*, 24 September 1980; *St. Petersburg Times*, 19 June 1981; *Tampa Bay* (May 1980): 53; "Florida Cities," *Florida Trend* (July 1974): 74.

65. "Barren Isle Looks to Future as Urban Area," *St. Petersburg Times*, 20 July 1981; *Tribune*, 28 June 1981; "Harbour Island," *Tribune*, 24 September 1981.

66. *Tribune*, 28 June 1981.

67. Quoted in Boyle, "Trouble in Paradise," 81.

68. *Tampa Times*, 19 June 1981.

69. Tom Ankersen, "Coping with Growth: The Emergence of a Florida Environmental Policy (M.A. thesis, University of South Florida, 1982); Jeff Klinkenberg, "Does 'Perfect Ecosystem' Outweigh Stadium?" *St. Petersburg Times*, 25 June 1982; "Saving Tampa Bay," *St. Petersburg Times*, 25 June 1982; Luther Carter, *The Florida Experience* (Baltimore: Johns Hopkins University Press, 1974); *Tampa Times*, 1 August 1967; *Morning Tribune*, 3 August 1957; John D. MacDonald, *Condominium: A Novel* (Philadelphia: Lippincott, 1977); Nelson Manfred Blake, *Land into Water—Water into Land* (Tallahassee: University Presses of Florida, 1980).

70. *Daily Times*, 13 January 1947.

71. John D. MacDonald, *Bright Orange for the Shroud* (Greenwich, Conn.: Fawcett Books, 1965), 114.

72. *Tribune*, 28 June 1981; Robert Catlin, "A Proposal for Mass Transit in Tampa and Hillsborough County," *Florida Environmental and Urban Issues* 9 (1982): 10–14; Research Department, *St. Petersburg Times*, 1980 Census.

73. Hillsborough Population and Housing, *1980 Census Summary* (Tampa: Division of Planning, 1982), 4–5; *Population: A Comprehensive Analysis for the Tampa Bay Region*, 37–39.

74. *The Seventh Census of the State of Florida, 1945* (Tallahassee, Fla.: Commissioner of Agriculture, 1946); U.S. Bureau of the Census, *U.S. Census of Population, 1960: Florida*, Table 6; U.S. Bureau of the Census, *1980 Census of Population and Housing: Florida*, Table 2.

75. "I-75 Bypass to Open Rural East," *Tampa Times*, 3 June 1982; U.S. Bureau of the Census, *1980 Census of Population and Housing: Florida*, 7.

76. *Population: A Comprehensive Analysis for the Tampa Bay Region*, 37–39; *1980 Florida Statistical Abstract* (Gainesville: University of Florida, 1980), 4–5.

77. *St. Petersburg Times*, 20 September 1982; "Florida and the Elderly: The Economic Romance May Be Ending," *Florida Trend* (August 1982): 54–59.

78. *Hillsborough Population and Housing*, 4–5; Gayle Everette Davis, "Riot in Tampa" (M.A. thesis, University of South Florida, 1976).

79. *Tampa Comprehensive Plan 2000* (Tampa, 1976).

81. "Good Life *Is* Getting Better—But Be Careful," *Tribune*, 19 July 1981.

82. Quoted in "How Tampa Stacks Up," *Tribune*, 11 October 1981.

6

DALLAS-FORT WORTH

MARKETING THE METROPLEX

by Martin V. Melosi

In popular circles it is customary to think of Dallas and Fort Worth primarily in terms of their rivalry with each other. No one epitomized that rivalry better than Amon G. Carter, Sr., successful businessman, publisher of the *Fort Worth Star Telegram*, and the preeminent Fort Worth booster. The oft-told story goes that whenever Carter went to Dallas on business he brought a sack lunch with him to avoid contributing ever so slightly to the Dallas economy. The stereotyping of the cities as unique urban types contributed mightily to the rivalry legend: Fort Worth—"Cowtown"—is "where the West begins"; it is the consummate Texas city, ten gallon hats and all. Dallas—"Big D"—is "where the East runs out." Dallas has acquired the reputation of being southern but with an eastern taste for culture and formality; "the Athens of the alfalfa fields." How could cities so different, yet so close geographically (with downtowns only thirty-five miles apart), help but clash?

The rivalry legend has lost much of its intensity in recent years. The death of Amon Carter in 1955 and the opening of DFW Airport in 1974 signaled a détente, if not a spirit of cooperation, in northern Texas. The fixation on the rivalry and its demise has turned attention away from the basic similarities in the cities' growth and expansion, political life, and community spirit. Unlike American cities of the eastern seaboard in the preindustrial era, neither Dallas nor Fort Worth were established along navigable waterways or natural transportation routes. They existed because their tenacious and aggressive founding fathers brought transportation facilities to them— by hook or by crook. Dallas and Fort Worth were built by men with an intense desire for economic gain. This desire was so powerful that it influenced not only the economic fortunes of the communities but every aspect of city life on the north Texas plains.

The Sunbelt phenomenon of the post–World War II era accelerated rather than initiated the growth of Dallas and Fort Worth. By the turn of the century both cities were already moving toward regional economic dominance in the Southwest. With large populations and substantial economies they exploited the region's agricultural base and influenced the development of its natural resources, especially petroleum.

The origins of Dallas and Fort Worth demonstrate some striking similarities. Established in 1841 near the three forks of the Trinity River, by the 1870s, with the coming of the locally subsidized railroads, Dallas had become a county seat and regional business center for cotton, cattle, sheep, wool, wheat, and hides. Soon the city became commercially linked to St. Louis and eastern cities and its population soared from three thousand in 1873 to forty thousand in 1890.

The next spurt of growth came with the oil boom in east Texas. The city broadened its economic base and became the oil capital of the state in the 1930s and 1940s. Local bankers financed numerous oil ventures and local factories manufactured oil-field equipment.

Fort Worth began as a frontier army outpost, Camp Worth, in 1849 and soon became the county seat of Tarrant County. The cattle drives in the early 1870s pushed the population over three thousand, but it tumbled to about six hundred as a result of the Panic of 1873. In 1876 unrelenting local pressure in the form of money and political persuasion brought the Texas and Pacific Railroad to Fort Worth. Cotton, wheat, and especially beef were the most important commodities. Swift and Armour located meat-packing plants in the city in 1902. After 1917 Fort Worth served as a petroleum refining center and as a pipeline terminal for west Texas. World War I reinjected the military into the city's increasingly diversified economy with the opening of a training site at Camp Bowie.[1]

Dallas and Fort Worth began, therefore, as typical commercial cities, dependent on the products and resources of their region for economic growth. The timing of their emergence as commercial centers coincided with that of many inland areas of the South and West. The two young cities also shared a determination to make their own luck, to exploit what was available, in a physical environment with little apparent advantage for city building.

By World War II both cities had established solid economic bases built on commerce, trade, finance, and some modest manufacturing. The war, however, brought about a major economic transition for the whole region, stimulating an important surge of industrialization. Manufacturing became the essential ingredient that transformed the two cities economically, demographically, and physically.

Throughout the 1940s and into the 1950s, manufacturing ac-

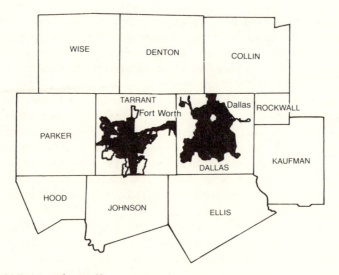

MAP 6.1. The Dallas–Ft. Worth SMSA

counted for the greatest increase in employment of any segment of the Dallas economy. Between 1940 and 1953 the total manufacturing employment in Dallas County jumped 184 percent—three times the national average. By 1953 more than 34 percent of the non-agricultural jobs were in manufacturing compared with only 17 percent in 1940. Manufacturing employment had increased more rapidly since 1940 than in any leading industrial center save Los Angeles. In the Southwest only Houston showed greater manufacturing strength than Dallas. Substantially as a result of this new dimension of economic growth, Dallas County gained more than 270,000 people between 1940 and 1953.[2]

Wartime production was the primary stimulant to the emergence of Dallas as an industrial center. Like other inland cities, Dallas benefited from the federal government's policy of decentralizing production. Dallas was attractive because it had a relatively well developed transportation system with ten railroads, nine major highways, and three airlines. Particularly important to Dallas's wartime economy was an aviation plant on the western edge of the city. It was shut down in 1945, but two new plants opened later that produced aircraft parts and missiles. Manufacturing produced a county-wide boom as suburban communities such as Garland, Carrollton, and Grand Prairie became the primary manufacturing sites in the area.[3]

Without a port, Dallas was limited to light industry, so the city was neither marred by extensive pollution nor dependent on scarce energy sources such as high-grade bituminous coal. Leading industries included women's and sports apparel, storage batteries, automobile accessories, beverages, and food specialties. By 1975 metropolitan Dallas had 112 planned industrial districts covering more than twenty thousand acres. Companies such as Texas Instruments, Inc., made Dallas a leader in high technology. About one-quarter of the area's manufacturing labor force is employed in computer and electronic firms or in research facilities such as those at Southern Methodist University. Although Dallas has lost leadership in the petroleum industry to Houston, the oil business still thrives in the north Texas city, which claims approximately 123 petroleum-oriented firms with assets of $1 million or more.[4]

Fort Worth has become even more dependent on manufacturing than Dallas. The aircraft industry, which grew directly out of World War II, accounts for approximately half of manufacturing employment in the city. Like Dallas, Fort Worth benefited from the federal policy of moving vital industries inland to areas with adequate population, plenty of space for factories, and year-round flying weather.

The opening of Consolidated Vultee Aircraft Corporation's Convair plant in March 1942 signaled the start of Fort Worth's major industrial development. The plant was the largest single industrial operation in the Southwest at the time, and had the largest work force in the nation's aircraft industry. Between 1942 and 1953 it produced more than three thousand airplanes and supported fifty-two subcontractors, twenty-four of which were located in Texas. Not surprisingly, Amon Carter was instrumental in the plant's location. According to one story, Carter became ill in the midst of the effort to persuade the government to locate the plant in Fort Worth. President Roosevelt sent flowers to the ailing booster who replied: "Thank you, Mr. President, for those wonderful roses and kind sentiments. But I must warn you that if Fort Worth doesn't get the bomber plant, the next flowers will not be roses but lilies. I won't be able to survive such a blow." World War II also brought Fort Worth several other defense-related facilities, including Tarrant Field (now Carswell Air Force Base), a marine air station at Eagle Mountain Lake, a U.S. Public Health Service hospital, and an army quartermaster's depot.

The acquisition of the Convair plant and related aircraft/defense facilities did not prove to be a wartime fluke. Fort Worth experienced serious postwar cutbacks in defense contracts, but the aircraft industry rebounded in the next decade. In 1951 Bell Aircraft announced plans to move its entire helicopter manufacturing facility from Buffalo, New York, to the Fort Worth area. Federal aviation and military facilities also expanded nearby.

Dallas participated in this growth as well. For instance, Chance Vought relocated in Dallas in 1948. The company transferred 1,300 employees from Stratford, Connecticut. Several auxiliary industries followed thereafter. The aircraft industry not only stimulated new industrial growth in Dallas and Fort Worth, but linked the cities in a common economic market.

The aircraft industry has maintained its role as a central component of the Fort Worth economy (less so in Dallas). In the 1960s General Dynamics (formerly Consolidated Vultee) employed about twelve thousand workers, and Bell Helicopter employed about six hundred. In addition, the regional office of the Federal Aviation Administration (FAA) employed 1,400 in the same period, and Carswell AFB employed another 5,700.[5]

Building on the foundation established by the aircraft industry, Fort Worth developed a broad-based manufacturing capability. In 1949, the city produced 216 commodities in over seven hundred factories. The gradual shift of some segments of the garment industry from the East to the Sunbelt led to Fort Worth's leadership in the manufacture of sportswear, work clothes, and western garb in the South and West. By the end of the 1950s, Fort Worth also was the South's leading producer of air conditioning equipment and packaged candy. In 1960 there were eight hundred industrial plants within the city; by 1963 almost one thousand. More than 90 percent of these firms, however, had fewer than fifty workers. The largest establishment outside of the aircraft industry was the General Motors plant, which opened in nearby Arlington in 1953.[6]

Manufacturing in the Dallas–Fort Worth metropolitan area (the "Metroplex")[7] continues to be essential. In 1977 manufacturing provided almost 20 percent of the area's earnings, matching the national average and exceeding the state average by 5 percent. The principal manufacturers include electronics, aircraft, apparel, oilfield equipment, food processing, automotive equipment, printing, and publishing.[8]

Manufacturing provided the underpinnings of the economy of the Metroplex, but the growing service sector brought it maturity and diversity. Retail and wholesale activities are central to this growth and have helped take the cities beyond regional markets to national and even international markets.

Of the two, Dallas is better known as a retailing center. Dallas County sales topped the $1 billion mark in 1954—a fivefold increase from 1940. In 1976 retail sales were close to $9 billion, which ranked Dallas eleventh among the twenty most populous SMSAs. The Dallas area has more than 260 shopping centers and several regional malls. Fort Worth has not fared as well in retailing as Dallas. In the twenty years after 1948 the downtown area's share of retailing dropped from 39 to 11 percent as suburban shopping areas garnered most of the trade. In the metropolitan area, however, retail sales have been growing steadily.[9]

At the heart of Dallas's retailing is the fashion industry. Beginning in the mid 1930s, the fashion industry in Dallas concentrated in sports clothes and casual wear. Eventually it expanded into high-fashion lines, especially through the influence of the world-famous Neiman-Marcus stores, which opened soon after the turn of the century. In 1950 Stanley Marcus inherited control from his father and aunt and launched a major expansion program. One author described "Mr. Stanley" as "a paragon of neatness and subdued elegance—qualities that by no coincidence are also the chief physical characteristics of the . . . stores . . . [that] make up the Neiman-Marcus operation."[10]

The strength of the Dallas fashion business as well as much of the area's other retailing is built upon a thriving wholesale industry, including the impressive Dallas Market Center, which annually attracts more than forty thousand domestic and foreign buyers. Designated in 1969 as a Permanent International Trade Fair by the U.S. Department of Commerce, the center includes home furnishings and decorative marts for household trade, a huge Apparel Mart, a Market Hall, and a World Trade Center. By the end of World War II Dallas was the nation's fourteenth largest wholesaling center, and by the late 1970s the wholesale-retail sector was the region's second largest contributor to personal income.[11]

Agricultural products remain central to wholesale trade with cotton most notable in Dallas and grain and livestock in Fort Worth. Since the 1960s, the relative importance of livestock to the Fort Worth economy has declined, but the Fat Stock Show, premier event since 1896, serves as an annual reminder of a golden age.[12]

Banking and finance are strongly identified with the north Texas twins, especially in Dallas where the banks prospered with the cotton and petroleum trades. Local institutions lent substantial monies to trucking companies, many of which relocated their headquarters in the city. Republic Bank's decision to loan funds to Texas Instruments at the start of World War II has paid untold dividends for the Metroplex.

In the last decade, banking and finance have taken on an increasingly important role in the economic life of the region. The two largest lenders in Texas, Republic National and First National, are located in Dallas, each with deposits in excess of $7 billion. The Dallas–Fort Worth SMSA has more than two hundred commercial banks and ranks seventh nationally in deposits. The growth of insurance companies is equally impressive with more than 260 headquartered in the area.[13]

One further gauge of Dallas–Fort Worth's economic vitality is the importance of the Metroplex as a corporate headquarters for such companies as American Airlines, Diamond Shamrock, and National Gypsum. Even the Boy Scouts of America maintain their main office in Big D. Between 1971 and 1976, the number of major firms based in Dallas increased by 25 percent, and by the mid 1970s Dallas ranked third as a corporate headquarters for companies worth over $1 million. Today the city ranks fourth in the number of publicly held corporations on the New York and American Stock Exchanges.

The establishment of major corporate offices in the Dallas–Fort Worth region is a visible sign of the migration of businesses from northern and eastern cities to the Southwest. A survey of several corporate migrants indicated that their companies relocated in the area because they were looking for a favorable business climate, a good residential environment for their executives, and a setting that provided an image compatible with their firm's reputation. These relocations meant more jobs, more investment, and more spending. According to James Byrd, chief economist for a Dallas holding company, such new arrivals create a multiplier effect that generates three to five jobs for every new employee coming from outside the area. Byrd estimated that in 1978 the movement of headquarters and regional offices to Dallas–Fort Worth created about three thousand new jobs. He further estimated that half of the region's growth in recent years resulted from the influx of new employees.[14]

Regardless of whether the Dallas–Fort Worth economy grew primarily because of internal or external forces, there is little doubt about its diversity and vitality. Built upon exploitation of the agricultural hinterland, a manufacturing base acquired during World War II, and thriving service economy with regional and national markets, economic fortunes have been central to shaping municipal images. The reputations of Dallas and Fort Worth as cities on the make go well beyond the accountant's balance sheet in influencing the growth and goals of both communities.

In large measure, the impressive population growth in the Dallas–Fort Worth region followed the typical pattern experienced by most major cities in the twentieth century: movement away from the urban core into the outer suburban ring. Both cities exhibited impressive growth throughout the late nineteenth and early twentieth centuries. The Great Depression slowed the rate of growth considerably, while World War II stimulated it once again. The city of Dallas expanded through the 1960s, but Fort Worth began to stagnate ten years earlier. Whereas the central cities grew by 20 percent during the 1960s, the outlying suburban ring grew by more than 62 percent. First signs of this movement of people occurred in the growth rates of Dallas and Tarrant counties. Between 1930 and 1960, for example, Fort Worth's share of the total population of Tarrant County dropped from 82.7 percent to 66.2 percent. By 1960 there were thirty-three municipal incorporations in the county, almost half of which had emerged in the 1950s. The out-migration to the suburbs has been most impressive since 1960, particularly to the north of Dallas and to the west and south of Fort Worth. Arlington and Richardson have emerged as important independent cities. By the mid 1970s, the overall growth of the Dallas–Fort Worth area made it the largest SMSA in Texas with more than 2.7 million people.

The two cities drew their population from somewhat different sources. In the 1940s and 1950s, Fort Worth tapped nearby rural areas for much of its growth. The rural population of Tarrant County dropped from 20 percent in 1940 to 3 percent from 1957 to 1968, and nineteen of the twenty-six counties in north-central Texas lost population during the 1950s. Dallas, by comparison, was more successful in attracting out-of-state people. A 1963 study indicated that 56 percent of Dallas's increase in population in the 1950s came from in-migration, the highest figure for any city in the state. Some of the changes in population were due to annexations rather than internal growth. In the 1960s, annexation accounted for 7 percent of the increases in Dallas and 30 percent of the increases in Fort Worth.

Population growth in Dallas and Fort Worth has not depended on a large influx of identifiable ethnic or racial groups as was the case in nineteenth-century eastern cities. Until the recent suburbanization of whites, the percentage of black population actually declined relative to white population. In 1910 blacks constituted 20 percent of Dallas, but by 1950 the figure was only 13 percent. Since then the black population has increased: to 19 percent in 1960, 25 percent in 1970, and 30 percent in 1980. In Fort Worth the increase has been more gradual, from 18 percent in 1910 to about 23 percent in 1980.

In neither Dallas nor Fort Worth are other racial and ethnic groups well represented. Whereas Mexican-Americans made up 18 percent of Texas' population in 1970, they constituted only 6 percent of the Dallas–Fort Worth area population. For the eleven-county region in 1980, blacks constituted 14 percent of the population but persons of Hispanic origin only 8 percent.[15]

The large-scale economic and demographic growth that Dallas–Fort Worth experienced after World War II had a profound impact on the cities' physical development and quality of life. As the economic influence of Dallas and Fort Worth extended into the hinterland and then into the new suburbs, so did political control. The availability of open or unincorporated land surrounding the cities allowed for extensive territorial growth, something unachievable in the more densely populated and developed East.

Although neither city rivaled area giants such as Oklahoma City or Jacksonville, Florida, their physical growth was impressive and transformed the cities in many ways. Until 1930 Dallas had not grown beyond the east bank of the Trinity River. In that year, engineers straightened the riverbed, erected high levees, and transformed the reclaimed bottomland into an industrial park. The city then spread its boundaries across the west bank of the river to surround Oak Cliff, the dominant southside community. In 1942 Dallas covered just forty-two square miles, but by 1970 its area had grown by more than 530 percent to 266 square miles. In Fort Worth the pattern was similar. Between 1873 and 1940 the city had made only twenty-four annexations; from 1940 through 1966 it made 188, creating enclaves of the River Oaks, White Settlement, and Lake Worth areas. Between 1940 and 1970, Fort Worth expanded from approximately sixty square miles to 205 square miles, an increase of 242 percent. Acting under Texas law, Fort Worth and Dallas also "reserved" territory for future expansion. For example, in 1961 Fort Worth reserved about 250 square miles, which allowed the city to keep the areas from incorporating or being absorbed by other cities. This method also allowed Fort Worth to maintain control without extending costly services to the residents.[16]

Without effective mass transit Dallas and Fort Worth have become particularly dependent upon automobiles, a circumstance that has had a profound effect on their physical development. Taxis and buses are the only remnants of a public transportation system once based on streetcars. Bus travel, the only form of mass transit left after the trolleys ceased operations in 1956, declined steadily in the 1950s. Whereas 20 percent of the trips taken in Dallas County in 1950 were by bus, that number dropped to 5 percent by 1964. In 1969 only 17 percent of the people traveling to and from the central business district in Dallas took the bus. Meanwhile, according to a 1971 estimate, 233,000 vehicles entered or left Dallas–Fort Worth daily, and the volume continued to increase for the rest of the decade.[17]

Automobile usage caused the expansion of low-density construction in the metropolitan area. Predictably, development has occurred along radial highways fanning out from Dallas and Fort Worth. Major highway development began in the 1940s and culminated with the initiation of the interstate highway system in 1956. By the mid 1960s, the highway network consisted of freeways radiating out from the cores of the two cities with ever-concentric loops at various distances from the downtown. The Dallas–Fort Worth Turnpike is the most obvious link in the metropolitan area's one-dimensional land transportation system. Opened as a toll road in 1957, it connects the two cities and symbolizes their growing interdependence.

In January 1974 Dallas–Fort Worth Regional Airport opened, marking a major turning point in the history of air transportation in the area. At its opening "the air harbor to the world" was the largest anywhere (eventually surpassed by Montreal's new facility) and the third busiest. Situated midway between the two cities, it spans more than 17,000 acres, an area larger than Manhattan Island.

The size and design of the airport created a lot of controversy about noise and facilities. Larger problems included airport financing and the reluctance of major airlines to move all their operations to DFW Airport from close-in Love Field. To urban historians Blaine Brownell and David Goldfield, "The Texas-sized airport is an interesting case of spatial overkill. Its amorphous sprawl is exceeded only by its ugliness." The principal architect for the airport, Gyo Obata, countered such criticism, arguing that "the humanizing thing about airports is not that they are pretty but that they are easy to use—to hell with monuments."

To the business and civic leaders of Dallas and Fort Worth, the beauty of DFW Airport was its ability to attract new economic growth. The airport has inspired a billion-dollar land boom in the surrounding areas and has accelerated the decentralization of the Metroplex. Developer Kenneth M. Good stated in 1972 that the airport "is probably the most significant project in the U.S. in the last 20 years in terms of its impact on real estate values." In nearby Coppell, Texas, in 1967 land was selling for $1,000 an acre, but by 1972 it sold for $10,000 an acre. In 1969, a prime site in Irving sold for $5,000; three years later it sold for more than $50,000. The area sprouted various commercial centers and new "towns," many of them constructed with little regard for proper planning or effective zoning. The result has been massive commercialization with little attention to careful residential development. In suburban Southlake, contractors built housing along the noise zones at the ends of runways. Longer-range problems include inattention to parks, open spaces, and adequate services, amenities that could make the new communities more attractive to potential residents.

Efforts at cooperative planning have been difficult, in part because the airport crosses the boundaries of four municipalities and directly affects at least nine other cities. The regional Council of Governments (COG) attempted to alleviate some of the problems by coordinating the activities of approximately twenty towns and cities around the airport. One of its biggest achievements was the establishment of the Joint Airport Board with power to block hazzards to air traffic. COG also formulated a model noise ordinance over the opposition of local builders.[18]

The decentralization of Dallas–Fort Worth did not foreshadow a significant deterioration of the inner cities. Although the central business districts (CBDs) lost their dominance over retailing, they did not fall into disuse. In some areas, downtown areas deteriorated into rundown warehouse districts or blighted residential neighborhoods, but in others, businesses relocated and revitalized small areas.

Beginning in the 1950s, downtown Dallas underwent a face-lift as financial and administrative offices relocated in a newer business district. In 1954, workers completed the forty-story Republic Bank Building; in 1955, the twenty-nine-story Adolphus Tower; and, in 1959, the forty-seven-story Southland Building. In 1958, business leaders, determined to revive downtown according to a professional plan, organized the Central Business District Association. Construction soon began on the $50 million Exchange Park, three miles north of the original CBD, and on the Main Place project, envisioned as a ten-acre complex in the heart of the city. Since World War II, more than thirty new office buildings have been erected downtown.

In the early stages of downtown rebuilding, planning lagged well behind development. Although the streets were too narrow and too meandering to accommodate the increased flow of traffic into the area, little attention was paid to street improvement. Parking space was also a major problem. Moreover, with most attention going to the commercial benefits of the building program, civic leaders raised few questions regarding the quality of life. They expressed little concern about what commercial redevelopment meant to inner-city residences. Designs of the downtown placed too little emphasis on parks and open spaces, on meeting areas for people, and on recreational facilities. Also, with the exception of hotels, the downtown lost much of its after five social and cultural activity. Nightspots and restaurants migrated to shopping centers in outlying areas.

Although federal aid was available for urban renewal and public housing, the rebuilding of downtown Dallas came about largely through local initiative and local funding. In this conservative southwestern city, urban renewal and redevelopment had bad connotations. They were considered likely to undermine private enterprise, invite Washington influence, and weaken the leadership of the local business elite. W. T. Overton, president of a major development company, stated in 1964: "We think it's the responsibility of businessmen to solve the redevelopment problems of our cities here. If the businessman doesn't assume this responsibility, the federal government will." Responding to the threat of federal intervention, private investment in building topped $207 million in the 1950s and early 1960s. Private development was a slow process, but local civic and business leaders considered it to be a reasonable trade-off to maintain local control.[19]

The selection of Erik Jonsson as mayor of Dallas proved to be an important step toward achieving the revitalization of the city. A New York native, born of Swedish immigrants, Jonsson is best known as the principal founder of Texas Instruments and as an effective business and civic leader. The city council appointed him mayor in February 1964 to fill a vacancy, and he subsequently won three consecutive terms. Jonsson found the city deteriorating physically despite redevelopment and set about to reverse the trend. "For a few years there was a vacuum," he stated. "The old bulls of Dallas had grown tired, and some younger ones didn't have the stuff. Dallas was not spending enough money and trouble to keep abreast of what was coming."[20] Seeking a systems approach to government, he initiated Goals for Dallas. Patterned on the 1960 Goals for Americans program of the Eisenhower administration, Goals for Dallas was boosterism at its most grandiose.

The program was the closest thing to a comprehensive plan for the city since 1943. In that year a $40 million Master Plan had set the pattern for much of Dallas's early expansion. Goals for Dallas, however, was geared more effectively to modern concerns, and despite its obvious emphasis on traditional business and civic interests, it gave more attention to city design, historic preservation, and ecology.

The program greatly accelerated the redevelopment program of the city. Goals for Dallas was an outgrowth of the efforts of some 120,000 people. The initial report came out in 1966, and an updated version appeared eleven years later. Elitist in approach, the plan strongly emphasized growth and governmental efficiency for the city, with less emphasis on social concerns. Housing, for example, was omitted in the original Goals.[21]

In Fort Worth a similar cycle of inner-city deterioration and revitalization took shape after World War II. Victor Gruen, a Vienna-born architect and planner, drew up a plan for the city in 1956. It called for a refurbished downtown encircled by an expressway leading to peripheral garages and other road links. The garages would be less than a three-minute walk from downtown. The core area would lure pedestrians with lush foliage, fountains, statues, malls, parks, sidewalk cafés, and small transit vehicles. The proposal carried an estimated cost of $100 million, and therein was the rub. Although Fort Worth leaders appointed study committees, the plan was underfunded. The Gruen proposal did provide a broad framework, and portions of it have been incorporated into the revitalization of the downtown. As Cliff Overcash, president of Leonard's department store, noted, the Gruen plan is

> a philosophy, not a blueprint, and we are being eclectic in our use of it. The way it has worked out, much of what we have done seems to follow the Gruen Plan. Much, on the other hand, doesn't. We are, after all, a unique city—we're called "the most typical" Texas city—and what we have done, and are doing, here is a matter of our own dreams.

The views of Overcash and the Downtown Fort Worth Association reflected a desire to draw specific ideas from the plan without full implementation. Efforts at revitalization have led to more than twenty major developments, including the Fort Worth National Bank—somewhat reminiscent of Rockefeller Center in New York City—and a major convention center. There is also the unique privately owned subway that Leonard's department store operates to bring people downtown from an outer parking lot.[22]

Although the city eventually accepted more general federal aid than Dallas, urban renewal created a political storm. Conservative opponents not only viewed urban renewal as a road to federal intervention but also as a program bent on undermining the traditional economic interests of the community. Proponents saw urban renewal as a method of establishing a broader economic base and making Fort Worth less dependent on defense contracts. Despite the political hoopla, Fort Worth has been able to rebuild a good portion of its inner city to a greater degree than many communities of comparable size.[23]

While downtown revitalization has been a tribute to the tenacity of business leadership in Dallas and Fort Worth, it has distracted attention from serious problems of housing blight. The reluctance to use federal aid for urban renewal and public housing has left many lower-class dwellings in a sorry state. Despite claims of improved housing conditions Dallas, especially, has great disparities between the physical surroundings of the affluent and the poor.

Housing blight strongly correlates with housing segregation. In October 1974 the Council of Municipal Performance reported that Dallas was one of six cities with the most racially segregated housing in the South. Of these, Dallas was the only major city. The overwhelming majority of Dallas's black population and much of its Mexican-American population live south and west of the downtown area in Oak Cliff (annexed in 1904), West Dallas (annexed in 1952), and South Dallas. It is estimated that 72 percent of Dallas's 265,495 blacks live in the south and southwestern portions of the city. The location of minorities near but not in the immediate inner-city area has made it easier to separate downtown revitalization programs from housing problems. The *Dallas Morning News* estimated in 1973 that there were 65,000 substandard housing units in Dallas. West Dallas, with 90 percent of its 55,000 people minority members, has been particularly hard hit by poor housing conditions. This low-income, industrial neighborhood within view of the downtown has suffered high unemployment and poor living conditions for many years. The little public housing that does exist is mostly in this area and in Oak Cliff, including one gigantic but dilapidated 3,500-unit project. A shocked Muhammad Ali toured the neighborhood and purportedly said, "I ain't goin' in there, or gettin' out of this car. Take me back to Dallas!" Change has been slow because of a lack of commitment on the part of city officials and a corresponding lack of local funds.[24]

It is not surprising that in cities where flourishing economies and dynamic physical growth became commonplace the leadership would reflect and encourage these trends. Political power in Dallas and Fort Worth has typically been concentrated in the hands of those people most willing and able to sustain growth and expansion. City leadership after World War II resembled that of the first group of settler-boosters who, through force of will, legislative manipulation, and money, brought the railroads to the north Texas plains. As the cities have become more complex so have the power structures, but an elitist, business-oriented leadership has continued to guide the destiny of the area. Its major goals have been clean government, fiscal stability, economic prosperity, the preservation of middle-class values, and law and order. Pluralistic interests, democratic government, community innovation, and human services, especially for the disadvantaged, have carried lower priorities.

To speak of community leadership in Dallas is to speak of the Citizens Council. The Citizens Council arose in the depression years as a result of the aggressive efforts of Dallas businessmen to get the Texas Centennial celebration placed in their city. At the head of the delegation was R. L. ("Uncle Bob") Thornton, Sr., a self-made banker with a folksy style that belied a razor-sharp mind and an iron will. Thornton and his cohorts raised $3.5 million and walked away from Austin with the prize, much to the chagrin of Amon Carter and the good people of Fort Worth, San Antonio, and Houston. As one journalist noted in 1964:

> The Centennial was hugely successful for Dallas, and can be said to have marked a turning point in the city's history. Dallas—and the state—suddenly discovered the past. Dallas realized too, as it regarded the works of art that had been assembled for the Centennial, that it was a city almost without culture. It was not the Athens of the Southwest, as it likes to call itself . . . it was simply a big Dubuque with money.[25]

To Bob Thornton, the Centennial meant something quite different. Raising the $3.5 million had been difficult. Thornton reflected: "Those were dydamic [sic] days, but there was no organization. We had to have men who could underwrite . . . Sometimes you'd get a bunch together, they couldn't say 'yes' or 'no.' We didn't have time for no proxy people—what we needed was men who could give you the boss talk. Then I saw the idea. Why not organize the 'yes' and 'no' people?" He did just that. First he went to see Nathan Adams, head of the First National Bank in Dallas and director of fourteen industries in the region. As the story goes, Thornton burst into Adams's office and declared, "Nate, what we need is the boss men organized so we can act quick . . . dydamic kind of organization . . . stupendjious effort . . . people doin' things!"[26]

In 1937 the Citizens Council of Dallas was born. Initially it included one hundred members (later expanded to nearly two hundred) drawn from the major businesses of the city. Membership was permanent and by invitation only. It was limited to corporate chief executive officers, and no proxies were allowed at meetings. "If you don't come, you ain't there!" insisted Thornton. Procedural rules and formal organization took a back seat to action—immediate and dramatic action if necessary.

From its impromptu origins, the Citizens Council went on to become the most vital force in the civic and political life of the city. To its adherents the council is an informal group of right-thinking businessmen with a selfless interest in the welfare of the city, who have supported efficient city government, charitable activities, culture, economic growth, and stability. In 1979, a staff writer for the *Wall Street Journal* observed that Dallas

> is a contented city because it works. Policemen don't strike in Dallas. The parks and streets are clean. Unemployment is among the lowest in the country, and there is $400 million in construction under way downtown. The city has a balanced budget and a $7 million cash reserve for emergencies. Dallas works so smoothly because, probably more than any other major city in the country, it is run by businessmen. Its entrepreneurs, bankers, executives and developers are cheerily confident that they know what's best for the 900,000 people who live here.

The Citizens Council's paternalism has raised many questions about its role in city affairs and even its justification for existence. To some, the Citizens Council is simply a benevolent oligarchy. To others, it is a civic machine, a businessman's boss system. As one community leader noted, "You get the banks, the utilities, then insurance, the big stores, and the papers. Once you got them, you don't need anyone else." Critics have called the council an "invisible government" that rules the city like the doges of medieval Venice or the princes of the Italian Renaissance.[27]

Warren Leslie, in a well-publicized and highly controversial book, *Dallas: Public and Private*, characterized the Citizens Council as "a collection of dollars represented by men." In a light-hearted poke at Dallas in *Texas Monthly*, Harry Hurt III expressed a not entirely facetious view of the Citizens Council:

> . . . Dallas was ruled for many, many years by an arch conservative white oligarchy. . . . Men of the Citizens Council made all the major decisions for Dallas. . . . They elected all the important politicians and told them what to do. They promoted

the city with their own time and money. They, in turn, were dictated to only by their wives, the true behind-the-scenes powers in Dallas. They held final dominion over the city by controlling its high society, its marriages and divorces and debutante balls.

Stanley Marcus, a past president of the council and maverick liberal among the conservatives, pointed out that sterility might be the price of efficiency:

> There is no municipal graft in Dallas, no fixed traffic tickets, no dishonesty, no pull with any of the city offices. Things cannot be fixed up by the mayor's office. There is just no place you can go or must go for a payoff, as in many other cities. People here want to run an honest and a safe city, with a safe Board of Education. But when you get such safety you are apt to get sterility and a lack of progress. This is the price you pay. Our leadership has been singularly lacking in men of wealth who have a genuine concern for intellectual freedom . . . We just have had authoritative leadership that has given respectability to certain drives and causes, but not leadership for excellence in education and the arts. Now we have a large but homogenous group of businessmen intent on unity and conformity.[28]

As an organization dominated by bankers and other business leaders, with few if any professionals, city officials, labor representatives, or minorities, the Citizens Council operates without public accountability and with the belief that it knows what is best for the city.

In an intangible sense, the image of the city has meant a great deal to the civic/political leadership. The Citizens Council has operated under a variety of motives to assure a positive image for the city. As one journalist noted: "The Citizens Council performs its good works not necessarily for their intrinsic value but in the booster spirit." Typically, chief booster Bob Thornton once admitted: "I'll be glad to do anything I can to help [the symphony], as long as you don't ask me to attend any concerts."[29] The council has accepted a kind of noblesse oblige in dealing with city affairs, but, as businessmen, members know that a good image promotes profits. This is not to suggest that the efforts of the Citizens Council have been directly linked to particular money-making schemes or crass business ventures—activities upon which its leadership would frown—but the council does believe that a good business climate requires a good city image.

Nothing threatened to tarnish the reputation of the city as seriously as the assassination of John F. Kennedy on 22 November 1963. Newspapers and magazines throughout the country revived sectional animosities and questioned the extent to which the environment of Dallas contributed to the tragedy. Some branded Dallas as "the city of hate" or "the hate capital of the United States." In a recent issue of *Texas Monthly*, Gregory Curtis reflected on the tragic shooting in light of the 1981 assassination attempt on President Ronald Reagan. The assailant, John W. Hinckley, Jr., is the son of a conservative oilman from Highland Park (Dallas). Curtis noted that in 1963 Dallas was blamed for what was a national tragedy, but not in 1981. "Back then," he noted, "it was easy to assume that all Texas, and Dallas in particular, stood against the new social order Kennedy represented."[30]

The feeling that Dallas was to blame for the assassination of President Kennedy was linked to the high visibility of such local political reactionaries as Dan H. Smoot, publisher of the *Dan Smoot Report*; retired general Edwin A. Walker; eccentric oilman billionaire H. L. Hunt; and various members of the John Birch Society. The city has also been a major center of religious fundamentalism.

The Dallas right wing came under particularly strong attack after the assassination because it had been so vocal in its criticism of the Kennedy administration. Although the president received a friendly reception from most Dallasites, right-wingers, especially H. L. Hunt, had shown their disapproval of the impending visit with public harangues and outrageous charges in the local newspapers. Particularly noteworthy was an inflammatory anti-Kennedy advertisement that appeared in the *Dallas Morning News* on the day of the assassination.

Attacks on Dallas made the city defensive. The Citizens Council, in particular, was worried. Erik Jonsson, president of the council and soon to be mayor of the city, attempted to quell the recriminations. But the council itself, as the body that epitomized the political/civic power in Dallas, became a focal point of the criticism. In reality, the council had tried to disassociate itself from the extreme right by cosponsoring a luncheon for Kennedy on the day before the assassination. After the tragedy the council continued to keep its distance from the far right, primarily by working for the defeat of arch-conservative Republican congressman Bruce Alger, whom it had previously supported. According to a commentator in *Nation*, "Ridding Dallas of Alger seemed a good way of ridding the city of its assassination guilt." The Citizens Council had retained ties with the far right for many years, but when its own power was questioned and the image of the city threatened, those connections were severed.[31]

The role of the Citizens Council has gone well beyond boosterism or the maintenance of a favorable business climate for the city. The council has wielded exceptional power in city politics as well. The Citizens Charter Association (CCA), a subsidiary of the Citizens Council, endorsed more than 90 percent of the city's successful council candidates, selected all but two mayors (one of whom was a maverick club member), controlled the school board, and orchestrated major fund drives. The CCA supported the council-manager system of government because it undermined partisan municipal politics. It also defended at-large election of city council members, which weakened opposition factions within the city and prevented minority representation.[32]

While maintaining a sizable portion of their economic and civic influence in recent years, the political power of the Citizens Council and its CCA has steadily eroded. The election of Wes Wise, a former TV sportscaster and political independent, as mayor in 1971 proved to be a major setback. Wise went on to defeat CCA candidates again in 1973 and 1975 by margins of 18,000 and 15,000 votes, respectively. In 1975 the CCA also lost its overwhelming dominance of the city council, electing only six out of eleven members, and two of the six, both black, were not considered particularly loyal to the CCA. Significantly, 1975 marked the first city election in which candidates ran for office from single-member districts. Following a four-year lawsuit by a group of minority citizens, a federal judge ordered the election held with eight single-member districts and three at-large positions.[33]

The CCA's power weakened not only because of the apathy of the Citizens Council and the redistricting plan, but also because of changing conditions in the city. By the late 1960s voters demonstrated an unwillingness to blindly support the CCA and the Citizens Council. Priorities had shifted, in some cases, toward social needs and the poor. For example, in 1968 a new order of young white citizens, the League for Educational Advancement in Dallas (LEAD), allied themselves with black voters in the school board elections. Business organization and alignment also was changing in Dallas. Several banks joined holding companies and national mergers absorbed several businesses, weakening their local roots and interests. Within the Citizens Council, efforts to recruit young leaders and educate them had not been totally successful. The Citizens Council's role in Dallas politics, however, has not ended. In a 1974 issue of *D*

Magazine, the editors declared: "The Old Guard *is* losing its grip—from age (just shy of 60 on the avearage), from apathy, from hard-headedness, in some cases, from death. Its power is diminishing in scope, in depth, in intensity. The oligarchy is still *the* game in town, but it's no longer the only game."[34]

Although Fort Worth business leaders did not develop a political structure as sophisticated as the Dallas Citizens Council, they nonetheless guided their city's progress. Until 1955, Amon G. Carter personified civic leadership in Fort Worth. Born in Crafton, Texas, in 1879, "Mr. Fort Worth" was a self-made man who held a variety of jobs in his youth. In 1905 he moved to Cowtown and assumed control of the city's newspaper business.

Carter became a booster of the most extreme form, not only for his city, but for west Texas in general. Biographer Jerry Flemmons noted that Carter was not simply the voice of the *Star-Telegram,* but also "cheerleader" for the entire region:

> He was recognized nationally as foremost exponent of the best of Texas: the joyous, expansive, unrestrained celebration of life, the genuine unfettered friendliness, the rugged individualism. And also of the worst: the doctrine that everything here is bigger and better, the loud, boisterous public displays, the practiced pretense of uncluttered ignorance. Those who disliked Amon said he was an embarrassment, that he played a role no longer true of Texas. His supporters said he behaved as outsiders *thought* Texans were, so what was the harm?[35]

Because of his drive, influence, and commitment to Fort Worth, Carter became involved in virtually every major effort at business expansion and civic development until his death in 1955. He was particularly adept at attracting new industry and branch offices of national firms to the city. He enthusiastically promoted aviation, education, charities, and recreational facilities. Although he was the best-known public critic of Dallas, Carter worked with local leadership on projects of mutual benefit, though always with careful consideration of what Fort Worth's share would be.

Rarely operating through official channels, Carter, a one-time Chamber of Commerce president, assumed the role of city advocate and spokesman. It was not unusual for him to fly to Washington to press a case for his city. John Nance Garner once said tht Amon Carter wanted the government of the United States to "run for the exclusive benefit of Fort Worth and, if possible, to the detriment of Dallas." Former senator Tom Connally observed: "The gates open when he comes to Washington and the Treasury Department puts on extra guards because they know he will take back some money for a civic improvement in West Texas."[36]

The flamboyance and style of Amon Carter often clouded the fact that he wanted for Fort Worth what the Thornton oligarchy wanted for Dallas. His death did not threaten that goal, it simply produced a different configuration of leadership that was no longer dominated by a single person or a single way of doing things. Post-Carter leadership in Fort Worth is difficult to discern because the vacuum that he left has taken time to fill. Since the 1920s businessmen and professionals had provided the leadership and the city council and the mayors had played supporting roles. Various groups had spoken for the community; periodically the Chamber of Commerce acted as spokesman for citywide projects. In the 1940s and 1950s ad hoc groups, such as the Committee for a Greater Fort Worth (later the Fort Worth Improvement Committee) endorsed slates of candidates. The Fort Worth Downtown Association lobbied for programs to improve trade activities in the CBD. Sometimes prominent, wealthy citizens—the "Fort Worth Club Crowd"— pressed for civic projects to their liking. Tom Curtis, formerly an editor and reporter for the defunct *Fort Worth Press*, argued that between Carter's death and about 1960, "several local captains of business jockeyed for position . . . It was taken as the natural order of things," he concluded, "that a business elite should run the town."[37]

New leadership began to solidify in the 1960s. From within Seventh Street—the business establishment, so-called because the *Star Telegram* and many banks and utilities kept offices there—three potential heirs to Amon Carter emerged: H. B. Fuqua, chairman of the board of Fort Worth National Bank and head of Texas Pacific Coal and Oil Company, and Marvin and Obie Leonard of Leonard's department store. Surprisingly, "Babe" Fuqua, an oil man with state and national connections, emerged as the most powerful. Like Carter and other conservative business leaders, Fuqua sought to keep taxes low and the local business climate healthy. Also like Carter, he was adept at raising funds for all sorts of community projects. Intolerant of liberals, minorities, or anyone else who had a different vision for Fort Worth, Fuqua knew "who was good for what" and he didn't mind "twisting arms." Fuqua formed the Good Government League (GGL) similar to the Citizens Charter Association of Dallas. The GGL, however, never had as tight a grip over Fort Worth politics as the CCA did in Dallas. Wealthy mavericks found that they could thwart the power structure, as in the case of iron-works owner De-

Witt McKinley, a right-wing, antiestablishment type who became mayor in 1967.

Fuqua was never the reincarnation of Carter, for diversification had made the city less susceptible to one-man rule in the late 1960s and 1970s. The Seventh Street crowd encountered competition from various citizens' groups, including a "Town Hall" movement that has resulted in mass citizen meetings, neighborhood action groups, and study committees. The Town Hall Association has attempted to meld officials of city hall with business and civic activists, thus it has hardly proven to be truly grass-roots organization. The debate over urban renewal in 1966 is a good example of the limits of the Town Hall Association's influence. With the backing of the mayor, the majority of the city council, the Chamber of Commerce, Town Hall leaders, and others, the city reversed its old policy and endorsed urban renewal for its blighted areas. The voters, however, rejected renewal four to one in a referendum that brought together elderly homeowners, other senior citizens, far-righters (opposed to federal intervention), populist elements from the lower-income sectors of the city, and a large number of business and professional people. The biggest issue was why developers from outside of the city should benefit from urban renewal projects.[38]

Antiestablishment backlash has occurred in Fort Worth for several reasons. First, Seventh Street failed to remain unified in its goals and fell into disarray in the early 1970s. The emergence of the Town Hall Association, despite its links to the power structure, helped to decentralize policy planning for the city. Neighborhood councils also attempted to take a greater hand in city and county government. In 1969 Fort Worth began "sector planning," which has helped to reinforce the importance of neighborhood, as opposed to citywide, developmental interests. In city elections, the implementation of single-member districts in the mid 1970s weakened central authority. Therefore, the ability of new populists such as DeWitt McKinley or Woodie Woods (a plumber and councilman noted for challenging the city's relationship with the Southwestern Exposition and Fat Stock Show) to challenge the Old Guard has grown.[39] Whether a change in election practices will open up the system, or conversely give the mayor more authority, remains to be seen, but growth as the central goal is as yet unchallenged.

Despite the internal struggles for leadership, both cities retained an aversion to outsiders (especially ones from Washington) having much say in municipal affairs. This has been more true of Dallas than Fort Worth, where Amon Carter and others actively sought defense contracts, military installations, and governmental offices for their city. Although Fort Worth has not participated in every federal program offering grants or matching funds, it has not shied away from those that seemed most beneficial to economic growth. In the case of Dallas, the reluctance to accept financial assistance from Washington has been more strident, at least until the mid 1970s. Underlying this opposition is the belief that accepting federal funds weakens local control and reorders the city's priorities. Under business leadership, locally initiated capital investment in streets, sewers, and public and private building ventures offered long-term benefits to the city as a whole and to the business community in particular. In the 1960s and 1970s, if not before, federal funding was primarily available for ongoing social programs. Dallas rejected aid under such programs as Title I of the 1949 National Housing Act, and in 1960 shied away from the subsidized urban renewal and public housing program offered through Lyndon Johnson's Great Society. Dallas was, in fact, one of only four major cities that refused participation in the federal school lunch program. Participation in such programs, it was feared, could force the city to contribute its own funds to projects outside the mainstream interests of the business leadership—programs for the poor and minorities—and threaten capital investment projects. It is significant that until 1972, the share of Dallas's general revenue coming from federal sources was less than 3 percent.[40] Lester Potter, president of Lone Star Gas and chairman of a citizens' slum prevention committee, rationalized: "As great as our federal government is, the problems of our cities are too complex and individually distinct to be directed from Washington."[41]

Pragmatism began to crack the ice in the late 1960s. In 1967 John Stemmons argued: "There are millions in Federal aid going to cities for urban renewal, and we're not getting a dime—because we're so holy." Others began to realize that the federal taxes of Dallas citizens were paying for projects everywhere but in Dallas. Mayor Erik Jonsson, hardly a supporter of federal intervention, saw the need to accept funding for urban renewal to expand the city's redevelopment program. By 1972 a great number of business leaders had come around to Jonsson's way of thinking. In trying to improve the image of Dallas, tarnished by the JFK assassination, too many of them had accepted the rhetoric of Big D as the mecca of the Southwest and had chosen to ignore the real problems facing the city. Fully a third of the population was living in poverty areas and major crime was on the increase. In 1967 Dallas ranked fourth in murder and nonnegligent manslaughter. Dallas leaders also began to realize that by trying to go it alone other Sunbelt cities such as Houston and Atlanta were, according to Dallas Chamber of Commerce president E. O. Cartwright, "wresting the initiative from us in the South." He concluded that Dallas "has just been out sold." According to the ever-quotable Stanley Marcus: "Economic determinism is forcing changes that wouldn't even have been considered before. I think our business leaders are coming around to the view that our arch-conservatism has hurt the city economically. I'm sure some liberals here would prefer that we change for humanistic reasons; frankly, I don't care how change comes about so long as it does come about."[42]

Dallas business leaders did not relinquish their free-enterprise principles simply because they wanted to surpass Houston or Atlanta. In the 1970s the availability of revenue sharing made federal aid more acceptable to the Dallas leadership. Richard Nixon's New Federalism called for a "new partnership between the federal government and States and Localities." Revenue sharing was attractive to the Dallas leadership because it required no readjustment of priorities such as those expected under Great Society programs. Although the new approach to federal spending inspired local debates over how to allocate funds—social programs versus capital improvements, "day-care centers or sewers"—it was perceived as complementary to the city's goals rather than competitive with them. In practice Dallas has had little inclination to direct federal monies into low-income areas. Several officials became aware of the need to establish or bolster services for the poor and disadvantaged, but could not agree on the method. Some saw geographic targeting of aid as a throwback to the old urban renewal schemes. Others believed that targeted development involved questions of equity in dispersing funds. Other officials did not even consider poverty and related problems as serious enough to justify new and larger expenditures. Since the poor have traditionally had little voice in local government, the city's priorities are not likely to change.

Dallas's acceptance of federal funds did not mean a fundamental shift in the philosophy of independent action. The goals of the business elite have gone virtually unchallenged. While Dallas has a growing number of social problems, the city is still run with efficiency and useful attention to the physical plant. The city fills potholes within three days, regularly inspects and cleans sewers, and maintains sidewalks and bridges.[43]

Dallas–Fort Worth's response to transportation developments in recent years demonstrates that economic growth remains the major goal of the business leadership. The development of a Trinity River Canal to link north Texas with the Gulf of Mexico was a dream that business and civic leaders had long cherished—an opportunity to turn land-locked Dallas and Fort Worth into port cities. After World War II Congress appropriated funds for the construction of reservoirs on the upper Trinity, approved a plan for a navigable waterway to Galveston Bay, and established an Army Corps of Engineers district office in Fort Worth. The state created the Trinity River Authority in 1955 and a Trinity River Canal Association kept local interest alive. Despite opposition from the Bureau of the Budget, Congress authorized the project in 1965, but the proposed canal still required further cost reviews.

Slowly the canal project seemed to be moving toward reality in the late 1960s. The Trinity River Authority and the Trinity Improvement Association (formerly the Trinity River Canal Association) linked interests in the project. Support also came from several of the region's congressmen, the mayors of both cities, the Citizens Charter Association, and from the downtown business establishments.

But the local leadership had not counted on the breadth of grassroots opposition to the project. Opponents no longer had to argue strictly along economic lines. Armed with the National Environmental Policy Act of 1969, concerned citizens could force the backers of such projects to present environmental impact studies, effectively delaying if not killing the projects.

In 1972 opposition began to take shape on local college and university campuses. A group of students from Navarro Junior College and two professors at Southern Methodist University assumed leadership. In April they organized the Citizens Organization for a Sound Trinity (COST) to actively oppose the project in court and later at the polls. The cliché about politics making strange bedfellows applied in this case. The "battle for the Trinity" did not simply pit developers against environmentalists. Some Dallas businessmen felt that the project would not be economically profitable. Republican congressional candidate Alan Steelman believed that the "billion dollar ditch" would lead to heavy pollution and increased crime. He won his race by a large margin.

Proponents of the canal trotted out the traditional reasons for supporting growth projects and attempted to demean the opposition. They bankrolled an expensive advertising campaign, which claimed that the canal would greatly improve the economy of the region, create needed jobs without threatening the purity of the water, and even improve recreational facilities in the area. Spokesmen labeled opponents as "environmental extremists."

The issue came to a head in a 1973 bond election for $150 million in seed money toward the $1.6 billion project. This money would come out of the pockets of the taxpayers in the seventeen-county region through which the Trinity flowed. As COST often charged: "Your money, their canal." They asserted that the project would destroy prime breeding grounds for shrimp, crab, and menhaden at the mouth of the Trinity and that it would pose a major threat to drinking water. The results sent shock waves through the local political establishment. Voters turned out in large numbers to defeat the bond issue and thus the canal. Opponents won ten counties with large majorities coming from the major cities. Final totals showed 54 percent against the bond. In some Dallas and Fort Worth precincts the issue lost by more than six to one.[44]

The defeat was stunning. Some commentators, however, have made too much of the claim that the defeat of the Trinity project signaled the demise of business influence in Dallas and Fort Worth politics. While it is clear that the old oligarchies can no longer unilaterally determine the future of their cities, the goals of economic growth and expansion were not abandoned. The process by which DFW Airport was created illustrates the ongoing vitality of the business-booster-development mentality. The idea of a joint airport for the two cities was first broached in 1927, but local rivalry, financial problems, jurisdictional disputes, and the development of separate municipal airport facilities in each city forestalled the effort. Before the economies of both cities expanded and diversified and before the major migration of people to the Southwest swelled the region, neither city believed that a regional airport was important enough to make concessions to its rival. State and federal aviation authorities, however, continually urged the cities to cooperate.

In 1947 Fort Worth decided to build its own modern airport. The city chose a site near where the Civil Aeronautics Administration (CAA) wanted the regional airport—between the two cities but slightly closer to Fort Worth. Six years later, Amon Carter Field (or Greater Fort Worth International Airport) opened, but it never lived up to expectations. By 1969 five and a half times as many passengers departed from Dallas's Love Field as from Carter.

Love Field, hemmed in by the city, was too small to service the whole region or to meet the future economic needs of the Metroplex. The Federal Aviation Administration (FAA), formerly the CAA, was hesitant to finance improvements at Love because of noise and safety hazards. In August 1962 the Civil Aeronautics Board (CAB) initiated the Dallas–Fort Worth Regional Airport Investigation. Dallas officials feared the CAB might recommend joint operation of Fort Worth's Amon Carter Field, but the 1964 report called for a partnership to construct a new airport in the same general area. In 1967 state representatives from both cities introduced legislation to create the North Central Texas Airport Authority.

As the project accumulated funding and began to take shape, officials from both cities grew more enthusiastic. Appearances belied the years of squabbling. At the official opening of DFW Airport in September 1973, the heated controversy seemed to have never existed. Fort Worth mayor R. M. Stovall declared that the airport "has focused attention on the Dallas–Fort Worth area beyond our most ambitious expectations." It truly seemed that DFW Airport had permanently put a hyphen between Dallas and Fort Worth as two independent goals for economic growth and prosperity were melded into one.[45]

School desegregation in Dallas is an important example of how business leaders attempted to deal with a major social issue. Soon after the *Brown* v. *Board of Education* (1954) decision, the Dallas branch of the National Association for the Advancement of Colored People (NAACP) started legal proceedings against the local school board. Throughout the 1950s plaintiffs and the school board were in and out of the federal district courts. After much deliberation, the Fifth Circuit Court accepted the so-called stair-step plan in 1961. According to this system, schools would integrate one grade per year until the whole system was desegregated. The school board decided to appeal no further and the stair-step plan went into effect.

Four years earlier, the Citizens Council, although blind to many racial problems, attempted to prepare the way for Dallasites to accept desegregation of the schools and integration of public places. Little attention had been given to the black community prior to 1954 even though ghetto and slum conditions were bad and some violence had erupted, especially in South Dallas when neighborhoods began shifting from white to black. But in 1957, civic and business leaders chose to face reality—legal attempts to repulse desegregation would certainly fail, and Dallas could become another Little Rock. The inability to resist the federal courts for much longer, coupled with rumors of potential sit-ins in Dallas, stimulated the Citizens Council to action. Maintenance of at least outward signs of harmony and a fear of the loss of business revenue were tangible enough reasons to seek a peaceful solution to the problem.

The first step of the Citizens Council and Mayor Thornton was to arrange a secret meeting to work out an integration plan for public places. Hand-picked black leaders attended, and the group decided to send black men and women downtown in April 1957 to patronize the more fashionable retail stores as a symbolic gesture toward desegregation. Dallas citizens did not receive this effort with complete acquiescence, but disturbances were minor and the council's gradualist approach made a successful start. Over the next few years the Citizens Council built upon this modest beginning by staging a visit to the fashionable Zodiac Room restaurant in Neiman-Marcus (1961) and by producing a film, narrated by Walter Cronkite, called "Dallas at the Crossroads," showing the consequences of not accepting integration. Sam Bloom, an advertising man who headed the Citizens Council's desegregation program, said about the film: "If you're going to sell a concept to a community you have to make it palatable. When we showed people what had happened in other cities, our concept became palatable."

Locally and nationally Dallas's efforts at peaceful desegregation were roundly applauded. W. Dawson Sterling, president of the Southwestern Life Insurance Company and member of the Citizens Council, summed up this feeing of exhilaration: "The way that integration has come about is another indication of the real nature of Dallas. Many of the white people were opposed to it. But they cooperated in seeing to it that there were no ugly incidents." A 1966 study authored by Walter Schiebel for the Dallas schools declared: "Desegregation of the Dallas Schools was accomplished in the course of ten short years with a minimum of commotion and stress. This may be viewed as just short of miraculous."

But the absence of a major conflagration in Dallas did not imply that desegregation was an accomplished fact or that the problems of minorities had disappeared. The stair-step plan remained in operation until September 1965, by which time four grades had been desegregated. At that point the plan was accelerated to have all elementary, junior high, and high schools desegregated by September 1967. In that year district officials declared that a unitary system had been achieved. But in October 1970 a suit filed in the federal district court charged that a dual system was being maintained through neighborhood school assignment plans, school building sites, and staffing practices. In July 1971, Federal Judge William Taylor declared that elements of a dual system remained: Dallas Independent School District (DISD) had seventy schools with 90 percent or more white students, forty with 90 percent or more black students, and forty-nine with 90 percent or more minority students. The jurist again instructed the district to eliminate the dual system.

Under the leadership of Nolan Estes, the Harvard-educated wunderkind superintendent who served from 1968 to 1978, several new ideas appeared. Never as committed to immediate desegregation as liberals hoped nor as radical as conservatives feared, Estes tried a "confluence of cultures" approach that paired secondary schools and integrated elementary schools through the use of closed-circuit television through which black and white students would communicate. The plan provoked laughter among some educators. Busing was a sterner solution. In the mid 1970s, the business community was brought back into the picture with the introduction of the Dallas Alliance, a business community service organization that helped write a compromise desegregation plan including some busing and the maintenance of some segregated schools. Despite footdragging, Dallas seemed to be moving toward a workable desegregation plan by the end of the 1970s. Recently, the Supreme Court ordered complete integration of the Dallas school system, noting the city's history of discrimination. The issue, however, has not been resolved and the court battle continues.[46]

The efforts at desegregation represented only one aspect of the racial question in Dallas. Community leaders had yet to effectively confront the increasing problem of white flight or the unrest in the black ghettos and Mexican-American barrios. The actions of the business leaders in helping to smooth the way for school desegregation unfortunately were not part of a comprehensive plan for dealing with minority interests or the problems of the poor.

In Fort Worth, the road to desegregation of the schools followed a similar path as in Dallas. Prior to 1961 the Fort Worth Independent School District (FWISD) maintained a dual system. An NAACP lawsuit prompted a federal court order that the FWISD submit a desegregation proposal. As in Dallas, the proposal incorporated a stair-step plan to begin in 1963. School officials declared that Fort Worth was completely desegregated in 1967. Although the stair-step plan was implemented, school district boundaries—following neighborhood lines—were not changed, which meant that de facto segregation still existed. During the school year in 1969–1970 80 percent of Fort Worth's black children attended predominantly black schools; in 1970–1971 the figure dropped somewhat to 67 percent. In 1970 the NAACP began another round of lawsuits to generate a new plan. The Fifth Circuit Court supported the NAACP's position and ordered a revision in 1971. School officials produced a new proposal in that year, which included some busing with "cluster" schools. Throughout the 1970s, however, litigation continued unabated.[47]

Most large cities traditionally have had a problem maintaining a sense of community. This seems less true for Dallas and Fort Worth. From their nineteenth-century beginnings both cities have taken great pride in what they believed to be their unique attributes—Cowtown's western flair, Dallas's style and sophistication. They also took pride in vigorous economic growth and physical expansion, which their business leaders touted as signs of success and progress. The rise of Dallas and Fort Worth as regionally dominant centers was a matter of pride. Dallas and Fort Worth came to represent what was dramatic and energetic about the emergence of Sunbelt cities, but they also suggest the limits of a leadership with too limited a vision and too narrow a focus on image.

NOTES

1. George S. Perry, "Dallas and Fort Worth," *Saturday Evening Post*, 30 March 1946, 23; "Can Feudists Grow Together?" *Business Week*, 9 March 1967, 101; Jan Morris, "Fort Worth, the Eternal City," *Texas Monthly* 10 (June 1982): 150ff.; "A Different Look at Dallas, Texas," *U.S. News and World Report*, 3 February 1964, 42–43; James Street, "Dazzling Dallas," *Holiday* 13 (March 1953): 106; Carol Estes Thometz, *The Decision-Makers: The Power Structure of Dallas* (Dallas: Southern Methodist University Press, 1963), 9–10; Robert Wallace, "What Kind of Place Is Dallas," *Life*, 31 January 1964, 68; Joanne P. Austin, "Dallas–Fort Worth: The Southwest Metroplex," *Texas Business Review* 52 (September 1978): 186, 191; Thomas McKnight, *Dallas* (Garden City, N.Y.: Nelson Doubleday, Inc., 1964), 13; William L. McDonald, *Dallas Rediscovered: A Photographic Chronicle of Urban Expansion, 1870–1925* (Dallas: Dallas Historical Society, 1978); August O. Spain, "Fort Worth: Great Expectations—Cowtown Hares and Tortoises," in Leonard E. Goodall, ed., *Urban Politics in the Southwest* (Tempe: Institute of Public Administration, Arizona State University, 1967), 46–47, 49; James Howard, *Big D Is for Dallas: Chapters in the Twentieth-Century History of Dallas* (Austin, Tex.: University Co-operative Society, 1957), 1–3; "The Dallas–Fort Worth Region," in *Twentieth Century Cities*, part 4 of Association of American Geographers, *Contemporary Metropolitan America*, John S. Adams, ed. (Cambridge, Mass.: Ballinger Publishing Co., 1976), 11–12. See also Martin V. Melosi, *Dallas–Fort Worth: Politics, Economy, and Demography since World War II*, Public Administration Series: Bibliography (Monticello, Ill.: Vance Bibliographies, June 1982).

2. Tom Lee McKnight, *Manufacturing in Dallas: A Study of Effects* (Austin, Tex.: Bureau of Business Research, University of Texas, 1956), 4, 8, 12, 18, 167–172; Opal Hill Munz, "Dallas, USA," *Texas Industry* 20 (October 1954): 22.

3. David Botter, "Big D Swings Out," *Texas Industry* 13 (November 1946): 12–14; Munz, "Dallas, USA," 24; "Railroad Orphan Gets Its Rights," *Business Week*, 13 November 1954, 178, 180; McKnight, *Dallas*, 36–37.

4. "Dallas," *Nation's Business* 63 (January 1975): 32–33, 40; Paul R. Porter, *The Recovery of American Cities* (New York: Sun River Press, 1976), 54; Botter, "Big D Swings Out," 13–14.

5. H. C. Green, "Planning a National Retail Growth Program," *Economic Geography* 37 (January 1961): 24; Opal Hill Munz, "Aircraft Produc-

tion High in Texas' Economic Sky," *Texas Industry* 18 (January 1952): 12–15; Lewis Nordyke, "Industry Likes Fort Worth," *Texas Parade* 19 (January 1959): 8; Spain, "Fort Worth," 49; Oliver Knight, "Fort Worth's First 100 Years," *Texas Industry* 15 (June 1949): 18–19; Opal Hill Munz, "Fort Worth Thar She Grows," *Texas Industry* 18 (October 1952): 40; "Economic Analysis and Land Use Requirements, Fort Worth, Texas" (Fort Worth: City Planning Department, 27 March 1963), 14, 19; Austin, "Dallas–Fort Worth," 191.

6. Knight, "Fort Worth's First 100 Years," 18–19; Nordyke, "Industry Likes Fort Worth," 11; Munz, "Fort Worth Thar She Grows," 39; William B. Alderman, "Just Look at Fort Worth Now," *Texas Parade* 24 (December 1963): 18; Robert H. Talbert, *Cowtown-Metropolis: Case Study of a City's Growth and Structure* (Fort Worth: Potishman Foundation, Texas Christian University, 1956), 158; Spain, "Fort Worth," 49–50; "Economic Analysis and Land Use," 21, 23, 24, 54–55.

7. The Metroplex is the eleven-county SMSA that includes Collin, Dallas, Denton, Ellis, Hood, Johnson, Kaufman, Parker, Rockwall, Tarrant, and Wise counties.

8. Austin, "Dallas–Fort Worth," 187.

9. Opal Hill Munz, "Fort Worth Roundup," *Texas Industry* 13 (January 1947): 11; "The Dallas–Fort Worth Region," *Twentieth Century Cities*, 15–21; Talbert, *Cowtown–Metropolis*, 134–135, 146; Austin, "Dallas–Fort Worth," 188–189.

10. John Bainbridge, *The Super-Americans* (Garden City, N.Y.: Doubleday and Co., Inc., 1961), 126 (quote); "The Merchant Prince of Dallas," *Business Week*, 21 October 1967, 115–118, 123.

11. Austin, "Dallas–Fort Worth," 189; Michael Ennis, "Rags to Riches," *Texas Monthly* 9 (January 1981): 96ff.

12. Al Reinert, "The End of the Trail," *Texas Monthly* 6 (November 1978): 170ff.

13. Alderman, "Just Look at Fort Worth Now," 18; Austin, "Dallas–Fort Worth," 190; Munz, "Dallas, USA," 21; "Dallas," *Nation's Business*, 39–42; "Economic Analysis and Land Use Requirements," 13; John Merwin, "The Dallas Economy, 2000: Business As Usual?" *D Magazine* 3 (January 1976): 68.

14. Doug McInnis, "Booming Host to Big Corporations," *Christian Science Monitor*, 12 October 1979; John Rees, "Manufacturing Headquarters in a Post-Industrial Urban Context," *Economic Geography* 54 (October 1978): 341; "Dallas," *Nation's Business*, 32; Austin, "Dallas–Fort Worth," 192.

15. Prior to 1970, Dallas and Fort Worth had separate SMSAs. "Economic Analysis and Land Use Requirements," 81–87; Porter, *Recovery of American Cities*, 44, 106; Howard, *Big D Is for Dallas*, 21–22; Spain, "Fort Worth," 51–52; Talbert, *Cowtown Metropolis*, 47; Fort Worth National Bank et al., *Population and Growth Trends of the Fort Worth Area, 1950–2000* (June 1958), 5; Oliver Knight, *Fort Worth: Outpost on the Trinity* (Norman: University of Oklahoma Press, 1953), 217.

16. Spain, "Fort Worth," 51; "A Different Look," *U.S. News and World*

Report, 42; Howard, *Big D Is for Dallas,* 13; John William Rogers, *The Lusty Texans of Dallas,* enlarged ed. (New York: E. P. Dutton and Co., Inc., 1960), 370.

17. "The Dallas–Fort Worth Region," *Twentieth Century Cities,* 3–9.

18. "Airport for 2001," *Time,* 24 September 1973, 92; "Aviation's Future Down in Texas," *Business Week,* 29 September 1973, 22–23; William Broyles, "Airport!" *Texas Monthly* 1 (December 1973): 76; David R. Goldfield and Blaine Brownell, *Urban America: From Downtown to No Town* (New York: Harper & Row, 1972), 340 (quote); "The Land Boom at a Texas Airport," *Business Week,* 11 March 1972; 116–117 (quoting Good); "Airport!" *Texas Observer,* 19 October 1973.

19. "Dallas Develops Its Downtown," *American City* 79 (October 1964): 146–147; "Dallas," *Nation's Business,* 32; Rogers, *The Lusty Texans,* 370; *New York Times,* 4 July 1959; "What Your City Needs to Grow," *Nation's Business* 52 (September 1964): 32 (quote).

20. Richard L. Williams, "Troubled Cities," *Smithsonian* 9 (November 1978): 66.

21. "Dynamic Men of Dallas," *Fortune* 39 (February 1949): 162; V. R. Smitham, "Dallas Prepares for the Future," *National Municipal Review* 33 (February 1944): 67; Dorothy Webb, "City Design Is a High Priority in 'Big D,'" *Nation's Cities* 14 (August 1976): 15–18; James R. Bobo et al., "Metropolitan Goals Programs," *Town Planning Review* 47 (January 1976): 43–55; *Goals for Dallas* (Dallas, 1966); *New Goals for Dallas* (Dallas, 1977); "Dallas Scores," *American City* 82 (November 1967): 130–132; "Dallas," *Nation's Business,* 33–34.

22. "Footprints in Fort Worth," *Time,* 19 March 1956, 26 (quote); "Basic Plan to Vitalize Fort Worth District," *American City* 71 (June 1956): 132–133; "Master Plan for Revitalizing Ft. Worth: Central Cure," *Business Week,* 17 March 1956, 70–74; R. Elliott, "Fort Worth: Cowtown-Turned-Now Town," *Texas Parade* 31 (July 1970): 37.

23. "The Ghosts of Urban Renewal Haunt Fort Worth's Leaders," *Texas Observer,* 31 March 1967, 9.

24. Williams, "Troubled Cities," 64–66 (quote); *New York Times,* 24 November 1973; "The Dallas–Fort Worth Region," *Twentieth Century Cities,* 27; Howard, *Big D Is for Dallas,* 22; Shirley Achor, *Mexican Americans in a Dallas Barrio* (Tucson: University of Arizona Press, 1978), 48–50, 128–129; Thometz, *The Decision-Makers,* 65. See also *D Magazine,* April 1977, June 1981.

25. Wallace, "What Kind of Place Is Dallas," 69.

26. "Dynamic Men of Dallas," *Fortune,* 162; Stanley Walker, *The Dallas Story* (Dallas: Dallas Times Herald, 1956), 340.

27. Warren Leslie, *Dallas: Public and Private* (New York: Grossman Publishing, 1964), 68–69; "Power in Dallas: Who Hold the Cards?" *D Magazine* 1 (October 1974): 49; *Wall Street Journal,* 24 September 1979 (quote); "A Different Look," *U.S. News and World Report,* 46; Street, "Dazzling Dallas," 109; *New York Times,* 19 January 1964.

28. Leslie, *Dallas,* 63; Harry Hurt III, "Houston Is Better than Dallas,"

Texas Monthly 6 (February 1978): 80; Richard A. Smith, "How Business Failed Dallas," *Fortune* 70 (July 1964): 158–159 (quoting Marcus).

29. Wallace, "What Kind of Place Is Dallas," 69.

30. Gregory Curtis, "Behind the Lines," *Texas Monthly* 9 (May 1981): 5.

31. "Dallas Superpatriots Are No Nuttier than Anyone Else, It Turns Out," *Texas Observer*, 27 November 1970; Harry Hurt III, "Welcome, Mr. Kennedy, to Dallas," *Texas Monthly* 9 (April 1981): 156ff.; "A Different Look," *U.S. News and World Report*, 43; *New York Times*, 24–28 November 1963; 19 January 1964; Smith, "How Business Failed Dallas," 157–159; Saul Friedman, "Tussle in Texas," *Nation*, 3 February 1964, 114–116 (quote).

32. "Power in Dallas," *D Magazine*, 49–50; Smith, "How Business Failed Dallas," 211–214.

33. *New York Times*, 13 April 1975; "Dallas: Up the Establishment," *Newsweek*, 3 May 1971, 32.

34. Kronholz, "Company Town," 26; Lee Clark, "Battle of Ideas in Dallas," *Texas Observer*, 10 May 1967; Jim Atkinson and John Merwin, "New Power," *D Magazine* 4 (September 1977): 60ff.; "Power in Dallas," *D Magazine*, 47 (quote).

35. Jerry Flemmons, *Amon: The Life of Amon Carter, Sr. of Texas* (Austin: Jenkins Publishing Co., 1978), 19–20. See also Knight, *Fort Worth*, 220–222.

36. Tom Curtis, "Who Runs Cowtown?" *Texas Monthly* 4 (March 1976): 30; Knight, *Fort Worth*, 223.

37. Curtis, "Who Runs Cowtown?" 28–30.

38. Ibid., 30–64; Spain, "Fort Worth," 54–64.

39. Howard W. Hallman, *The Organization and Operation of Neighborhood Councils: A Practical Guide* (New York: Praeger, 1977), 8, 31.

40. Robert Bradley et al., "New Federalism and the Texas Urban Poor," *Texas Business Review* 54 (March–April 1980): 111–113.

41. *New York Times*, 4 July 1959.

42. Dennis Farney, "Change in 'Big D,'" *Wall Street Journal*, 17 November 1967.

43. "A City That Still Works," *Time*, 27 April 1981, 48.

44. Dave McNeely and Lyke Thompson, "The Unholy Trinity Incident," *Texas Monthly* 1 (June 1973): 42–43; D. Clayton Brown, *Rivers, Rockets and Readiness: Army Engineers in the Sunbelt: A History of the Fort Worth District, U.S. Army Corps of Engineers, 1950–1975* (Washington, D.C.: Corps of Engineers, 1979), 84, 102–109.

45. "Airport!" *Texas Observer*; Stanley H. Scott and Levi H. Davis, *A Giant in Texas: Dallas–Fort Worth Regional Airport, 1911–1974* (Quanah, Tex.: Nortex Press, 1974), 1–50; James H. Winchester, "The Great Fort Worth–Dallas Controversy," *Flying* 68 (May 1961): 85–86; "Designing an Airport to Fit People," *Business Week*, 26 October 1968, 112; "Airport for 2001," *Time*, 92; *New York Times*, 30 January 1966; Broyles, "Airport!" 74.

46. William W. Beck and Glenn M. Linden, "Anglo and Minority Perceptions of Success in Dallas School Desegregation," *Phi Delta Kappan* 61

(January 1979): 379; William R. Carmack and Theodore Freedman, *Dallas, Texas: Factors Affecting School Desegregation* (New York: Anti-Defamation League of B'nai B'rith, 1962), 6–21; Steve Kenny, "The Struggle for Power," *D Magazine* 9 (June 1981): 136–140; *New York Times*, 8 September 1961, 19 January 1964, 16 December 1976; Ronnie Dugger, "Dallas: Another Little Rock?" *Nation*, 11 January 1958, 27; "Integration: Sign of the Zodiac," *Newsweek*, 7 August 1961, 26; Walter J. E. Schiebel, *Education in Dallas: Ninety-Two Years of History, 1874–1966* (Dallas: Dallas Independent School District, 1966), 159; Lee Clark, "Dallas' Oligarchy and Fateful '68," *Texas Observer*, 1 March 1968; Nolan Estes, "On Eliminating Institutional Racism," *Phi Delta Kappan* 60 (December 1978): 302–303; Jim Atkinson, "Nolan Estes on the Tightrope," *D Magazine* 3 (April 1978): 46ff.; "Dallas: A Scandal Bigger than One City?" *Phi Delta Kappan* 62 (January 1980); 306, 361; "Desegregation in Dallas Derailed," *Texas Observer*, 10 September 1971; Tracy Curts, "Is White Flight Ruining the Dallas Schools?" *D Magazine* 4 (August 1977): 76ff.; Anchor, *Mexican Americans*, 64–65.

47. Joyce E. Williams, *Black Community Control: A Study of Transition in a Texas Ghetto* (New York: Praeger, 1973), 149–152; Alwyn Barr, *Black Texans: A History of Negroes in Texas, 1528–1971* (Austin: Jenkins Publishing Co., 1973), 212–213.

7

HOUSTON
THE GOLDEN BUCKLE OF THE SUNBELT

by Barry J. Kaplan

Houston, Texas, is one of the fastest-growing, major urban areas in the Sunbelt, with a metropolitan population of 2,891,146 in 1980, an increase of 44.6 percent since 1970. The city's economic prosperity, based primarily on its oil and petrochemical industries and guided by a glittering, often gaudy, boom mentality, has earned it the nickname of "Golden Buckle of the Sunbelt." But more than just rapid population growth and economic prosperity has earned Houston this title, for the city epitomizes many of the political and economic developments characteristic of the region.[1]

Founded in 1836, Houston stands at the headwaters of Buffalo Bayou, a small stream that meandered some fifty miles before emptying into Galveston Bay. At the mouth of the bay, clinging to a narrow, sandy island, lay Galveston, Texas' leading port. Throughout the last decades of the nineteenth century, Houston and Galveston were commercial rivals. Galveston had a deepwater port, but Houston had better rail connections. By 1900, Houston's population of 44,000 exceeded Galveston's by 7,000, but the lack of a port inhibited further growth. Buffalo Bayou, despite intermittent dredging and improvement efforts, could not accommodate ocean-going vessels, so Houston remained an exchange point between the rail lines and barges that transferred goods to Galveston. The competitive balance between the two cities suddenly changed, however, on 4 September 1900, when a major tropical hurricane and a six-foot tidal wave hit Galveston Island and virtually destroyed the city. The storm demolished over one-half of the buildings and killed over five thousand people. Never again would Galveston rival its inland neighbor.

With its major competitor vanquished by nature, the Houston business and political community, aided by the federal government, acted quickly to capture regional leadership. After the Galveston disaster, Congressman Tom Ball of Houston convinced Congress to approve a one-million-dollar appropriation for a ship channel from the Gulf to Houston via Buffalo Bayou. In 1909, the city ensured the completion of the channel by matching subsequent federal spending on the project, and the channel opened in late 1914.[2]

Throughout the modern period, the Houston Ship Channel has remained a critical component in the city's economic base. Although the waterway is often overshadowed by Houston's popular images as the energy capital of the world and the center of the nation's space programs, Houston is also one of the nation's leading ports. In 1979 it ranked first in foreign trade tonnage, second in dollar value of foreign trade, and third in total cargo tonnage. Over one-half of the bulk imports were crude oil and petroleum products, while grains accounted for slightly over 50 percent of the total bulk exports. Houston's major trading partner is Saudi Arabia, one reason for the increasingly strong ties between local businessmen and bankers and their counterparts in the Middle East. The port and the adjacent industries provide over 180,000 jobs for the area's workers. These industries represent over $8 billion in capital investments. The port and the energy-related companies, moreover, have had a multiplier effect on the city's economy. Houston has become a major manufacturing center: the sixth largest in the United States in both value added by manufacture and value of shipments.[3]

The second crucial ingredient for Houston's twentieth-century boom was the discovery of oil on 10 January 1901 at the Spindletop fields near Beaumont. This discovery made Houston the oil capital of the United States. As twentieth-century industrial technology shifted its reliance from coal to petroleum, Houston prospered. After the Spindletop discovery, oil companies extended pipelines to the Houston Ship Channel. Protected from the devastating storms that frequently strike the Gulf Coast, the channel was a superb location for oil refineries and oil-related concerns. By the end of the 1920s, more than fifty businesses had grown up along the channel.[4]

This waterway and the expanding oil-related industries that lined its banks were the major factors in the tenfold growth of Houston from a small city in 1900 to a metropolitan center of 467,000 in 1945. By that year, Houston was on the verge of an economic takeoff based upon its oil and gas centered economy, assisted by federal expenditures, facilitated by a favorable business climate, unhampered by government restrictions, and guided by an intelligent and aggressive entrepreneurial elite.

While the national government bolstered the local economy with the freeway program and later NASA, the private sector reaped the benefits of a good business climate and the growing world re-

liance upon oil and petroleum products. Based upon its early proximity to oil and gas deposits and the federal government's purchases
of petroleum for the military during World War II, postwar Houston
became the heart of the expanding petroleum and petrochemical industry. Today the Houston area possesses close to one-quarter of the
refining capacity and over one-half of the petrochemical manufacturing capacity in the United States. In addition, over two-thirds of
the world's oil tools are produced in Houston. Such towering edi-
fices as the Penzoil Building, One and Two Shell Plaza, the Tenneco
Building, and the Conoco Towers punctuate the Houston skyline
where twenty-nine of the thirty largest energy companies have their
offices.[5]

Houston benefited greatly from the staggering increases in oil
prices after 1973. These price boosts fattened the profits of the city's
energy corporations and stimulated the search for new energy supplies, using equipment and services supplied by Houstonians. As political scientist Richard Murray noted, "Houston may be a one horse
town, but Houston's horse . . . has been a far better steed to ride in
the turbulent 1970s than mounts available to other American
cities."[6]

A technological factor assisting growth in Houston and other
Sunbelt cities is air conditioning. First introduced in 1923, but not
used on a mass scale until after World War II, air coolers negated the
hot, humid climate and removed a major deterrent to population
growth and economic expansion.

Perhaps the major reason, however, for the growth of business
activity in Houston is what the Houston Chamber of Commerce
calls the "nation's best economic climate." One study gave Texas
that rating based upon labor legislation favorable to management,
the small size and efficiency of the state government, a low per-
capita debt, a moderate cost of living, and minimal unemployment
compensation payments required of employers. Texas is also a right-
to-work state and has banned mass picketing and secondary boy-
cotts. As a result, union membership accounts for only 13 percent of
the Texas labor force, compared to a national figure of about 28 percent.[7] Moreover, the state exacts no personal or corporate income
taxes. Property taxes, the city's main source of income, are very low;
about 2 percent of the assessed market value of the property.

The economic boom and rapid population growth in Houston
are products of geography, technology, and government assistance.
They are also the products of an optimistic and aggressive entrepreneurial elite, which, by popular consensus, has been free to
create an urban monument to the business culture. Houston may be

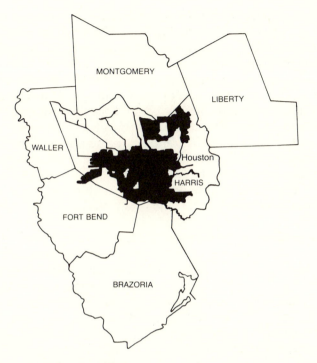

MAP 7.1. The Houston SMSA

one of the last bastions of corporate capitalism, popularly known in Texas as "free enterprise." This phrase is somewhat misleading, however, because in Houston the government is not a neutral observer of the marketplace. Rather, it is an active agent of business growth.

This version of capitalism makes Houston a prime frontier for those on the make, speculators, wheeler-dealers, people with dreams, modern Horatio Algers, and builders of tomorrow. The private sector is the driving force in the city. In this atmosphere, the government provides a minimum of basic services and assists business growth. Citizens who want more than the minimum of public services go to the private sector to obtain support. The emphasis on individualism, capitalism, and economic growth has created a city that believes in the American dream.

These values are apparent in the lack of government planning and public land use controls in the city. Houston is a product of twentieth-century technology, particularly the private automobile, which, along with private investment by the business community, has created a polynuclear city. Although the city has a planning department, it is not very active, due in part to political realities and inadequate funding. On the average, Houston annually spends about $.32 per person for city planning. In comparison, Kansas City spends $7.24; Dallas, $1.53; Los Angeles, $1.37; and Baltimore, $2.79. Of course these cities have higher tax rates. Voters in Houston have rejected zoning twice, and the city council blocked implementation two other times. Given the absence of this often controversial planning tool, the government has limited influence over private land use, compared to other American cities. Although the Houston City Council passed new legislation in 1982 controlling commercial development and land use setbacks, basic public planning is based primarily on control of water and sewer lines that direct urban expansion.[8]

Urban planning in Houston has been the province of the private sector, which has produced, among other things, the planned elite community of River Oaks and one of the largest medical facilities in the world—the Texas Medical Center. The center, which includes a public hospital, is the site of research in heart and cancer treatment. Trailing only the construction firm of Brown and Root, the medical center is the city's second largest employer with over 26,000 employees and 8,600 students.[9]

Without a strong city planning department and without the land use controls of other American cities, the public sector has allowed businessmen to plan the city through the profit mechanism. This investment planning has resulted in a sprawling, low-density city, linked by a massive freeway system that delineates city sectors. As a result of limitations on the role of government, construction costs and times are lower in Houston, making the city conducive to home ownership. A majority of Houstonians own their own homes, although like other American cities Houston is segregated by race and income.

Since three-quarters of Houston has been built since 1945, the city's physical plant is relatively new and highly decentralized. Private construction has created numerous subdivisions, often possessing community recreational facilities like pools and tennis courts. Multifamily apartment units are rarely more than two to three stories high and often include pools and other recreational facilities. The heavy reliance on the automobile and the lack of an effective public transit system has created a city designed by and for the personal car.[10]

Houston's polynuclear urban form is a product of this post–World War II transportation technology and the decisions of Houston's business community. The freeway system is a basic loop (Interstate 610) connected to the other freeways running north to south (Interstate 45 and Interstate 59) and east to west (Interstate 10). The central business district has expanded from the site of first settlement at the confluence of Buffalo and White Oak bayous, but the other nodes are products of the free market and transportation technology. The famous Galleria, located on Houston's desirable west side, is next to Interstate 610 and between Interstate 10 and Interstate 59. The Galleria is a multifunctional area encompassing major retail, hotel, office, dining, and recreation facilities, with numerous condominiums and private residences nearby. The medical center on south Main Street near the South Loop, Greenway Plaza next to Interstate 59, the Energy Coordinator paralleling Interstate 10 in the city's West Houston region, and the Farm-to-Market 1960 community are other major nodes in the metropolitan region. Essentially the east side of the city remains the province of heavy industry around the ship channel and the residence of minority groups, while Houston's west side has attracted middle- to upper-income white residents and office/retail complexes.

Houston's progrowth policies have created a viable private sector that continues to expand, despite recessionary national trends. Employment in Houston increased by 70,000 between 1976 and 1981, while unemployment was only about 5 percent by 1982. The figure may continue to rise as the unemployed from other states flock to Houston. Between 1970 and 1980, Houston climbed from seventy-sixth to sixteenth place in national per-capita income ranking. At least 125 companies employ one thousand or more people. From 1975 to 1980, Houston led the nation in housing starts and in the last two of those years total construction in the Houston area topped $2 billion. Since 1970, over two hundred companies have moved headquarters or other major operations to Houston. In the early 1980s, according to the Chamber of Commerce, over one thousand people a week came to Houston in search of jobs.[11]

This economic boom makes population increases before 1945 seem insignificant. From about 600,000 people in 1950, Houston's population increased to approximately 938,000 in 1960. By 1970 it was 1.2 million and in 1980 the census figures placed Houston's municipal population at 1.6 million. By 1980, Houston was the nation's fifth largest city and it should surpass Philadelphia in the 1980s to become the nation's fourth largest. Aside from some highly publicized but statistically insignificant gentrification of selected inner-city neighborhoods on Houston's west side, Houston's population growth has been in the so-called vital fringe. Unlike most cities, especially in the Northeast, Houston has not been seriously hemmed in by incorporated suburbs or recalcitrant unincorporated areas under county jurisdiction. Over half of the SMSA population remains in the central city. To be sure, Houston has its incorporated suburbs, such as Pasadena and Bellaire, but thanks to an aggressive use of liberal state annexation laws, the City of Houston has been able to capture much of the peripheral growth within its corporate limits.[12]

In addition to its 556 square miles of land, Houston has extra territorial jurisdiction (ETJ), which reserves an additional two thousand square miles for future annexation. In 1945 the city boundaries encompassed about 73 square miles, but by 1949 its land mass had doubled to 159.70 square miles. Numerous annexations since 1949, especially in 1956, 1965, and 1978, tripled the size of the city. The combination of ETJ and liberal annexation laws stymies the incorporation of suburban municipalities and allows the city to enlarge its tax base while avoiding fiscal strangulation by peripheral governments.[13]

This annexation power has hidden the growth of Houston's black and Hispanic populations. Because the city has been able to expand its boundaries and add the predominantly white populations on the urban fringes, the percentage of nonwhites is not as high as in other cities. Between 1950 and 1960, the black population in Houston increased from 125,400 to 215,037. By 1970 that figure was 316,922, and in 1980 it had increased to 440,257. Proportionally, however, from 1950 to 1980 the percentage of blacks in Houston only increased from 21 percent to 27.6 percent. Blacks generally live in the older parts of the city, but those upwardly mobile have imitated their white counterparts by moving to newer communities on the urban fringe.[14]

The Hispanic population is far more difficult to count because of the large number of undocumented workers and the different labels that the census placed on that group. In 1980, 281,244 people identified themselves as being of Spanish origin (compared to 149,727 Hispanics reported in the 1970 census), an increase of 87.9 percent, the fastest rate of any major population group. In 1960, Hispanics constituted 7 percent of the population; in 1970 they had jumped to 12 percent; and by 1980, they accounted for at least 17 percent of the city's population, not including the many illegal aliens who are often overlooked by the census. Hispanics concentrate in the older areas of the city, especially along the ship channel on the city's east side.[15]

Because of Houston's low density (about 3,300 people per square mile) and segregation by income and race, nonwhites are not visible on Houston's posh west side. The traditional black ghettos are the Third, Fourth, and Fifth wards in the city, but blacks, and to a lesser extent Hispanics, have been moving into previously all-white areas since the 1950s. As minorities move into these communities, the earlier inhabitants flee to the urban periphery. Although the minority communities have benefited from Houston's economic growth, they still have higher rates of unemployment, crime, and other negative indexes. Their incomes are lower than those in white communities. City services, generally minimal in order to reduce taxes, are inefficient in minority areas. Some of these communities lack paved streets and sewer service. The paucity of city services, although slowly being rectified, dates to the time when nonwhites were outside of the political process and power rested in the hands of a small group of businessmen.[16]

Houston's movers and shakers traditionally have been its businessmen who did not draw a fine line between their private interests and the interests of the city. To them, they were one and the same. From the early twentieth century to the late 1950s, a combination of elected officials and a half-dozen entrepreneurs guided the city. Dana Blakenhorn, a writer for the *Houston Business Journal*, described the scene:

> In the 1950s, Jesse Jones, Gus Wortham, Judge [James A.] Elkins, and others would drop by George Brown's private suite, number 8F in the Lamar Hotel, to drink, play cards or dominoes and to swap stories. Between them, the men in the "8F crowd" could run Houston, Texas, and the nation. They were friends with both senate majority leader Lyndon Johnson and house speaker Sam Rayburn.[17]

Jones was the owner of the afternoon *Houston Chronicle*, the former head of Roosevelt's Reconstruction Finance Corporation, and allegedly the owner at one time of half of downtown Houston. Judge Elkins was the founder of one of the city's major law firms and the guiding force behind the First National City Bank. George and Herman Brown founded and ran the construction and engineering firm of Brown and Root and controlled vital gas transmission pipelines. Wortham was the founder of the American General Life Insurance Company. Another member of the group was former Texas governor William P. Hobby, representing the family-owned *Houston Post*.

These men and their allies controlled the economic and political fortunes of the city of Houston. Their protégé, Watergate prosecutor Leon Jaworski, remembered when

. . . Jesse Jones, for instance, would meet Gus Wortham, Herman Brown and maybe one or two others and pretty well determine what the course of events would be in Houston, politically, particularly, and economically to some degree. I witnessed it then. I sat at the feet of these men. I was up in 8F often.[18]

The 8F Crowd could choke off campaign contributions to hostile office-seekers while raising huge war chests for the candidates with whom they agreed on basic economic and political issues. They concentrated their interest on bond issues and other aspects of city government that directly affected the economic status of the city. They set the city government on a course that encouraged rapid and essentially unregulated economic activity.

The last political campaign in which the 8F Crowd was able to exert its influence was the 1955 mayoral election between the flamboyant incumbent, Roy Hofheinz, and former mayor Oscar Holcombe, "the old Grey Fox." Holcombe had been first elected to that office in 1921 and had won an additional ten terms over a thirty-six-year period. Although the 8F Crowd supported Hofheinz in 1952, by 1955 his aggressive style turned the group to Holcombe, who won the election. In 1957, however, 8F support was not enough. Holcombe lost the election to newcomer Lewis Cutrer, partly because of the growing presence of black voters and partly because of the expanding nature of the city, which made it increasingly difficult for any one group to control the heterogeneous and numerically large electorate.[19]

Although the 8F Crowd no longer exists except in memory, political power in Houston is still based in the business community. That power is more diluted and it is increasingly shared with other groups, especially blacks and Hispanics. According to political scientists Robert Thomas and Richard Murray, "The city is run by a union of the city government and . . . the growth and development elite, who are defined as bankers, realtors, apartment owners, developers, investors, builders and large law firms." This progrowth faction consists of people "whose very good livelihoods depend on a local government that will continue to make the 'right' policy decisions." Surprisingly, the oil and gas industry remains aloof from local Houston politics, preferring to concentrate on the national and international policies crucial to its interests.[20]

The major campaign advantage for a Houston politician is the ability to raise sufficient funds. *Texas Monthly* reported in 1980 that Walter Mischer, chairman of the largest bank holding company in

Texas, was the "heir to the mantle of George R. Brown and James Elkins and, before them, Jesse Jones." According to the magazine, Mischer's money guaranteed the election of Houston's last three mayors prior to 1981. Financial support is critical in a city with 1.6 million people spread out over close to six hundred square miles. Only the media is able to reach and shape public opinion. During the 1970s, winners in mayoral contests spent between $750,000 and $1 million to obtain office, with most of that going for advertising.[21]

Other reasons for the preeminence of businessmen and developers in the power structure of the city are the legal framework of city elections and the popular consensus favoring economic growth and free enterprise. Houston has a nonpartisan municipal ballot and its campaigns are relatively short, technically lasting only thirty days from filing to voting. Even counting prefiling activities, the mayoral contest lasts no more than six months. Both the ballot and the timing discourage the rise of unknown candidates and the creation of local political organizations. Instead, candidates mount personal media campaigns, generally devoid of issues, and the best-known personality who conveys a positive media image usually wins.

On questions of growth, most Houstonians unite behind the policies of the community's business leaders. In part this has been true because of the city's traditional convervatism, which equated most government intervention in the economy with socialism. For example, in the last zoning campaign (1962), the antizoners branded land use controls as both socialistic and communistic. The recent victories of Fred Hofheinz (1973 and 1975) and Kathy Whitmire (1981) indicate that there is an additional factor that goes beyond right-wing rhetoric. People in Houston generally support the idea of economic growth and free enterprise. A large percentage of Houston's population, both white and black, has moved to the city in the past thirty years in the expectation of improving its economic condition. The culture and values of the city support the concept of unlimited economic opportunity provided by the business community. This consensus on the role of the private sector enables the business community to pursue a policy of economic growth. The citizens of Houston believe, as do the business leaders, that rapid growth is in their own best interests, as well as in the interests of the city.[22]

Blacks have played only minor roles in Houston politics. The white primary devalued the black vote until the Supreme Court outlawed it at the end of World War II. Thereafter, as blacks began to participate in the political process, the city's ability to annex white suburban areas, coupled with the at-large structure of the city council, generally offset growing black and Hispanic social and economic pressure. There have been indications that a modification of the traditional power structure has occurred.

In the mid 1970s, Fred Hofheinz (the son of Roy Hofheinz) won the mayor's post with the help of a coalition of minorities and white liberals. In 1979 the Justice Department of the United States ruled that Houston could continue to annex white suburban areas only if it modified its system of at-large elections. The department contended that at-large systems, coupled with annexation, discriminated against minorities by diluting their voting strength. This forced Houston to restructure its city council and to allow minorities more representation.[23]

Despite the victories of Fred Hofheinz and Kathy Whitmire and the revamping of the city council, the growth in minority voting clout does not automatically represent a challenge to the dominant business ethic of the city. Although power is increasingly shared with minorities and special interest groups, the minority leaders are often businessmen who share the basic values of their white contemporaries. The nexus of black political power in Houston is the Harris County Council of Organizations, which represents over eighty black business and civic organizations. Politically, blacks have obtained local and national representation but their power seems to be more symbolic than effective. For instance, Barbara Jordan became nationally known as a congresswoman from Houston, but her larger-than-life image was more stylistic than ideological; it was a reflection of the business consensus in Houston politics. Her congressional voting record tended to be liberal, but her stands were not dogmatic. Essentially she espoused a "solid, traditional political platform," fitting her role as a protégée of Lyndon Baines Johnson.[24]

Hispanics and labor leaders have not yet made their influence felt. The new generation of Hispanic leaders has developed a community or neighborhood base, but, due to the large number of illegal aliens and cultural traditions, the Hispanic community has not yet fully utilized its voting power. Union political activity, limited though it is, has been a minor factor in local politics in northeast Houston, close to the industries that line the ship channel.

Today, the downtown business establishment has been flexible enough to reach a consensus with the politically active special-interest groups. This establishment, represented by the Houston Chamber of Commerce, has managed to create a consensus on the efficacy of continued economic growth, thus limiting potential conflict. In fact, under the guidance of Louie Welch, a former mayor of Houston, the chamber has become a major political force in the city and has spearheaded a number of planning projects, ranging from mass transit to future studies.[25]

An illustration of the style of Houston politics appears in the changeover from an at-large system to a combination ward-based and at-large system. Until 1979, the voters elected eight council-members at large. This procedure prevented minorities from holding office. After the Justice Department ruling banning the at-large system, local special interest groups and minorities proposed a twenty-member council with only four at-large seats. The Chamber of Commerce, according to Rice University sociologist Chandler Davidson, opposed single-member districts, fearing a dilution of its influence. The chamber, therefore, backed a nine-and-five plan for a fourteen-seat council, including five at-large officeholders. Under this proposal, the citywide councilmembers required the support of only three district representatives to obtain a majority. The city adopted this compromise plan, and this illustrates the savvy and pragmatism of Houston's business leaders. Rather than blindly fight the Justice Department, the chamber sponsored a plan that conformed to Washington's demands but was not as radical as the sixteen-and-four plan. The city's voters then had the choice of voting for the federally discredited eight-member system or the new nine-and-five plan. Of course, the new plan won. Although the new council was the most diverse in Houston's history (three blacks, one Hispanic, and two white women among its fourteen members), a combination of at-large members and some district members has produced policies not radically different from its predecessors.[26]

From 1977 to 1981, the powerful office of chief executive was in the hands of Jim McConn, a former builder/developer, who withstood a series of scandals to win reelection in 1979. In 1981, however, McConn ran a poor fourth in the November primary. His successor is city comptroller Kathy Whitmire, who won a smashing victory (62 percent) in the mayoral runoff against Harris County's "law and order" sheriff. While many commentators perceived her victory as the beginning of a new era in Houston politics, that is really not the case. Rather than being the liberal politician who was going to buck the system, as some of her supporters hoped, Whitmire is a conservative who wants to revamp municipal government along the principles of business management. Rather than expanding the scope of government, the new mayor is simply attempting to make the government more efficient in the provision of existing services.[27]

That is going to be a difficult task. Whitmire inherited a government burdened by an image of mediocrity and facing serious problems. The lack of a mass transportation system has been exacerbated by increasingly clogged freeways. Because of Houston's rapid growth, an additional four hundred cars charge into Houston's traffic every day. According to *Texas Business*, at least one manufacturing firm recently abandoned plans to open a Houston facility because it concluded that the transportation problems would reduce employee productivity and slow the transfer of raw materials.[28]

Indicative of Houston's political style and basic values, it has been the private sector rather than the government that has begun to deal with service issues like transportation. The business establishment spearheaded the creation of the Metropolitan Transit Authority (MTA) in 1979, funded by a one-cent sales tax approved by the voters. This metropolitan authority is the first step, but its image of poor service has hampered its efforts. Problems with the new Grumman Flxible and General Motors' buses aggravated the situation. In 1982, the chamber unveiled its Regional Mobility Plan, a twenty-year, sixteen-billion-dollar plan to improve mobility in the Houston region. Furthermore, the MTA under its new director, Alan Kiepper, is planning the construction of an eighteen-mile, spine-corridor, heavy-rail system.[29]

Kiepper, who oversaw the construction of Atlanta's mass transit system, has been trying to improve bus service while supervising park-and-ride service, contraflow lanes, and other plans. How successful MTA and the chamber will be in implementing their plans without federal assistance remains to be seen. But given Houston's enterprising private sector and strong economic base, it is quite possible that in the long run Houston's traffic problems can be contained.[30]

Another problem arising from Houston's rapid growth is wastewater treatment. Presently, 70 percent of the city is under a sewer moratorium that limits wastewater hookups to five units per acre. Although the city's wastewater division is racing to keep up with Houston's growth, a new plant will not be able to treat Houston's wastes before 1984. Related problems, as in other American cities, include pollution of the groundwater and the atmosphere.[31]

Another problem is caused by Houston's geographic characteristics. Located on the Gulf plain only a few feet above sea level, Houston is plagued with the unusual and threatening problem of subsidence as well as flooding. Parts of Houston sank 7.5 feet between 1942 and 1973 as a result of pumping underground reserves for local consumption. Although subsidence has been slowed around the ship channel and in southern Harris County, sinkage is increasing in West Houston—the Galleria shopping area has settled a foot since 1973. Subsidence, local geologic conditions, and rapid growth have increased the incidence of flooding, always a problem in low-lying Gulf areas. In 1979, tropical storm Claudette created floods that caused an estimated $500 million in property damage. The last hurricane to hit Houston was in 1961, and unless the government and the private sector redouble their flood control efforts, some experts warn that the next hurricane will be a major disaster.[32]

Other problems include the provision of fresh water, an understaffed police force often accused of brutality, and a solid waste department that is unable to pick up the garbage due to political infighting and poor management. Yet Houston has great promise and its unique reliance on the private sector offers this country another way besides government to deal with urban ills. In Houston's expanding west side, private developers and corporations have formed the West Houston Association to plan the region in cooperation with county authorities. Their goal is planning, but through the business sector. In August, William C. Harvin, chairman of the board of the Houston Chamber of Commerce, called for an expanded role for the private sector to meet the problems of the future. "We have reached the point now," Harvin declared, "that there has to be more comprehensive planning and there has to be some architect for the future of the city. The private sector must seize the initiative. Whether by default or desire, I submit, that must become the role for the Chamber. . . . instead of simply reacting . . . we can anticipate what's going to happen in the city and see to it that proper plans are carried out."[33]

If any city can implement private planning and meet the needs of the future through private enterprise, Houston is that city. A city that emphasizes individualism and free enterprise, a private city in the sense that urban historian Sam Bass Warner, Jr., used that term, Houston is the product of enterprising businessmen who implemented new technology and conducted their affairs with a minimum of government interference. Although partially a product of federal governmental policies, Houston's culture and values emphasize the role of free enterprise in creating and maintaining the nation's fifth largest city. The ability of the city's business/political elites to meet the urban service problems while diversifying its economy will be a test of Houston's corporate government and traditions. The success or failure of the Golden Buckle will be a testimony to the efficacy of the business culture and its commitment to the city. If it is successful, Houston will be the premier American city by the next century, offering other cities an alternative to traditional public sector activities. If it fails, the Golden Buckle will just be another case of what could have been.

NOTES

1. Melinda Beck and Ronald Henkoff, "A City's Growing Pains," *Newsweek*, 14 January 1980; *Houston Chronicle* (hereafter cited as *Chronicle*), 31 December 1980; George B. Tindall, "The Sunbelt Snow Job," *Houston Review* 1 (Spring 1979): 3–13; Barbara McIntosh, "Houston: Boomtown, U.S.A.," *Houston Post* (hereafter cited as *Post*), 24 September 1978, 15 February 1981. Various reports and pamphlets of the Houston Chamber of Commerce, Rice University Center, and the U.S. Census Bureau are used throughout this essay but are not cited specifically.

2. David McComb, *Houston: The Bayou City* (Austin: University of Texas Press, 1969); Marilyn McAdams Sibley, *The Port of Houston* (Austin: University of Texas Press, 1968); Joanne Harrison, "Galveston, 1900," *Houston City* (July 1980): 70ff.

3. Port of Houston Authority, *Port of Houston Handbook* (1980); Warren Rose, *the Economic Impact of the Port of Houston* (Houston: Houston Center for Business and Economics, 1965); *Chronicle*, 19 April 1981; *Port of Houston Magazine* (March 1981); *Houston Monthly Statistical Summary* (February 1981).

4. McComb, *Bayou City*, 113–118.

5. Ibid., 203–205; James Stafford, "Behind the NASA Move to Houston," *Texas Business Review* 36 (April 1962); *Chronicle*, 16 June 1980; Richard Murray, "Politics of a Boomtown," *Dissent* (Fall 1980): 500–504.

6. Murray, "Politics of a Boomtown," 500.

7. *Chronicle*, 15 February 1981; *U.S. News and World Report*, 27 November 1978, 47; Alfred J. Watkins, "Good Business Climates, the Second War between the States," *Dissent* (Fall 1980): 476–485; George N. Green, "The Union Movement in the Southwest," *Dissent* (Fall 1980): 485–492; Richard Murray, "Houston: Politics of a Boomtown," *Chronicle*, 1 February, 29 March 1981.

8. Barry J. Kaplan, "Urban Development, Economic Growth, and Personal Liberty: The Rhetoric of the Houston Anti-Zoning Movements, 1947–1962," *Southwestern Historical Quarterly* 84 (October 1980): 133–168; *Post*, 21 April 1980; *Chronicle*, 5 October 1978.

9. Nicholas Lemann, "Super Medicine," *Texas Monthly* (April 1979): 110–130ff.; *U.S. News and World Report*, 27 November 1978, 47–48; Charles O. Cook and Barry J. Kaplan, "Civic Elites and Urban Planning: Houston's River Oaks," *East Texas Historical Journal* 15 (1977).

10. George Fuermann, *Houston: The Once and Future City* (Garden City, N.Y.: Doubleday and Co., 1971), 20–25; James E. Buchanan, *Houston: A Chronological and Documentary History* (Dobbs Ferry, N.Y.: Oceana Publishers, 1975); Howard La Fay, "Texas!" *National Geographic* 157 (April

1980): 457–460; Houston Planning Department, *Housing Analysis: Low-Moderate Income Areas* (1978); *Post*, 15 November 1980; *Chronicle*, 15 November 1980.

11. Watkins, "Good Business Climates"; Green, "The Union Movement"; Murray, "Politics of a Boomtown."

12. Texas Commerce Bancshares, *Texas Facts and Figures*, 10th ed., A-9; Houston Planning Commission, *Land, Population Growth* (1951); R. L. Polk Co., *Houston City Directory* (1970); Murray, "Politics of a Boomtown," 500.

13. *U.S. News and World Report*, 27 November 1978, 47–48.

14. Chandler Davidson, *Biracial Politics: Conflict and Coalition in the Metropolitan South* (Baton Rouge: Louisiana State University Press, 1973); Barry J. Kaplan, "Race, Income, and Ethnicity: Residential Change in a Houston Community, 1920–1970," *Houston Review* 3 (Winter 1981): 178–203; *Chronicle*, 27 March 1981.

15. Houston Public Library, *Invisible in Houston* (1978); *New York Times*, 17 December 1977; Beck and Henkoff, "A City's Growing Pains"; *Post*, 12 June 1979; *Chronicle*, 27 March 1981.

16. *Chronicle*, 6 April 1980; *Post*, 12 June, 30 December 1979; Richard West, "Only the Strong Survive," *Texas Monthly* (February 1979): 94–105ff.; William Broyles, "The Making of Barbara Jordan," *Texas Monthly* (October 1976): 129.

17. Dana Blakenhorn, "Houston's Founding Fortunes," *Houston Business Journal*, 19 March 1979, 3.

18. Craig Smyser, "Houston's Power," *Chronicle*, 27 (quote), 28–30 June, 1 July 1977.

19. Ken Parker, "Return of the 'Old Gray Fox': The Political Decline and Revival of Mayor Oscar F. Holcombe, 1940–1947" (Unpublished research paper, University of Houston, 1981).

20. *Post*, 24 September 1978, 30 December 1979 (quote); Murray, "Politics of a Boomtown," 502; Patricia Sharpe, "The Kingmaker," *Texas Monthly* (February 1980): 60–64; Stan Redding, "Louie Welch," *Chronicle*, 3 February 1980, *Texas Magazine* section; Lynn Bracewell, "Sanctuaries of Power," *Houston City* (May 1980): 50–55, 90.

21. Sharpe, "The Kingmaker," 60; Murray, "Politics of a Boomtown," 502; Smyser, "Houston's Power."

22. Murray, "Politics of a Boomtown," 502–503; Kaplan, "Houston Anti-Zoning Movements," 159–164; Willie Morris, "Houston's Super-Patriots," *Harper's Magazine* 223 (October 1962): 48–56; Don E. Carlton, "McCarthyism in Houston: The George Ebey Affair," *Southwestern Historical Quarterly* 53 (October 1976); Buchanan, *A Chronological and Documentary History.*

23. Chandler Davidson, "Reforming a Reform: The Attack on Multimember Districts," in Merle Black and John Shelton Reed, eds., *Perspectives on the American South*, vol. 1 (New York: Gordon and Breach Science Publishers, 1981), 143–149.

24. Walter Shapiro, "What Does This Woman Want?" *Texas Monthly* (October 1976): 134–135ff.; Broyles, "The Making of Barbara Jordan," 127, 132 (quote).

25. Smyser, "Houston's Power"; Reddings, "Louie Welch."

26. Davidson, "Reforming a Reform."

27. *Post*, 12 June 1979; *Chronicle*, 22 March 1979; Murray, "Politics of a Boomtown"; Kaye Northcutt, "Wish You Were Here," *Houston City* (December 1980): 54–58ff.

28. Geoffrey Leavenworth, "Houston: Will It Choke on Its Own Success?" *Texas Business* (December 1980): 28–36; John Bloom, "Letter from Houston: The Good, the Bad, and the Ugly," *Texas Monthly* (August 1979): 68–70.

29. *Wall Street Journal*, 11 July 1980.

30. Patrick Jankowski, "MTA's New Driver," *Houston* (August 1982).

31. Joel Warren Barna, "Factory Air," *Houston City* (September 1980): 32–38ff.; Bloom, "Letter from Houston," 68–70; Leavenworth, "Houston: Will It Choke," 29–33; Alan Waldman, "Water Hazards," *Houston City* (June 1980): 52–57.

32. Ryan Bernard, "The Last Wave," *Houston City* (July 1980): 65–69ff.; Beck and Henkoff, "A City's Growing Pains."

33. 5 August 1982 text courtesy of the Houston Chamber of Commerce.

8

OKLAHOMA CITY

BOOMING SOONER

by Richard M. Bernard

Oklahoma City's modern history began in 1947. Since the city's founding on a spring day fifty-eight years earlier, the citizens of the one-day Sooner capital had placed their hopes for prosperity in the hands of the area's business leaders. In 1947 those men moved to secure the future for themselves and their fellow citizens.

"Born grown" in the Indian Territory land run of 22 April 1889, Oklahoma Station, as it was then known, exploded from a one-building railroad stop to a town of twelve thousand in one remarkable afternoon. After several decades of uncertainty accompanying the general rowdiness of frontier life, Oklahoma City experienced a second take-off in the 1920s. Based on vast petroleum discoveries in and around the city, this boom might have thrust the Sooner capital into regional leadership in the Southwest had not wind and Wall Street intervened. Instead of experiencing prosperity, the state suffered a decade of dust and depression. Revived, however, both in patriotic spirit and in pocketbook by the Second World War, postwar Oklahoma Cityans again looked optimistically to the future and turned to their business leaders for guidance.

Established before the municipal government, the Oklahoma City Chamber of Commerce won the people's respect over the years. But in 1947 a revitalized chamber began to act vigorously to insure their livelihoods. Beginning with the city elections in the spring of that year, the chamber took steps to renew its hold over government. The chamber's leaders offered funeral director Allen Street as a candidate for mayor, and the voters dutifully ratified their selection. In April, Street began the first of his twelve years in office, pledged to continue the harmony that his predecessor had nurtured between city hall and the business community. It was, in fact, the Chamber of Commerce, backed by elected officials, that would control the city's, and indeed the region's, postwar maturity.

Under the leadership of the chamber's managing director, Stanley Draper, one of the nation's most remarkable urban builders, businessmen acted in 1947 to tie the area's economic development to air transportation. That year, the chamber guaranteed the landings of a steady stream of commercial carriers by securing a Federal Skyways Flight Pattern centered on the city's Will Rogers Airport. This advance followed the wartime acquisition of Tinker Field, a major maintenance and refueling base, and the 1946 capture of the Civil Aeronautics Administration's training school for air traffic controllers. These efforts secured Oklahoma City's place in the air age and foreshadowed the enormous growth and industrial expansion that lay ahead.

The city government supported the chamber in its development promotions, and in 1947 that elected body took the first steps toward massive annexation and urban renewal programs that would soon merit national acclaim. The council began consideration of the Bartholomew Plan, which governed postwar development, and, in a separate move, adopted a major street design that committed the city to today's modern freeway system. Symbolic of the times, the lethargic old trolleys ceased their intracity runs the same month that Street took office.

But the city's business leaders did not control all change. In the fall, the United States Supreme Court heard arguments in the case of *Sipuel* v. *Regents of the University of Oklahoma*. The resulting court order, requiring the admission of Ada Sipuel, a black woman, to the university's law school in Norman, hastened an end to the nation's Jim Crow era and set the stage for integration in nearby Oklahoma City.

Thus, by the end of 1947, all of the major events in the city's postwar history were in motion. Business leaders had reinforced their hold over the area's destiny by securing a friendly government, initiating a substantial economic development program, and laying the groundwork for enormous territorial expansion and urban redevelopment. Only in the realm of civil rights was the chamber unaware of the portents of change, yet even there businessmen, not politicians, would make the inevitable adjustments for progress.

Postwar Oklahoma City was the nation's most homogeneous urban area and one of its most socially conservative. Aside from the oil derricks on the lawn of the state capitol, journalist John Gunther found the city most distinctive for its Waspish complexion. He noted that it has the highest percentage of native-born whites among all major U.S. cities, though he delighted in reporting also that it was the only locale to require wartime venereal disease testing of its entire adult citizenry (a result of the liberties granted local service-

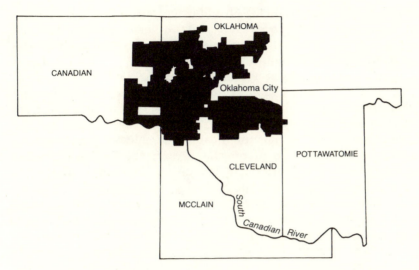

MAP 8.1. The Oklahoma City SMSA

men). From a population of only 200,000 in an urban area of fewer than a quarter million before the war, Oklahoma City grew to over 240,000 in a metropolitan region of just under 400,000 by mid century. The city was about 91 percent white and the suburbs about 96 percent, figures that changed little in the next four decades. American Indians made up less than 2 percent of the urbanized population. Upper- and middle-class families made their homes on the north and northwest sides of the city; blacks, most of whom were quite poor, lived on the east side; working-class whites scattered about but dominated the area below the North Canadian River, which bisects the community.

Conservative, Democratic, and overwhelmingly Protestant (predominantly Baptist and Methodist), the city, which like many claimed to "buckle the Bible Belt," boasted over two hundred churches including at least one with a then shocking neon sign. Oklahoma offered virtually no night life and tolerated no legal liquor, although bootlegged booze was easy to find. It was an outgoing, friendly city that lacked great extremes of wealth. It was a family town of rodeos, Split-T football, and barbecues, a southwestern roasting of "anything that doesn't move or squeak."[1]

Oklahoma City was also a businessman's town, with a frontier predilection against governmental activity, a deep-seated distrust of organized labor, and a polite indifference to minorities. Constant reinforcement of these conservative values came from the Oklahoma

Publishing Company (OPUBCO) and its powerful owner, E. K. Gaylord. Called the "town's boss man" and the "leading press lord of his state," Gaylord personally supervised the city's two daily newspapers, its leading radio outlet, and its first television station. Until the day he died in 1974 at age 101, Gaylord held decisive influence over public opinion in Oklahoma by limiting the scope of reporting and editorially stressing widely shared conservative views on politics, economics, society, and religion. His front-page editorials in the *Daily Oklahoman* (perhaps the most memorable being an extended series exposing a Russian submarine threat in the Caribbean, which the rest of the nation overlooked) denounced liberalism in all alleged forms and set the political tone of the city and state.[2]

Despite his immense power, Gaylord did not rule alone. Through most of the postwar period, the publisher shared community decision making with four other men: Stanley Draper and board chairmen Dean A. McGee of the Kerr-McGee Corporation, Donald S. Kennedy of Oklahoma Gas and Electric Company, and Charles A. Vose, Sr., of the First National Bank. Upon E. K. Gaylord's death, his son Edward L. Gaylord took over the family businesses and joined the inner circle. Many believe that he also replaced his father as the most powerful man in the state.

There are several reasons why Oklahoma Cityans turned over public leadership to this unelected, elite corps and the Chamber of Commerce that it controlled. Free enterprise reigned supreme in the Sooner State where people put more faith in successful businessmen than in their detractors. Because of the city's low percentage of industrial workers, labor unions were weak. Racial minorities and immigrants were scarce, and a tax-conscious electorate kept down the number of civil servants. In other words, virtually none of the usual groups to challenge urban business leadership could muster much strength in Oklahoma City. Few politicians dared oppose the centralized authority of the chamber and the Gaylord media. Why should they? A conservative populace steeped in deference was uninterested in alternatives.

After a period of turmoil in the 1930s, Oklahoma City officials closed ranks behind the chamber during the administration of Mayor Robert A. Hefner (1939–1947). Aside from his work on a new city reservoir, which today bears his name, Hefner assumed a symbolic role as head of government in classic council-manager system. Serving mainly as a conciliator between the city council and the chamber, Hefner left planning and policy development to the latter and general administration to the city manager. When the seventy-three-year-old mayor and former judge decided to retire, he "asked the business group to look around and agree upon a man to succeed me." That man was Allen Street.[3]

The mild-mannered Street emulated Hefner's low-keyed approach to governing. Oklahoma City grew and prospered during the Street administration, but the credit belonged to the chamber and not to the mayor. Yet, despite his inoffensiveness, Street met considerable opposition in his reelection bids from a friend, maverick councilmember Walter M. Harrison. Harrison, the "Old Skipper" to his readers, had been managing editor of the *Daily Oklahoman* before breaking with Gaylord. In the mid 1950s, he ran a weekly northside newspaper. Street led Harrison by only 4,300 votes in the 1951 primary, after which Street's aides convinced Harrison that the mayor's heart condition could not withstand a rugged runoff campaign. The sympathetic Harrison withdrew. A wiser Harrison led Street in the 1955 primary by campaigning on several issues, including the "under cover control of the council by *The Daily Oklahoman*, the First National Bank and the Chamber of Commerce." Such a frontal attack on the business elite by a major candidate was unique in Oklahoma City's modern history. Despite Gaylord's ridicule and the refusal of the OPUBCO papers and stations to cover his campaign, the "Old Skipper" almost won the runoff. Street took 20,592 votes to Harrison's 19,505.[4]

Standing apart from these political wars was an unelected figure of more importance. Caretaker of the city's business interests for nearly a half century was the gnomelike North Carolinian Stanley Draper. Hired as the chamber's membership secretary in 1919, he emerged as the guiding figure by the mid 1920s and served as managing director (1931–1967) and executive vice-president (1967–1969). Draper became the region's prime vehicle for economic growth as he pioneered industrial procurement, territorial expansion, and urban renewal. Under Draper, the chamber's agenda became the city's agenda, so much so that in 1967 the state House of Representatives designated him "Mr. Oklahoma City."[5]

Draper began the chamber's industrial recruitment program in 1920 when he attracted Taggart Bakery to the city. Under his leadership over the next ten years, the city won a name change from Oklahoma Station to Oklahoma City, gained a centralized state highway system through the capital, multiplied convention business sixfold, created the area's first public construction trust to finance the Stockyards Coliseum, and initiated Will Rogers Airport. During the depression, he began work on the reservoir that became Lake Hefner. At the war's outset, the chamber set its sights on either a major military installation or an aircraft factory, but Draper obtained both Tinker Field and a Douglas Aircraft assembly plant. After V-J Day, Tinker absorbed the bomber factory and hinted at major personnel reductions. Draper then convinced the Civil Aeronautics Administration to locate its training center in Oklahoma City and thereby minimized unemployment problems.[6]

In the late 1940s, Draper concentrated on highway development and water procurement, which he believed were essential to retain Tinker, by far the state's largest employer, and to solicit manufacturers. Relying on the chamber's planning department, which dwarfed the city's own agency, Draper produced designs for a network of interstate highways. Coordinating city, county, and state governments with the lure of federal funding, Draper kept his promise to the Pentagon for defense highways around Tinker as the first links in the system. This action unleashed a chain of displacements culminating in a new state fairgrounds, a relocated black high school, and an industrial park. By the late 1960s, the chamber had initiated five major highway projects. A decade later, the interstate road system was complete except for a central expressway and a northwest passage around the city, both of which faced prolonged neighborhood opposition.[7] In the meantime, the city inaugurated an elaborate pumping system to bring water to nearby Lake Stanley Draper. Although Oklahoma City's rainfall was well below the nation's average, Draper's foresight prevented any need for water rationing in the Sooner capital. In the late 1970s and early 1980s, no other major city escaped that burden.[8]

Draper's greatest accomplishment was his successful promotion of economic growth. An industrial development program "unequaled in the U.S." germinated in 1945 when the chamber founded the profit-making Oklahoma Industries, Inc. Beginning with the construction of a warehouse for the locally based TG&Y department stores, Oklahoma Industries sold and leased development property on very favorable terms. Purchasing the land secretly, allegedly to prevent price inflation, the firm handled over 350 commercial and industrial projects between 1954 and 1964, highlighted by the arrival of Western Electric and General Electric branch plants.

In the 1960s, Oklahoma Industries begot new, nonprofit successors that were able to exploit a recent change in state law permitting public development trusts to raise funds by issuing bonds without voter approval. Operating under county commissioners, these agencies copied a system widely used in the South and sold low-interest but tax-exempt bonds to bankers and other investors. The proceeds went to purchase potentially valuable property. When private firms bought, or more commonly leased, the land and facilities owned by the trusts, their payments went to reimburse the bond-holders. In effect, the companies financed expansion at the low interest rates accorded industrial revenue bonds, and thus saved millions over commercial borrowing. Moreover, by renting their land and buildings, the companies left ownership in the hands of the non-profit trusts and thereby avoided ad valorem taxation. The Oklahoma City Industrial and Cultural Facilities Trust (1962) used this approach to finance construction for such divergent concerns as Ling-Temco-Vought and the National Cowboy Hall of Fame. Between its founding in 1966 and 1982, the Oklahoma Industries Authority (OIA) floated $250 million in bonds. Its help proved instrumental in the addition of General Motors, Firestone Tire, Dayton Tire, Lear-Siegler, and Hertz Rent-a-Car to the city directory, if not to the tax rolls. According to OIA chairman Edward L. Gaylord, the trust's bonding authority was "the only thing in the last twenty-five years to attract new business to Oklahoma." Chamber director Paul Strasbaugh estimated that the OIA's past efforts accounted for twelve percent of the city's 1981 employment.[9]

But the industrial development program has had its critics. As early as the mid 1960s, businessmen in competition with OIA-supported companies questioned the propriety of the government favoring one firm over another. How could nonsubsidized businesses compete with those blessed with low-interest financing and tax concessions? Later, school districts complained of lost property tax revenues, a contributing factor to the state's then embarrassingly low teachers' salaries. Others questioned the potential for conflicts of interest in decisions made by trustees who stood to benefit by their own actions.

No one directly challenged the trusts, however, until 1978 when state attorney general Jan Eric Cartwright removed the tax exemption of companies located on trust properties. His opinion, since sustained by the state supreme court (although again under challenge), cited the Oklahoma constitution's requirement of equal apportionment of taxes. Cartwright also disallowed sales-tax exemptions on industrial equipment purchased by the trusts and obtained a state supreme court order opening the OIA's records as a means of investigating alleged conflicts of interest among trustees.

Recently, independent journalists reported that several OIA directors, notably Chairman Gaylord, banker Charles Vose, utility man Donald Kennedy, and soft-drink distributor Stanton Young, owned shares in companies that did business with the OIA, a violation of state law. Drawing heavily on Kerry Kelly's investigative series in the now defunct *Oklahoma Journal*, KOCO-TV doggedly reported every known detail of these charges in spite of losing nearly $100,000 in advertising from Vose's First National Bank and the OPUBCO newspapers. Gaylord claimed that no member of the trust ever voted on funding for one of his own companies, but Attorney General Cartwright responded that nearly all firms aided by the OIA had some tie to one or more of the trust's directors, a view endorsed by a local investigative reporter. According to University of Tulsa finance professor Michael Joehnk, the state "leads the nation" in industrial revenue bond abuses, and even OIA general manager Jess Metheny admits that "I can't stand on a stack of Bibles and say everything has been white." [10]

The OIA's allies accused Cartwright of destroying its industrial development program by forcing the state to renege on promises of tax concessions to new businesses. Attorneys for the trust accused Cartwright of "strident rhetoric" and "downright slanderous statements" painted with a "tar brush." In August 1982, Cartwright lost his bid for reelection when a Gaylord-backed candidate defeated him in the Democratic primary. Gaylord has attacked KOCO-TV for resorting to the "communistic tactic" of the "big lie" and for "picking on top civic leaders." Meanwhile, pressure on local journalists became intense. In 1976, Gaylord's radio station WKY pulled an overeager reporter off his OIA investigation. Station KTOK, faced with threats of advertising cancellations, discouraged a reporter from producing a documentary on the trust, but later changed its position and allowed another to proceed. Because of their efforts, reporters Vince Orza (KOCO-TV) and Terri Watkins (KTOK) received threats to their careers. [11]

Only a few politicians have dared to challenge the industrial development program. One of these, attorney Merton M. Bulla, ran for mayor in 1959, questioning utility rate hikes and contract negotiations with the Federal Aviation Administration (successor to the CAA). Backed by organized labor, Bulla at first appeared to have run second in the March primary and won a runoff spot. His success, however, proved illusory. Despite the lack of legal sanction for a recount, third-place finisher James H. Norick secured one from a county election board that included his supporters. In the second tally, Norick passed Bulla by one vote. The board then denied Bulla a second recount. This action limited the voters' choice to two candidates acceptable to the business community. Norick, a printing company executive, won. [12]

Controversy marked Norick's first administration as the chamber led the city into a massive annexation program during times of racial and political strife. On New Year's Day 1959, Oklahoma City

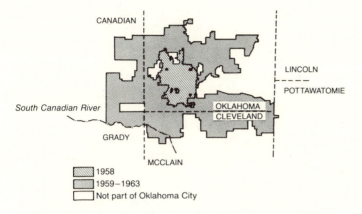

CANADIAN

LINCOLN

POTTAWATOMIE

South Canadian River

OKLAHOMA
CLEVELAND

GRADY

MCCLAIN

1958
1959–1963
Not part of Oklahoma City

MAP 8.2. Oklahoma City Annexations, 1959–1963

SOURCE: Thomas M. Ballentine, "The Oklahoma City Annexation Program, 1958–1963, Purposes, Processes and Planning Implications," M.A. thesis, University of Oklahoma, 1964, p. 31.

encompassed eighty square miles, about 40 percent more territory than a decade earlier. In the next two years, the Sooner capital grew to 430 square miles, and by 1963, the year that Norick left office, the city covered 641.5 square miles, reflecting an astonishing four-year growth rate of over 700 percent. For a brief time in the 1960s, Oklahoma City was the nation's biggest city in land area, nearly three times the size of Chicago. At 637 square miles, it remains today the largest aside from those that have consolidated boundaries with counties or other larger units of government (see Map 8.2).

The chamber planned, financed, and executed the entire annexation drive. The city council played no role in this process except that of voting to add the properties that the chamber designated.

Two factors motivated the chamber leadership. As early as 1943, Draper had fretted over suburban incorporations and the resulting uncontrolled peripheral development that he thought would damage the area's economic growth. The chamber had placed Tinker Field east of the city's boundary, a move that had allowed private developer W. P. ("Bill") Atkinson to construct and incorporate Midwest City next to the base. Fearing that Atkinson's suburban residents might constrict Tinker's flight patterns and thereby jeopardize the base's existence, Draper fumed about the need for the chamber and its city to control more land. He sought to protect Tinker, Will Rogers Airport, and nearby lakes and to provide enough room for industrial expansion within the city proper.

Then there was the problem of maintaining a solid tax base for the central city. As well as any urban leader in America, Draper foresaw the flight of businesses and wealthy taxpayers to the suburbs and the accompanying loss of city revenues. He sought to prevent Oklahoma City from ever becoming landlocked by incorporated suburbs and financially strangled like so many northern cities.

Aided by the laxity of state laws and the economic clout of the chamber, Draper persuaded a hesitant city council and a reluctant Mayor Norick to gobble up most of the surrounding territory. Norick and four councilmen preferred a go-slow approach, but chamber leaders impressed upon them both the urgency and workability of their program. In Oklahoma, big-city annexation was easy and cheap. The law allowed municipalities to take contiguous property on receipt of a petition from a majority of the resident owners or one from 75 percent of the legal voters plus the owners of 75 percent of the land in value. The chamber rounded up signatures for these petitions, sometimes purchasing key properties to gain the proper percentage of signers. A city could also add land without the owner's permission if the municipality bordered the desired property on three sides. The chamber calculated land purchases to surround and capture recalcitrants. Finally, under easily invoked emergency conditions, a major city could capture territory with only one reading of an annexation ordinance, and this Oklahoma City did to allow property owners no time to fight incorporation. The city's cost was minimal because Oklahoma law did not require a full extension of services to the acquired land.

At first, the chamber's planning department plotted the annexation, parcel by parcel, with little opposition. Councilmembers fell in line and few citizens complained, largely because the chamber kept its operations under wraps until action was complete. When Oklahoma City reached the outskirts of neighboring towns, however, those communities went on the counterattack. Edmond, Norman, and other suburbs that previously had had little desire to expand, annexed fringe areas in part to provide relief for threatened farmers and in part to assure their own independence. The chamber's well-financed legal arm overwhelmed many of these efforts, but not all. In Edmond, called by one journalist "a microcosm of the Sun Belt," city attorney Robert T. Rice blocked Oklahoma City's expansion to the northeast almost single-handedly by supervising his town's annexation of over fifty square miles. Other cities made remarkable headway by confronting landowners with the limited alternatives of joining either city or suburb. One such community, El Reno (population 15,448), now contains more land area (126 square miles) than

Boston and St. Louis combined. In the end, the suburbs succeeded in adjoining the city on most sides and stopping its expansion. By the time the dust settled, an area equivalent to the size of three counties fell within the municipal boundaries of the city and suburbs.[13]

Although territorial acquisition outstripped population growth, the influx of newcomers in the third quarter of the century was almost as notable. People flocked to this petroleum oasis, drawn by climate, lifestyle, and, until 1982, by profits on oil and gas production that generated thousands of jobs. The mid 1981 city unemployment rate stood at 2.6 percent, second lowest in the nation, though the falling petroleum market has since pushed that figure upward. As a result, the Sooner capital and its suburbs exceeded state and national growth rates in every postwar census. In 1960, the city counted 325,000 in a metropolitan population that passed the half-million mark. Ten years later, 370,000 people called Oklahoma City home, about 100,000 more than lived in outlying areas. In the most recent accounting, however, the suburban population surpassed the city total for the first time. The city reached 400,000 but another 430,000 bedded down in neighboring towns and housing additions, which now stretch thirty miles in most directions from downtown. White-collar workers predominate on the city's north side, but they also push into the northern and western suburbs and south of the river as well. Wealthier families have moved westward, but more and more they are discovering Edmond to the northeast. Blue-collar whites permeate the south side, but spread both northward and southward into the suburbs. To the far southeast, however, income and educational levels rise in the vicinity of Norman and the University of Oklahoma. Fewer than 15 percent of the city dwellers are black, and nearly all of these live on the east side. Some have bought homes in the eastern suburbs, but blacks still constitute only 4 percent of the suburban population. Indians, who are widely scattered, represent 3 percent of the area's population.

Until 14 August 1958 black people were the least advantaged and most quiescent citizens of the metropolitan region. Restricted by both law and private agreements to the run-down homes of the city's east side, postwar blacks lived segregated lives. City ordinances, upheld in court as late as 1944, prohibited blacks from moving into blocks with white majorities, and houses around the black area carried deeds that allowed for their sale only to Caucasians. Some blacks did live elsewhere, but most were born on the east side (or in one of the four hospitals that admitted blacks) and grew up there. They attended segregated schools, churches, and movie theaters. They played and read in all-black parks and libraries, and they learned to call friends from "colored" phone booths. As adults, they worked at menial jobs when they could, but some entire industries, notably oil, virtually banned them. A few blacks, nearly two hundred at the close of the war, became professionals, but there were never many of these, and most were teachers or ministers. When death came, and it arrived much sooner for blacks, they found their rest in segregated cemetery lots. Blacks lacked the voting strength to change these conditions, and at any rate, many recognized black leaders preferred the rewards of segregated politics to the uncertainties of confrontation.[14]

Given such a heritage, black and white Oklahomans greeted with remarkable calm the United States Supreme Court's 1954 school desegregation ruling in *Brown* v. *Topeka Board of Education*. In fact, physical resistance to integration was so lacking in this border state that its absence became newsworthy. A courageous Governor Raymond Gary integrated state offices and with the help of the legislature immediately eliminated the state's dual educational funding system. The Oklahoma City School Board voted unanimously to end the legal mandate for segregation. Such measures seemed enough to whites, but for blacks they marked only the beginning.[15]

The real turning point in the city's race relations came on that late summer night in 1958 when school teacher Clara Luper drove eight black children downtown to Katz Drug Store. All took seats at the soda fountain, and, when the management refused service, they remained to initiate the nation's first civil-rights sit-in demonstration, a year and a half before the better-known Greensboro incident. Three days later, Katz gave in and the Oklahoma City desegregation movement had its first triumph.

Over the next six years Luper and the NAACP Youth Council that she advised led an extensive campaign of sit-ins, protest marches, and negotiations with business leaders, including a seminal 1961 meeting between the city's two most powerful women, Luper and Mrs. John A. Brown, owner of the city's largest department store. Other black organizations joined in and new leaders, such as E. Melvin Porter, emerged. The main targets were whites-only eating establishments, and from August 1960 to the following July blacks attempted to boycott all downtown stores in order to force dry-goods merchants to pressure restaurateurs to desegregate. The boycott failed because blacks had virtually nowhere else to shop, but the larger movement succeeded. In July 1964, before passage of the federal Civil Rights Act, black leaders surveyed local dining places and declared victory when they found no racial bans.[16]

In March 1960, Governor J. Howard Edmondson formed a state commission to soothe tensions in Oklahoma City and elsewhere. By contrast, Mayor Norick and the council refused to act on the issue of civil rights and forefeited leadership to individual businessmen. Doubtless their inaction prolonged the conflict. However, a new council, elected in 1963, feared the impact of the movement on the area's image and economic growth and took action. Having "learned the lesson of Little Rock" where industrial expansion stagnated, these new leaders urged racial moderation. They supported city manager Robert Tinstman in establishing a municipal human relations commission, barring discrimination in city hiring, and improving police/community relations. In 1964, the council approved a public accommodations ordinance similar to the recent federal law. In 1969, a new council also took its cue from Washington and passed a mild Fair Housing Ordinance.

One bit of unfinished business remained: school integration. The end of de jure school segregation brought little practical change due to a formal policy of neighborhood schools and an informal one of busing outlying black children to black neighborhoods. To remedy this injustice, black optometrist A. L. Dowell sued in October 1961 for admission of his son to Northeast High, the white school in his attendance district. A year later the suit went to federal district Judge Luther Bohanon, who over the next fifteen years personally forced Oklahoma City schools to integrate as thoroughly as those of any other large American city. While critics screamed and hung the judge in effigy, Bohanon rejected proposal after proposal from the school board and ordered the pairing of white and black schools, accompanied by massive busing. School integration began in 1967, with the final desegregation plan taking effect in 1972. Not until five years later was Bohanon sufficiently convinced of the school board's good faith to withdraw from the case. Educational results remain unclear, but opponents point to the resegregation of city schools resulting from white flight to suburbs and "Christian" academies. Enrollment in the public schools dropped from 75,000 in the mid 1960s to 40,000 today while the black student proportion climbed from 15 percent in 1961 to over one-third in 1981.[17]

By the late 1960s, the civil-rights movement, both nationally and locally, focused on economic concerns. Following the well-publicized Memphis sanitation strike, Oklahoma City's black leaders endorsed a garbage workers' strike in August 1969. Characteristically, business leaders settled the dispute. Stanton Young and Paul Strasbaugh, then Draper's assistant at the Chamber of Commerce, negotiated on behalf of the city and reached a compromise agreement with the strikers. The nation's Black Power movement, however, never made inroads in Oklahoma City where moderates retained control. As in other southern and border cities, blacks in the Sooner capital concentrated on building black businesses and electing candidates to public office. In 1964, state senator Porter joined Oklahoma City representatives Archibald Hill and John B. White and Tulsan Curtis Lawson as the first blacks elected to the Oklahoma legislature since 1908.

The time was right for the emergence of black political leadership, for the city's politics were in flux. In addition to the annexation and civil-rights controversies, businesses and press spokesmen accused the Norick council of shortsightedness, contentiousness, and misbehavior. The last charge applied to city hiring and the letting of noncompetitive contracts. OPUBCO alleged in particular that some councilmen had built personal machines by forcing the city manager to employ their supporters in the sanitation department and elsewhere.

In 1962, citizens concerned about inefficiency, corruption, and the city's lack of power in the state legislature formed a grass-roots reform organization, the Association for Responsible Government (ARG). Although most were professionals or businessmen, the ARG founders were not part of the local elite. They were less wealthy and less socially prominent. Many had attended out-of-state colleges and were new to Oklahoma City. Yet within a year, these people enlisted over five thousand members in their good government movement.

ARG entered the 1963 city elections. They drafted nonpolitical civic leaders (the "best men") to run for office and financed their campaigns with membership fees and donations from sources kept secret from the candidates. The organization arranged to disband right after the runoff and to stay dormant until the next primary election two years later. ARG's leaders hoped that such a strategy would insulate the new officeholders from all undue influences, including their own.

ARG scored its first coup by persuading the highly respected president of Oklahoma City University, Dr. Jack S. Wilkes, to head its ticket and a second in convincing Frank C. Love, number two man at Kerr-McGee, to run for a council seat. The presence of such an insider reassured the business establishment. Against Mayor Norick and four independent ward candidates, ARG fielded a complete slate pledged vaguely to dignity and reform. Despite their initial distrust, most business leaders followed the *Daily Oklahoman* and endorsed the ARG men. The reformers swept every contest and, counting Mayor Wilkes's tie-breaking vote, they captured control of the council, 5 to 4.[18]

On issue after issue the mayor's vote proved decisive, because the council, deeply divided over personalities and procedures, frequently split its votes. "Holdover" councilmembers often threatened the removal of city manager Tinstman as a blow against dictatorial "slate government." Tinstman's tenure, in fact, depended on full attendance by the ARG forces at each council meeting. In this charged atmosphere, Mayor Wilkes suddenly resigned in June 1964 to accept the presidency of Shreveport's Centenary College. His departure left the choice of an interim successor to the warring council.

Following a two-week donnybrook, the two factions compromised on lawyer and gentleman-historian George H. Shirk, an unaffiliated civic leader with views compatible to ARG, business leaders, and at least two of the independent councilmembers. Legal niceties required the council first to annex Shirk's home in order to make him a city resident, then to add him to the council (one member "resigned" temporarily), and finally to appoint him mayor. In a forty-five-minute procedure, Shirk became chief executive on a 6 to 9 vote.[19]

These were boom times for the chamber, sonic boom times to be exact. In 1964, business leaders spread a rumor that Washington had promised Okahoma City the nation's first supersonic landing facility. In return, the city would have to endure eight sonic booms daily as air force jets tested the population's noise tolerance. The Federal Aviation Administration (FAA) began the tests without the city's approval, only to face a 7 to 0 council demand for suspension. Within twenty-four hours, however, Draper and his group convinced the ARG-led council that its "implied criticism of the FAA could well cost us our future." More concerned about growth than serenity, the council immediately rescinded its action. The booms continued for six months, after which 4,600 people followed plumber Woodrow W. Busey to court where they sued the FAA for damages. The government paid dearly, the chamber quietly dropped talk of the airport, and Busey became a local folk hero.[20]

Shirk faced the voters in 1965. ARG again ran a full aldermanic slate in an attempt to knock out their holdover opponents. The reformers asked Shirk to accept their banner, but he refused so ARG made no mayoral endorsement. Running without a platform, the popular incumbent handily defeated a lesser opponent. ARG candidates swept three of the four contested races and gained a 7 to 1 council majority. The organization failed only on the working-class south side, which sent independent small-businessman Bill Bishop to fight alone at city hall. OPUBCO backed no candidates, but business leaders seemed satisfied by the outcome.[21]

Shirk endorsed chamber policies with enthusiasm and even became the OIA's administrative head after leaving office. Under pressure from Washington, the mayor sponsored cooperation among area governments to create the Association of Central Oklahoma Governments (ACOG). Key federal redevelopment funds depended on formation of such an intergovernmental agency. Shirk also watched as the courts gave Oklahoma cities more power through legislative reapportionment, but the shift proved of little practical importance since Oklahoma's urban, suburban, and rural populations differ little in political philosophy. Reapportionment did result in black representation, a stronger voice for cities, and the election of a few more suburban Republicans, but the new alignment had little effect on policy outcomes.[22]

The death of ARG's northeast ward councilmember Guy James in 1966 led to a historic milestone, the appointment of the city's first black councilmember, Dr. Charles N. Atkins. Two circumstances accounted for this unexpected council action. First, imminent reapportionment would soon split the city's four wards into eight single-member districts and guarantee black representation. Second, many feared the election of A. L. Dowell, whom whites had considered too aggressive since he had filed the school desegregation suit. Councilmember James had barely beaten him in 1965. To hedge against Dowell's "radicalism," the council, therefore, picked the least objectionable of several prominent blacks for the vacant post. Dowell then promptly unseated Atkins at the next election.[23]

ARG entered the fray one last time in 1967. It sponsored ad man Ray Ackerman for mayor against a rejuvenated Norick, who ran on a promise of "straight government, not slate government" and refused to take a stand on the key issue of urban renewal. E. K. Gaylord, upset by the creeping socialism of LBJ's Model Cities Program, published a front-page editorial attacking urban renewal advocate Ackerman for doing business with the city. Actually, printer Norick, not Ackerman, held city contracts, but only the few who read the nascent rival *Oklahoma Journal* had this information. Norick won by 782 votes.

ARG also endorsed four prorenewal council candidates in five races, leaving a new south side ward to the independents. Three ARG people won, including Patience Latting, who became the first woman on the city council. Their victories gave the organization a 5 to 3 council majority that denied Mayor Norick his tie-breaking vote.

Still, businessmen, who for once were ahead of Gaylord's position on an issue, feared independent attacks on urban renewal. This concern proved groundless, however, because the antiredevelopment opposition could not unite. The negative positions of the two south side councilmembers on several desegregation issues precluded any coalition between them and Dowell, the other independent. The chamber's redevelopment plans were safe.[24]

Urban renewal began as a chamber effort to obtain federal funds for the rebuilding of downtown. In 1948, a healthy central business district had claimed 75 percent of the region's retail sales, but the following year Mayfair, first of the modern shopping centers, opened and the outward rush began. Between 1954 and 1965 downtown lost seventy-seven businesses and saw its portion of area sales drop to a mere 11 percent. Alarmed as early as 1957, the chamber sent a delegation to Pittsburgh to study the revitalization of that city's Golden Triangle. Within two years of their return, these businessmen coaxed enabling legislation from the state, and renewal efforts began.[25]

The first steps, passage of a $39 million bond issue and creation of a public redevelopment agency, required city approval, and the latter ignited controversy when Mayor Norick fought the council for the right to appoint the members of the new Oklahoma City Urban Renewal Authority (OCURA). With Norick out of town in November 1961, the council approved its own balanced five-member board that included a labor leader and a black educator. At first, chamber leaders were aghast at this development, but they soon regained momentum and co-opted the council's appointees. Later, after ARG came to power, the chamber insisted on the selection of businessmen for the renewal agency.

OCURA needed seed money to hire a director and finance the planning necessary for federal applications. To supply these funds, the chamber formed its own Urban Action Foundation (UAF) which extended credit to the city agency and aided in staff and design selection. When the first OCURA director quit in 1966, UAF loaned its own head to the city authority until OCURA filled the position permanently with the chamber's general council, James B. White. Such helpfulness speeded up the entire program while insuring that urban renewal served the interests of the business establishment.[26]

Redevelopment centered on the much-heralded Pei Plan (1964) and its successor, the Central Oklahoma City Plan of 1974. The blueprints covered enormous territories, 528 and 1,420 acres, respectively, and called for the demolition and reconstruction of most of downtown and the east side. Even before Pei and Associates submitted their proposals, however, the chamber went to work. In February 1963, Draper and his colleagues, operating through OCURA, filed an application for federal funds to expand the University of Oklahoma Medical Center complex in the east side black neighborhood near the state capitol. Chamber officials started with this program instead of one for downtown because they thought it would be the most acceptable to the Kennedy administration in Washington. Business leaders wanted to tear down the central business district next, but a funding deadline prompted a hurried request for the east side John F. Kennedy residential project. Finally, in December 1967, HUD approved the chamber's centerpiece, Project 1-A, and downtown redevelopment began.

In 1970, workers completed the Mummers' Theater (which promptly went bankrupt) as the first among thirty new and renovated downtown buildings. In effect, urban renewal completely leveled the core of the city to replace the old buildings with modern structures of exposed steel and glass. OCURA funded buildings, streets, parks, heating systems, and an underground walkway. By 1980, the authority had spent some $500 million ($300 million downtown), including money for support services for relocated businesses (the nation's first such program) and construction of 786 housing units. OCURA's director claimed success by noting the nearly 500 percent increase in property values during the 1970s. Critics, however, fumed over the elite's autocratic control of land use, citing, as an example, the location of a "courthouse" parking garage three blocks from the county courthouse, but next to Charles Vose's First National Bank. They also noted that the underground concourse conveniently connected buildings owned by key influentials. Moreover, the new 786 residential units fell far short of the agency's own conservative estimates of 4,212 units needed to rehouse the displaced.[27]

In virtually all matters involving urban renewal, the chamber could count on the support of ARG, but by the 1970s the chamber needed new allies. The last ARG councilmembers left office in 1971 at which time personality politics engulfed city elections.

Councilmember Bill Bishop had long symbolized south-side defiance of ARG and the chamber, both of which frequently ignored his working-class constituents. Councilmember Patience Latting, meanwhile, had demonstrated her own brand of independence. Labeled by the *New York Times* as a Claudette Colbert look-alike who "handles politics like F.D.R.," Latting, the daughter of a banker and wife of an oilman, had gained public attention as a PTA lobbyist. In

1966, she had used her master's degree in statistics to help a federal district court reapportion the state legislature. Once in the council, Latting had become a gadfly, demanding open meetings, competitive contract bidding, conflict of interest rules, and an end to sloppy building inspections and turn-key public housing. She had frequently clashed with Bishop, whose construction firm held noncompetitive public housing contracts with city agencies.

Much to the surprise of political observers, both Bishop and Latting made the 1971 mayoral runoff. Faced with an awkward choice in a brutal campaign, most chamber members sat out the election. Former ARG councilmembers endorsed their colleague Latting, but Mayor Norick and former mayor Shirk joined independent councilmembers in announcing support for Bishop. OPUBCO remained neutral, and Latting won 59 percent of the vote. She swept all but the southside wards, and Oklahoma City became the largest municipality up to that time to elect a woman chief executive.[28]

Latting retained her office for over a decade despite politically dangerous power plays in 1973 and 1975. Two years after her own triumph, she engineered a successful purge of her council opponents. Only the omnipresent Bishop survived her wrath. The *Daily Oklahoman*, by this time an advocate of massive redevelopment, applauded her maneuvers because the losers had favored piecemeal zoning with greater neighborhood control over development.[29] Seven months after her reelection in 1975, the Latting-led council rejected pay hikes for city policemen, prompting virtually the entire force to resign. The resulting compromise agreement favored the city and angered organized labor. That settlement, together with Latting's unheeded call for a ban on political activities by city workers, caused intense hostility from government employees. In 1979, former state senator Phil Lambert capitalized on this sentiment and almost rode union support to victory over the incumbent. The mayor won a bare 50.2 percent endorsement. During her years in office, Latting's administration maintained the status quo in a competent, moderate manner.[30] In 1983 Latting retired, and District Attorney Andrew Coats, an OPUBCO favorite, succeeded her.

Through the Latting years, and indeed through the entire postwar period, one word captured the essence of Oklahoma City politics and life. *Growth*, unchallenged and unquestioned, has summarized the desires of most of the citizens of central Oklahoma. An inscription at the base of a downtown memorial to the original pioneers of 1889 best expresses the city's mood: "Passerby—Look about you and ask this question: Where else within a single life span has man built so mightily?"

All this expansion has caused some things to change. Liquor, for example, is now legal, if more tightly regulated than in any other state, and God-fearing Oklahoma Cityans now divorce at a rate exceeded nationally only by Reno and Las Vegas. The city's conservative political environment, however, remains much as it has always been. Politicians are now as apt to be Republican as Democrat, but their outlook is unchanged. The Gaylord family still controls the print media, and Edward L. Gaylord and his colleagues at the Chamber of Commerce continue to make the area's major decisions. True, these men now share more of their power with elected officials, but even today the city ventures no important actions without their consent. In Oklahoma City, business leadership remains as sacred as chicken-fried steaks with white cream gravy and Sooner football victories over Texas.[31]

NOTES

1. John Gunther, *Inside U.S.A.* (New York: Harper & Bros., 1947), 876–885; Milton MacKaye, "The Cities of America: Oklahoma City," *Saturday Evening Post*, 5 June 1948, 20ff.; quotation from Debs Myers, "Oklahoma City," *Holiday* (May 1950): 114–129.

2. Kenneth A. Cox and Nicholas Johnson, "Broadcasting in America and the F.C.C.'s License Renewal Process: An Oklahoma Case Study," Federal Communications Commission Report, 1 June 1968, 170–234; *New York Times*, 8 March 1953, 6 March 1973, 1 June 1974; "Survival of the Fittest," *Time*, 3 May 1968, 53–54.

3. Clifford Earl Trafzer, *The Judge: The Life of Robert A. Hefner* (Norman: University of Oklahoma Press, 1975), 208–209.

4. *Daily Oklahoman*, March–April 1947, 1951, and 1955; *North Star* (Oklahoma City), February–April 1955; Roy P. Stewart, *Born Grown: An Oklahoma City History* (Oklahoma City: Fidelity Bank, 1974), 127–128; Horace Thompson, "Municipal Government in Oklahoma City, Oklahoma: An Outline of the History of Municipal Operation under the Council-Manager Form, 1927–1959," Report to the City Manager, April 1959 (mimeo).

5. James M. Smallwood, *Urban Builder: The Life and Times of Stanley Draper* (Norman: University of Oklahoma Press, 1977), 227.

6. James N. Eastman, Jr., "Location and Growth of Tinker Air Force Base and Oklahoma City Air Materiel Area," *Chronicles of Oklahoma* 50 (Autumn 1972): 326–346.

7. Ronald Laird Stewart, "The Influence of the Business Community in Oklahoma City Politics" (M.A. thesis, Oklahoma State University, 1967). In the 1981 fiscal year, Tinker Field employed 22,600 civilians and spent $522 million, with over half that amount remaining in Oklahoma County. "Military Defense Key Contributor to Healthy State Economy," *Oklahoma Business* (July 1981): 11–13.

8. "Update/Oklahoma Growth"; Stewart, "The Influence of the Business Community," 37.

9. "Update/Oklahoma Growth"; Smallwood, *Urban Builder*; Neal R. Peirce, *The Great Plains States of America* (New York: W. W. Norton, 1973), 246–279; John R. Doxey, Jr., "The Role of Inducements in Industrial Development in Oklahoma" (M.R.C.P. thesis, University of Oklahoma, 1965), 71–73, 88; "Oklahoma City: Plains, Planes and Plans," *Industrial Development and Manufacturers Record* 132 (April 1963): 45–59; *The Oklahoma Journal*, 21 September 1980; Odie B. Fauk, *The Making of a Merchant: Raymond A. Young and the TG&Y Stores* (Norman: University of Oklahoma Press, 1980), 232–237; *The Wall Street Journal*, 29 June 1982; Paul Strasbaugh, Report to the Board of Directors of the Oklahoma City Chamber of Commerce, 7 May 1981, 4.

10. *Wall Street Journal*, 29 June 1982.

11. *Oklahoma Journal*, 21–27 September 1980; KOCO-TV notebooks and videotapes on OIA stories, Vince Orza, reporter, February–June 1981; KTOK newsscripts, 8 May 1981–2, June 1981; KEBC thirty-minute documentary on the OIA, Bob Sands, producer (tape, n.d.); *Oklahoma Observer*, 25 March, 25 April 1980, 25 March 1981; *Oklahoman*, 20 May, 19 June 1981; interviews with Orza (KOCO-TV), Terri Watkins (KTOK), and Bob Sands (KEBC), Oklahoma City, June 1981.

12. *North Star*, 26 March 1959; *Oklahoman*, March–April 1959.

13. Thomas McClellan Ballentine, "The Oklahoma City Annexation Program, 1958–1963, Purposes, Processes, and Planning Implications" (M.R.C.P. thesis, University of Oklahoma, 1964); interview with Robert T. Rice, Edmond, 14 December 1980; Smallwood, *Urban Builder*, 195–207; Patti Case, "The Other Side of Paradise," *Oklahoma Monthly* (July 1981): 48.

14. National Urban League, *A Study of the Social and Economic Conditions of the Negro Population of Oklahoma City, Oklahoma* (New York, June–July 1945); Allan A. Saxe, "Protest and Reform: The Desegregation of Oklahoma City" (Ph.D. dissertation, University of Oklahoma, 1969), 14–59.

15. Monroe Billington, "Public School Integration in Oklahoma, 1954–1963," *Historian* 26 (1964): 521–537.

16. Clara Luper, *Behold the Walls* (Oklahoma City: Jim Ware, 1979); Arthur L. Tolson, *The Black Oklahomans, A History: 1541–1972* (New Orleans: Edwards Printing Co., 1972), 190–197; Jimmie Lewis Franklin, *The Blacks in Oklahoma* (Norman: University of Oklahoma Press, 1980), 55–61; Chester M. Pierce and Louis Jolyon West, "Six Years of Sit-ins: Psychodynamic Causes and Effects," *The International Journal of Social Psychiatry* 12 (Winter 1966): 29–34; Saxe, "Protest," 58–260.

17. Scot W. Bolton, "Desegregation of the Oklahoma City School System," *The Chronicles of Oklahoma* 58 (Summer 1980): 192–220; *Oklahoman*, 24 May 1981.

18. *Oklahoman*, March–April 1963; George J. Mauer, "Oklahoma City: In Transition to Maturity and Professionalization," in Leonard E. Goodall, ed., *Urban Politics in the Southwest* (Tempe: Arizona State Uni-

versity Center for Public Affairs, 1967), 88–109; Stanley P. Wagner, "Oklahoma City Government Reform," *Oklahoma City Magazine* (April 1964): 10ff.; Marshall H. Bord, "The Politics of Administration: Oklahoma City, Oklahoma" (Ph.D. dissertation, New York University, 1969); Stewart, *Born Grown*, 130–131.

19. *Oklahoma City Times*, 16 June 1964.

20. John Lehr, "The Era of Supersonic Morality," *Saturday Review*, 6 June 1964, 49–50; "Learning to Love the Boom," *Time*, 7 May 1965, 64, 67; "Sonic Boom Town," *New Republic*, 22 August 1964, 5–6.

21. *Oklahoman*, March–April 1965; *Oklahoma Journal*, 17 March 1965; Mauer, "Oklahoma City," 98–99.

22. Gerald Alan Starr, "Organizational Functions and Conflicts in a Regional Council of Governments: An Application of Parsonian Theory" (Ph.D. dissertation, University of Oklahoma, 975); John M. Wood, "The Oklahoma Legislature," in Alex B. Lacy, Jr., ed., "Power in American State Legislatures," *Tulane Studies in Political Science* 11 (1967): 131–171; Richard D. Bingham, "Reapportionment of the Oklahoma House of Representatives: Politics and Process," *Legislative Research Series*, no. 2 (Norman: University of Oklahoma, Bureau of Government Research, 1972); David R. Morgan and Samuel A. Kirkpatrick, "Legislative Reapportionment and Urban Influence in the Oklahoma Legislature," *Oklahoma Business Bulletin* 40 (March 1972): 5–9; idem, "Urban-Rural Divisions within the Oklahoma Legislature," *Oklahoma Business Bulletin* 40 (April 1972): 5–9.

23. *Black Dispatch*, (Oklahoma City), 30 September 1966.

24. *Oklahoman*, March–April 1967, especially editorial on 1 April 1967; *Oklahoma Journal*, March–April 1967. For replies to the *Oklahoman* editorial, see *Oklahoma Journal*, 3–4 April 1967.

25. Oklahoma City University Business Research Center, "Impact of Urban Trends and Community Accomplishments on Downtown Oklahoma City" (April 1977): 14–16; Oklahoma City Chamber of Commerce, *Building toward Our Centennial, 1989* (4 December 1980), 31–33.

26. Oklahoma City University Business Research Center, "Impact," 50–52, 83–84.

27. Ibid.; *Oklahoma Journal*, 4 April, 21–27 September 1980; KOCO-TV files.

28. *Oklahoman*, March–April 1971; *Oklahoma Journal*, March–April 1971; *New York Times*, 14 April 1971.

29. *Oklahoman*, March–April 1973.

30. *Oklahoman*, March–April 1975, 1979; Charles R. Greer, "Public Sector Bargaining Legislation and Strikes: A Case Study," *Labor Law Journal* 29 (April 1978): 241–247; Richard M. Ayers, "Case Studies of Police Strikes in Two Cities—Albuquerque and Oklahoma City," *Journal of Police Science and Administration* 5 (March 1977): 19–31.

31. Nan Birmingham, "Sitting Pretty in Oklahoma City," *Town and Country* (February 1977): 109ff.

9

SAN ANTONIO
THE VICISSITUDES OF BOOSTERISM

by David R. Johnson

San Antonio is a city struggling to regain its former grandeur. Once the largest city in Texas, it lost that distinction and all that it implied in economic power and prestige when in the 1930 census both Dallas and Houston surpassed it. Bad luck and a lack of imagination combined to cause this decline in status. Located in south central Texas, San Antonio was isolated from the major oil fields that were the key to prosperity for other cities in the state. Houston and Dallas, more fortunately situated, became the principal beneficiaries of the oil boom. Furthermore, Houston's successful struggle to become a major port together with Dallas's wholesaling hegemony over north central Texas and Oklahoma gave those cities more sophisticated economic bases upon which to build their prosperity. Both Dallas and Houston thus created local economic environments that fueled startling growth. San Antonio's development lagged behind. Businessmen in San Antonio had no imaginative responses to the changing economic structure of the state and region. Instead of aggressively participating in the booming oil industry, they adopted the more conservative strategy of enhancing San Antonio's role as a center for defense, tourism, and regional services.

Military spending and tourism have been the backbone of the local economy since World War I. The military has a long-standing relationship to San Antonio dating back to the frontier era. Fort Sam Houston, founded in 1879, served as an important training center during the Spanish-American War and World War I. The Great War also expanded San Antonio's commitment to things military when the army decided in 1917 to train its first aviators at a new facility, Kelly Air Force Base. Brooks, a military medical center, was established that same year.

Once accustomed to a diet of federal funds, postwar San Antonians hungered for more. The city provided free land to the air force to build two more bases, Randolph in 1928 and Lackland in 1941.

By the 1930s many local businessmen and politicians had become committed to the idea of the military as a linchpin in the area's economy.

Tourism was the other major "industry." San Antonio's climate and history had attracted tourists since the late nineteenth century. They had come to enjoy the warm winters, the decaying Spanish missions, and, above all, the Alamo. Hotels, restaurants, brothels, and gambling houses relied heavily on the tourists for their livelihoods. In the late 1930s, a WPA project transformed the San Antonio River, which winds through the downtown, into a major tourist attraction. One of the most successful renewal projects of the New Deal, the riverwalk not only boosted tourism, it also enhanced the economic vitality of the downtown.

But military bases and tourism were insufficient props for vigorous economic expansion in the interwar period. Neither could compare to oil as a boom industry capable of generating extensive population growth.

World War II gave San Antonio a chance to recoup its former glory by infusing over 150,000 new residents into the city. After the war, however, continued growth became a crucial issue. How would the city sustain wartime prosperity?

The search for an answer to that question became the central theme of San Antonio's postwar development. However much individuals or groups might disagree over details, the desire for growth has conditioned and directed economic and political affairs since the halcyon days of the Second World War. San Antonio failed to overtake its upstate rivals, but that failure was not due to a lack of serious effort.

San Antonio's postwar economic problems have their roots in the narrow range of choices forced on the city by a small coalition of businessmen and politicians. Shortly after 1945, this coalition, which was committed to continuing the city's role as a service center, seized political power. The group's attempts to implement its own vision of growth shaped San Antonio's economic development for almost twenty years. Not until the early 1970s did fundamental changes in the city undermine that vision and destroy the ruling coalition. The failure of a once domineering growth consensus then provoked a long and acrimonious debate that culminated in the emergence of a somewhat different consensus late in the decade. During the 1970s, moreover, the political context in which economic issues were resolved changed dramatically, ensuring that future growth policies will have wider support than has been true at any previous time.

MAP 9.1. The San Antonio SMSA

Rapid wartime growth provided the context for political and economic change after 1945. The needs of thousands of new residents severely strained an already overburdened municipality and threatened to fragment the metropolitan area politically. Local politicians were incapable of dealing with these problems. San Antonians, in 1914, had restructured political power by substituting a commission form of government for the old ward system. Over the next two decades the commissioners created a powerful, corrupt political machine that largely ignored the legitimate needs of local residents. They had become adept at winning elections and perpetuating their own power, but they were incapable of coping with the problems presented by the wartime population explosion that followed Pearl Harbor.

Businessmen, angered by the incompetence of the politicians and determined that San Antonio should capitalize on its new opportunities, began to agitate for another change in the structure of local government. Their disenchantment with the commissioners dated from the late 1920s, but the machine's skill and the deferential attitude of most citizens had frustrated the business community's attempts at change. After World War II, however, population pressures mounted and caused sufficient local concern to give businessmen another opportunity to implement their ideas. The result was a reform movement that transformed local politics.[1]

The movement began officially in 1946 when Edward G. Conroy and A. C. ("Jack") White founded the Council-Manager Association. Conroy, a powerful figure in San Antonio's Parent-Teacher Association, and White, a hotel owner who was president of the Chamber of Commerce, had the backing of the business community in this venture. Local leaders such as Walter W. McAllister, Sr., president of the city's largest savings and loan association, provided both financial and moral support for the new organization. The litany of the association's complaints against the commissioners summarized the business community's concerns. Conroy and White criticized the city's outdated tax asessment rolls, its lack of adequate urban planning, its deteriorating public services, and its failure to annex newly developed subdivisions. Their solution to these problems was explicit in the name of their new organization: San Antonio should substitute council-manager government for the inefficient, ineffective commissioners.

By 1951 the reformers had marshalled enough public support to defeat the commissioners' machine decisively. This new voting coalition, made possible by population growth, dominated San Antonio politics for over two decades. White-collar workers living on the city's north side combined with federal employees from the military bases on the south side to elect White as mayor. The new coalition did not need the votes of San Antonio's lower-class Mexican and black populations to maintain its power. Those groups had traditionally supported the now defeated commissioners' machine. The reformers' victory thus signaled an end to lower-class ethnic influence in local politics and marked the emergence of middle- and upper-class political power in San Antonio.[2]

Simultaneously with their electoral victory, the reformers changed the structure of city government. At the time of the mayoral election, voters approved the creation of a charter revision commission comprised of individuals selected at large. Within two months this body recommended a referendum to obtain public approval for the council-manager system. The Council-Manager Association spearheaded the subsequent campaign to transform local government. Backed by a $40,000 budget and supported by the new voting coalition, the association swept to victory in October 1951.[3]

Victory brought new difficulties, however. Mayor White discovered that political power was more attractive than reform. His conception of council-manager government emphasized a strong role for the mayor, an interpretation at odds with that of several prominent reformers, including W. W. McAllister. Substantive city problems took a back seat to politics in the subsequent battle over whose view would prevail. The new government did annex eighty square miles of unincorporated subdivisions (the largest such annexation in the city's history), but it held other issues in abeyance for two years while the power struggle continued. White appeared to triumph in 1953 when he and his candidates for the council won handily, but their victory was short-lived.[4] White's opponents regrouped and marshalled their forces for another assault. Their efforts not only defeated the mayor but also created a new political machine that persisted for some twenty years.

In December 1954, Thomas Powell, president of the Chamber of Commerce, called a meeting of San Antonio's middle- and upper-class civic leadership to prepare for the upcoming municipal elections. Those who attended included presidents, past presidents, and vice-presidents of important service organizations such as the Optimists, Lions, and Kiwanis clubs; officers of businessmen's associations such as the Chamber of Commerce and the San Antonio Manufacturers Association; leaders of such reform organizations as the Citizens Committee, the Taxpayers League, and the Research and Planning Council; publishers and editors of the local press; leading divines from the Jewish, Methodist, Catholic, Baptist, and Presbyterian churches; and a smattering of representatives from women's clubs, the Bar Association, and the Bexar County Medical Association. In all, fifty civic leaders attended and agreed to form the Good Government League (GGL). They elected Frank Gillespie, Sr., a prominent automobile dealer, president and appointed a steering committee to handle organizational details.[5]

According to its sponsors and spokesmen, the GGL was to be a nonpartisan political organization dedicated to the election of individuals who would act in the best interests of all San Antonians. General supervision of the GGL was in the hands of a board of directors; but in practice the executive committee ran the organization, and the nominating committee performed the critical function of screening potential candidates for public office. Throughout the lifetime of the GGL, the composition of the nominating committee and the details of its deliberations remained secret. The GGL specified that candidates had to be sufficiently wealthy to serve without significant salaries. They had to eschew further political ambitions and had to represent the GGL's concept of the "community as a whole." Perhaps most important, potential candidates were expected to demonstrate a commitment to urban growth and economic expansion. These criteria served to reduce the range of acceptable candidates to representatives of the city's social and economic elite.

The structure of aldermanic elections, the powerful financial resources of the new organization, and the lack of any organized opposition combined to make the GGL the dominant force in local politics from 1954 to 1973. Because the mayor and council were elected at large, opponents of the GGL faced enormous problems with campaign financing, access to publicity, and voter recognition of candidates. The GGL had the resources to overcome these difficulties. Once it selected its slate, the GGL marshalled all its resources and influence to elect it. Victory normally followed victory. Between 1955 and 1971, the GGL-endorsed candidates won seventy-seven of eighty-one council races. The self-effacing, civic-minded GGL became one of the most successful political machines in America.[6]

As in most such political organizations, the leadership conducted the public's business behind closed doors and beyond the glare of publicity. The city council simply ratified decisions already made elsewhere. Under these circumstances the GGL's progrowth and development philosophy determined the course of public events. Businessmen were the most influential members of the GGL, and their plans for San Antonio's future guided the city's growth. With political and economic power so closely intertwined there was little debate over the soundness of their designs.

After its overwhelming victory in the spring elections of 1955, the GGL set out to implement a program that had three essential elements: improving city services, preventing metropolitan fragmentation of government, and attracting new business.

Improving municipal services required larger sums of money than current taxes could provide. In order to deal with this fiscal problem, the city council authorized a series of bond elections during the late 1950s. The GGL used its access to the local media and its financial resources to mount highly successful publicity campaigns in support of each bond referendum, and the people responded. By 1958, voters had approved $42 million for use in public works improvements.

The distribution of these funds among particular projects illustrated the GGL's priorities. Over one-third ($15 million) of the money went to storm drainage projects. Property damage, and occasional drownings, made drainage a major local issue. Water runoff during rain storms was (and still is) a serious problem that affected the livability and safety of many neighborhoods. Since the defunct commission machine had done little to ameliorate the drainage problem, the GGL's efforts were long overdue. Of course, improvements in this area of services also enhanced the city's attractiveness to potential new residents and businesses.

Street improvement received 45 percent of the monies from bond issues. The distribution of these funds indicated, however, that the GGL was more interested in building roads as stimulants for urban growth than in repairing old streets in already settled neighborhoods. The bulk of the bond money was earmarked for the purchase of rights-of-way for expressways.[7] Since 1946, the Chamber of Commerce had advocated a vigorous highway-building program. Until the emergence of the GGL, however, the chamber had been unable to attract sufficient political support for its views. Thus, when the Federal Highway Road Act of 1956 made possible a massive, national road-building program, the business leaders had the crucial support they needed. The chamber prepared and presented to the Texas Highway Commission a comprehensive plan for expressway construction in the San Antonio metropolitan area. Loop 410 was a crucial element in the plan. This beltway road would follow a route that was largely beyond the settled areas of the city. By handling large volumes of people and goods efficiently, the loop promised to act as a magnet to attract new growth toward it and as an anchor for development beyond it. Interstate 10, which bisected the loop, would similarly promote growth in areas to the north of San Antonio. Both roadways were essentially complete by 1965.[8]

Local businessmen displayed a keen appreciation for the economic possibilities of the new highway network. Subdivisions appeared on both sides of the loop even while it was under construction. Following a national trend, shopping malls and single-family homes appeared simultaneously with the new roadway. In 1960, Wonderland, the first shopping center on the northwest side of the city, opened for business at the intersection of Interstate 10 and the loop. North Star Mall, which also opened in 1960, sprang up directly north of downtown at the intersection of the loop with San Pedro Avenue. A third mall, Central Park, opened in 1968 directly across from North Star. By the late 1970s continued population growth had justified two more malls on the loop, one at the far northeast corner and the other on the far northwest side. Development along Interstate 10 to the north proceeded slowly at first because of the continued availability of land within the loop. Once that land had been occupied in the 1970s, however, subdivisions began to spring up around the more northerly interstate exits. This remarkable growth more than fulfilled the Chamber of Commerce's expectations regarding the use of highways to promote economic opportunities.

While pursuing its goal of improving public services, the GGL also sought to implement the second element of its program: the prevention of metropolitan fragmentation within Bexar County. Eight new municipalities incorporated in the 1950s, five of them between 1955 and 1957. The GGL sought to eliminate further such splintering by taking advantage of favorable provisions in state annexation laws. City governments had to read annexation ordinances twice before final passage. After the first reading, the area under consideration could not be claimed by another municipality, nor could it incorporate unilaterally. In September 1959 the city council held the first readings on ordinances annexing 330 square miles of territory. The city had no intention of actually annexing those areas because it could not afford the expense of providing services to them. But by giving the ordinances their first reading the council reserved those areas for future expansion.

Annexation opponents from around the state complicated the GGL's local campaign against fragmentation. In 1963 the legislature responded to its complaints by passing a new annexation law that created the concept of extra territorial jurisdiction (ETJ). Under its provisions, cities obtained the power to regulate development in their ETJ, which was defined as unincorporated land contiguous to a city. The extent of ETJ varied according to central city population; in San Antonio's case, ETJ extended five miles beyond the city limits. Various restrictions reduced the ease with which new subdivisions could be annexed. The most important of these required that any land within the ETJ that was to be annexed had to be contiguous to the existing city limits.

The GGL managed to devise a scheme that essentially bypassed the intent of the new law while staying within its technical limitations. City manager Jack Shelley proposed, and the council accepted, a plan to annex major roads extending outward from the city. This permitted the city to measure the boundaries of its ETJ from these highways rather than from the original city limits, thereby significantly expanding the field of potential annexation.[9] By 1972, when the last GGL-sponsored annexation occurred, San Antonio's land area had increased to nearly three hundred square miles. Through the GGL's efforts San Antonio had managed to expand its boundaries to include over 80 percent of Bexar County's population and to retain the bulk of the area's economic development.

The third aspect of the GGL program—attracting new businesses to San Antonio—proved to be the most difficult. The city continued to rely very heavily on tourism and its military bases for its economic well-being. Inadequate rail connections, the absence of nearby industrial raw materials, and the presence of a largely unskilled, poorly educated labor force made San Antonio a relatively unattractive location for major industries.[10] The business community sought to overcome these disadvantages in two ways. First, the GGL continued its program of improving city services. Second, various interest groups within the private sector—with the GGL's enthusiastic support—sought to expand San Antonio's role as a service center. Although this effort did not generate uniform success, it did achieve two of its principal objectives: the acquisition of a medical complex and a new state university. In both cases the GGL/business coalition demonstrated the ability to enlist the state legislature's aid in promoting local growth.

The idea of a major medical center, including a school of medicine, originated with a group of business and civic leaders who in 1947 established the San Antonio Medical Foundation. For the next twelve years the medical foundation worked assiduously within the local business and medical communities to create support for its goal. By the late 1950s a consensus emerged on the desirability and location of the proposed facility. Some major developers who owned land in unincorporated areas to the northwest of San Antonio worked with the Chamber of Commerce and the medical foundation to convince the Bexar County Medical Society to support placement of the proposed complex near its properties.[11] The San Antonio Medical Center was thus intended to act as a major spur to physical growth in addition to being a source of employment and prestige.

The coalition working for the medical center finally triumphed in 1959, when the state legislature approved a medical school for Bexar County. Since the legislature conveniently failed to specify a site for the new facility, the decision on its location was left to the University of Texas Board of Regents, who would supervise the school. After a decent display of impartiality, in which three separate teams of advisors recommended three different locations, the regents announced that the facility would be built on land donated by the northwest San Antonio developers. The GGL helped matters along by obtaining voter approval of a $5 million bond issue for construction of the school.[12]

Actual building at the UT Health Science Center did not begin until 1966. In the meantime, private enterprise took advantage of this new growth anchor. The area around the school's site became a magnet for hospitals, health-related businesses, and housing subdivisions. By 1979 sixteen major facilities employing over 10,000 people spread over the square-mile complex. The economic impact on San Antonio exceeded $1 billion annually.[13] Medicine ranked as the city's third most important industry, and the medical complex was a major triumph for San Antonio's boosters.

Although successful, the campaign to establish a branch of the state university system in San Antonio had less economic impact. The effort to achieve this goal began in 1966, when the GGL ventured into county and state legislative elections for the first time. As usual, the GGL's candidates won, and they immediately began the campaign for a branch campus. Their 1967 attempt failed, but re-

newed efforts brought victory. In June 1969, the governor, surrounded by representatives of the GGL, signed the bill into law at a
ceremony in front of the Alamo.[14]

In a scenario strongly reminicent of the decision regarding the
medical center's location, the UT Board of Regents considered various sites for the new university. As in the previous decision, debate
revolved around the issue of growth. John Peace, a UT regent whose
business associates had extensive land holdings north of San Antonio, offered to donate land for the university. Since the site Peace
suggested was fifteen miles north of the downtown, in an area that
was almost totally undeveloped, his offer stirred some opposition
among people who had had the impression that the new branch was
to be an urban university. The regents, however, had close political
ties with the landowners surrounding the proposed site, and they
found Peace's arguments compelling. San Antonio would, presumably, grow toward the university that bears its name.[15]

The university has yet to fulfill its destiny as a magnet of urban
development. Various problems have prevented the school from
achieving its sponsors' purposes. Slow, costly construction, combined with niggardly appropriations from the legislature, delayed the
school's opening until 1975, but more fundamental problems arose
in the interim. First, the coalition that had dominated local politics
and economic policy fragmented fatally between 1971 and 1974.
Second, new political forces with different policy objectives arose to
challenge basic assumptions about growth and development. Together, these events produced a major crisis over San Antonio's
future.

A variety of problems led to the demise of the GGL in 1975.
Ironically, the organization's success contributed to its disintegration. Since its inception, the GGL had prided itself on a public harmony that derived from the organization's commitment to the
whole community's welfare. In this ideal world there were no special interest groups, no privileged individuals. Reality belied that vision, however. Businessmen dominated the city council and all the
important agencies in charge of city services and policy making
from 1955 to 1971. In the process of seizing upon the economic opportunities that the GGL's program offered, local businessmen began to develop competing interests that eventually had devastating
impact on the GGL itself. Disarray replaced harmony as the businessmen fell to fighting among themselves over the fruits of urban
development.

The GGL's disintegration began in a controversy over annexation, an issue that had been one of the key components of the GGL's

program. Early in 1972 the city manager proposed that the council annex several new subdivisions. This suggestion caused an unprecedented controversy in which some north side builders protested that the proposal represented an unwarranted governmental intrusion on their property rights. According to these protesters, the city should annex new subdivisions only when it was convenient for the builders. Other businessmen, however, regarded the proposal as a rational step in the city's goal of orderly and timely growth. The controversy continued through the year, and the council's eventual decison to proceed with annexation alienated important builders with extensive subdivision investments on the north side.[16]

While the annexation problem roiled local political discussions, yet another controversy appeared. A consortium of prominent local and state businessmen proposed the construction of an entire new community, to be called Ranchtown, on the far north side. With a projected population of over eighty thousand residents within thirty years, this proposal attracted considerable comment. Environmentalists and local officials objected that Ranchtown posed a threat to San Antonio's water supply, which was drawn from the Edwards Aquifer. The aquifer was an extensive, natural, underground water collection and filtration formation. Any development on that formation might permanently pollute the city's only source of cheap, pure water. Furthermore, the sheer size of the project bothered even the GGL. The organization could muster only lukewarm support for Ranchtown, thereby angering developers who had expected (and until now had always received) enthusiastic support for their plans. As public opposition grew and the GGL hedged, these developers became increasingly unhappy with their erstwhile allies.[17]

These two controversies had provoked a fatal split within GGL ranks. Essentially, two groups of developers emerged: one more interested in downtown, the other more committed to further north side expansion. The latter group demanded that their candidates for city council and mayor receive the GGL's blessing as their price for continuing to support the organization. When that demand was not met, the north side developers seceded from the GGL and ran an independent ticket in the 1973 election. The independents won, but their victory inaugurated an era of heated political controversy. The internal amity of the GGL had been shattered at a time when other important changes in San Antonio were also revising the nature of local politics.[18]

The emergence of a viable middle class among Mexican Americans struck yet another blow to the business community's dominance. San Antonio's economic and political elite had traditionally ignored the problems of the city's ethnic groups, but the elite's efforts did encourage a general prosperity in which minorities shared. That prosperity, in turn, fostered the emergence of a powerful, ethnic political force in the city.

Kelly Air Force Base made a crucial contribution to this development. Originally founded in 1917 on the city's southwest side, Kelly remained a small installation until 1940 when the nation's military buildup caused enormous expansion. During the war, the air corps designated Kelly as a major logistics center responsible for training, maintenance, and supply functions. In the process, Kelly became San Antonio's largest employer.[19]

Initially, Kelly's civilian employment was overwhelmingly Anglo. Beginning in the 1950s, however, the base hired increasing numbers of Mexican Americans from the west side neighborhoods contiguous to the northern edge of Kelly. The base eventually became the largest single employer of Mexican Americans in the United States.[20]

Most of these employees were blue-collar workers, but an increasing number of them moved into white-collar jobs during the 1980s. The economic impact on the Mexican-American community was great. The median income of Mexican-American families living in the census tracts near Kelly exceeded the group's city average by more than $500 in 1970.[21]

Once these employees had acquired their new economic status, they turned to activities typical of the middle class. They sought more education for themselves and their children, and they became heavily involved in community affairs. Many became officers in local parent-teacher associations, in community betterment societies, and in parish social welfare organizations. By the late 1960s they had become important neighborhood leaders. And, as a group, they held a low opinion of the city's dominant political leadership.[22]

That low esteem derived from the neglect of the service needs of their neighborhoods. Such neglect was not deliberate, for unlike many political machines of the past, the GGL had pursued an evenhanded policy in distributing services. There is no evidence that poor neighborhoods received less than their per-capita share of city expenditures or that well-to-do neighborhoods gained more. Neither was the GGL's tax assessment policy apparently unfair to poor neighborhoods. The service distribution problem arose because the west side neigbhorhoods had more severe needs. The GGL's policy of equitable per-capita distribution of tax revenues had the effect of perpetuating historic patterns of inequality. The money available was not commensurate with the scope of the problems facing west side residents. Population increases compounded the difficulties. New residents on the west side placed greater strains on public services. At the same time, the mushrooming growth of the north side aggravated drainage problems that the GGL had long ignored. New streets, parking lots, and houses decreased the amount of open land available to absorb water runoff. Since north side land is more elevated than that on the west side, water that should have stayed northward instead rushed to the Spanish neighborhoods and caused extensive flood damage.[23]

GGL indifference to west side complaints about service problems—especially drainage—helped to create a defiant mood among Mexican-American leaders. All they needed was a catalyst to propel them into political activism. That catalyst appeared in 1973 in the person of Ernesto Cortes. Cortes, a graduate of Saul Alinksy's Industrial Areas Foundation in Chicago, had learned the techniques for effective neighborhood organization, and he chose to apply those lessons to his native city. Cortes began by working with west side community leaders, especially those associated with the Catholic church.[24] Fortuitously, Cortes's campaign to organize Mexican-American neighborhoods began shortly after the local Catholic diocese experienced a significant leadership change. Prior to this period, Mexican Americans had been excluded from the upper levels of the church hierarchy, but San Antonio received its first Mexican-American bishop, Patrick Flores, in 1970. Flores was committed to using the church's financial and moral resources to promote his parishioners' concerns.[25] In 1974, following yet another flood, Cortes found a receptive environment for his drive to organize the west side. A combination of community discontent, Cortes's campaigning, and Flores's encouragement led to the formation of a new organization, Communities Organized for Public Service (COPS). This new organization obtained financial support from a local interdenominational church council and drew its leadership (other than Cortes) from civil servants working at Kelly. COPS adopted a federated structure, acting as an umbrella organization for neighborhood associations joined together to seek common goals.[26]

COPS quickly demonstrated that its members had a very different approach to public policy issues than that of the coalition that had dominated San Antonio for so long. Spokesmen for COPS demanded that the city council concentrate its attention on inner-city problems. Furthermore, COPS regarded continued north side development as detrimental to the city's future. Growth should be encouraged, COPS conceded, but within Loop 410 rather than beyond it. The city should attempt to entice new industries that would pay adequate wages, and such new enterprises should locate close to inner-city neighborhoods whose residents need better jobs. In sum, COPS's agenda for San Antonio's future emphasized policies that would redirect the growth patterns and assumptions of the previous twenty years.[27]

COPS had appeared on the local political stage at a point when the GGL's disintegration had left public affairs in disarray. In the absence of united opposition, COPS was able to create an image of a successful, well-organized federation that had the political clout to promote its interests. This achievement was all the more impressive when considered in the context of the Mexican-American community's voting record. Less than 40 percent of all registered voters were Mexican American, and fewer than half of those registered typically voted.[28] COPS was engaged in an effort to improve that record, but progress was slow. Thus COPS had to achieve its goals through its organization and tactics rather than through any concrete power at the ballot box. North side developers were appalled, but they had no effective way to squelch this extremely capable enemy. Using Saul Alinsky's tactics of careful grass-roots organization, concrete issues, thorough research, and confrontations with public officials, COPS quickly compiled an impressive series of victories. The city council, no longer dominated by the GGL and badly flustered by COPS's tactics, approved a large number of improvements for west side neighborhoods.[29]

The political chaos occasioned by the GGL's disintegration and the rise of COPS became even more widespread when the United States Justice Department objected to the city council's 1972 annexation of some north side subdivisions. By adding the Anglo residents of this new territory, the city had lessened the chances of minority group members winning citywide elections. The 1975 amendments to the 1965 Voting Rights Act, however, gave the Justice Department the authority to challenge political changes, including annexations, that might dilute minority political power. This authority could be applied retroactively, and the department did so in 1976. San Antonio had the choice of deannexation or adoption of a district electoral system that would guarantee minority representation on the city council. Faced with this choice, the council called a referendum on the district idea, and voters narrowly approved it in 1977. The proposal had the overwhelming endorsement of the city's ethnic minorities, while the Anglo north side voters were only mildly supportive of the idea. COPS's efforts to turn out a large vote on the west side probably determined the outcome.

With councilmanic elections now based on local districts, San

Antonio's ethnic neighborhoods had direct access to political offices for the first time since 1914. Nothing demonstrated the new order of things more dramatically than the composition of city government following the 1977 campaigns. Five Mexican Americans and one black constituted a majority of the new council. (During the heyday of the GGL, San Antonio's minority groups had been permitted a single representative each.) The business community could no longer dictate public policies affecting urban development and growth. On the other hand, the new political majority did not have economic power commensurate with their strength at the polls. With political and economic resources split into opposing camps, the city lacked a workable consensus.

In the absence of agreement, conflicting interest groups quickly polarized the community. The ethnic majority on the city council attempted to implement their constituents' views by passing ordinances imposing restrictions on north side growth, encouraging investment in inner-city industrial sites, and approving more services to neighborhoods on the west, east, and south sides.[30] Businessmen responded with bitter denunciations, threats of law suits, and plans for continued north side development. For a time, neither side displayed any willingness to negotiate. Instead, both sought confrontation.

One public battle between COPS and the Economic Development Foundation (EDF) epitomized the confrontational attitudes of the opposing camps. Organized in 1974 by a small but powerful group of businessmen drawn from the ranks of relative newcomers to San Antonio, the EDF's sole concern was to diversify San Antonio's economic base. Since the Chamber of Commerce had not been particularly successful in this regard, such an effort was sorely needed. EDF launched the city's first national promotional campaign to attract a variety of enterprises to San Antonio. Part of the strategy of this campaign was to emphasize the fact that the local labor force was largely nonunion and that wages fell far below national averages. In 1977 COPS issued a strong denunciation of this approach, charging that the EDF was trying to sell San Antonio as a cheap labor town. COPS demanded that the foundation work to attract industries that would pay high wages.[31]

Surprisingly, the ensuing debate, though high-spirited, marked the beginning of an effort to forge a new consensus about San Antonio's future. The most important representatives of opposing development policies were now locked in a public confrontation. Whoever won would achieve at least a moral victory that could tilt any future consensus in their favor.

EDF won this power struggle by using the threat of urban stagnation, a situation that would benefit no one but that would disproportionately penalize the city's poorer neighborhoods. The threat became credible when a major company announced that it had changed its mind about relocating in San Antonio because of community conflicts over what new industries to attract. Next the Fantus Corporation, which specializes in industrial relocation, announced that it could not recommend San Antonio to its clients due to ethnic and political strife in the community. Using these announcements, EDF boxed COPS into a corner. Businessmen spoke alarmingly about the negative economic effects that would follow if COPS did not develop a more reasonable attitude. Outmaneuvered in an arena where it had no practical knowledge or resources, COPS capitulated in an informal treaty ceremony in 1978. Superficially an agreement that both sides would work to make San Antonio a more attractive place for new industries, the "treaty" in effect neutralized COPS as a disruptive element in the EDF's campaign to diversify and improve the local economy. COPS agreed that San Antonio should attract as many new industries as possible, that higher-paying jobs should be a goal rather than a precondition in seeking new firms, and that no business should be discouraged from moving to the city. Once this battle was won, the EDF returned to its major concerns and began to compile an impressive record of successes in attracting new enterprises to the area.[32]

COPS also suffered another, more severe rebuff in 1978. The city council authorized a bond election seeking voter approval for a wide range of service improvements. However, by allocating the bulk of the proposed projects to the west, south, and east sides, the council's ethnic majority ensured that the election would become a referendum on COPS's continuing control of the city. Although COPS worked hard, Anglo voters on the north side turned out in large numbers to defeat the bond issue.[33]

These twin defeats did not reduce COPS to impotence, nor did they signal the end of ethnic political power. Each side in the confrontation over San Antonio's future had learned that it could not dominate the other, thus opening the door to compromise. It would, however, be a compromise favoring the business community, which now controlled the initiative in recreating a consensus about growth. Capitalizing on their momentum, businessmen involved in the EDF called for a new organization that would embrace the interests of all San Antonians and that would work to improve the local economy. The result of this proposal was United San Antonio (USA), founded in January 1980. Many community leaders, businessmen, and politicians attended the first meeting and expressed hope that USA would "act as a forum for widely divergent groups which, during the 1970s, represented images of divisiveness and controversy."[34] COPS remained aloof from USA, but it may have miscalculated in doing so. Determined to create an image of USA as truly representing all San Antonians, the chairman of that body has recently enlisted the cooperation of the Mexican-American Unity Council. The council, which began as an antipoverty agency in the late 1960s, has become a major force in west side economic development. It enjoys considerable credibility among Mexican Americans because of its achievements, and its current philosophy regarding San Antonio's future is generally in accord with the views of the EDF and USA. The businessmen working to recreate the appearance, and perhaps the substance, of community harmony seem to have adroitly outmaneuvered COPS.[35] Cooperation, after nearly a decade of controversy, is once again to be the norm.

Whether that cooperation will prevail remains unclear. USA has no clearly defined role in economic development—that remains the EDF's special mission. Instead, USA seems to exist to assure prospective new industries that San Antonio is "united in its desire for new business" and to reassure local businessmen that they have at last reconstituted a consensus on future growth. Political power is relatively well balanced between competing interests, a situation that has introduced a note of caution in policy debates once notable for their raucousness. Serious problems remain unresolved in the city's lower-class neighborhoods, but access to political power ensures that the poor will no longer be ignored in decisions regarding the allocation of resources. Development continues, and seems to be accelerating, on the north side. The local consensus that continued economic expansion in a tranquil political environment is desirable acquired another important ally in the spring 1981 elections. Henry Cisneros won election and became the first Mexican-American mayor of a major American city. Cisneros is an urbane, skilled politician who is committed to an alliance with San Antonio's business community. By temperament and ambition, he is well suited to the needs of the new consensus on future growth.

San Antonio does not easily fit prevailing stereotypes about rapid urban Sunbelt growth. After an extraordinary increase in population during the 1940s, the city's growth rate declined until the 1970s. A narrow economic base that relied too heavily on defense, tourism, and service industries prevented San Antonio from sustaining its spectacular increase of the forties. During the era of the GGL, public and private economic initiatives remained fixated on the expansion of service functions. Innovative diversification occurred elsewhere, particularly in cities such as Dallas and Houston. Recent developments, especially the emergence of a strategy of economic diversification guided by the EDF, indicate that the city's fortunes may be changing significantly. Whether San Antonio is on the verge of breaking from its traditional economic base remains to be seen. Until that occurs, San Antonio will continue to be a very large, but also very poor, city in which the benefits of growth do not accrue equitably to all its residents.

NOTES

1. John A. Booth and David R. Johnson, "Power and Progress in San Antonio Politics, 1836–1970," in David R. Johnson, John A. Booth, and Richard J. Harris, eds., *The Politics of San Antonio: Community, Progress, and Power* (Lincoln: University of Nebraska Press, 1983).

2. Lorin Peterson, *The Day of the Mugwump* (New York: Random House, 1961), 196.

3. *In Search of Good Government* (San Antonio: Crumrine, Inc.), 10; Arnold Fleischmann, "Sunbelt Boosterism: The Politics of Postwar Growth and Annexation in San Antonio," in David C. Perry and Alfred J. Watkins, eds., *The Rise of the Sunbelt Cities*, vol. 14, Urban Affairs Annual Reviews (Beverly Hills, Calif.: Sage Publications, 1977), 155–156.

4. Peterson, *Day of the Mugwump*, 197–198; *In Search of Good Government*, 11, 16–17; Fleischmann, "Sunbelt Boosterism," 157–158.

5. *San Antonio Express*, 8 December 1954 (hereafter cited as *Express*).

6. Ibid., 13 January 1955; Luther L. Sanders, *How to Win Elections in San Antonio the Good Government Way, 1955–1971* (San Antonio: Urban Studies Department, St. Mary's University, 1975), 14–17; L. Tucker Gibson and Robert R. Ashcroft, "Political Organization in a Nonpartisan Election System" (unpublished paper, Southwest Political Science Association meeting, 1977), 6–7; Booth and Johnson, "Power and Progress in San Antonio Politics," 46.

7. *San Antonio News*, 18 September 1958.

8. Ibid., 1 June 1956; *San Antonio Light*, 18 January 1966 (hereafter cited as *Light*).

9. City Planning Department, *Economic Base Study of San Antonio and Twenty-Seven County Area* (San Antonio: City Planning Department, 1964), 9; Fleischmann, "Sunbelt Boosterism," 158–161.

10. Howard W. Davis, "A Case Study of Industrial Location," *Land Economics* 45 (November 1969): 444–452.

11. *South Texas Medical Center at San Antonio* (San Antonio: n.p., n.d.), 5–7.

12. Ibid.; "South Texas Medical Center," *The Ewing Halsell Foundation Biennial Report* (San Antonio: Ewing Halsell Foundation, 1979), 31–35.

13. *South Texas Medical Center at San Antonio*, 5–7; *San Antonio Express-News*, 24 June 1967 (hereafter cited as *Express-News*); *Light*, 5 October 1975, 26 February 1978, 12 December 1978.

14. *Express*, 20 April 1967, 6 June 1969, 14 August 1974; Booth and Johnson, "Power and Progress in San Antonio Politics," 47.

15. *Express*, 26 February 1971; *Express-News*, 18 November 1979; Ronnie Dugger, *Our Invaded Universities* (New York: W. W. Norton, Inc., 1974), 283–288.

16. Fleischmann, "Sunbelt Boosterism," 162–163.

17. Sidney Plotkin, "Democratic Change in the Urban Political Economy: San Antonio's Edwards Aquifer Controversy," in Johnson, Booth, and Harris, eds., *The Politics of San Antonio*.

18. *Express*, 31 Janaury 1973; *News*, 11 November 1976; *Light*, 12 November 1976; *North San Antonio Times*, 9 December 1976.

19. *Light*, 14 July 1963.

20. *Express-News*, 17 August 1975.

21. Tentative conclusions based on analysis of census tracts surrounding Kelly Air Force Base.

22. John H. Lane, Jr., "Voluntary Associations among Mexican Americans in San Antonio, Texas: Organizational and Leadership Characteristics" (Ph.D. dissertation, University of Texas at Austin, 1968), 120, 144–145, 59.

23. Robert L. Lineberry, *Equality and Urban Policy: The Distribution of Municipal Services* (Beverly Hills, Calif.: Sage Publications, 1977), 94–98, 102, 134. Lineberry's conclusions do not apply to the problems of drainage on the west side, a problem the GGL never adequately addressed. Regarding this neglect, see the *Express*, 23 August 1974, and Charles L. Cotrell, *Municipal Services Equalization in San Antonio, Texas: Explorations in Chinatown*, vol. 2 (San Antonio: St. Mary's University, Department of Urban Studies, 1976).

24. *Light*, 21 December 1975; Calvin Trillin, "U.S. Journal: San Antonio," *New Yorker*, 2 May 1977, 92–93.

25. *Express*, 6 April, 3, 5 May 1970.

26. *Express-News*, 9, 16 November 1975.

27. *Express*, 22 November 1976.

28. L. Tucker Gibson, "Mayoralty Elections in San Antonio" (Paper presented at the Southwestern Political Science Association, April 1978), 12–13.

29. Paul Burka, "The Second Battle of the Alamo," *Texas Monthly* (December 1977).

30. Robert Brischetto, Charles L. Cotrell, and R. Michael Stevens, "Structural Change and Voter Participation in the Political Culture of San Antonio in the 1970s," in Johnson, Booth, and Harris, eds., *The Politics of San Antonio*.

31. *Express*, 27 October, 20, 21 November, 16 December 1977.

32. *Light*, 31 May 1978.

33. Brischetto, Cotrell, and Stevens, "Structural Change and Voter Participation," 178–180.

34. *Express*, 3 January 1980.

35. *Express-News*, 18 October 1981.

10
ALBUQUERQUE
CITY AT A CROSSROADS

by Howard N. Rabinowitz

World War II helped transform numerous small western towns into sprawling metropolises. Although journalists and politicians have recently discovered the shift of people and political power to the so-called Sunbelt, historians have been slow to seek the causes and consequences of the urban West's remarkable postwar expansion. Western historians rarely venture past the turn of the twentieth century and when they do it is usually to examine nonurban matters. And with few exceptions, urban historians have limited themselves to the history of a handful of large eastern and midwestern cities in the years prior to 1920. As a result, economists, political scientists, and sociologists have taken the lead among social scientists in examining such issues crucial to the postwar development of western cities as city-suburb relations, annexation, land-use planning, and growth policies.[1] Yet each of these issues requires careful historical investigation if we are to understand the phenomenon of rapid growth in the urban West.

The experience of the Albuquerque SMSA since 1940 reflects what has been happening throughout most of the urban West. In 1940 New Mexico's Bernalillo County had 69,391 residents, 35,449 of whom were concentrated in Albuquerque, the state's largest city. Ten years later when the county was designated the Albuquerque SMSA, its population had grown to 145,673, on its way to 262,199 in 1960 and 315,774 in 1970. In the latter year it ranked ninety-sixth out of 233 SMSAs, although Albuquerque itself was the nation's fifty-eighth largest city with a population of 243,751. A mix of economic, cultural, and locational factors continues to attract not only midwestern and eastern Anglos, who are primarily middle class, but also large numbers of predominantly lower-class Hispanics from small northern New Mexican villages and, of course, from nearby states and Mexico. Thus census figures for 1980 show the city again growing at a faster rate than the county, with a population of

331,767, nearly 34 percent of whom are Hispanic. (Although the proportion of Hispanics is down about a percentage point from 1970, that group remains the city's primary minority element by a large margin; the percentages of blacks and American Indians showed slight increases but only to 2.4 percent and 2.2 percent, respectively.) Along with the rapid growth so typical of western cities has come a relationship between city and suburb that not only separates the Albuquerque SMSA from most of its eastern and midwestern counterparts, but even from many older Sunbelt SMSAs. A look at Albuquerque's recent history will reveal much about the forces shaping the patterns of growth throughout metropolitan America.

During the late nineteenth century, the railroad created a network of new or expanded communities throughout the west. With obvious exceptions such as Los Angeles and Denver, most of these places enjoyed only moderate growth until World War II. Like its Sunbelt contemporaries Tucson and Phoenix, Albuquerque on the eve of the war was basically what it had been since the railroad brought it into being in 1880: little more than a small town that attracted tourists and health seekers and served as a trading and distribution center for a limited hinterland. World War II and the cold war that followed, however, led to the establishment and rapid expansion of Kirtland Air Force Base and Sandia and Manzano bases, which specialized in special weapons development and atomic research. By the mid 1950s the military and military-related activities so common in the region had replaced the declining Santa Fe Railroad as the city's most important source of economic growth. The federal government further stimulated the local economy by continuing its prewar policy of establishing regional offices for numerous federal agencies, a policy that had already given the city the nickname "Little Washington." Growth was also generated by the expansion of the University of New Mexico from 1,800 students in 1940 to over 5,000 in 1950 and more than 20,000 by the mid 1970s. The opening of the university's school of medicine, together with the construction or enlargement of several public and private hospitals, enhanced the city's long-standing reputation as a health center. The continued success of the tourist industry, especially after the rediscovery of Indian crafts, also helped sustain growth. Albuquerque's future growth seems further assured by its pleasant climate; amply water supply (especially rare among western cities); location astride major highway, rail, and air routes (new airlines are added every year at the greatly expanded Albuquerque International Airport); and proximity to rich natural resources. Though the city has been hurt by the recent decline in the demand for uranium, the in-

MAP 10.1. The Albuquerque SMSA

flux of new electronic firms has picked up some of the slack. In short, despite rosy predictions about the city's prospects for industrial expansion, Albuquerque can be classified as a typical postindustrial city dependent upon a government- and service-oriented economy that in 1970 had only 7 percent of its work force in manufacturing jobs.[2]

The SMSA is atypical, however, in that as late as 1970 it consisted of a single county totally dominated by a central city whose share of the SMSA population had grown from 51.1 percent in 1940 to 77.2 percent in 1970. During the same period the percentage of residents in the central cities of most of the country's largest metropolitan areas declined so that by 1973 in only twenty-one of the top eighty-five SMSAs did central-city population represent as much as 60 percent of the total metropolitan population. The percentage was 34 percent in the major eastern cities, but even in the sample's eighteen western cities the mean was only 44 percent. Although the South, including Texas, had the greatest concentration of metropolitan population in its central cities, fewer than half of its twenty-seven cities exceeded the 60 percent mark.[3]

The city of Albuquerque was until 1975 one of only two incorporated places in the entire SMSA, the other being the village of Los Ranchos de Albuquerque, population 1,900 in 1970. The absence of incorporated suburbs that so trouble most other cities was due to several factors, including a 1963 law (recently repealed) that forbade the incorporation of communities within five miles of the central city, the poverty of the small villages in the area, and the fact that many areas outside of the city were satisfied with their access to city and county services. As recently as 1976, the last in a series of attempts to incorporate the adjacent South Valley failed dismally.[4]

A final cause for the absence of incorporated communities also helps account for the remarkable growth of the central city. This, of course, has been an aggressive policy of annexation so typical of many Sunbelt cities. As early as 1940 the city administration, local newspapers, and the Chamber of Commerce expressed concern about the proliferation of new subdivisions just outside the city limits. In response, they launched a Greater Albuquerque campaign to bring these areas into the city in time for the taking of the 1940 census. "Not only should Old Town be a part of the present city of Albuquerque, but so should all the territory adjacent to the city," declared the *Albuquerque Journal* in one of its frequent editorials on the subject. "To all intent and purposes," it continued, "the entire built up community that surrounds Albuquerque is Albuquerque, and should officially become so."[5] The failure to bring in these new areas encouraged the city commission to revise its previously liberal policy of extending services to noncity residents. As one commissioner put it, "If we continue to extend water and fire protection outside the city, why will people want to come inside the limits?"[6] The withholding of city services did lead to a few small annexations, but as late as 1946 the *Journal* was still complaining that

> the growth in the last few years has been more rapid outside the city than within. It has resulted in areas being developed without adequate water, sewer and other services. It is becoming a detriment to health and physical appearances of greater Albuquerque. . . . We need some program whereby we can be brought together in one big municipality and improvements extended to all areas.[7]

With the aid of favorable state legislation, such a program was soon undertaken, with dramatic results. In 1940 the city comprised an area of eleven square miles. This was increased to sixteen square miles in June 1946 and to twenty-four square miles in October 1948. By 1950 the city limits had more than doubled, and by 1973 they covered an area of 82.2 square miles. Today Albuquerque sprawls over more than 105 square miles.[8] Prior to 1950 much of the annexed land already contained sizable populations; after 1950 and especially during the early 1960s most of the land was empty and was brought into the city at the request of developers who hoped that city services would make their subdivisions more attractive. This new acreage was primarily on the east side of the Rio Grande in an area commonly known as the Heights, which stretched for miles from east of downtown toward the foothills of the Sandia Mountains. There are no accurate figures with which to gauge the impact of annexation on city population growth during the 1940s, although at least twenty thousand residents were immediately added when the city tripled in area between 1946 and 1950. Census data for subsequent years provide a firmer picture of annexation's role, although in this case most of the new residents arrived after annexation had occurred. In 1960, 23,646 of the city's 201,189 residents lived in areas annexed during the previous decade; ten years later, however, 234,036 of the city's 243,751 people lived within the boundaries of the 1960 city.[9]

Not surprisingly, widespread annexation produced a socioeconomic pattern quite unlike that found in most SMSAs outside certain parts of the Sunbelt. The central city was able to maintain a middle-income base either by annexing already heavily populated middle-class Anglo subdivisions or else by annexing largely undeveloped land before it drew middle-class migrants from within the city's original boundaries. Unlike most cities, particularly those in the East and Midwest, Albuquerque was able to catch most members of the fleeing middle class.[10] It is true that generally low-income areas such as Barelas, Martineztown, and Old Town were also added to the city, but their presence was more than balanced by the addition of middle- and upper-income areas and by the number of semi-rural, low-income districts still outside the city. As a result, the socioeconomic status of central-city residents (as expressed in median years of schooling completed, median income of families and unrelated individuals, and percentage of persons employed in managerial and professional jobs) has been consistently higher than that of the rest of the SMSA.

It needs to be added that although the city's indicators have improved with each census, those of the surrounding territory have increased more rapidly, thus steadily reducing the gap since 1940. Nevertheless, the 1970 census still found city residents with a median income of $7,737 versus $7,371 for the entire SMSA; 12.6 years of schooling versus 12.5, and 34.9 percent in professional and managerial positions versus 32.3 percent. The contrast with the central city was greatest in the urban fringe. Almost three-fifths of the fringe's 53,000 people were concentrated in the heavily Chicano South Valley, where residents had 10.3 years of schooling and a median income of $5,543. Almost 30 percent of the residents were under the poverty level compared to only 14.2 percent within the city. The North Valley, which contained over ten thousand residents, enjoyed a much higher socioeconomic status than the South Valley, due mainly to the presence of several wealthy Anglo enclaves, but as a whole still lagged considerably behind the city.

These findings support sociologist Leo Schnore's hypothesis that in younger SMSAs the central cities will have higher socioeconomic status than the suburbs in contrast to the pattern of suburban superiority found in older SMSAs. The so-called Tucson-Albuquerque type he isolated in the 1950s and 1960s is still alive and well in the Albuquerque of the 1980s, even though, as he predicted, the gap is narrowing between city and suburbs.[11] As the contrast between the North and South valleys suggests, however, we must not lose sight of the significant disparities within the suburban ring. But that is a subject for another essay.

What can be examined here, however, is the general character of city-suburb relations. This has already been touched on in the discussion of annexation, but it needs to be emphasized that the process of annexation has not always gone without opposition. As one county resident put it in 1940, "Up to date I haven't heard of people living outside the city begging to be admitted."[12] And indeed many residents of places annexed during the late 1940s were practically dragged into the city after prolonged court battles, petition drives, and lobbying efforts. There was especially strong resistance from residents of Old Town, the original settlement of Albuquerque founded in 1706 but later overwhelmed by the new railroad town. Proponents of annexation stressed the benefits of improved public services for Old Town and the impact of sanitary advances, a "bigger 1950 census total," and a richer historical heritage for Albuquerque.[13] Opponents countered that "annexation will substantially increase taxes on every owner of real property in Old Town, will mean payment of a sewer tax, [and] will mean higher occupation license fees for business." For good measure they added that "the present city administration is arrogant, overbearing, and dictatorial."[14] This opposition proved unsuccesful, but noncity residents subsequently have been better able to resist several other efforts at annexation and especially to thwart attempts at city-county consolidation.

Consolidation was considered at least as early as 1940,[15] but the issue came to a head during a lackluster campaign in 1973. Unlike most recent consolidation campaigns elsewhere, neither ethnicity nor class was a motivating factor due to the relatively even distribution of the SMSA's minorities and to the heavy concentration in the county of low-income people, most of whom were Chicano. Advocates of consolidation argued that the rapid growth of the previous thirty years had produced a wasteful duplication of urban services.

City voters in a light turnout cast a slight majority in favor of consolidation, but irate county voters turned out in large numbers to overwhelmingly defeat the proposal.[16] The negative arguments were those generally found in such campaigns and centered around a feared increase in taxes and loss of political power. More interesting, though, were the fears of county residents that their semirural way of life would be destroyed by rigid city building restrictions. Since they already enjoyed most city services, including libraries, buses, and water, the county dwellers felt that consolidation would not offer sufficient advantages to offset these fears.[17] In short, county residents, be they Anglo or Chicano, rich or poor, felt and continue to feel along with most suburbanites that the ideal situation is proximity to city life so as to enjoy its benefits while at the same time avoiding the burdens that city residents must bear.

Consolidation is not a dead issue, however, although there are signs that if it is to be successful it will have to be done on a piecemeal basis that involves specific governmental functions rather than an immediate wholesale merger. Some functional consolidation has already taken place. In 1940 there were separate and totally independent boards of education and superintendents for the city and county schools. Five years later the county system turned over its largest district to the city board and in 1949 the two systems were consolidated under the progressive leadership of the city superintendent, John Milne.[18] Currently there is a good deal of discussion about the value of combining the Albuquerque Police Department and the Bernalillo County Sheriff's Office in the name of economy and greater efficiency. Such a merger would be particularly significant. During the 1973 referendum the county sheriff was one of the most vocal opponents of city-county consolidation because of the effect it would have had on his position and his patronage-ridden department. The recent leasing of the Bernalillo County Medical Center to the University of New Mexico for $1 per year could be a further factor in any consolidation effort. Removing education, hospital administration, and possibly police protection from the purview of county government would leave that government with little reason to exist. The fact that inefficiency and scandal characterize the administration of its remaining functions would further weaken the forces opposing consolidation. Perhaps symbolic of the future course of consolidation was a favorable 1981 bond vote on the construction of a city-county office building.

The consolidation issue has implications for the broader issues of planning and controlled growth. As early as 1947, the *Albuquerque Journal* observed that

Albuquerque in its years of rapid growth has been built without any planning. The result has been that the city has not the
physical appearance that it should possess. Blighted areas exist
where they should not have been allowed. Business or commercial areas have encroached upon residential districts. It
will take years of effort to overcome these defects.[19]

Yet despite the passage of state legislation in 1947 allowing municipalities to establish planning commissions, the city did not have a
permanent planning department or zoning ordinance until the early
1950s, and until the late 1960s developers and boosters controlled
land-use policy.[20] Under a new coalition of professionals and businessmen that had ended Boss Clyde Tingley's longtime control of
the city commission in the early 1950s, subdivisions were laid out in
checkerboard fashion on the city's outskirts and a highly destructive
urban renewal program was initiated downtown. By the mid 1960s
this new governing clique, which drew its support from the recent
migrants in the Heights and included both Anglos and middle-class
Hispanics, was at the peak of its powers and could boast among its
most forceful members the future U.S. senator Pete Domenici. As
elsewhere, however, the late 1960s brought an increased awareness
of the weaknesses of uncontrolled growth. Calls for limited growth
came from environmentally conscious migrants and longtime residents who claimed that urban sprawl, pollution, and destruction of
old landmarks were undermining the quality of life. One outcome of
this reaction was the adoption of the city's first comprehensive plan,
issued in four parts in 1975.

Another manifestation of this increased interest in limited
growth and greater public planning was the conflict between the
five-member city commission (elected at large) and its less growth-
oriented city manager over growth policies that led to the adoption
of a new charter in 1974. Four months after voters rejected the more
radical remedy of city-county consolidation, city residents decided
to return to the district-based, council-mayor form of government
that they had abandoned in 1917, though this time it was to be on a
nonpartisan basis.[21] And capping this era of reexamination of the traditional "bigger is better" approach of the public and private sectors
was the election in the fall of 1977 of Democratic mayor David
Rusk, the son of the former secretary of state. Rusk, who had come
to the city a few years earlier as a federal bureaucrat, ran on a platform that supported the comprehensive plan, downtown revitalization, improved mass transit, and strong mayoral leadership. He opposed construction of another bridge across the Rio Grande, which

separates the city's populous east side from the developing West Mesa. The ease of his election over Harry Kinney, the conservative, more progrowth incumbent, was surprising and still defies easy analysis. Although Democrats had about one and one-half times as many registered voters as the Republicans, many of the Democrats were conservatives who lived in the Heights and normally voted Republican in national and state elections, while others were poor Hispanics with a history of low voter turnout. And unlike the situation in other states with large Hispanic populations, New Mexico's Hispanics, especially members of the growing middle class, traditionally give a generous share of their vote to Republicans. Thus Kinney enjoyed considerable support among both Democratic and Republican Hispanics, support that should have been particularly effective in a technically nonpartisan election against a newcomer with little prior political experience. But Rusk was able to fashion a winning coalition based on voter dissatisfaction with the incumbent and the support of well-organized, young, middle-class activists. Many of the latter were, like Rusk, relatively new residents who realized that Albuquerque needed to take forceful action in order to successfully guide its transformation from an overgrown small town or refuge from suburbia into a true city. Only then could the city make the most of its choice site and almost unlimited opportunities for "the good life." After taking office, Rusk pushed ahead plans to make downtown a thriving commercial, cultural, and residential district, sought to encourage a sense of neighborhood identity, pressed for acquisition of land on the city's periphery to guarantee the preservation of open spaces, and announced a slowdown in the expansion of city services to prospective leap-frog subdivisions.

Despite some successes, Rusk ran into strong council and public opposition, especially over the issues of downtown revitalization and increased taxes to improve mass transit and the police department. Furthermore, he made a number of poor appointments and was indecisive on several key matters, including the location of a major new hotel in the Heights rather than downtown and the need for new bridge crossings over the Rio Grande. More damaging, however, was the seemingly minor decision to save money and improve other services by partially disbanding the city's weed and litter force. A rainy summer in 1981 left the city with a weed eyesore that became the primary early issue in Rusk's reelection campaign and, along with streets torn up to replace a decaying 1950s infrastructure, served as a symbol to the voters of seemingly declining services in the face of rising user fees. In an officially nonpartisan race that was devoid of serious discussion of crucial issues, Rusk finished third to two Republicans: Harry Kinney, whom Rusk had soundly defeated four years before, and Gordon Sanders, a conservative, shoot-from-the-hip, local TV and radio broadcaster cut in the Jesse Helms mold. Sanders drew laughs with his numerous folksy quips and cheers for threatening to fire high-priced bureaucrats, but he had little of substance to say about the city's future.

Rusk is bright and articulate and his farsighted agenda was a good one, but he got too far ahead of a public that he failed to educate about the complex new realities of life in a rapidly changing Albuquerque. In a sense, then, Rusk's defeat was due to the same combination of forces—personal limits as a politician, years of neglect of tough problems by predecessors, and an escapist, resentful public—that had previously brought down Jimmy Carter, whom Rusk greatly admired.

In the runoff necessitated by the failure of either Kinney or Sanders to garner 40 percent of the vote, Kinney won by a surprisingly small margin of 54 percent. Sanders's first try for office brought out a record 50 percent of the voters, who were united across ethnic, party, and class boundaries by a growing dissatisfaction with local government and who had a penchant toward easy answers to complex problems. Kinney, an engineer who, as the first mayor under the new charter and a former chairman of the old city commission, was seen as a part of the business-professional establishment that had been running the city since the early 1950s, was put in the ironic position of defending much that Rusk sought to accomplish. He even came out strongly for controlled growth, though on the basis of his more than twenty-five-year progrowth record in local government it is not immediately evident what he meant by the term. Nevertheless, such positions, together with understandable reservations about Sanders's ability to run the city, led most of Rusk's supporters to switch to Kinney and assure his victory.[22]

Whether or not Kinney has truly converted, the success of any advocates of controlled growth will depend on their ability to rally an often apathetic public against the ever-vigilant progrowth forces and to overcome somehow the decentralization of power in the metropolitan area. Though power is not as fragmented as in most metropolitan areas, the lack of coordination among city government, county government, two flood-control districts, the intercounty council of governments, and the autonomous Albuquerque Public Schools (until recently, the only local body engaged in systematic long-range planning and whose acquisition of further school sites under Superintendent Milne helped determine the direction of urban growth) has made it difficult in the past to institute positive measures and prevent destructive tendencies.

In Albuquerque's favor is the fact that the immediate future will bring little change in its dominance of the SMSA, though in the wake of the 1980 incorporation of Rio Rancho future efforts at incorporation by both high- and low-status areas can be expected. Annexations will continue, albeit on a reduced basis, and the socioeconomic gap between the city and the rest of the SMSA will actually increase as a result of the post-1970 addition of Sandoval County to the Albuquerque SMSA. Sandoval's population of about 22,500 in 1975 contained some high-status residents in the small incorporated villages of Corrales and Jemez Springs and in the developer's dream of Rio Rancho, but overall its socioeconomic indicators in 1970 were much lower than those of the SMSA as defined in 1970. Sandoval, for example, had 41.2 percent of its workers in white-collar jobs versus 60.7 percent for Bernalillo County; median years of schooling completed were 10.3 versus 12.5; and median income was 60 percent of Bernalillo's. Sandoval is growing faster than Bernalillo largely because its percentage increase in net migration is twice as great, but even the continued influx of high-status people will require at least another decade for it to match Bernalillo indicators. By that time some form of metropolitan consolidation may well have taken place.

Meanwhile the critical issues in local politics will continue to revolve around the often conflicting claims of the economy and the environment and will pit against each other the proponents and opponents of planned growth. What is most interesting here is that the low-income areas of the suburban ring will have the most to gain economically and the most to lose culturally. Will the heavily Chicano, native-born New Mexicans currently tied to a semirural way of life join with the developers and Chamber of Commerce boosters in the fight against middle- and upper-income Anglo newcomers dedicated to the preservation of what is unique about Albuquerque? The answer to that question will determine much of what happens to the Albuquerque SMSA during the remainder of the century.

As it stands, Albuquerque now threatens to repeat the mistakes of the 1950s but this time on the burgeoning west side—for which two new bridge crossings have finally been approved and where the policies of the comprehensive plan are being challenged—and in the new satellite downtown that is emerging around the two regional shopping centers constructed during the 1960s in the Northeast Heights off Interstate 40. To make matters worse, the city council has suffered a notable decline in quality during the past two elections and an increasing hardcore minority of residents is determined to vote against all bond issues or even innocuous charter revisions. The new council initially rejected a Rusk-initiated auto-emission program aimed at alleviating the city's deplorable air pollution problem. It has since approved an alternative plan but its eventual implementation is still in doubt. Similarly unclear is the status of a strong sign ordinance that sought to deal with the city's visual pollution. Reaganomics and growing public hostility threaten the nascent preservation movement, and the closing of schools with declining enrollment demonstrates how the lack of coordination between city government and the Albuquerque Public Schools system is undermining the health of older neighborhoods. In short, it is questionable as to how long Albuquerque's dominance of its metropolitan area will make up for the city's uninformed privatistic population and a serious deficiency in leadership and long-range planning.

NOTES

NOTE: Parts of this essay originally appeared as "Growth Trends in the Albuquerque SMSA, 1940–1978." They are reprinted with the permission of the *Journal of the West* (July 1979), copyright 1979 by the *Journal of the West, Inc.*

1. For exceptions see Kenneth T. Jackson, "Metropolitan Government versus Political Autonomy: Politics on the Crabgrass Frontier," in Kenneth T. Jackson and Stanley K. Schultz, eds., *Cities in American History* (New York: Alfred A. Knopf, 1972), 442–462, and some of the works cited in the introduction.

2. The statistical information is from various publications of the U.S. Bureau of the Census and is not cited specifically. For useful background material see Marc Simmons, *Albuquerque: A Narrative History* (Albuquerque: University of New Mexico Press, 1982); Erna Fergusson, *Albuquerque* (Albuquerque: Merle Armitage Editions, 1947); idem, "Albuquerque: A Place to Live in," in Ray B. West, Jr., ed., *Rocky Mountain Cities* (New York: W. W. Norton and Co., 1949), 151–178; "Albuquerque: Bombs Build Boom Town," *Business Week*, 13 May 1950, 58–61; Neil M. Clark, "The Cities of America: Albuquerque," *Saturday Evening Post*, 8 April 1950, 26–27ff.; Alan J. Oppenheimer, *The Historical Background of Albuquerque* (Albuquerque City Planning Department, 1962, mimeo); Albuquerque National Bank, *Albuquerque Progress*, various issues 1934 ff.; *Albuquerque Journal*, 19 August 1982 (hereafter cited as *Journal*).

3. San Antonio, Memphis, Austin, Jacksonville, and El Paso had higher percentages of the SMSA population in the central cities. Advisory Commission on Intergovernmental Relations (ACIR), *Trends in Metropolitan America* (Washington, D.C., February 1977), 3, 14–16.

4. *Journal*, 5 November 1960, 20, 22 September 1963, 11 November, 6 December 1945. See also Irene Fisher, *Bathtub and Silver Bullet* (Placitas, N.M.: The Tumbleweed Press, 1976).

5. *Journal*, 23, 30 (editorial) January 1940.

6. Ibid., 21 February 1970.

7. Ibid., 9 January 1946, 12 June 1940; *Albuquerque Progress* 13 (June 1946): 3, 13.

8. E. H. Chacon, *Annexations to the City of Albuquerque* (Albuquerque City Engineer's Office, Department of Public Works, 1967); *Journal*, 24 February 1978.

9. *Journal*, 22 August 1948, 25 January 1950.

10. See Jackson, "Metropolitan Government," 442–462; ACIR, *Trends*, 3.

11. See Leo Schnore, "Measuring City-Suburban Status Differences," *Urban Affairs Quarterly* 3 (September 1967): 95–108; idem, *Class and Race in City and Suburbs* (Chicago: Markham Publishing Co., 1972); John D. Kasarda and George V. Redfern, "Differential Patterns of City and Suburban Growth in the United States," *Journal of Urban History* 2 (November 1975): 43–66; John J. Harrigan, "A New Look at Central-City Suburban Differences," *Social Science* 51 (Autumn 1976): 200–208.

12. *Journal*, 21 June 1940 (letter).

13. See ibid., 18 February 1948, 11 April 1949.

14. Ibid., 11 April 1949 (quote). Annexation opposition can be found in the Albuquerque City Commission minutes for August–September 1948 and January 1949. See also *Journal*, 27 January 1950.

15. *Journal*, 5, 7 December 1940, 21 September, 16 November, 24 December 1950; City Commission Minutes, July–September 1952, January 1953.

16. City residents voted 12,533 for consolidation and 10,072 against. County dwellers were 1,392 for and 7,477 against. Daniel D. Weaks, "An Analysis of the Consolidation Effort in Albuquerque-Bernalillo County," Studies in Urban Affairs no. 19 (Albuquerque: Albuquerque Urban Observatory, 1973, mimeo), 86.

17. Ibid., passim; *Journal*, 10, 14, 23 January 1940, 19 June 1950.

18. *Journal*, 11, 12 December 1940, 21 March, 28 April, 1, 2 May 1945; Tom Wiley, *Public School Education in New Mexico* (Albuquerque: Division of Government Reserach, University of New Mexico, 1965), 91.

19. *Journal*, 20 June 1947 (editorial), 28 August 1948.

20. Oppenheimer, "Historical Background," A-16; City Commission Minutes, 17 November 1953; Dorothy I. Cline, *Albuquerque and the City Manager Plan, 1917–1948* (Albuquerque: Division of Research, Department of Government, University of New Mexico, 1951), 33.

21. Paul L. Hain et al., "From Council-Manager to Mayor-Council: The Case of Albuquerque," *Nation's Cities* 13 (October 1975): 10–12.

22. *Journal*, 7 October, 11 November 1981.

11

LOS ANGELES

IMPROBABLE LOS ANGELES

by David L. Clark

It struck me as an odd thing that here, alone of all the cities in America, there was no answer to the question, "Why did a town spring up here, and why has it grown so big?"—Morris Markey, *This Country of Yours*, 1932

Los Angeles is today in population the second largest urban area in the nation and the sixth largest in the world. Were it an independent country, Los Angeles would rank twelfth among the nations in production. The city is the world's leading center of entertainment, popular culture, and aerospace technology. Few developments in humanity's past have been more improbable than the rise of Los Angeles to its present position.

Two thousand miles of mountains and deserts isolate Southern California from the nation's main centers of population and industry. Reviewing future possibilities for economic expansion in 1945, the War Production Board concluded: "Those mountains and dry lands constitute the great wall of California. They are barriers that separate the West Coast industrially from the other states. California is an economic island."[1]

Not only is Southern California an island, it is a desert island. Its streams could provide water for only a small fraction of the present population. It lacks coal and iron, the sinews of the industrial revolution. Settlers found no local forests to provide lumber for construction. Compounding the city's distance from major markets, resources, and trade routes, Los Angeles also lacked the sort of natural harbor with which San Francisco and San Diego are blessed. Almost everything found in Los Angeles today has been created artificially or imported.

Through a combination of advertising and engineering, Los Angeles created the conditions that nature did not provide. From its unlikely beginnings as a small and isolated pueblo, Los Angeles built a major metropolitan area by constructing an artificial harbor, transporting water, and importing orange, palm, and eucalyptus trees. The city developed unique industries unhampered by geography.

Los Angeles pioneered a new type of city and economy. It was the predecessor of the Sunbelt and the first postindustrial metropolis. Los Angeles brought in the money necessary for an expanding economy not through exporting goods, but by drawing in people. The migrants did not come just for factory jobs, of which the city had few to offer, but in the pursuit of hopes and dreams. Los Angeles became the nation's dream spinner and faith healer: the City of the Second Chance.

The manufacturing activities that Los Angeles developed—entertainment and aerospace—perpetuated the earlier patterns more often than changing them. Both activities avoided the region's historic limitations. Neither required much in the way of raw materials. Shipping distance was of no importance if the export was but a canister of film, or an electronic signal, or if the product itself could fly.

The city's unusual pattern of growth had strong consequences for the social, political, and even religious life of the community. Los Angeles lacked traditional, established, social elites, perhaps to its benefit. It became a city in which it was difficult to be a nonconformist because of the lack of clear standards against which to rebel. Newcomers could not be absorbed into the majority, for they were the majority. In every decade social patterns were broken. The result was more personal freedom but also more loneliness, which sometimes found outlet in charismatic religious and political movements. Political parties did not take root deeply, and as a result politics centered on personality and media coverage rather than organizational loyalty.

The geography of Los Angeles made it a borderland between different cultures and ethnic groups. Los Angeles stands on a frontier between Europe and Asia and between Anglo and Hispanic cultures. As a borderland it has been an arena for conflict as well as assimilation.

The two main themes of Los Angeles history thus originate from the city's geographical position. These themes—the improbable economic development of a resource-poor island on the land and the tension between acceptance and conflict in a racial and cultural borderland—are the features to be found constantly throughout the city's past. They have had marked effects upon the economic, social, labor, religious, and political characteristics of Los Angeles in every era of its existence.

MAP 11.1. The Los Angeles–Long Beach SMSA

Los Angeles, although founded in 1781, truly began with the real estate boom of 1887. In one year the town's population grew by nearly five times, from 11,000 to 50,000, irrevocably setting the community on a course of "grow or perish." Population growth preceded and created economic expansion, rather than following it in the late-nineteenth-century pattern of the Northeast and Midwest.

The boom began in 1887 when the Santa Fe Railroad completed its line into Los Angeles and began to compete with the Southern Pacific, which had enjoyed a monopoly since 1876. The first boom set a standard of flimflam that subsequent enthusiasms have approached but never equaled. Some promoters attached oranges to Joshua trees. Other astute developers donated portions of their land for the creation of colleges, and many local institutions of higher learning owe their origins to this early real estate speculation. The boom collapsed when banks refused to take real estate as security. And for good reason, since developers had laid out a half-million lots at a time when the county recorded only 650 manufacturing jobs.

At this fateful juncture, Los Angeles made its "new beginning." At a meeting of business leaders on 15 October 1888, Harrison Gray

Otis, owner of the *Los Angeles Times*, spearheaded the creation of the Los Angeles Chamber of Commerce, which embarked on a course of continuous promotion, distributing two million pieces of literature within the next three years. From this time forward, Los Angeles advertised itself relentlessly as the golden land of promise and hope. Commercial leaders created the Rose Parade to draw national attention to Southern California's balmy weather by staging an outdoor event with fresh flowers in the middle of winter.

As a result of the chamber's efforts, Los Angeles outdistanced all other metropolitan centers in the United States in rate of population increase. From an ambitious small town of 11,000 in 1887, Los Angeles became by 1930 a city of 1,238,000, with another million suburbanites living in the county.

As many as one-fourth of the new residents of Southern California came for reasons of health or accompanied a relative who migrated for such reasons.[2] The medical science of the time prescribed a move to a dry, sunny climate as the last resort for many ailments, especially respiratory disorders. Many of those who came in hope of a cure later turned to faith healing, partly accounting for the wide variety of religious enthusiasms to be found in Los Angeles.

Tourism has been an integral part of the Los Angeles scene and economy since the 1880s, and today Los Angeles continues as a tourist Mecca. Busloads of Japanese disembark hourly at Grauman's Chinese Theater in Hollywood to marvel at the cemented footprints of the stars. Three of the nation's top five tourist attractions are located near Los Angeles. In 1981, 123.1 million visitors spent $8.8 billion in the Los Angeles area.

Present-day residents of the city may be surprised to learn that in 1920 Los Angeles possessed an urban transit system judged to be one of the best in the nation. It was not the automobile but the trolley that determined the city's shape. The Pacific Electric Railway system created, or allowed the creation of, the Los Angeles suburban lifestyle, which was aptly summed up by an electric railway ad in the early 1900s: "Live in the Country and Work in the City." Racing along at speeds of forty-five to fifty-five miles per hour, the Red Cars of the Pacific Electric made it possible for Los Angeles residents to live near the beach or in the midst of orange groves and to work downtown. The forty-two incorporated cities spreading out along the trolley lines within a radius of thirty-five miles of Los Angeles constituted the fastest growing urban area in the United States and the nation's largest interurban transit network. His lines, owner Henry Huntington said, "extended into the open country, ahead of, and not behind, the population." The Pacific Electric lost millions of dollars extending lines far ahead of demands for service, but the loss was compensated many times over by the profits from land sales by the Huntington Land and Improvement Company. In fact, the system was built not to provide transportation but to sell real estate.[3]

The trolley system was overbuilt and therefore costly to run. Mass transit requires a dense population if the system is to run efficiently and economically, but the Pacific Electric had shaped a city so dispersed that no transit system could ever break even serving it. Los Angeles had a population density far lower than that of other large cities, with a number of inhabitants per square mile in 1930 one-sixth that of Chicago and one-eighth that of New York.

Moreover, even while the Pacific Electric provided excellent transit service, Los Angeles became the first city to fully adopt the automobile. By 1930, Los Angeles County contained more cars per resident than any other community in the world. As early as 1937, 80 percent of all local trips were made in automobiles.[4] Private autos hurt the Pacific Electric by taking away business and clogging the streets on which the trolleys ran.

Los Angeles rejected the pattern of the concentrated, centralized, eastern city and chose instead to become a collection of suburban communities that strongly resembled the midwestern small towns from which 37 percent of the population had recently emigrated. The electric trolleys, which had originally encouraged dispersal, were rejected when they threatened to bring genuine urbanization. In the 1920s the city set a new direction for urban development and transportation. By the end of the decade Los Angeles had become the model for other cities in the West; after World War II it became the prototype of the mid-twentieth-century metropolis. In the 1950s and 1960s, the Los Angeles suburban lifestyle was established as the prevailing middle-class model in a thousand situation-comedy episodes produced in Southern California. Even "Duckburg," where Donald Duck and his nephews lived, was clearly a Los Angeles suburb, with single-family homes and freeways.[5]

Los Angeles in 1930 housed a higher proportion of its population (94 percent) in single-family homes than any other metropolis of comparable size. Seventy-two percent remained in detached dwellings in 1960, compared to 28 percent in Chicago, 20 percent in New York, and 15 percent in Philadelphia. Downtown Los Angeles in 1920 was the focus of commercial activity. Today downtown accounts for only 3 percent of the area's retail sales. Wilshire Boulevard's Miracle Mile in the 1920s was the area's first shopping center to be built away from the trolley tracks and the first to attract large branch operations from the downtown establishments. To the post-war suburban generation, downtown seemed almost foreign, the least typical part of the region.

On 30 December 1940, just in time to take visitors to the Rose Parade, the Pasadena Freeway opened, the first freeway in the western United States. By 1960, Los Angeles County had more than 250 miles of freeways. By the 1970s, five hundred miles of concrete ribbon extended across Los Angeles County, and two thousand miles spread across Southern California. The freeway building program was financed by gasoline taxes, pushed by lobbies of contractors and real estate developers, and supported by the hordes who headed west. New freeway construction expanded the area within a half-hour drive of downtown from 261 square miles in 1953 to 705 square miles in 1962, while suburbs grew like fruit on a branch along each new freeway extension. By 1980, the ten million people living within a sixty-mile circle of downtown Los Angeles operated eight millon motor vehicles.

Freeway construction came to a virtual halt in Los Angeles by the end of the 1970s, with less than half of the 1950 California Master Plan completed. Building costs had skyrocketed, and by the end of the decade almost any determined community could thwart the state department of transportation by demanding an Environmental Impact Report. Also, the realization grew that the primary result of a new transportation artery was not to relieve present congestion, but to induce new traffic to destinations that now became more accessible. Henry Huntington had demonstrated the process seventy years earlier. Highway engineers simply completed Huntington's work. Some have proposed a return to a mass-rail system, but high costs, questionable net energy savings, and community opposition to higher density development will apparently doom such plans.[6]

Los Angeles could not grow into the metropolis that it aspired to be on the basis of boosterism alone. The three great obstacles in the path of development were the lack of a good harbor, the absence of a water supply that could match future growth, and the shortage of energy for industry in a region without coal. The success of Los Angeles in overcoming these handicaps would eventually make it the metropolis of the Southwest, with one-third of the total population of the thirteen western states.

In 1889, Los Angeles began a ten-year struggle to secure federal construction of a breakwater that would protect shipping at nearby San Pedro. The extremely powerful Southern Pacific Railroad, how-

ever, wanted the federal appropriation to go to Santa Monica, an alternative Los Angeles harbor site where the company had monopo-
lized rail access.

The *Los Angeles Times* rallied the city time and again around
the uncompromising position that it would be better to abandon
harbor development for the present than to have a Southern Pacific
monopoly port permanently fixed at Santa Monica. The final drama
was played out in Congress where the adverse publicity that Los Angeles had brought to bear defeated the Southern Pacific's plans.

In 1908 the Great White Fleet, which Theodore Roosevelt sent
around the world to announce the entrance of the United States into
the Age of Imperialism, called at San Pedro, symbolically welcoming
Los Angeles into the new era of American commercial supremacy.
The city's hopes were fulfilled when the boom of the 1920s brought
the harbor into full use. Its new harbor allowed Los Angeles to export the production of the decade's tremendous oil strikes.

Today the ports of San Pedro and Long Beach together constitute
the world's largest man-made harbor and handle more than eighty
billion tons of cargo annually, 60 percent of the West's total. They
provide some 120,000 jobs directly and another 100,000 indirectly,
while one in four positions in the Los Angeles area depends on the
harbors in some way.[7]

In the course of the "Free Harbor" battle, the *Times* created a
united business community. With the prestige of the harbor victory
behind them, this group was able in the coming years to enlist widespread citizen support and to portray its foes, especially labor
unions, as the enemies of the city's development. The *Times* never
lost its position (which it holds to this day) as the prime spokesman
for the business community.

Water is the key to development throughout the arid West, and
Los Angeles became the great metropolis of the region primarily because it was the community most successful in concentrating local
control over that scarce and necessary resource. Los Angeles from its
birth held exclusive power over the Los Angeles River, the most reliable water source in the vicinity. Recognizing that additional supplies were the key to future growth, Los Angeles used its power base
to reach out for more water. Municipal leaders managed the new
flow with the same monopoly policy, and expanded the size of the
city by forcing other communities to accept annexation or die of
thirst. The city's western neighbors refer to this procedure as Los
Angeles Water Imperialism.

Southern California today holds 60 percent of the state's population but only 1.7 percent of its natural stream flow. Los Angeles

and its neighbors depend on the importatation of water through long, narrow aqueducts that cross hundreds of miles of surrounding mountains and deserts.

The primary builder of the aqueduct system was William Mulholland, who arrived in 1877 as an Irish immigrant with ten dollars in his pocket and a resolve to "grow with the country." Mulholland as head of the water department created a plan to tap the Owens River, which receives water from the melting snow of the eastern slope of the Sierra Nevada Mountains. The obstacles to the plan were imposing: the harsh terrain through which the aqueduct had to pass, the mountains through which tunnels had to be blasted, and the subterfuge through which the rights had to be obtained.

The final decision on the right of Los Angeles to the water of a valley more than two hundred miles away lay with President Theodore Roosevelt, who had to give the aqueduct right of way over federal land. The decision represented both the best and worst of that era: best in its great accomplishments and worst in the relations between the more and the less powerful. Roosevelt declared that the opposition of the "few settlers in Owens Valley . . . must unfortunately be disregarded in view of the infinitely greater interest to be served by putting the water in Los Angeles."[8] Los Angeles Water Imperialism was a part of its age.

Through subsequent annexation of the San Fernando Valley and other areas, Los Angeles maintained its policy of control over regional growth. Many smaller communities in need of water were absorbed, and the harbor area was annexed to protect the city's port investments and to control trade.

By the early 1920s, Mulholland's water and power projects, built to induce development, had succeeded beyond even the hopes of the city's boosters. The flood of water brought a genuine flood of new residents and new industries. As a result, the Owens Aqueduct, meant to supply the needs of Los Angeles for the next fifty years, ran short in ten, and Mulholland turned toward the Colorado River. The political impediments to the Colorado project loomed higher than the San Jacinto Mountains. Like the Owens Valley water war, the Colorado struggle continues today. The Colorado is the most bitterly contested river in the United States. The opposition of six western states compelled Los Angeles, which had previously annexed neighboring communities, to unite with them to form the Metropolitan Water District (MWD) of Southern California. In 1931, MWD's thirteen cities passed a $220 million bond issue to build the Colorado Aqueduct. The Reconstruction Finance Corporation financed the bond for the project, again indicating the importance of the role of the federal government in western water development. The first water from the Colorado arrived in Southern California in 1941, helping to make possible the aircraft boom of the war years. Today the MWD includes 131 cities and the majority of Southern California's population.

By 1963 Southern California drew half of its water from the Colorado, but in that year Arizona won a larger share of the river in a United States Supreme Court decision. Southern California in 1982 contains a population of nearly 14.5 million and continues to grow at the rate of 300,000 new residents every year. The prospect of losing more than half of the region's Colorado River water to Arizona has focused renewed attention on other sources. One possibility is a forty-three-mile peripheral canal around the Sacramento Delta, which would bring more state project water to Southern California and the San Joaquin Valley; but many fear that the canal would cause increased saltwater intrusion. Nor was Owens Valley forgotten in the continuing search for more water. In 1930 Los Angeles extended the aqueduct another hundred miles to the Mono Basin, and in 1970 the city added a "second barrel" to its original pipeline. Los Angeles intended to pump out even greater amounts, but angry Owens residents are today fighting with a weapon more effective than the dynamite they employed in the 1920s: the Environmental Impact Report. The real charm of the Owens Valley water is a characteristic that Mulholland first seized upon: gravity flow. As the water of Owens Valley drops 2,617 feet on its journey to Los Angeles it turns hydroelectric generators and creates electrical energy; on the other hand, state project and Colorado River water cost energy to pump.

Just as water is vital in an arid region, so is cheap electric power in a region without coal. The Los Angeles Department of Water and Power became the largest municipally owned electric utility in the United States. The department long maintained the city's biggest political machine, with campaign committees in every district to rally support for public power against the opposition of the private power companies. Low-cost electric power became the cutting edge of Los Angeles's industrialization as electricity drove three-fourths of the city's factory machinery during the 1920s. Water flowing through the Owens Aqueduct produced 97 percent of the electricity distributed within the city limits, and additional electric power arrived from the Hoover Dam in 1936.

The manufacturing and population booms that changed Los Angeles after 1940 outstripped the region's ability to generate electricity from water. Today Los Angeles obtains only 15 to 20 percent of its electricity from water power, and much of that comes from the Pacific Northwest.

The oil strikes of the 1920s opened for Southern California all the opportunities and conveniences of a society based on cheap energy. In that decade Los Angeles pumped one-fifth of the world's oil. Petroleum production was the city's largest industry, measured by value of product, while moviemaking held the top position in value added by manufacture.[9] By 1946, 90 percent of the energy consumed on the Pacific Coast came from oil and natural gas. Los Angeles County in 1940 produced twice as much oil as it consumed, but by 1970 both the county and the state imported one-third of the petroleum used locally. Los Angeles still pumps some eighty million barrels of oil yearly and remains a major refining center and manufacturer of petroleum equipment. The six largest corporations in California today are all oil producers; five of the six have their headquarters in Los Angeles.[10]

Southern California has no coal, but coal-produced electricity is delivered to the region from other areas, most notably the Black Mesa lands of northeastern Arizona leased from the Hopi and Navaho tribes. However, there have been growing protests against such arrangements as a form of "exporting pollution," and coal-rich areas now often wish to produce energy for local industrial development rather than for distant metropolises. Like the rest of the nation, Los Angeles looks to new technologies for a brighter energy future.

Agriculture has to a large extent shaped the economic, political, social, and racial composition of the Los Angeles area. Since the Spanish era, political power derived from the concentration of agricultural landholding has had a great, and often a dominant, influence over Southern California. Los Angeles and Orange counties held first and second place, respectively, in the nation in value of agricultural production from 1909 to 1949. As late as 1943, the city limits of Los Angeles included 100,000 acres of farmland, mostly in the San Fernando Valley.

Los Angeles retains strong links with its agricultural roots because much of the farm production of the Southwest is processed, canned, marketed, and shipped through the city and its ports. California today accounts for half of the nation's canned fruit and one-fourth of its canned vegetables. Although canning may employ more people in Los Angeles today than farming, Los Angeles County and Orange County farmers still received a half billion dollars in farm receipts in 1981, and agriculture remained by far the state's leading industry.

Southern California farmers found it necessary to engage in a long and costly process of experimentation to discover what crops and methods would work in a new and untested land with one of the most varied and confusing climates in the world. Growers tried to raise pineapples, bananas, sugarcane, tobacco, tea, coffee, silk, and opium.[11] The need for experimentation gave science, university research, and the federal government a greater role in Southern California than elsewhere.

By 1940 Southern California contained a quarter million acres of orange groves due to the successful introduction of the navel orange from Brazil and the Valencia from the Azores. Organized in 1893, the Sunkist citrus growers' cooperative made the rare and exotic orange a staple by using colorful advertising that promoted both oranges and Southern California at the same time.[12]

The unique agriculture of Southern California created a labor situation that has profoundly affected the region. Specialty fruit crops were not subject to the rapid strides in mechanization that by 1900 had transformed many farm activities; therefore the impetus to maintain a cheap labor supply in the region remained strong. Employers secured an adequate labor force without offering wages and conditions competitive with industry only by importing nonwhite groups who were not allowed to compete directly in the general economy. Thus, agriculture has to a large extent determined the racial mix of present-day Los Angeles. Farm labor practices spilled over to the neighboring urban areas, as nearly all manual labor was, and is, assigned to nonwhite groups. The connection between labor and race is one of the great continuities of local history.

The great exception to the general rule of nonwhite farm labor came with the dust bowl migration of the 1930s. The same attitudes and folk beliefs earlier applied to nonwhites quickly became attached also to the "Okies," suggesting that class, not race, was the key determinant of local reaction.

As the generally deplorable conditions of farm labor became worse during the depression, a wave of strikes broke out. Some of the organizational work was done by the Communist party. The "Red Squad" of the Los Angeles Police Department, organized to break up factory strikes and housed not in the police building but in the offices of the Chamber of Commerce, now went into action against farm workers. The Associated Farmers managed the anti-union drive. This organization included the Bank of America, the Southern Pacific Railroad, Pacific Gas and Electric, and Southern California Edison. The large agricultural, financial, and industrial interests in California have consistently stood together against farm labor. As strikes and repression grew in intensity, many hoped for or feared a revolution in California. What happened instead was World War II. The Okies left the fields for the aircraft factories and the decade of white farm labor ended.

When a wartime labor shortage appeared in agriculture, California turned again to Mexico. The *bracero* program, begun as a temporary measure in 1942, lasted until 1965 and brought nearly five million Mexicans to the state for temporary employment. Mexican workers were eager to come. After 1965 the *bracero* was replaced by the "green carder," who also worked under a temporary permit; by the undocumented worker; and by Hispanics born in the United States. In 1970, three-fourths of California's farm workers spoke only Spanish, and most earned less than $1,000 per year. Because of pesticide spraying, they had the highest rate of occupational disease in any California industry.

Cheap labor and more recently mechanization have encouraged the continuation of the large landholding pattern begun in Spanish times.[13] Since Proposition 13 drastically reduced property taxes in 1978, California's metropolitan areas have depended on the state for funds. Los Angeles County in particular, with a heavy burden of health service and welfare expenses, is tied to decisions made in the state legislature, decisions that are heavily influenced by the landholding and labor patterns prevalent in California agriculture. Before court-ordered reapportionment in the 1960s, agricultural interests dominated the state legislature even more completely. Such important powers as the Bank of America, Southern Pacific Railroad, the *Los Angeles Times*, and the major oil and utility companies own or hold mortgages on millions of acres. Agriculture uses 85 percent of California's water, and as supplies dwindle urban-rural wars may develop. Even while farm acreage in the Los Angeles area constantly shrinks as shopping centers and subdivisions replace orange groves, the political and economic power of agriculture continues directly to affect Los Angeles.[14]

With the invention of the movie camera, entertainment became a product to be manufactured. For the first time entertainment could have a universal impact and yet be concentrated in single place. Los Angeles became that place. In the process Los Angeles also became the creator of a new universal popular culture that would batter down the barriers of traditional societies. The movie and aerospace industries together gave Los Angeles world importance.

The movie industry was a perfect match for Los Angeles. It was not affected by the city's historic handicaps. High freighting charges were no problem because the only product to be shipped was a canister of film. Nor was there much need for raw materials. The industry caused virtually no pollution, most of its expenditures went for local salaries, and it tended to stay afloat in times of economic depression.

Movies reversed the previous status of Los Angeles as a cultural colony of the East, for people everywhere took their ideas of fashion and manners from films produced in Los Angeles. The movies popularized the Southern California style of casual dress, helping to make Los Angeles the nation's second largest garment industry center. The city's role in movie production also would make it a prime location for the creation of radio shows, television programs, and phonograph records. Movies gave the city more publicity than the Chamber of Commerce had ever dreamed of and fed into the community's speculative spirit and image as a place where fame and fortune waited around every corner.

The moviemakers came to Los Angeles for sunlight, because the early movie film and artificial lighting were not adequate for indoor shooting. Happily, film producers soon discovered within a fifty-mile radius of downtown Los Angeles an array of different landscapes perfectly suited to movie requirements. Whether a picture called for beach, mountain, desert, plains, or city views, all were within driving distance.

D. W. Griffith first came for winter filming in 1910, and five years later he put Los Angeles on the map as the movie capital with *Birth of a Nation*. For the next half century Los Angeles made 95 percent of the films shown in the United States and two-thirds of those screened in the world. The film companies that at first had required sunlight were obliged with the introduction of sound in 1927 to go indoors and to build expensive studios, which kept the movie producers anchored to Hollywood. Filmmaking would not emerge from the sound stage fortresses until portable equipment became common in the 1960s.

The Hollywood sign, put up originally in 1923 as "Hollywood-land" to promote a real estate development, came to symbolize movie glamour. Movies were the biggest industry in Los Angeles between the world wars. After sound entered film, local movie employment reached 100,000. The craft guilds of the studio workers made up the strongest outpost of organized labor in open shop Los Angeles before World War II.

The Industry, as it was known in Los Angeles, developed as a near-monopoly with complete control over its product. The eight studios that dominated Hollywood received 95 percent of all U.S. film rental receipts and owned 80 percent of the nation's metropolitan, first-run movie theaters at a time when ninety million Americans went to the movies every week.[15]

The profitable studio system broke down in the postwar era. In 1949 an antitrust suit forced the film studios to sell off their theater chains, and about the same time television began to usurp the movies' domination of popular entertainment. Television now accounts for 80 percent of the studio and location shooting down in Los Angeles. Although today with mobile equipment filmmaking takes place all over the world, three-quarters of all U.S. employment in motion-picture production is still located in Southern California, as is 69 percent of television employment. Los Angeles remains the Dream Capital.

The glamour and success of the motion-picture, radio, and television industries attracted the record industry. RCA, CBS Records, and other New York companies established major Los Angeles operations, and a dozen new California labels, most notably Capitol, sprang up and prospered. The recording industry is now larger financially than the film industry.

The future of the entertainment capital will lie with the coming revolution in distribution technology through cable TV, pay TV, fiber optics, satellite transmissions, and laser-operated discs. Cable companies Home Box Office and Showtime in 1978 spent $22.5 million on original programs, mostly produced in Los Angeles. Revenue from cable subscriptions and select systems may greatly expand the Los Angeles entertainment industry in the coming decades.

In 1930, less than a quarter of the city's residents had been born in its environs. The most numerous, and the most satirized, of the migrants who multiplied the town's population twenty-five times between 1890 and 1930 were the midwesterners. In spirit and appearance Los Angeles became something of a midwestern city, and H. L. Mencken accordingly designated it "Double Dubuque." The midwesterners brought with them Prohibition, the Republican party, a rural midwestern sympathy for the antiunion position of the *Los Angeles Times*, and a commitment to practical, state-supported higher education.

In the 1920s, Los Angeles–based Sister Aimee Semple McPherson was the first evangelist to make systematic use of radio. She founded the first religious radio station in the United States. Rather than repeating the standard themes of punishment and retribution, she chose to emphasize a message of hope and acceptance in what was, for newcomers, often a very lonely town. Anticipating the techniques of today's media crusades, Sister Aimee took the revival meeting—America's most genuine folk festival—into the electronic age.

Los Angeles has been a bloody industrial battlefield. Though it was not truly a manufacturing city, Los Angeles became a focal point of national attention because of the intensity of its class struggle and the completeness with which management organized for the pur-pose. of keeping labor unorganized. The bitterness of the labor con-flict in Los Angeles was due primarily to General Harrison Gray Otis and his *Los Angeles Times*. Under the *Times*'s leadership, the Chamber of Commerce and the Merchants' and Manufacturers' Association formed a solid phalanx of employers. Until the 1960s, the 1910 labor-related bombing of the *Times* building was the news-paper's "bloody shirt," to be dredged up whenever the subject of la-bor unions arose. For nearly thirty years after the explosion, Los An-geles remained an open shop city.[16]

New Deal legislation that protected the right to organize and the influx of branch plants more accustomed to unions helped to bring an end to the era of the open shop. The industrialization of the Los Angeles work force through the phenomenal expansion of the aircraft industry provided an even greater boost to local union growth after 1940. Ninety percent of the city's aircraft workers were union members by 1955. The success of the *Times* and the Chamber of Commerce in bringing industry to Los Angeles destroyed their cherished industrial freedom—freedom from labor unions. The city became too big and heterogeneous to be controlled as it had been in the time of General Otis. Yet a legacy from that era remained in 1970 when only 24.1 percent of the Los Angeles work force was orga-nized, compared to 34.8 percent in San Francisco.[17]

Unionization has largely failed to reach the large numbers of Mexicans and Asians employed in the Los Angeles garment indus-try. The California Division of Labor Enforcement in a 1978 inves-tigation found that 90 percent of the nearly one thousand garment factories surveyed were in violation of major sections of the labor code, including child labor laws.[18] Such workers are threatened with deportation if they demand better conditions. Resolving the issue of the undocumented workers and organizing professional groups that have proven difficult to unionize are the main challenges now facing Los Angeles labor.

The aerospace industry transformed Los Angeles as did no other single activity or development. It gave Los Angeles a manufacturing foundation, created the nation's highest concentration of scientific and technological expertise, and made of the booster city a base camp for the exploration of space. Aircraft production was as suited to Los Angeles as was moviemaking, for it too sidestepped the historic dis-advantages of the city's position as an island on the land. As with movies, the weather was an advantage, allowing flying at all seasons of the year and making possible outdoor storage and assembly.

Between the two world wars, half of the aircraft industry shifted from the Northeast to Southern California. The great expanses of flat, cheap land that the city offered were ideal for airports and aircraft plants. The aircraft makers placed their plants on the periphery of the Los Angeles suburbs. The need for specialized suppliers and skilled aircraft workers became greater as aircraft grew more complex, therefore the Los Angeles lead in airplane production would prove cumulative, as it had in moviemaking.

The willingness of local business leaders to boost a fledgling industry played a vital role in early aircraft development, especially for the Douglas Aircraft Company, which was the only Los Angeles plane-making firm to survive the depression. Douglas received backing from *Times* owner Harry Chandler, successor to General Otis. In 1932 Douglas won the Transcontinental and Western Airlines design competition for a new commercial airliner. The DC-3, carrying twenty-one passengers at a speed of 190 miles per hour, marked an enormous technological advance over the Ford and Fokker trimotors of the time. Because of its reliability and economy, the DC-3 became the workhorse of commercial aviation, soon carrying 95 percent of all civilian air traffic in the United States and 60 percent in the world. With the DC-3 in production, the Douglas company on the eve of World War II employed more than a third of the nation's aircraft workers.

Lockheed Aircraft was purchased out of bankruptcy in 1932 and plans to move the company east were canceled after consideration of Los Angeles's advantages. North American Aviation, owned by General Motors, moved to the city in 1936. John Northrop, who had worked for both Douglas and Lockheed, began his own company in Los Angeles in 1939. Airplanes pulled Los Angeles out of the depression. In stark contrast to other big cities, in 1939 Los Angeles employed one-fifth more manufacturing workers than it had in 1929. Los Angeles's early lead in what was in 1940 a still small industry would bring an unexpected bonanza as U.S. aircraft production expanded from 5,856 planes in 1939 to 96,318 in 1944. During World War II, Southern California supplied approximately one-third of the U.S. aircraft produced. Aircraft production, which had employed one thousand workers in Los Angeles in 1933, by 1943 employed 280,000. Total employment in the city's factories and shipyards tripled from 205,000 in 1940 to 638,000 in 1943.[19]

While wartime production created a half million new jobs, Los Angeles lost 150,000 men to the draft, and defense contractors ran short of manpower. Yet, at first the aircraft companies resisted hiring women. Vultee Aircraft claimed that every time a woman walked through the plant the company lost $250 in decreased productivity as men turned to look. But by 1943 manufacturers were finally compelled to open their doors to "Rosie the Riveter," and 113,000 women made up nearly half of the city's aircraft labor force.

Women workers were not the only answer to labor shortages, for the aircraft boom created still another migration to Los Angeles. Between 1940 and 1944, 780,000 new residents arrived. A special census taken in April 1947 revealed that one-third of the city's population had not lived there seven years earlier. Los Angeles remained a community in which nearly everyone was from somewhere else. As in the 1930s poor whites, notably the Okies, led the influx, but the procession was now integrated. The number of the city's blacks doubled by 1944 and tripled by 1950.

The spectacular growth of the city's aircraft industry under the pressures of wartime necessity made Los Angeles a great industrial employer, but it also laid the foundations for its future as a center of science and technology. The Second World War in addition greatly increased the role of federal assistance, already an important factor in western development. During the war, the federal government became Los Angeles's most important customer, and it has remained so, for only the national government could afford to support the area's new scientific research programs.

The end of the war brought a rapid drop in aircraft employment. From a peak of 280,000 the number of aircraft workers in Los Angeles declined to 55,000 by 1946. The city only emerged from its postwar depression when aircraft orders increased with the Korean War and the cold war. By 1950, aircraft factory employment was up to 100,000, but by 1955 it had grown to 275,000, almost reaching the wartime peak. By 1967 the aerospace industry supplied 350,000 jobs in Los Angeles and a half million in Southern California.[20]

The growth of the aircraft industry in the 1950s and 1960s made the western United States, with Los Angeles in the lead, into a vast military, industrial, technological, and educational complex. Since 1950, defense has been the nation's largest industry with approximately $2 trillion spent on the military in the last three decades. These expenditures have been concentrated disproportionately in the South, the Southwest, and the Pacific Coast states. Although the name Sunbelt is generally employed today with regard to the developing areas of the South and West, the label Space Crescent, suggested by *Nation* in 1964, may provide a more appropriate term. The heart of the crescent lies in the West as the territory that begins at Cape Canaveral runs from Houston to Southern California and up the Pacific Coast to Seattle and takes in the air bases and electronic and missile complexes that spread throughout the arid West.

Washington's role as the reallocator of national resources multiplied many times over after 1940 with the concentration of the aerospace industry in the western region. The West, with one-sixth of the national population, in the 1950s received one-third of the military prime contract awards, one-half of all defense research and development contracts, and two-thirds of all missile appropriations.[21] Between 1945 and 1960 the number of scientists, technicians, and engineers living west of the Mississippi tripled to over 400,000. The Space Crescent became the nation's latest boom town frontier.

The heavy concentration of aerospace and defense business in a traditionally conservative region encouraged the new middle class of Space Crescent technicians and managers to develop into the most dynamic force behind the nation's current conservative trend. It is perhaps ironic that conservatives, opposed in principle to Big Government, should grow in strength from the aerospace and defense sector, which has been the major cause of government growth since 1940. But that pattern is consistent with the region's history. Fiscally conservative aerospace managers lobby for federal defense appropriations today just as their western predecessors did for dam and irrigation projects.

California, and in particular Southern California, claimed by far the greatest share of the new development. More than $100 billion was spent in California for defense between 1945 and 1965. Los Angeles County alone received more than $50 billion in defense appropriations, doubling the number of the county's manufacturing jobs.[22] Aerospace accounted directly for 40 percent of all manufacturing employment in Los Angeles County and for one-half to three-quarters of the factory jobs in the other coastal counties of Southern California.

The influence of the aerospace sector spreads far beyond those jobs directly connected to the making of airplanes. About 12,000 firms in the Los Angeles area are linked with the aerospace industry, mostly through subcontracting. For example, a 1962 Bank of America survey found that 69.2 percent of the employment in the production of photographic equipment in Southern California depended on aerospace work, as did 83 percent of the jobs in electrical machinery production, 47.2 percent of those connected with metal-working machinery, and even 11.7 percent of the employment in the making of cardboard containers.

The aerospace industry caused the Los Angeles area to continue its rapid growth. During the 1950s, Los Angeles County received more new residents than any other county in the nation. Even more striking was the growth of peripheral areas, especially the San Fernando Valley and Orange County. The San Fernando Valley more than tripled in population during the 1950s. Many of the valley's residents worked at the Lockheed plant in Burbank or for one of the many subcontractors spread over the valley floor. Orange County, with only four hundred aircraft workers in 1950, had 5,100 by 1956 and 73,500 by 1968. The electronics industry made up 40 percent of Orange County's manufacturing employment by 1965. Orange County's population more than tripled in the 1950s from 216,224 to 703,925 and doubled again in the 1960s to 1,421,233. In the 1970s, the neighboring four counties increased their populations by more than a third. The pattern of growth through dispersion represented the continuation of a historical course dominant in Los Angeles from the time that the Pacific Electric trolleys first made it possible.

In the late 1950s, the aircraft industry became the aerospace industry, transformed by a change in primary emphasis from airframe assembly to research and electronics. The West in general and Southern California in particular landed an even larger share of research and development contracts than they had previously for aircraft production. Competition centered not so much on price as on technical capability, since Washington was often asking for instruments whose feasibility had not yet been demonstrated. Naturally, therefore, the government favored the Southern California companies with the best record for producing high technology items.

As the aerospace sector shifted its center of gravity from assembly lines to laboratories, the leading aerospace companies, institutes, and universities of the Space Crescent merged into a scientific and educational complex that University of California president Clark Kerr in 1963 called the "knowledge industry." The University of California at Los Angeles serves as an example of the development of the knowledge industry within the context of the growth of Los Angeles. The origins of UCLA date back to the founding of the State Normal School in 1881 on a site donated in order to increase the value of the surrounding real estate. By 1924 the school had acquired a full four-year course of instruction, and graduate training began in 1934. Each step had the endorsement of Southern California leaders, but the expansion of UCLA met with opposition from the northern part of the state. Feelings about UCLA's expansion were intense. University of California regent Edward Dickson of Los Angeles declared that delay in establishing graduate study at UCLA represented "a stigma, an insult to all the people of Southern California" and that the region was "on the verge of an open outbreak against the University of California . . . we may look forward to years of warfare."[23] The city's many midwestern migrants were particularly active in demanding a large and important state university in the land-grant college tradition.

The university's primary function was to meet the region's increasing demands for technology, knowledge, and skills. During the 1950s, when public school enrollment in California doubled, UCLA supplied more than a thousand new teachers a year. Vern Knudsen, founding dean of the university's Graduate Division, designed all of the early Hollywood sound stages. He was the only architectural acoustics expert west of the Mississippi River at the time. The School of Engineering, originally designated as the School of Aeronautical Engineering, was created in 1943 specifically to meet the needs of the aircraft industry. As the aerospace industry grew, relations between the federal government and the university became more extensive. In 1969 UCLA carried out $47 million in federally funded research.

By the mid 1960s, California had added twenty-one state colleges, seventy-seven junior colleges, and eight campuses to its university, forming a network of higher education unequaled by any other state. Public education now employs more than 400,000 Californians.

The regional concentration of the aerospace industry has continued and even intensified in recent years. Two-thirds of all employment related to space projects is now located on the Pacific Coast, as is 42 percent of all aerospace work. Southern California gained over 100,000 new aerospace jobs between 1976 and 1980 as the industry came out of its most recent period of depression. Aircraft engineers are again in demand as Northrop builds the center fuselage section of the Boeing 747, Rockwell prepares to put the B-1 into production, and other Los Angeles firms take on new business either directly or through subcontracting. One-fourth of Seattle-based Boeing's work is subcontracted to Southern California.

Southern California's Rockwell Corporation is the prime contractor for the space shuttle and Vandenburg Air Force Base, north of Santa Barbara, will be the shuttle's home port. Vandenburg already has launched over four hundred satellites. TRW in Torrance is developing a system of telecommunication satellites. Hughes Aircraft employs 55,000 workers in Southern California on more than a thousand different projects. Lockheed is responsible for a major portion of the NASA Space Telescope project. These programs will bring an expansion of scientific knowledge and its corresponding economic growth to high technology export industries.

A 13 May 1979 *Los Angeles Times* listing of California's largest corporations indicated that seven of the top seventeen were engaged in aerospace and electronics. Much of the industry is also made up of small and medium-sized firms, many of which were founded by imaginative engineers who split from the giants. Southern California has developed the nation's highest concentration of scientific talent. By 1960, 37 percent of the world's Nobel Prize winners lived in California.

As the local aerospace industry continued to grow in the 1970s, Los Angeles became the nation's leading manufacturing center. During the decade Los Angeles's economy grew 40 percent faster than did that of New York. Chase Econometrics, the forecasting subsidiary of Chase Manhattan Bank, expects Los Angeles to retain its status through the 1980s. The Center for the Continuing Study of the California Economy in Palo Alto predicted in a 1979 report that California's economy will continue to grow faster than that of the rest of the nation through the 1980s. The report estimates that the state will add three million new jobs in the 1980s, half of which will be developed in the Los Angeles basin. Most economic forecasters anticipate that high technology, entertainment, and tourism, the areas in which Southern California is strong, will continue growing for the remainder of this century.

In the aftermath of World War II, many observers of the Southern California scene predicted that the boom years had ceased, but that prophecy, made many times before, once again proved false. The spread of suburban tract housing and shopping centers in the postwar era did more to change the physical landscape of the region than any transformation occurring in other periods of growth.

Southern California doubled in population between 1949 and 1965, growing from 5.5 million to eleven million. During World War II Los Angeles received nearly a million new residents and played host to many of the eight million soldiers given a government tour of the state. Many would return to California when the war ended.

A very different group of migrants were the exiles from Europe. Einstein's reaction regarding the United States expressed the feelings of many of the new arrivals: "We were exiled into Paradise." Thomas Mann and Bertolt Brecht lived in Los Angeles. Mann sounded like a Los Angeles booster when he marveled in a letter to Hermann Hesse: "I wish you could see the country around our house and the view of the ocean; the garden with its palm, olive, pepper, lemon and eucalyptus trees,—the sky is bright almost all year long and sheds an incomparable all beautifying light."[24] Many of the exiles who had come seeking political freedom left again during the McCarthy era.

The newcomers and their children changed the age and educational profile of the community. The median age of the county's population dropped while the proportion who had completed college rose dramatically. Black and white migrants came from the South, and whites arrived from the industrial centers of the eastern and north central states. The midwestern element was still strong, but no longer dominant.

Because of the demographic swing from middle age to youth, young people increasingly set the tone and spirit of life. Overcrowding and strained services, especially in the public schools, were major problems of the new population boom. In 1948, 27,000 children in Los Angeles had to attend school on a double shift basis.

After the war, Rosie the Riveter moved to the suburbs. Postwar suburbia concentrated more on raising children than had any previous communities. The "baby boom" peaked in 1957 when women averaged 3.7 children each. Parents sought comfortable surroundings for child rearing far removed from the recent trials of war and depression. The availability of flat land, pleasant climate, cheap gasoline, and freeways allowed Los Angeles to spread its suburbs far in all directions. Henry Huntington's dream of a solid city from the mountains to the sea came true, although without his bright red trolleys. The suburbs at first jumped over farmlands, creating curious checkerboard patterns with houses planted among orange groves, but as the real estate beneath the orchards became too valuable for growing oranges, developers sometimes uprooted a thousand trees a day. In 1948 a Los Angeles suburbanite could purchase a small but comfortable house for about fifty dollars a month. By 1963 Southern California was the scene of nearly one-fourth of all the home-building activity in the United States and contained a quarter of the nation's real estate agents.

For example, suburban Lakewood was one of the many communities that developed under the stimulus of aerospace employment. The nearby Long Beach Douglas plant employed 48,000 people, yet little affordable housing existed in the area. Lakewood grew from bean fields in 1949 to a population of 57,000 by 1954 and developed a new pattern of intergovernmental relations that would encourage further dispersal. Under the threat of annexation by neighboring Long Beach, Lakewood incorporated as a separate municipality and invented the Lakewood Plan. The unique feature of the arrangement was that rather than having to create entirely new police, fire, and other departments, a costly and difficult process, the new city simply contracted with Los Angeles County for a package of services, including law enforcement and fire protection. When Lakewood incorporated on 16 April 1954 as the fifteenth largest municipality in California, its first city hall consisted of a storefront office equipped with a desk, a typewriter, a table, and some folding chairs. Yet the full range of municipal services was immediately available through contract arrangements. The contract system made municipal incorporation far easier, with the result that thirty new cities in Los Angeles County incorporated in the next ten years. Today the county contains eighty-one separate municipalities. The creation of new cities tended to spread services and population over a wider area.[25]

By the late 1950s and early 1960s the main scene of suburban growth had shifted to the San Fernando Valley. As late as 1949, 70 percent of the valley floor was zoned for agriculture. Between 1944 and 1960, the valley population grew five times, from 170,000 to 850,000. Today the San Fernando Valley contains 1.5 million residents. The city of Los Angeles annexed most of the valley at the time of the building of the Owens Aqueduct. Were it a separate political unit today, the San Fernando Valley would be the sixth largest city in the United States.

In the postwar era, the lack of strong party organization, the steady stream of new migrants, and adroit manipulation of fears about Communism allowed the continued domination of local politics by personality and media coverage. Mayor Fletcher Bowron won election in 1938 in a cleanup campaign that formed a backdrop to the politics of the postwar period. City government in Los Angeles had reached a low point of corruption under the administration of Mayor Frank Shaw in the mid 1930s. As Raymond Chandler put it: "Law is where you buy it in this town." Two political bombings shook Los Angeles into action, and Frank Shaw became the first mayor of an American city to be removed by a recall campaign.[26]

In later years the Los Angeles Police Department would be criticized for the straitlaced conformity that the department imposed on its members. That tendency was a product of the rigorous house cleaning necessary after the demise of the Shaw regime. Police Chief William Parker built a new department in which the bribing of a police officer is virtually unknown.

The postwar period also brought another form of rigorous conformity. In the late 1940s the tone of Los Angeles politics adapted to the atmosphere of fear engendered by the cold war. The civil defense coordinator of Riverside told the residents of that community to arm themselves in order to repel invasion from Los Angeles refugees should the area be hit by a nuclear attack.

The situation abroad was used to discredit domestic American radicals and progressives. West coast labor leader Harry Bridges endured prolonged grilling by the House Un-American Activities Committee, which wished to deport him to his native Australia or to jail him under the Smith Act as a Communist. The chairman of a loyalty oath board declared: "Of course the fact that a person believes in racial equality doesn't *prove* that he's a Communist, but it certainly makes you look twice, doesn't it? You can't get away from the fact that racial equality is part of the Communist line."[27]

The business elite in Los Angeles compounded the acrimony and strife of the McCarthy era. The Chamber of Commerce and the Merchants' and Manufacturers' Association were no longer secure in their control over a city whose major industries—aircraft and entertainment—did not depend for credit or favor on the downtown Old Guard and whose workers were included in the ranks of organized labor. The new residents pouring into Los Angeles were better educated. They would not simply take the *Times* ballot recommendations into the voting booth and rubber stamp its list. Such changes might have toppled the old, conservative power structure, were it not for the insecurities of the incoming population. These new Angelenos were often young couples trying to meet mortgage payments. Frequently, they were dependent on the aerospace industry and through it on the defense sector. They had problems and fears that could be exploited to political advantage, especially the fear of Communism.

The *Times* attacked public housing in Los Angeles by alleging Communist infiltration into the city's Housing Authority. Municipal plans for public housing on Bunker Hill, immediately west of downtown, stood in the way of major business and real estate interests who wished to extend the financial district into that hilly secton of decaying Victorian mansions. Important interests also feared that the housing project would cause a downtown concentration of working-class families under the influence of a coalition of liberals and labor supporters in the Housing Authority. Public housing would threaten the traditional pattern of private real estate speculation that had been so much a part of the city's growth and economy. Private real estate development was at the heart of the *Times*'s financial structure due to the land and buildings that the company owned and the tremendous volume of advertising generated by house sales.

As the public housing battle extended into the Korean War,

Communism rather than housing became the main issue. A building industry publication headlined its editorial on public housing "Striking Back at Housing Pinks" and charged that "pinko politicians" were promoting "communistic housing projects" that would "consume necessary defense materials."[28] In a 1952 advisory referendum, Los Angeles voters turned down public housing three to one. Mayor Bowron, noting that the city had already signed contracts and spent considerable sums, nevertheless continued the Bunker Hill project.

Because of his positive stand on public housing, the *Times* turned against Mayor Bowron's bid for reelection in 1953. Norman Chandler, now owner of the *Times*, met with business leaders and chose lackluster congressman Norris Poulson to run against Bowron. When the mayor denounced the *Times*'s plan to foist its candidate upon the city in a manner reminiscent of General Otis's former domination of local affairs, the newspaper compared Bowron to "the anarchists who bombed the *Times* Building 43 years ago."[29]

The climax of the campaign came shortly before election day when the House Subcommittee on Government Operations conducted hearings in Los Angeles on the Housing Authority. In a televised session Police Chief Parker detailed the past left-wing associations of the authority's public relations director whom Bowron had refused to fire. Mayor Bowron was turned out of office by a narrow margin.

Mayor Poulson is chiefly remembered for denying Nikita Khrushchev the chance to go to Disneyland and for taking the occasion of a banquet toast during the Soviet premier's visit to the city to deliver a lecture on the evils of Communism. According to Ed Davis, later chief of police and during this period the police department's lobbyist with the city council, the power of the *Times* during Poulson's era was such that a *Times* representative would nod or shake his head to council members during meetings as an instruction on how to vote.[30]

In the place of public housing, Bunker Hill is now the site of the Music Center, expensive apartments, the Security Pacific Bank building, and other financial skyscrapers. The Chicano residents of Chavez Ravine were forcibly removed to make way for planned public-housing units. Officials promised that the displaced families would be the first tenants admitted, but the city gave Chavez Ravine to the Dodgers for a baseball stadium.

Poulson finally lost the office of mayor in 1961 in the course of the political resurrection of Sam Yorty, a saga strange even by local standards. Yorty was regarded in the 1930s as Southern California's most eloquent radical. According to Dorothy Healey, then vice-president of the Communist Cannery and Agricultural Workers' Industrial Union, Yorty was a favorite speaker at the union's meetings: "Sam loved alliteration and would use phrases like 'the princes of privilege.' He was a great speaker against capitalism. Sam was redder than a rose in those years."[31]

Yorty broke with the Left when the reform coalition chose Judge Bowron rather than him as their candidate against Frank Shaw in 1938. When he heard the news Yorty declared, "Those god damned commies knifed me in the back."[32] His sharp turn to the Right dates from this event. In the 1940s he ran without success for Congress, the U.S. Senate, and mayor. His 1954 senatorial campaign against liberal Republican Tom Kuchel carried the Southland's red-baiting tradition to new extremes. After losing in 1954, failing to gain the Democratic senatorial nomination in 1956, and attacking Democratic presidential candidate John Kennedy for his Catholic religion in 1960, Yorty was generally given up as politically dead. However, in the 1961 mayor's race his maverick style and populist stance sparked the interest and support of George Putnam, the city's most popular and flamboyant newscaster. Residents found the duo of Yorty and Putnam fresh and exciting in comparison with the faceless Poulson. Illness further hampered the incumbent. Yorty won by making a great show of attacking the *Times* and portraying himself as the champion of the little guy.

Sam Yorty distinguished himself as the only mayor of an American city unable to pronounce his community's name correctly. His successful reelection campaign in 1969 against black city councilman Tom Bradley held echoes of the 1954 contest with racial overtones added to the charges of radicalism. Bradley was a twenty-year veteran of the Los Angeles Police Department and very much a moderate. In 1973 Yorty repeated the same charges but without their previous effect. Low voter turnouts in the white conservative outer regions of the San Fernando Valley, Hispanic votes that had been lacking in 1969, and the solid support of the liberal Jewish west side and the black south central district gave the election to Tom Bradley.

As mayor Bradley has been a popular figure, easily winning reelection twice. He has made more personal appearances than any other political figure in recent memory. No ethnic parade, festival, or business opening is complete without the mayor, a tall and commanding figure as he wears a kimono, sombrero, or whatever costume is called for. Bradley's style is a logical extension of the submergence of party structures and their replacement by personal popularity.

Tom Bradley's tenure has not been marked by any bold, innovative policy. The only major controversy centered on the former UCLA track star's determination to bring the Olympic Games to Los Angeles in 1984, a project hampered by local apathy and resistance. Bradley has kept his liberal and black support without challenge while working closely with the leading business interests to promote a new high-rise downtown. He has also, as leader of a city in which race is the most volatile issue, provided a symbol of unity.

The main cold war protégé of the *Los Angeles Times* and the most skilled at portraying opposition as treason was Richard Nixon. His protection by the near monopoly media power of the *Times* allowed Nixon to be ruthless in his treatment of opponents and encouraged him to regard any criticism as a personal affront. The spirit of Watergate was born in postwar Los Angeles.

In 1946 Richard Nixon ran against incumbent Jerry Voorhis for Congress in the Twelfth District east of Los Angeles. Nixon never accused Voorhis directly of complicity with Communism. The young Republican charged, however, that Voorhis was supported by radical and left-wing elements, and told an American Legion post that there was a plot afoot "calculated to gradually give the American people a Communist form of Government."[33]

After defeating Voorhis, Nixon served on the House Un-American Activities Committee (HUAC) and in 1950 ran for the Senate against Helen Gahagan Douglas, a congresswoman since 1944 and the wife of actor Melvyn Douglas. It was Mrs. Douglas who gave Nixon the name "Tricky Dick" for his cleverly worded statements that gave the impression that his opponent was up to her ears in subversion without ever actually making the charge. Mrs. Douglas was labeled the "Pink Lady." The *Times* charged her with "apathy toward the menace of Communism in this country" because of her votes against the HUAC, but adroitly displayed its most inflammatory accusations in the form of quotes, without giving an equal chance to Mrs. Douglas to reply. Thus the paper featured many statements such as that of a "civic leader" who declared that to vote for Mrs. Douglas was to "turn against our American way of life for Communistic slavery." As the Korean War raged, with heavy U.S. casualties after the entrance of Communist China into the conflict, Nixon asked, "Doesn't she care whether American lives are being snuffed out by a ruthless aggressor?"[34] With such methods and support Nixon won easily, and was on his way to a national career.

The most famous of the witch-hunts and inquisitions of the anti-Communism crusade were directed against the entertainment industry. Hollywood offered the perfect target for this and every other era of political repression, because nowhere else could be found names with so much prominence but so little power. Because of its dependence on popularity and image, no other group was so vulnerable to criticism. Hollywood and HUAC were natural partners in the era's mad dance of accusation and confession.

The Communist party was very active in Hollywood in the 1930s, but was effective only as a supporter of groups such as the Hollywood Anti-Nazi League, whose purposes coincided with widely held views. During the war, many considered support of the Russian ally no different from assistance to Britain.

In 1947, the House Un-American Activities Committee began hearings on Communist involvement in the movie industry. In the first round of HUAC hearings Hollywood put on a brave front. Then step by step movie people made concessions which ended ultimately in total capitulation. Dore Schary, production chief of RKO and later of MGM, considered himself an outspoken liberal. He told HUAC that he would not judge the qualifications of employees on political grounds, yet he drew up the Waldorf Declaration. In this statement the studios gave in to pressure to fire the group of writers known as the Hollywood Ten, who had refused to cooperate with the House committee.

As chairman of the producers' group created to enforce the new blacklist, Schary asked the Writers' Guild for its support and promised that the ban would end with the condemned Ten. Yet in the next three years, hundreds of screenwriters, actors, and directors were blacklisted by Schary and other studio chiefs. No one could be safe from accusation. Avoidance of political activity provided no security, far from it. What was demanded was "effective anti-Communism," which in practice meant active support of any group of subversion-hunters who might otherwise complain to one's employer. It was no longer necessary to be a Communist to deserve blacklisting. It was enough to oppose the blacklisters. There was no room left for a civil liberties viewpoint.[35]

The Fund for the Republic took a survey of television and radio executives in 1955 and discovered that virtually none of them believed that the blacklist served any useful purpose.[36] Yet although they privately held the blacklisters in contempt as greedy, misguided, or simply crazy, the executives, like Dore Schary at MGM, still carried out the purge. The real support for blacklisting did not come from any independent power held by those who issued the lists and the threats. Those people were a ragtag group of sloppy researchers at best. The support for the system was commercial cowardice.

In the 1960s the effectiveness of the charge of subversion waned. The *Santa Barbara News Press* won a Pulitzer Prize for a series of articles revealing the operations of the John Birch Society in Southern California. The *Los Angeles Times* ran an editorial against the Birch Society in March 1961 and declared as unacceptable the "smearing as enemies and traitors those with whom we sometimes disagree."

When Richard Nixon ran against incumbent governor Pat Brown in 1962, the old methods failed to achieve their former success. The state Democratic chairman appeared on television to expose a misleading Nixon pamphlet, "California Dynasty of Communism," which portrayed Brown as subservient to the Soviet Union. A new medium was available through which unfounded accusations could quickly be refuted. Moreover, although the *Times* endorsed Nixon in 1962, it failed to give him the type of support that it had provided him against Douglas and Voorhis a decade earlier. The *Times* made no accusations linking Brown with subversion, and it reported the charges and replies of each side. The 1962 campaign revealed the extent to which the earlier stifling of opposition through insinuations of treason had depended on the protection of media monopoly.

In the 1960s Los Angeles experienced surges of political upheaval, as did the rest of the nation. In 1968 Senator Robert Kennedy won the California presidential primary. Minutes after his victory announcement at the Ambassador Hotel in Los Angeles he was shot down. With the normal democratic process short-circuited, the politics of confrontation grew more violent. Many Los Angeles area colleges served as battlegrounds between protesters and the police. Even the students of the usually conservative campus of the University of Southern California staged a march on city hall after the May 1970 Kent State shootings.

The 1970s saw an enormous price explosion in Southern California real estate. Housing demand increased as the baby boom generation matured and formed new households, and migration to the area resumed when the aerospace industry came out of its early 1970s slump. In 1970 the average Southern California home sold at the national median price of $32,000. By mid 1981 the average U.S. home price came to $74,000, but in the Los Angeles five-county area the figure had shot up to $118,000.[37] Skyrocketing prices led to sky-high tax assessments. This is the situation that led Howard Jarvis to launch his emotional campaign for property tax reduction through Proposition 13. Passed in 1978, this initiative restricted property taxes to 1 percent of assessed valuation. Although the centerpiece of the campaign was the beleaguered homeowner, the greater part of the $7 billion tax reduction went to commercial property. Proposition 13 also limits future rises in property tax assessments to only 2 percent per year unless the parcel is sold. This provision creates an ever-widening gap between the tax bills paid by those who move and those who do not. Proponents of the measure had also promised that landlords would reduce rents if Proposition 13 passed. Many apartment owners, however, had paid too much for recently acquired property, counting on a rapid further speculative increase in real estate prices. The new owners, caught in a squeeze by high mortgage interest rates, responded by suddenly raising rents. It was not surprising that demands for rent control soon followed.

Santa Monica, a Los Angeles area community with 80 percent of its population comprised of renters, had defeated a rent control measure in early 1978, just before Proposition 13, but the next year the city passed the stiffest rent control law in the nation. The Los Angeles City Council also passed a rent control measure, although it is milder than that of Santa Monica. Rent control, like Proposition 13, rewards those who stay in place. The motto of Southern California politics as the 1980s opened was "I've got mine, so to Hell with the rest of you."

The last two decades have also brought change to the *Los Angeles Times*, the metropolis's most important political voice. In 1960 Otis Chandler took control with the goal of making the *Times* the best newspaper in the nation. It certainly became the most profitable. Daily circulation doubled to a million, the largest home delivery circulation of any paper in the nation. The *Times*, which captured 93 percent of the newspaper advertising in its territory, has led all U.S. papers in volume of advertising since 1955. Two-thirds of all Times-Mirror Corporation revenue now comes from outside Los Angeles. These sources include 329,000 acres of timberland for the production of newsprint, a half interest in the 348,000-acre Tejon Ranch, and other newspapers, television cable companies, and publishing firms.

In his 1979 study of the U.S. media, David Habersham said that "no other publisher in America improved a paper so quickly on so grand a scale." Under Otis Chandler the editorial budget of the *Times* rose from $3.6 million in 1960 to $19 million in 1976. In the quality of its reporting the *Times* today ranks even with the *Washington Post* and trails only the *New York Times*.[38]

The paper has changed in other ways also. The *Times* has exposed various local abuses, including labor law violations. The inaugural edition of the paper's new Fashion section rather surprisingly featured a long exposé on labor conditions in the garment industry.[39] The *Los Angeles Times* has the financial power to criticize groups that a smaller paper might fear to offend. In its November 1982 election ballot recommendations, the *Times* endorsed Democrats, and often liberal ones at that, in twenty-four out of thirty-one partisan races.

Yet the newness of the new *Times* has been exaggerated, perhaps out of gratitude and relief at the passing of the old bastion of civic reaction. It should not be expected that the nineteenth largest corporation in California would publish extensive and basic criticism of the surrounding social, political, and economic order. In the real estate section, one still finds the old *Times*. When architecture critic John Pastier repeatedly panned the new downtown (in which the Times-Mirror Corporation has extensive holdings) as a "contemporary Stonehenge," he was fired.

The *Times* is the greatest single force for moderation in Los Angeles today. No longer the hungry, fighting paper of General Otis's era, the *Times* is a satisfied power that does not expect to benefit from any sudden change in the status quo. Thus it opposes and helps to block that populist radicalism, recently represented by Howard Jarvis, that has always supplied the American Right with its main striking force. The *Times* opposed Proposition 13 as a radical change. Like many other large institutions, including public television station KCET, the *Times* practices corporate public-relations liberalism as the policy best suited to the protection of its interests. The *Times* and KCET give the impression that critical examination of society and its institutions is taking place. Yet they do not go beyond the individual exposé to systematic investigations of corporate relations such as the interlocking ties between the great landholding units and the state's other large institutions in the areas of transportation, finance, industry, commerce, and education. Just as KCET broadcasts no Southern California version of class relations (no "Upstairs, Downstairs" with American accents), the *Times* does not investigate the role of racial divisions among workers in maintaining the present economic structure, or the unearned increment in the value of real estate favored by tax-supported projects. The region's dominant newspaper and public television outlet preempt the role of critical and structural interpretation without performing it. The result is to give those who believe that such examination should be carried out the assurance that the matter is being taken care of.

Los Angeles by its geographical position is a racial and cultural borderland between the Far East and Europe and between Anglo and Hispanic America. With proximity to cheap labor supplies from

Asia and Mexico, Southern California agriculture drew on one group after another to perpetuate the plantation style of landowning that began in the Spanish period. In every era, nonwhites have performed the community's manual labor. The close connection between race and labor, when linked to the borderland position created by geography, provides a continuous theme to the Los Angeles historical experience.

As a border territory Los Angeles has been the scene of both assimilation and conflict, mostly the latter. Within the context of the area's borderland history, the relocation of 112,000 Japanese Americans during World War II (often referred to as a "tragic mistake") appears less as a mistake than as the culmination of a trend, brought to fruition under wartime pressure.

After the war new opportunities opened for the Japanese. Many did not return to Little Tokyo but spread to other parts of the city. American-born Japanese entered professional occupations. Young Japanese Americans now fully participate in the larger community, to the point that nearly half marry outside their own ethnic group. For the older Japanese, assimilation has brought with it a disappointing loss of distinctive group character.

There are today over 850,000 blacks living in Los Angeles County. When Los Angeles was created in 1781, the majority of its founders were black or mulatto. The first black mayor of the city was Francisco Reyes in 1793. The American conquest and gold rush, however, filled California with a new population, and Los Angeles did not again have a substantial proportion of blacks until the massive industrialization of World War II created factory jobs attractive to poor southern job seekers. The number of blacks in Los Angeles County nearly tripled from 75,000 in 1940 to 218,000 in 1950. By the latter year blacks outnumbered Asians four to one, and the focus of racial prejudice shifted accordingly. By 1970 the black population of Los Angeles County had risen to 750,000, a ten-fold increase in three decades.

Los Angeles in the 1950s was one of the first large municipalities in the United States to elect blacks to the city council. The County Human Relations Commission, established in 1943, and the state Fair Employment Practices Commission, created in 1959, worked against discrimination in employment, while the California legislature in 1963 passed the Rumford Act to prohibit racial discrimination in housing. By 1964 an Urban League "statistical portrait" rated Los Angeles the best of sixty-eight cities surveyed for black housing, employment, and income.

White reaction to the new fair housing law revealed a bitter con-

flict that the Urban League's statistics has not discerned. In the postwar era, while middle-class whites moved out to the burgeoning
suburbs, a rapidly growing black population and less prosperous
whites competed for space in a more limited turf. Blacks expanded
southward along Central Avenue amid the surrounding antipathy of
neighborhoods that were determined to remain white. Such a community was Lynwood, separated from black Watts by the traditional
dividing line of the Southern Pacific railroad tracks. In its 10 April
1962 issue, *Look* magazine named Lynwood the "All American
City," while its black neighbors called it "lily-white Lynwood."
Democratic officeholders in this overwhelmingly Democratic area
found themselves in serious trouble over their party's support of fair
housing. Thus a 1963 congressional by-election brought a two-to-
one Republican victory in a district with a two-to-one Democratic
registration edge. Fair housing was virtually the only issue in the
campaign.

In November 1964 an initiative measure on the California ballot to overturn the fair housing law passed by a vote of two to one.
Blacks were embittered by the open rejection that the large margin
of victory symbolized. An oral history project on black domestic
workers has indicated that young blacks raised in Los Angeles did
not compare their situation with that of the rural South, as their parents often did, but with the white affluence that they saw around
them and on television.[40] The crushing electoral defeat seemed to
push any hopes of attaining that affluence farther away.

In August 1965 racial hostility turned an incident into a riot. On
11 August the California Highway Patrol arrested a black youth for
drunk driving. His mother and a woman bystander became involved
in a scuffle with the police that attracted a large angry crowd. Over
the next six days rioters burned white-owned businesses over an
area of eleven square miles, causing property damage of more than
$40 million. Thirty-four people were killed, twenty-eight of whom
were black, and another 1,032 were wounded or injured. Police arrested nearly four thousand, while a force of 13,900 National Guards-
men held south central Los Angeles under military occupation by
the end of the week.[41]

The outcome of the Watts Riot, as it became known, was not
the pillaging of white neighborhoods but further economic distress
in black Los Angeles. Most of the burned-out stores, in particular the
large chain operations, were never rebuilt. Blacks now had to travel
to other areas to shop or pay higher prices at the small stores that
remained. The business life of the section was further depressed, for
the hollow buildings of "Cinder Alley" could offer no jobs.

The largest black business in the country, Motown Industries, an entertainment firm with over $58 million in sales in 1979, is located in Los Angeles. A black middle class lives in areas such as Baldwin Hills and Leimert Park. But the anger and despair that burst forth in 1965 have not disappeared. Affirmative Action programs have benefited mainly those who already hold white-collar or professional status, not the unemployed subproletariat. Except for the building of Martin Luther King Hospital, the economic conditions of south central Los Angeles have not improved since 1965.

The majority of the children currently attending elementary school in the Los Angeles Unified School District are Chicano. Two and one-half million Hispanics live in Los Angeles County today, where they outnumber blacks three to one. Yet despite their growing numbers, Chicanos in Los Angeles lack even the political representation that blacks have achieved. Currently there are no Chicano city council representatives. Chicanos were difficult to organize partly because they scattered throughout California's farm lands where they worked as seasonal laborers. Today 85 percent live in urban areas, but tremendous obstacles to effective action still remain.

The most significant difference between Chicanos and other non-Anglo groups in Los Angeles is that the Mexican immigrant's homeland lies only 150 miles away. Indeed, the Southwest is really a borderland or transitional zone between the United States and Mexico. Understandably, Mexican migrants hold more firmly to their language and culture than most other arriving groups have done.

The Chicano population of Los Angeles today is almost entirely a product of immigration from Mexico since 1910. At the time of the American conquest of California in 1846 the state held no more than 7,500 Hispanics, who were overwhelmed by a new population of 350,000 arriving with the gold rush. In 1900 there were ten times as many Chinese in California as Mexicans. Federal action cut off the region's previous cheap Oriental labor supply and later acts virtually stopped the flow of new population from Europe. However, the Los Angeles Chamber of Commerce, Sunkist, and growers throughout the Southwest successfully resisted any attempt to ban the arrival of Mexican farm workers. The imposition of limits on European and Asian immigration and the absence of restrictions on Mexican did much to determine the ethnic balance of the Southwest today.

During World War II prejudice against Chicanos erupted in the form of the so-called Zoot Suit Riots. The participation of Chicanos in the American political system began after the war. The strong liberal, labor, and progressive movement of the immediate postwar years in Los Angeles opened up the chance for Chicanos to build alliances. Thus in 1948 and 1949 the Community Service Organization, an outgrowth of Saul Alinsky's Industrial Areas Foundation in Chicago, registered 12,000 new Hispanic voters in the Ninth Council District. Working in an ethnically mixed area, Ed Roybal put together a coalition of Armenians, Russians, blacks, and Jews, as well as Chicanos, to become the first Hispanic on the city council since 1881.[42] Since Roybal's election to Congress in 1962 no other Chicano has gained a council seat.

When the postwar progressive coalition fell apart under the impact of the anti-Communism crusade, Chicanos were particularly subject to political suppression through the threat of deportation. The 1952 McCarran-Walkers Immigration and Nationality Act included a long list of grounds, some rather vague, on which the government could take away the citizenship of naturalized citizens and deport them as aliens. The provision had no statute of limitations, so a naturalized citizen was open to reprisal at any time.

The Chicano leaders deported included an organizer of the shoe workers' union and another labor leader who had sought to create cultural and ethnic units within trade union locals. In all, twenty-two o the Los Angeles Chicanos threatened with deportation were labor organizers.[43] Chicanos, more so than other groups, were thus silenced and intimidated, thereby bringing to an end the promising postwar Hispanic resurgence. By the time the long night of the McCarthy era finally ended, memories of the postwar progressive coalition had died, and nonwhites were committed to ethnic separatism rather than alliances.

In the 1969 Los Angeles mayor's race Chicanos failed to give Tom Bradley sufficient support against Sam Yorty, costing Bradley that election. Even today, the dominant political coalition in Los Angeles is composed of the politically well-organized, black south central district and the liberal west side Jewish section. Chicanos remain outside that coalition and politically impotent, although the Latino share of the total Los Angeles County population has grown from 7 percent in 1950 to 27 percent in 1980.

Because of their young population profile, the Hispanics are gaining on whites at a net rate of 50,000 persons annually. Even if all future Hispanic migration to Los Angeles were cut off, the difference in population profiles between whites and Hispanics would bring continued ethnic change.[44]

New Asian communities in Los Angeles have arisen from a change in legislation as well as events in Southeast Asia. In 1965 a new Immigration and Naturalization Act abolished the previous system of quotas based on national origins. In the first ten years of the new system 832,453 Asians entered the United States, with the largest proportion coming to Southern California. Asians now make up 6 percent of the population of Los Angeles County.

Recent Asian immigrants have become the new middle class in Los Angeles, excelling in two areas: education, in particular technical fields such as engineering and computer sciences, and small business. Like the Japanese of the prewar period, the new Asian businessmen often command a substantial advantage over competitors by having available to them the unpaid labor of their families.

Second- and later-generation Asians have done outstandingly well in the educational system. They have the lowest high school dropout rate and the highest college attendance rate of any racial group. For the past thirty years, Asians have outperformed whites in the schools and on standardized tests, indicating that cultural attitudes stressing performance play a greater role in educational success than any special white-based body of knowledge, as is sometimes suggested. It should also be noted, however, that Asians in the labor force generally earn less than do whites with equal educational standing. And some recent Asian immigrants who lack educational advantages have been used, in a manner reminiscent of the early Chinese experience, against other workers.

Ventura County's giant Egg City chicken ranch employed Vietnamese refugees as strikebreakers, prompting the response from a Chicano organizer for the United Farm Workers that "the problem with the Vietnamese is that they're a captive labor force."[45] The problem and reaction indicate the continuity of the region's racial and labor history.

Los Angeles appears to be evolving a structure that will include a large permanent black and brown underclass as the successor to a series of nonwhite groups who have occupied the lowest strata within the framework of the region's traditional relationship between race and labor. Asians primarily fill the role of a middle strata of shopkeepers and technicians.

The city's school population indicates the future racial composition of Los Angeles. Whereas whites made up the majority of elementary school pupils in 1966, by 1979 they constituted only one-fifth of the total in the Los Angeles Unified School District. The Community Analysis Bureau predicts that soon, with the exception of a few enclaves, the only important areas within the city limits to retain a predominantly white Anglo population will be West Los Angeles and the San Fernando Valley.[46] Younger and more affluent whites continue to move to the periphery of the urban area. The four counties surrounding Los Angeles remain predominantly white.

Between 1967 and 1977, 450,000 more people moved out of Los Angeles County than moved into it. By the late 1970s aerospace and electronics were booming again, and between 1977 and 1980 Southern California received a net migration of 600,000 for an overall population of 13.8 million. The five-county Los Angeles area grew by a net of one million inhabitants, including both immigration and births, to reach a figure of 11.5 million. The 1970s witnessed a continuation of the previous pattern of population dispersal, but on a broader scale. Los Angeles County acted as a gateway, drawing in newcomers while sending its own residents to the four neighboring counties, which increased their populations by an average of one-third during the decade. Orange County in 1980 contained 1.9 million residents. Its total population gain during the 1970s was second in the nation after Houston.

Population dispersal has not ended with higher transportation costs. Rather than residents moving back into the central city, jobs have moved out to the suburbs, especially high technology firms that are highly competitive in drawing personnel and that have no need for proximity to heavy industrial facilities. The five-county Los Angeles area today includes nearly half of all the industrial plants in the western United States.

During the 1970s the number of jobs in the area grew by 1.4 million, while the population increased by one million. Without the economic boost from increased aerospace orders in the latter part of the decade, the maturing baby boom generation would not have been able to find employment. As long as room must be found for new generations in the job market and for groups on the bottom of the scale, growth will be necessary for a healthy society.

Two-thirds of the foreign trade of Los Angeles today is with Asia. The economic expansion of the Pacific Basin has propelled the volume of commerce passing through the harbors of Los Angeles from less than $5 billion in 1970 to $39 billion today. If Mexico eventually succeeds in using its oil and gas revenues for industrial growth, considerable new trade with Southern California will result.

While other metropolises follow the Los Angeles pattern of deserting the central area, Los Angeles is experiencing what many hope will be a downtown renaissance. In the last dozen years new construction has changed the city's skyline. While aerospace activities spread to the outer suburbs, banks and insurance companies have congregated in the center because of the importance of information exchange and personal contact. Nearly half of all the financial employees in Los Angeles work in the downtown area.

Los Angeles is criticized today to an extent that nearly matches its booster propaganda of an earlier age. Yet the city is also widely imitated in the most sincere form of flattery. Reprints of the Los Angeles text spread across the country, particularly in the Sunbelt or Space Crescent. If Los Angeles no longer appears quite so eccentric, it is because the rest of the country has come to resemble the place once thought to be the nation's oddball. Suburban sprawl, electronic evangelism, informal dress and lifestyles, and economies based on services and technologies have become widespread.

The basic censure leveled at Los Angeles is that the city, by its sheer spread and size, has violated its own dream by flooding the neighborhoods in a sea of pink stucco. Yet those who do not find community feeling in Los Angeles may not know where to look. Harry Carr, a reporter for the *Times* in the 1930s, explained it best when he said, "You can't understand Los Angeles unless you understand that it's not a town, it's a lot of towns." Maps and directories of the Los Angeles area name 180 separate communities. Los Angeles County alone contains eighty-one incorporated cities, twelve of which have populations of over 100,000 each, and the continuous metropolitan area spreads over four neighboring counties. Few people describe themselves as living in Los Angeles, and many heatedly deny the accusation. They live in Canoga Park, Eagle Rock, Venice, Brentwood, Hollywood, or San Pedro, although each of those areas lies within the Los Angeles city limits.

Los Angeles does not lack community, it simply ignores conventional geographic definition. Bonds often form around interests. For example, those who work in the film, record, and television industries form a community of sorts transcending geographical boundaries. They are of Hollywood, although most likely they do not live there. An oral history project revealed that migrants from the village of Ziquitaro, Mexico, had reconstituted the social ties of their village in East Los Angeles, without living in the same neighborhood. Some areas blend geography and interests. Venice, for example, is a self-defined community, whose artists and other low-income residents have fought for a decade to fend off invasion from neighboring affluent Marina del Rey. Rustic Topanga Canyon has its community feeling kept alive by the common danger of fire and mudslides. A 1969 survey for the city planning department belied the city's impersonal reputation. Eighty-five percent of the respondents said that they were happy with Los Angeles as a place to live and work, and two-thirds agreed with the statement, "I feel a part of my neighborhood."[47]

Los Angeles still lacks the natural resources and proximity to population and industrial centers that one would expect for a city of its size. In the years ahead, the problems of water and energy that the Owens Aqueduct once solved will have to be solved again, as will the tension between conflict and assimilation in a racial borderland. Los Angeles will always live a dangerous existence, struggling with nature's declaration that a metropolis should not exist here. The lesson to be learned from the Los Angeles experience is that the future is open and anything is possible.

NOTES

1. *Los Angeles Times*, 18 July 1945 (hereafter cited as *Times*).

2. John Baur, *The Health Seekers of Southern California* (San Marino, Calif.: Huntington Library, 1959), 176.

3. *Los Angeles Examiner*, 12 December 1904; Huntington Land Co. Files, Huntington Library, San Marino, Calif.; Robert Fogelson, *The Fragmented Metropolis* (Cambridge, Mass.: Harvard University Press, 1967), 104–107.

4. Automobile Club of Southern California, *Traffic Survey* (Los Angeles, 1937), 31.

5. Giovanni Brino, *Los Angeles: La Citta Capitalista* (Florence, Italy: Edizioni Medicea, 1978), 254–263.

6. Eugene Lelong, "Air Pollution in California from 1970 to 1974" (Ph.D. dissertation, UCLA, 1974), 61, 138; Charles Lave, "The Mass Transit Panacea and Other Fallacies about Energy," *Atlantic* 244 (October 1979): 40; Charles Lave, "Transportation and Energy: Some Current Myths," *Policy Analysis* 4 (Summer 1978): 297–307.

7. *Times*, 27 April 1980; Williams, Kuebelbeck, and Associates, *Economic Impacts of Waterborne Commerce through the Ports of Los Angeles* (Los Angeles, 1976).

8. *Times*, 28 June 1906 (quote); William L. Kahrl, "The Politics of California Water: Owens Valley and the Los Angeles Aqueduct," part 2, *California Historical Quarterly* 55 (Summer 1976): 112.

9. James Findley, "The Economic Boom of the 1920s in Los Angeles" (Ph.D. dissertation, Claremont Graduate School, 1958), 249.

10. *The Oil and Gas Journal*, 28 January 1980; *Times*, 13 May 1979.

11. John Baur, "California Crops That Failed," *California Historical Quarterly* 45 (March 1966): 41–68.

12. Josephine Jacobs, "Sunkist Advertising" (Ph.D. dissertation, UCLA, 1966), 101, 135, 365.

13. Robert Fellmeth, project director, *The Politics of Land: Ralph Nader's Study Group Report on Land Use in California* (New York: Grossman, 1973), 8, 12–13.

14. Security Pacific Bank, *Southern California: Economic Issues in the Eighties* (Los Angeles, 1981), 29.

15. Leo Rosten, *Hollywood: The Movie Colony, the Movie Makers* (New York: Harcourt, Brace and Company, 1939), 6.

16. Louis B. Perry and Richard S. Perry, *A History of the Los Angeles Labor Movement* (Berkeley: Institute of industrial Relations, 1963), 21; Grace Stimson, *Rise of the Labor Movement in Los Angeles* (Berkeley: Institute of Industrial Relations, 1955), 119, 266, 303.

17. Arthur P. Allen and Betty V. H. Schneider, *Industrial Relations in the California Aircraft Industry* (Berkeley: Institute of Industrial Relations, 1956), 3; *California Statistical Abstract, 1973*, 29, *1971*, 21.

18. *Times*, 29 January 1979.

19. Leonard Levenson, "Wartime Development of the Aircraft Industry," *Monthly Labor Review* 59 (November 1944): 919; Civil Aeronautics Administration, *U.S. Military Aircraft Acceptances, 1940–1945* (Washington, D.C., 1946), 2–3; U.S. Department of Labor, *Statistical Summary of Los Angeles* (Washington, D.C., 1943), 16.

20. California Employment Development Department, *Summary of Employment: Aerospace, California and Areas, Part B, 1949–1971* (Sacramento, 1976), 1–4.

21. U.S. Congress, Joint Economic Committee, *Background Material on the Economic Impact of Federal Procurement, 1966*, 89th Cong., 2d sess., 1967, 17, 21, 37.

22. James L. Clayton, "The Impact of the Cold War on the Economies of California and Utah, 1945–65," *Pacific Historical Review* 36 (November 1967): 471, 460.

23. Letter to G. C. Earl, 12 June 1933, in Edward A. Dickson Papers, Special Collections, UCLA University Research Library, box 20; Vern O. Knudsen interview, typescript, UCLA Oral History Program, 652, 664, 651, 707.

24. *Hermann Hesse—Thomas Mann Briefwechsel* (Frankfurt am Main: Suhrkamp Verlag, 1975), 150.

25. City of Lakewood, *The Lakewood Story* (Los Angeles, 1979); John Anson Ford (county supervisor 1934–1958), interview with author, 1979.

26. Ford interview; Charles Mercer, "50 Years at City Hall," Oral Histories of the Los Angeles Collection, UCLA; Raymond Chandler, *Farewell My Lovely* (New York: Vintage, 1976, originally pub. 1940), 116; Leonard Leader, "Los Angeles and the Great Depression" (Ph.D. dissertation, UCLA, 1972), 258.

27. Walter Gellhorn, *Security, Loyalty and Science* (Ithaca, N.Y.: Cornell University Press, 1950), 152.

28. *Southwest Builder and Contractor*, 27 July 1951, 7.

29. Robert Gottlieb and Irene Wolt, *Thinking Big: The Story of the Los Angeles Times* (Los Angeles: G. P. Putnam's Sons, 1977), 262–265.

30. Ibid., 258.

31. Dorothy Healey, "The Left and California's Politics in the 1930s" (Paper presented at Southwest Labor Studies Conference, California State University, Dominguez Hills, 20 April 1979).

32. Leonard Leader, "The Depression in Los Angeles" (Paper presented at Conference on Los Angeles between the Wars, UCLA, 4 November 1978).

33. Paul Bullock, "Richard Nixon's 1946 Campaign against Jerry

Voorhis," *Quarterly of the Historical Society of Southern California* 55 (Fall 1973): 319–360; Jerry Voorhis, address presented at the Upton Sinclair Centennial, California State University, Los Angeles, 20 October 1978.

34. *Times*, 1–5 November 1950.

35. Larry Ceplair and Steve Englund, *The Inquisition in Hollywood: Politics in the Film Community, 1930–1960* (New York: Anchor/Doubleday, 1980), 79–126.

36. John Cogley, *Report on Blacklisting*, vol. 1, *Movies* (New York: The Fund for the Republic, 1954), 17–18, 53, 157–160; idem, *Report on Blacklisting*, vol. 2, *Radio-Television* (New York: The Fund for the Republic, 1956), 242.

37. Security Pacific Bank, *Southern California: Economic Issues*, 5, 18.

38. David Halberstam, "The California Dynasty: Otis Chandler and His Publishing Empire," *Atlantic* 243 (April 1979): 69.

39. *Times*, 29 January 1979.

40. Cynthia Shaw, "Black Maids in Beverly Hills," Oral Histories of Los Angeles Collection, UCLA.

41. *The McCone Report: California Governor's Commission on the Los Angeles Riots* (Los Angeles, 1965), 12–13.

42. Norma Alvarado, "The Election of Edward Roybal to the Los Angeles City Council," Oral Histories of Los Angeles Collection, UCLA.

43. Patricia Morgan, *Shame of a Nation* (Los Angeles: Committee for the Protection of the Foreign Born, 1954), 38–39.

44. See David L. Clark, "Report on Literature Search: Illegal Aliens" (Community Analysis Bureau, City of Los Angeles, 1976), 1–7; David L. Clark, *Los Angeles: A City Apart* (Los Angeles: Windsor Publications, 1981).

45. Emma Gee, ed., *Counterpoint: Perspectives on Asian America* (Los Angeles: UCLA Asian American Studies Center, 1976), 132–133.

46. Los Angeles Unified School District, *Racial and Ethnic Survey: Fall 1979* (Los Angeles, 1980); Los Angeles Community Analysis Bureau, *Ethnic Clusters Map* (Los Angeles, 1980).

47. Hector Aguiniga, "Emigration from a Mexican Village to Los Angeles," Oral Histories of Los Angeles Collection, UCLA; David L. Clark, *L.A. on Foot*, rev. ed. (Los Angeles: Camaro Publishing, 1976), 58–60; Los Angeles Department of City Planning, Preliminary Citywide Plan (Los Angeles, 1970), 179.

12

PHOENIX

THE DESERT METROPOLIS

by Bradford Luckingham

The four leading urban centers in the desert Southwest are El Paso, Albuquerque, Tucson, and Phoenix. These Sunbelt cities are among the fastest growing in the country. They have been centers of life in the region and their spectacular growth since World War II appears likely to continue during the remainder of the century. Since the 1950s, Phoenix has been the major oasis in the desert Southwest.

In 1867 Anglo pioneers entered the Salt River Valley in central Arizona and admired the remains of the ancient canal system of the Hohokam, a people who had lived in the area prior to 1400. Homesteading the land, clearing out old irrigation ditches, planting crops, and negotiating supply contracts with nearby army posts and mining camps, the pioneers created an economic base for their community. Realizing that they were revitalizing the land of an ancient agricultural people, the settlers in 1870 named their townsite Phoenix, a fitting symbol of life rising anew from the remains of the past. Growth was slow but steady, and by 1900 the valley center contained a population of 5,544 and offered an impressive array of urban goods, services, and amenities. By then it was a railroad hub, the seat of Maricopa County, and the territorial capital.

But along with progress came problems. In 1900 little rain fell in the nearby mountains, and the flow of the Salt River dwindled to a trickle. Thousands of acres of land were forced out of cultivation, and many farmers and town dwellers moved away in search of a more promising place. Those who remained recognized that growth would be limited unless they solved the water problem. After much debate, they decided that a storage system was the answer.

Joining together, valley residents formed the Salt River Valley Water Users' Association, and this organization, taking advantage of the National Reclamation Act of 1902, supported the federal government in the construction of Roosevelt Dam, completed in 1911. Water management projects brought vital stability to the area, allowed irrigation control, and assured agricultural growth and prosperity. As the valley prospered, so did Phoenix. In the decade following 1910, the population of the capital city almost tripled from 11,134 to 29,053, and by 1920 it had surpassed Tucson and established itself as the largest city between El Paso and Los Angeles.

Local business and civic leaders, proud of their city and anxious to see it develop, conducted promotion campaigns to attract visitors and new residents to the Valley of the Sun. The campaigns emphasized the opportunities and the amenities available, especially the climate; Phoenix was boosted as a place "where winter never comes." As a result, thousands of people arrived in the resort city during the 1920s. Phoenix also served as the center of activity for hinterland towns, farms, ranches, and mining settlements, and by 1930 the city had become a regional urban center of 48,118. The Great Depression retarded progress, but the central Arizona oasis recorded a population of 65,414 in 1940.[1]

During the 1930s the federal government helped to alleviate distress in the city and the valley through New Deal programs, and during and after World War II the relationship between Washington and the Phoenix area grew stronger as the Arizona capital became a major military and high technology center. By 1942 the area housed three army camps and six air bases, including Luke Field and Williams Field, and a number of defense plants. A Phoenix-area location offered desert training grounds to the army, fine year-round flying weather to the air corps, and a protected inland location to defense plants, an especially important consideration in light of the federal government's program to decentralize the production of vital military materials. Phoenix business organizations, such as the Chamber of Commerce, worked closely with Arizona's representatives in Washington, especially Carl T. Hayden, to secure these valuable assets. Business leaders offered many inducements and every form of cooperation. Federal funds and projects stimulated the local economy. The major role played by Uncle Sam in creating the boom in the central Arizona oasis during and after World War II can hardly be overestimated.

During the cold war, military installations such as Luke and Williams Air Force bases continued to serve as part of the national defense effort, and former war plants looked not only to the military but to civilian markets as well. A multiplier effect took hold, and as more manufacturers moved to the area, they attracted others. Predominant were light and clean industries, especially electronics firms, which flourished in the low humidity climate so necessary to their success. Electronics plants used little water, and they produced

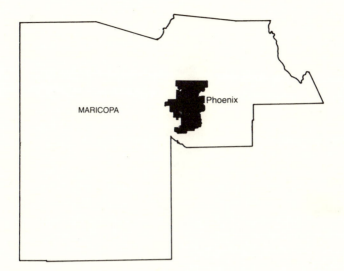

MARICOPA

Phoenix

MAP 12.1. The Phoenix SMSA

high-value, low-weight products that could easily be shipped over-land. Phoenix's relatively isolated location was no problem in electronics production because, as one observer declared, "a truckload is worth a million dollars." The city's modern transportation system included everything from trucking lines and major highways to transcontinental railroads and international airlines.[2]

It was important to tourist businesses in the "clean city" of Phoenix that pollution-free industries settle in the area. City developers encouraged smokeless plants in order to preserve "the sunshine and pure atmosphere" of the oasis. In the Arizona capital, the sun shone 85 percent of the time, a statistic that pleased manufacturers. Business could meet production schedules without being interrupted by adverse weather, absenteeism fell, and outdoor testing of particular products such as weapons systems went undisturbed as a result of "nature's battle plan." Executives and workers also appreciated the nearby mountains, the man-made lakes, and the active but casual year-round lifestyle that emphasized informal outdoor leisure living.[3]

By 1955 manufacturing had become the city's number one source of income with farming and tourism in second and third places. Between 1948 and 1960 nearly three hundred manufacturing enterprises opened their doors as manufacturing employment in the metropolitan area tripled. The annual income from manufacturing rose from under $5 million in 1940 to over $435 million in 1963. As a result, in this important sector urban rivals in the desert Southwest such as El Paso, Tucson, and Albuquerque were left far behind.

In the postwar years, Phoenix achieved economic diversification and the Valley of the Sun emerged as the metropolitan center of commerce and industry in the desert Southwest. Major firms in the Phoenix area in the 1950s included Motorola, General Electric, Goodyear Aircraft, Kaiser Aircraft and Electronics, AiResearch, and Sperry Rand. They represented the type of industry local promoters wanted to attract. They were clean and they employed thousands of trained workers—engineers, computer experts, and electronics technicians—and other highly skilled personnel.[4]

Phoenix booster organizations worked hard to attract and serve industry. For example, in September 1955 the Municipal Industrial Development Corporation, a group of determined business leaders, played a key role in bringing Sperry Rand to the Valley of the Sun by raising $650,000 in seventy-two hours. The organization bought the company a factory site, paid for improvements to a nearby airport, and arranged other inducements. Phoenix influentials also helped to establish Arizona as a right-to-work state to keep organized labor weak, and they succeeded in getting changes in state tax laws that made the "business climate" of the Phoenix area more attractive. Most important was the repeal in December 1955 of a state sales tax on products manufactured for sale to the federal government. The day after the legislature acted, Sperry Rand headquarters in New York announced that it would definitely locate its electronics aviation division plant and research center in Phoenix. The change also encouraged a number of other companies to move and inspired the expansion of several local electronics and aerospace firms that did business with the federal government.[5]

Urban leaders in the desert Southwest in the 1950s wanted their cities to develop economically, but some worked harder than others to realize their goal. Phoenix promoters often led the way, and businessmen in other cities noted the aggressive tactics they employed. In Phoenix, an El Paso businessman observed, "industrial scouts are met at the plane, entertained, offered free land, tax deals, and an electorate willing to approve millions in business-backed bond issues." By comparison, he lamented, "El Paso does nothing." As a result El Paso lost its spot as the "number-one city" in the region, and the businessman declared, "Unless we start hustling after new industry, we're going to wind up in serious trouble."[6]

Phoenix moved to the top of the urban hierarchy in the desert Southwest in the 1950s, and it secured its hold on that position during the next twenty years as manufacturing remained the most dynamic growth sector. By the end of 1977 the city had 74.5 percent of the total manufacturing employment in the state, and annual income from manufacturing in the Phoenix area had increased to $2.5 billion. Electronics and aerospace plants dominated the industrial landscape. In 1980 local leaders announced that the Valley of the Sun ranked third in the nation behind the Boston and San Francisco Bay areas as a high technology center. Other cities in the region could not keep pace with the promoters of the Arizona capital. As an El Paso influential put it in December 1978, "We want to be like Phoenix, but we don't have the kind of business leadership we need."[7]

By the end of 1955 the Salt River Valley Water Users' Association, known as the Salt River Project, had repaid its debt to the federal government for aid in construction of the Roosevelt Dam and the water management system it inspired continued to provide service to rural and urban dwellers in central Arizona. Over the years the Salt River Project had expanded in an effort to meet the water and power needs of the Phoenix area. By 1950 it had built seven dams to create valuable reservoirs and hydroelectric power, and the pattern for serving Phoenix and the Valley of the Sun in the future had been set.[8]

According to spokesmen, the most persistent problem faced by Valley of the Sun farmers since the 1950s is urban pressure. Prior to 1948, only 22,000 acres of irrigated land had been lost to subdivisions, but in the following decade an additional 32,000 acres were taken out of agricultural production and converted to residential and commercial use. Because urbanization and manufacturing used less water than agriculture, the developers did not worry about that precious commodity being lost when irrigated lands were transformed into housing and business sites. Increasingly, the land became worth more than the crops produced and many metropolitan area farmers sold out to developers. In some instances, land worth $250 an acre in 1940 was selling for $25,000 an acre in 1980.[9]

Agriculture, despite urban encroachment, has continued to be important to the welfare of the area. Maricopa County, one of the five top-rated agricultural counties in the nation in 1980, has remained far ahead of the counties surrounding El Paso, Tucson, and Albuquerque in the amount of acres cultivated and the market value of agricultural products sold. Agriculture, however, is declining. In 1980, agriculture was using 89 percent of the water consumed in Arizona, while the cities were using 7 percent and industry 4 percent. In the years ahead, more of the water supply will be diverted from agricultural to nonagricultural users. Moreover, the conservation of water is becoming a planning priority. A state groundwater law passed in 1980 regulates the use of water by irrigators, and it promotes more water management in the metropolitan areas. A higher water-use rate structure and a public education program implemented in Phoenix in recent years have resulted in a voluntary reduction in water consumption. The goal is to cut waste by making water conservation a way of life in the desert center. In addition, with the completion of the federally funded Central Arizona Project in the 1980s, which will bring Colorado River water to the region, the sprawling oasis should benefit from further allocations.[10]

During the 1950s, the tourist business in the Arizona center remained vital, and income from it rose considerably as facilities and services multiplied to meet the rush. Tourism continued as the Phoenix area's third biggest source of revenue, behind manufacturing and agriculture, and accommodations ranged from luxurious resort hotels to modest motels. By 1978 visitors were spending $1.4 billion a year in and about the city, and tourism had replaced agriculture as the area's second largest source of income. Traditionally most tourists came to seek relief from harsh northern winters, but thanks to the "miracle of air conditioning" some visitors even came in the summer. The mass production of air conditioners in the 1950s and the consequent "age of refrigeration" not only attracted manufacturers and brought an extended tourist season to Phoenix, it also made the city more comfortable for those permanent residents unable to leave for the coast or the mountains during the hot summer months. In addition, many of the military veterans who had served in the area, and many of the steadily increasing number of winter visitors, wanted to come back to live permanently in the air-conditioned oasis. An expanding job market and the Arizona mystique drew many to the booming metropolis. As a young executive from the East declared: "It's the life style that's so attractive. This is an informal place. A man's youth is not held against him. Society isn't as structured as in other places. You don't have to wear a tie. And then there's the open spaces, the mountains, and the lakes just a short drive away."[11]

As the population rose, the need for services increased. Metropolitan Phoenix not only continued to supply more tourists and its own growing population, but it also remained the trading and distribution hub for a vast hinterland of towns, farms, ranches, and mining settlements throughout Arizona and the Southwest. Employment increases within the services and trade sectors along with those in manufacturing and government accounted for a very sizable percentage of the total increase in employment registered in Maricopa County in the thirty years before 1980. By 1980, the services sector provided the most jobs and the importance of it to the local economy was clear.[12]

Phoenix also made gains as a cultural center during the postwar years. Although the Chamber of Commerce often emphasized the popular recreational facilities and events available in the area, a variety of cultural programs also benefited residents and visitors. Phoenix offered a Little Theatre, a civic opera company, an art museum, and a symphony orchestra. Elements of the growing population demanded quality, and they often received it. In the 1970s, the Phoenix Civic Plaza and the Scottsdale Center for the Arts presented a wide range of first-rate cultural offerings to citizens. In surburban Tempe, Arizona State College became Arizona State University in 1958, and offered excellent general programs as well as graduate courses in business and engineering. Student enrollment increased from 533 in 1945 to 11,128 in 1960 to 37,828 in 1980. During that time the institution increasingly served as an intellectual and cultural focal point in metropolitan Phoenix and the state of Arizona.[13]

During the 1950s signs of growth appeared everywhere in the capital city. The value of construction in the area, for example, jumped from $22 million in 1955 to $94 million in 1960. New city, county, state, and federal buildings reflected increased government activity at all levels, and the number of new private-sector structures was equally impressive. "All of Central Avenue [the "Main Street" of Phoenix]," noted a reporter, "is becoming a great commercial artery." Central Avenue "skyscrapers"—notably the twenty-story Guaranty Bank, the tallest building in the state—and sprawling subdivisions appeared during the decade. Developers created bedroom suburbs such as Maryvale and Arcadia; retirement communities, notably Youngtown and Sun City; and such large shopping centers as Uptown Plaza and Park Central. When Uptown Plaza opened in north Phoenix in August 1955, it was billed as "the largest single shopping center between Dallas and Los Angeles" and "dramatic evidence of the importance of suburban shopping centers in modern living . . . a symptom, and a healthy one, of a great demand for goods that will grow as metropolitan Phoenix grows."

There was more construction done in Phoenix in 1959 than in all the years from 1914 to 1946 combined. In that year a total of 5,060 dwellings, mostly single-family residences, were constructed, along with 429 swimming pools, 115 office buildings, 94 stores, 167 industrial buildings, and 15 educational facilities. Each year records were broken in practically every category, as the population, rising from 106,818 in 1950 to 439,170 in 1960, increased a remarkable 311 percent, the highest rate of population growth among the nation's fifty largest cities during the decade. In 1960 a Phoenix observer noted that "the mood is here; the word is out; this is the place. The city is going somewhere, and it is attracting more than an average share of people who want to go somewhere with it."

Explosive new growth and development prompted an exhibit of the exploitive but traditional philosophy of progress. Like the up-start western cities of nineteenth-century America, Phoenix and other boom towns of the Southwest in the mid twentieth century attracted men of enterprise, "new pioneers" willing to promote their cities for their own kind, with all, in their view, to share in the bene-fits. Reflecting on the "frontier spirit" that pervaded the area in the 1950s, a "new" Phoenix millionaire asserted: "This country pumps new life and energy and thinking into a man! Back East, there's nothing left to make the blood circulate; hell, it's all been done be-fore your time by your grandfather. For the big and small alike, out West there is release from the staid, old ordinary ways of life and thinking. The same thing is true today in Phoenix as in the Gold Rush, except in a more civilized way." The lure of Phoenix included the chance to "make it big," declared a reporter; in the growing des-ert center "new millionaires breed like forced hothouse flowers" and "behind them are more candidates on the heels of the initial successes."

By 1960 Phoenix not only retained its position as "the metropo-lis of Arizona," but it also became the largest city in the region. In 1960 the Phoenix and Tucson metropolitan areas constituted about 70 percent of Arizona's population compared to only about 50 per-cent in 1940; in 1960 the Phoenix metropolitan area alone contained about 50 percent of the state's population. Phoenix no longer faced any serious challenge from the other three major cities of the region, and during the next two decades the Arizona capital continued to set records as the fastest growing city in that section of the Sunbelt. By 1980 it ranked as the ninth largest city in the nation, up from twen-tieth in 1970, and it was recognized as a leader in the new urban America (see Table 12.1).[14]

As in the past, the 1980 population was largely Anglo. Blacks and Hispanics accounted for less than 20 percent of the total popula-tion in the Phoenix area. Hispanics continued to be the largest mi-nority group in the desert center with 14.3 percent of the total, while blacks constituted only 4.7 percent.

Annexation of land was vital to Phoenix's population growth. In 1940 the city had a population of 65,414 in an area of 9.6 square miles, and the totals by the end of 1955 were 156,000 population and twenty-nine square miles. At that time the city council in a *75th*

TABLE 12.1. Populations of Major Southwestern Cities, 1940–1980

	1940	*1950*	*1960*	*1970*	*1980*
Phoenix	65,414	106,818	439,170	584,303	789,704
El Paso	96,810	130,485	276,687	322,261	425,259
Tucson	35,752	45,454	212,892	262,933	330,537
Albuquerque	35,449	96,815	201,189	244,501	331,767

Anniversary Report to the people announced that "the rapid growth of Phoenix and its surrounding area has brought your city to a crossroads in its development." Phoenix, the report declared, "faced the choice of being a large city capable of planning for sound growth throughout the area and providing the types of services and facilities a large city requires or of being a relatively small city surrounded by a number of satellite 'bedroom' towns benefiting from a number of city facilities and services but making no financial contributions toward their costs." In May 1956 the city charted its course by approving a basic plan for the growth of a greater Phoenix. The plan consisted of a "stepped up year-round program of annexation," and the "development of a long range capital improvement program to take care of present and future needs of the growing city."

Although some outlying towns, notably Scottsdale and Tempe, resented this type of urban imperialism, the annexation program moved ahead. As the *Arizona Republic* asserted, "Phoenix faces a problem common to all growing metropolitan areas. It must keep pushing its limits out into the county as new housing and industrial developments are built up. Otherwise, the new areas will become incorporated and Phoenix will find itself hemmed in by a group of independent satellites." Efforts to "throttle the growth of the city" failed; indeed, in one operation in 1959 the city more than doubled in area and added over 100,000 people to its population.

An aggressive annexation policy helped Phoenix to increase its population sixfold between 1950 and 1980 and enabled the city to increase its physical size in square miles from 17.1 to 324.1 during the same period. In this manner Phoenix expanded and retained its influence in the metropolitan area; in 1980, 52 percent of the area population lived in the Arizona capital. As a local official put it, "We wanted to avoid the St. Louis model, where suburbs strangle the city." In Phoenix, "we didn't want white flight, or brain drain, or whatever you call it, so we annexed."[15]

The occupations of many of the heads of households who have arrived in Phoenix since World War II show a high percentage of educated, ambitious people who are interested in career opportunities and the quality of life available in the desert center. The majority of them have been young. Of family heads moving to the Phoenix area in 1977, 44 percent were under thirty-five years of age while only 12 percent were sixty-five years or older. They have envisaged growth and prosperity for themselves and Phoenix, and they have appreciated a local government that has claimed as its mission "a better, more beautiful, efficient community."[16]

For years Phoenix, under a council-manager system, had been governed in an undistinguished manner. To remedy this problem, reformers met in 1948 and designed changes to eliminate "corruption, crime, and vice," strengthen the city manager's position, and "remove politics from city hiring and firing." Voters enacted their suggested charter revisions later that year, but to the dismay of many reformers good government did not result. Reform opponents still held positions of power. In 1949, therefore, concerned citizens organized a Charter Government Committee (CGC) for the purpose of offering a slate of candidates committed to the implementation of the revised charter. Supported by newcomer Eugene Pulliam, since 1946 the owner of the city's two major newspapers (the *Arizona Republic* and the *Phoenix Gazette*), the CGC candidates, including department store executive Barry Goldwater, won easily. In every election during the next twenty years the Pulliam-Goldwater–inspired CGC ticket achieved victory. Businesslike, honest, growth-oriented, flexible, and pragmatic enough to meet any serious opposition, the remodeled city government succeeded because it reflected the ideals of most Phoenicians.

The CGC welcomed the All American City awards it won in the booming 1950s and 1960s, for they contributed to the desired image of Phoenix as a city with "a good, clean, competent government" run by the "right people." One observer noted that the "leadership of the CGC . . . reads like a list of the social and economic elite of the city." Another declared that the great majority of the supporters of the committee "are white, business-oriented, highly educated, and generally could be placed in middle- or upper-middle classes." Critics complained that the CGC-endorsed city council was "unrepresentative and stacked in favor of upper economic and social classes," but the opponents had little influence. Nearly all of the CGC candidates in the 1950s and 1960s were businesslike individuals who lived in the affluent north side areas of the city. Reflecting a philosophy akin to Republican conservatism, they easily won at-large, nonpartisan elections time and again. This trend, evident elsewhere in the urban Southwest during the period, seemed natural in the Arizona capital, and it was in keeping with observations by analysts that the average Phoenix citizen was "a family man . . . white in skin and white collar in occupation and very likely middle class in terms of both income and attitudes."

During the 1950s city services improved as population grew and the city expanded. The city upgraded its utilities and police and fire protection, and it contracted for new streets, sewers, parks, and public buildings. Sky Harbor Airport, purchased by the city in 1935 and developed into a jet-age facility over the years, became one of the busiest airports in the nation. Local leaders initiated a freeway system and a water development program, and citizens displayed their faith in the Phoenix government by voting millions of dollars in bonds for necessary improvements.[17]

Improvements, however, rarely kept pace with growth in the 1950s, and as the desert center expanded in size and population during the 1960s, urban problems became more apparent. Traffic congestion, high pollution levels, soaring crime rates, downtown decay, and questionable business practices, among other problems, intruded upon the good life of Phoenix. There existed few social welfare programs for the poor, and critics often expressed their disappointment that Phoenicians did not possess a greater social conscience. By 1965, the failure of the city's influentials to recognize and do something about negative conditions in parts of south Phoenix led outside reporters to view "the entire 'Southside' as a squalid slum . . . looking like a cross between a Mississippi Black Belt ghetto and a Mexican border town." The generalizations of such reporters were not entirely accurate because areas of south Phoenix contained a wide range of socioeconomic neighborhoods. In some parts of south Phoenix, however, could be found some of the worst slums in America, and they left a lasting impression on observers.[18]

Despite problems, the CGC served Phoenix well for two decades, but in the 1970s citizens of the growing metropolis called for a more open atmosphere, and candidates independent of the CGC won. The end of CGC domination came in 1975, when the mayor's office and four out of six council seats fell to non-CGC candidates. The CGC never recovered from that reversal, but critics, including minority leaders, continued to maintain that a larger council and a district system of elections were needed to meet the varied problems of the increasing population. They complained about a lack of services in some city areas, and a lack of neighborhood concern on the part of city council members elected at large. They kept asking for

TABLE 12.2. Populations of Phoenix and Neighboring
Communities, 1940–1980

	1940	1950	1960	1970	1980
Phoenix	65,414	106,818	439,170	584,303	789,704
Tempe	2,906	7,684	24,897	63,550	106,743
Mesa	7,224	16,670	33,772	63,049	152,453
Glendale	4,855	8,179	15,696	36,228	97,172
Scottsdale	1,000	2,032	10,026	67,823	88,412
Chandler	1,239	3,799	9,531	13,763	29,673

structural change in the political system, and finally in December
1982 in a closely contested special election Phoenix voters approved
a proposal to expand the city council from six to eight members,
with all of them to be elected from districts. The mayor would continue to be elected at large. The phenomenal growth of Phoenix
caused more than a change in political structure and style in recent
years; it also forced city, county, and state officials to be more responsive to the needs of the metropolitan complex.[19]

Over the years downtown Phoenix, with its high-rise building
development, continued to serve as the governmental, legal, and financial center of the urban area, but the sprawling city, a product of
the automobile age, kept spawning new focal points as residential
dispersal and the decentralization of business and industry increased. Nearby settlements, including Tempe, Scottsdale, and
Mesa to the east and Glendale to the west, became large satellites of
Phoenix. Small communities in 1940, these places thrived during
the next forty years, and as a result there emerged one vast, auto-
connected metropolitan complex, with the capital city in the middle
(see Table 12.2).

In the 1950s and 1960s each town retained an identity of its
own. Tempe was the home of Arizona State University, Mesa remained the "Mormon Capital of Arizona," and Glendale continued
as a farming community. Scottsdale, looking like "a western movie
set in which a director decides to replace horses with station wag-
ons," billed itself as "The West's Most Western Town" and became
famous as a winter resort for affluent tourists or "snowbirds." By the
1970s, however, it became increasingly difficult for them to maintain individual identities as each town experienced individual population explosions and building booms. Under the push of more peo-

ple, automobiles, housing tracts, shopping centers, and office and industrial parks, the urbanization of the desert continued.

Low-density urban sprawl remained part of the Arizona lifestyle; indeed, since World War II many newcomers to the sprawling Sunbelt center had moved from decaying, high-density, heavy-industry, massive-problem areas, and they welcomed the change, seeing Phoenix as a better place than the city they left. This feeling and the atmosphere it encouraged helped the Phoenix SMSA (Maricopa County) to increase its population by more than 700 percent between 1940 and 1980, easily extending its lead as the metropolitan center of the desert Southwest (see Table 12.3). In 1980, in fact, the Phoenix metropolitan area was the fastest growing among the top thirty SMSAs in the nation.[20]

As metropolitan Phoenix boomed, many people failed to appreciate the possibility that the good life might become more difficult to retain if rapid, uncontrolled growth damaged or destroyed the very environment they had sought. A few critics complained about the "Los Angelization" of Phoenix and the "Californication" of Arizona, but most of the mobile, ambitious Americans living in Phoenix viewed it as an urban area of great promise, a place resembling an earlier Los Angeles where opportunities and amenities seemed to await believers in the American Dream.

Rarely in the 1950s and 1960s did Phoenix and the other cities of the Valley of the Sun adopt plans predicated on growth management. Local citizens who advocated regulation of urban growth met

TABLE 12.3. Population Growth of Major Metropolitan Areas in the Southwest, 1940–1980

	1940	1950	1960	1970	1980
Phoenix (Maricopa County)	186,193	331,770	663,510	971,228	1,509,052
Tucson (Pima County)	72,838	141,216	265,660	351,667	531,443
El Paso (El Paso County)	131,067	194,968	314,070	359,291	479,899
Albuquerque (Bernalillo County with parts of Sandoval County added in 1960, 1970, 1980.)	69,391	145,673	276,400	333,266	454,499

with sharp criticism. Few took seriously those who wanted the latest newcomers to be the "last settlers" with the gates locked behind them.

Only in the 1970s with the appearance of problems relating to energy and the environment did controlled growth become a significant issue. By 1980 the "smaller is better" approach had not yet taken over, but steps to preserve the quality of life in and around the popular Sunbelt metropolis were under discussion. For example, civic leaders spoke often of the effort to revitalize downtown Phoenix and of the attempt to "infill" lands leapfrogged by earlier development. The construction in 1972 of the Phoenix Civic Plaza, a new convention and cultural center downtown, prompted the appearance of nearby hotels and office buildings, including the forty-story Valley National Bank Center. City officials and the Central Phoenix Redevelopment Committee encouraged people to live in the core area, but deteriorating schools, fear of crime, and problems with transients and drunks in a depressing skid row located near the Civic Plaza dampened the enthusiasm of many potential residents. Planners called infilling the answer to the high costs of urban sprawl. As late as 1980, 40 percent of the land within the city was vacant. Urging less sprawl and offering inducements, Margaret Hance, mayor of Phoenix since 1975, declared that "vacant properties within the city should be developed first, because the utilities, streets, fire stations, and parks are already in existence and can be used by additional thousands of people."[21]

Downtown revitalization and redirected growth were evident by 1980 in Phoenix and larger towns of the metroplex, all of whom suffered from problems similar to those challenging the capital city. Yet, metropolitan area critics were quick to point out that problems remained. Pockets of poverty that could "match misery for misery and squalor for squalor" with any city in America were still evident; smog often obscured the once-clear view of valley landmarks; debate over flood control and other water-related programs persisted; and mass-transit and freeway systems were grossly inadequate.[22]

Many local leaders considered transportation to be the most critical issue, especially the problem of funding. The cities of the valley, hurt by state-imposed spending limitations, have been unable to keep up with the demands made upon them for adequate transportation services. For example, Phoenix residents paid $53 million into the state highway fund in 1979 and 1980, but the city received only $12 million in return. In a city where more than 95 percent of all personal travel is by automobile, most observers agreed the situation was unfortunate, and Mayor Hance continued to call for more substantial state funding of local road programs, bus lines, and freeway projects. In a special session of the state legislature in the summer of 1981, representatives voted more funds to meet Arizona's "transportation crisis" and Phoenix benefited, but not enough to satisfy critics.[23]

The state legislature has sometimes mandated costly programs for local governments without providing enough funds to finance them. Recession, inflation, and tax revolts helped inspire state and federal cutbacks, and fewer dollars allocated to carry out assigned programs have served on occasion to erode the ability of Phoenix and other growing Arizona cities to function effectively. The state constitution prohibits deficit spending by local governments. Republicans from metropolitan Phoenix have dominated the state legislature since reapportionment, but local representatives often guard the narrow interests of their own particular districts within Maricopa County and hamper the goals of regional development. As a result, the state has not always proved responsive to metropolitan needs.[24]

Like the various Maricopa County representatives in the state legislature, local officials in the cities and towns of metropolitan Phoenix often disagree about what direction to take, particularly when the issue becomes who gets what. Since 1967, the Maricopa Association of Governments, a voluntary organization, has served as the principal federal grant clearing and metropolitan planning agency. It has provided a forum through which representatives of the nineteen incorporated cities and towns in Maricopa County could work together toward solving common problems in such areas as transportation, housing, land use, water and air quality, criminal justice, and social services. Its success has been limited. As one observer correctly declared, "MAG has been long on studies, but short on implementation—and for good reason. With no statutory authority, it can only recommend."[25]

Most local officials believe that "problems really must be solved by individual government units, working in cooperation with others." In 1980, Mayor Hance of Phoenix proposed that Valley of the Sun cities join in creating an intergovernmental agency to provide urban services throughout the metropolitan area, but other city leaders did not share her enthusiasm for the idea. "Political jealousies probably would emerge in a regional government," noted one, while another asserted that "written agreements are sufficient. Local control is still left with the cities and yet an area-wide cooperation is provided." Still another stated that "we do not need to build more government. We need to cooperate on issues of mutual interest such as transportation, but I am not sure another level of government should be created." The few in favor of a formal regional government want it to deal with the common concerns of the various municipalities and to manage orderly metropolitan area growth. The debate over the structure of government and related service issues seems endless.[26]

In 1980, Phoenix won another in a series of All America City awards for "citizen participation in government." Many residents of the Arizona capital and its suburbs serve on committees and belong to organizations dedicated to helping local officials preserve the area's wide appeal. Yet increased cooperation at all levels is needed between the private and public sectors in the interest of all. The rapid rise of this Sunbelt center has resulted in significant problems as well as benefits, making the contemporary scene a time in which crucial decisions concerning metropolitan progress and maturity must be made. The phenomenal growth experienced by the desert metropolis since World War II slowed considerably in the early 1980s because of the poor condition of the national economy, but Phoenix area boosters have expressed confidence that the boom will resume its fast pace in the near future. Some observers have suggested that metropolitan leaders should take advantage of this opportunity provided by the slowdown to pause and reflect on the future of the area. Indeed, in the 1980s, the major problem facing the Valley of the Sun's leadership is the evolving conflict between the area's two most cherished values—growth and the good life. Growth seems to be inevitable, but not the quality of life. The great challenge now facing metropolitan Phoenix is to handle that growth in ways that will improve life in the central Arizona oasis rather than harm it.

NOTES

1. Bradford Luckingham, *The Urban Southwest: A Profile History of Albuquerque, El Paso, Phoenix, and Tucson* (El Paso: Texas Western Press, University of Texas at El Paso, 1982); idem, "The Southwestern Urban Frontier, 1880–1930," *Journal of the West* 18 (July 1979): 40–50; idem, "Urban Development in Arizona: The Rise of Phoenix," *Journal of Arizona History* 22 (Summer 1981): 197–234.

2. *Arizona Republic*, 22 November 1942, 5, 10 January 1945, 11 March 1956, 10 March 1957, 1 January, 12 February 1961; Charles S. Sargent, "Arizona's Urban Frontier: Myths and Realities," in Charles S. Sargent, ed., *The Conflict between Frontier Values and Land-Use Control in Greater Phoenix*

(Tempe: Arizona State University Center for Public Affairs, 1976), 19–23; Charles C. Colley, "Carl T. Hayden—Phoenician," *Journal of Arizona History* 18 (Autumn 1977): 245–257; Tom McKnight, *Manufacturing in Arizona* (Berkeley: University of California Press, 1962), 325–330.

3. *Arizona Republic,* 16 November 1948, 22 May, 14 December 1954, 11 March 1956, 4 January 1958, 30 June 1960, 1 January 1961; McKnight, *Manufacturing in Arizona,* 312–340.

4. *Arizona Republic,* 11 March 1956, 1 January 1961; *Phoenix City Directory,* 1960 (Phoenix, 1960), 2–11; McKnight, *Manufacturing in Arizona,* 325–330.

5. *Arizona Republic,* 16 August, 10, 22 December 1955, 1 January, 1 February, 11 March 1956; W. Eugene Hollon, *The Southwest: Old and New* (New York: Knopf, 1961), 343–347.

6. *Arizona Republic,* 11 March 1956, 1 February 1958, 24 December 1961, 11 February 1962; Mark and Gertrude Adams, *A Report on Politics in El Paso* (Cambridge, Mass.: Joint Center for Urban Studies of the Massachusetts Institute of Technology and Harvard University, 1963), section V, 26–27.

7. *Arizona Republic,* 29 June 1980; *Phoenix Gazette,* 24 February 1981; *El Paso Times,* 22, 23 December 1978; Phoenix Newspapers, Inc., *Inside Phoenix, 1978* (Phoenix, 1978), 35; *U.S. Census of Manufacturing* (various years).

8. Stephen C. Shadegg, *Century One: One Hundred Years of Water Development in the Salt River Valley* (Phoenix: Salt River Project, 1969), 35–43; Courtland L. Smith, *The Salt River Project* (Tucson: University of Arizona Press, 1972).

9. *Arizona Republic,* 11 March 1956, 11 February 1962, 26 May 1980, 23 November 1980; G. M. Hermonson, "Urbanization of Agricultural Lands in Maricopa County, Arizona, 1950–1980" (M.A. thesis, Arizona State University, 1968).

10. *Mesa Tribune,* 9 October 1980; *Arizona Republic,* 29 October, 23 November 1980; *Phoenix Gazette,* 29 November, 1, 13 December 1980, 24 February 1981; Paul Bracken and Herman Kahn, *A Summary of Arizona Tomorrow* (New York: Hudson Institute, 1979), 15–17.

11. *Arizona Republic,* 21 November 1954, 11 March 1956, 11 February 1962; Phoenix Newspapers, Inc., *Inside Phoenix, 1978,* 69; Bert Fireman, "Urbanization and Home Comfort," in William R. Noyes, ed., *Progress in Arizona* (Tucson: University of Arizona Press, 1973), 3–4; Neal R. Peirce, *The Mountain States of America* (New York: Norton, 1972), 236–240.

12. Valley National Bank, *Arizona Statistical Review* 36 (September 1980): 13.

13. *Arizona Republic,* 11 March 1956, 11 February 1962, 5 January 1981; *Phoenix Gazette,* 24 February 1981.

14. *Arizona Republic,* 1 January, 25 August 1955, 11 March 1956, 4 January 1958, 1, 2 January, 4 March 1960, 1 January 1961, 11 February 1962; *Phoenix Gazette,* 15 June 1981; City of Phoenix and Maricopa County, Ari-

zona, *Land Use of the Phoenix Area* (Phoenix, 1959), 10–12; Neil Morgan, *Westward Tilt: The American West Today* (New York: Random House, 1961), 344–346, 354.

15. *Arizona Republic*, 9 May, 8 December 1955, 11 March 1956, 26 March, 1, 30 April 1959, 21 March, 24 May 1960, 11 February 1962; *New York Times*, 5 April 1975; City of Phoenix, *75th Anniversary Report* (Phoenix, 1956), 8; John D. Wenum, *Annexation as a Technique for Metropolitan Growth: The Case of Phoenix, Arizona* (Tempe: Arizona State University Center for Public Affairs, 1970), 127, passim.

16. *Arizona Republic*, 13 December 1954, 1 March 1956, 4 January 1958, 2 January 1960, 11 February 1962, 7 March 1981; *Phoenix Gazette*, 24 February 1981; Phoenix Newspapers, Inc., *Inside Phoenix, 1978*, 19.

17. *Arizona Republic*, 4, 15 August, 12, 18 November 1948, 1, 6, 7 November 1949, 5 January, 5 August 1954, 9 November 1955, 11 March, 9 February 1956, 24 May 1960, 26 December 1961, 11 February 1962; Leonard E. Goodall, "Phoenix: Reformers at Work," in Leonard E. Goodall, ed., *Urban Politics in the Southwest* (Tempe: Arizona State University Center for Public Affairs, 1967), 110–119; Brent Whiting Brown, "An Analysis of the Phoenix Charter Government Committee as a Political Entity" (M.A. thesis, Arizona State University, 1968), 9–37, 40–46.

18. Goodall, "Phoenix Reformers at Work," 123–124; Brown, "Phoenix Charter Government Committee," passim; Andrew Kopkind, "Modern Times in Phoenix," *New Republic*, 6 November 1965, 14–16.

19. *Arizona Republic*, 5 November, 10 December 1975, 3 November 1977, 15 April, 19 August, 4 September, 7, 26 October 1979, 11 February, 11, 13 July 1981, 2 December 1982; *Phoenix Gazette*, 24 February, 14, 15 July 1981, 2 December 1982.

20. Robert C. Hook, "Phoenix Yesterday and Today," *Arizona Business Bulletin* 13 (April 1966): 2–6; *Arizona Republic*, 13 June 1973, 9, 16, 21, 23 October 1980.

21. Sargent, "Arizona's Urban Frontier," 20–23; Jeffrey Cook, "Patterns of Desert Urbanization: The Evolution of Metropolitan Phoenix," in Gideon Golaney, ed., *Urban Planning for Arid Zones: American Experiences and Directions* (New York: John Wiley & Sons, 1978), 228–231, 236–238; *Arizona Republic*, 20 May 1979, 25 May, 12 September, 15 November 1980, 22 February, 6 May, 2 August 1981; *Phoenix Gazette*, 24 February, 19 March 1981.

22. *Arizona Republic*, 12 December 1971, 16 April 1979, 30 November, 1 August 1980, 30 January, 3 May, 19 September 1981; *Phoenix Gazette*, 19 November 1979, 25 September, 28 July, 1, 20 August 1980, 24 February 1981; Jay Brashear, ed., *The Urban Challenge* (Phoenix: Phoenix Newspapers, Inc., 1978).

23. *Arizona Republic*, 10 February, 10 December 1980, 4 January, 6 February, 8 April, 14 August 1981; *Phoenix Gazette*, 6, 24 February, 12 March, 8 April, 7 July 1981.

24. *Arizona Republic*, 31 December 1980, 29 January, 16 March, 5

May, 16 July, 26 September 1981; *Phoenix Gazette,* 6 February, 14 May 1981.

25. Maricopa Association of Governments, *Ten Years of Working To-gether* (Phoenix, 1977), 2–8; idem, *Planning for Growth* (Phoenix, 1980).

26. *Arizona Republic,* 6 April, 15, 16 July, 6 August 1980; *Phoenix Gazette,* 1 January, 22 September 1981.

13

SAN DIEGO

THE ANTI-CITY

by Anthony W. Corso

The transformation of an urban place to the stature of a metropolis is generally accompanied by an enormous influx of population, an expansion and diversification of industry and commerce, and the eventual manifestation of that somewhat elusive quality of life called "urbanity." This urban-growth model is one that has been the mainstay of historians, writers, and lyricists who describe and rejoice in the emergence of a cosmopolitan populace who devote their lives to the creation of great cities full of diversity, opportunity, and culture.

The history of San Diego as a contemporary addition to the galaxy of America's cities in a peculiar way contradicts this scenario of urbanism. The historical record indicates that San Diego has grown extraordinarily large in population and spatial size, but in so doing it resisted pressures to become a city in the classical or cultural sense. For some San Diegans this is the city's greatest tragedy; for others, it is its most desirable feature.

This division of perspectives has fomented numerous disputes among community and business groups since the turn of the century and remains the central topic on the city's political agenda. In the 1940s, the city's pulse beat to debates of "geraniums versus smoke stacks"; presently it palpitates to the arguments of growth versus nongrowth. Over the past four decades each side has witnessed its ascendancy to the pinnacle of power and its decline to impotence. Woe to the artless politician who failed to recognize the civic melodrama determining whether growth was to be or not to be.

For decades, San Diego remained a small, scenic tourist town that attracted those who sought an idyllic escape from the harsh midwestern and eastern winters and rigors of urban life.[1] This "divine isolationism" and the myth of San Diego as a protected coastal community have been continually reinforced in public debates about the city's future. Despite extensive growth and development since 1940 and the addition of hundreds of thousands of people, many citizens tenaciously hold on to an antiurban image of San Diego as a Sunbelt town, not a city. In this respect, San Diego might truly be described as an anticity city.

Students of San Diego's developmental and political history acknowledge the futility of its political wars and contests. The mistaken belief that growth decisions are fully lodged within the city power structure persists despite the overwhelming evidence that federal policies are pivotal determinants of the city's past trends and probable future.

The prewar history of San Diego is composed of interesting vignettes of would-be millionaires frustrated in their attempts to create a great metropolis. For many decades, San Diego remained a nice place to visit, but certainly not a place to work unless one was willing to pick oranges. Geographically off-centered, hemmed in by mountains to the east and the deserts of Mexico to the south, it defied even the most determined attempts at civic boosterism. Four decades of efforts to bring railroads and economic development to the city proved futile. Los Angeles remained the avaricious big sister capturing whatever investments eastern investors propelled to the far western hinterlands.[2]

No one disclaims the correlation between war and the awakening of San Diego. Shortly before World War II, the population stood at 200,000. By 1941, new and expanding aircraft plants and shipyards engulfed the city. Military bases mushroomed, and khaki and navy blues quickly replaced two-piece suits. An estimated 100,000 persons arrived in 1941 alone, and by 1942 the population had reached 380,000.[3] In response to the outcries of San Diego city fathers, who were attempting to accommodate the hordes, the federal government entered into a massive public/private program of community development that constructed housing projects on numerous sites throughout the city. In turn, San Diego relaxed its building codes to make allowances for the exigencies of the time. Thus, the city of flower gardens and cottages by the sea became an American bastion.[4]

In some ways, the termination of hostilities had more of a traumatic impact upon the city than had the declaration of war. Aircraft industries, shipyards, and military installations, which had become the foundation of the local economy, drastically declined. Richard Pourade, a preeminent local historian, refers to the city's "shock of transformation," during which the community nervously faced the future. The issue quickly became one of "geraniums versus smokestacks." Many business leaders felt that the future lay in developing

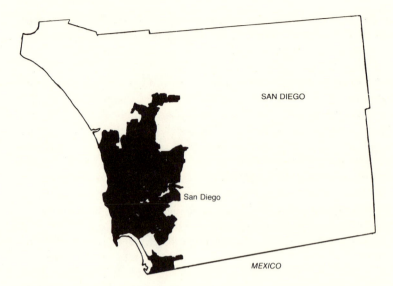

MAP 13.1. The San Diego SMSA

an economically vigorous community and in attracting commerce and business. Optimists argued that millions of persons had passed through the city on their way to war; certainly they would be back to establish roots and prime the pump. Not everyone agreed with such prognostications and recommendations.[5]

The "geranium" advocates envisioned a return to a low-profile style that accepted only tourism as a major industry. Harleye Knox, mayor of San Diego in the forties, became the arbitrator, arguing that both positions could be honored with the adoption of stringent developmental controls.

In the latter part of the 1940s, the view of the "geranium" advocates remained dominant, due largely to less spectacular increases in population (13,000 to 15,000 persons per year) and a slower pace of economic growth. San Diego did not experience a suburban boom like eastern cities. There was no central core city in the final stages of decay, inundated with an influx of poor from rural America. There was no ring of single-family homes with two-car garages strangling the downtown area. A few subdivisions did emerge at the edges of the canyons that finger their way throughout the region, but the dredging and development of Mission Bay, more as a tourist attraction than as a settlement, proved to be the only development of note.[6] The relative tranquility of the postwar forties, however, quickly gave way to the cold war expansionism of the 1950s. The outbreak of the Korean conflict in June 1950 renewed pressures to accommodate war workers, and San Diego began to expand once again.

San Diego's newsweekly, *Point*, captured the city's self-consciousness as a war town and the degree to which its future was linked to national defense policy. Without the least intention of cynicism it reported in 1951 that

> Though many city planners . . . have called attention to the insanity of jamming America's target cities with more people, there is a real scramble on now to build at least 20,000 more housing units in San Diego. With any luck, most of this development will take place several miles from bomb-worthy parts of town. Thus the women and children at least, will survive to mop up after the men.[7]

A rapid influx of population accompanied the Korean conflict; 240,000 additional persons moved to the city between 1950 and the 1960s and an equal number entered the outlying areas. The city population reached 573,224, and the SMSA passed the one million mark. This increase precipitated suburban sprawl as housing tracts appeared on each of the mesas within a fifteen-mile radius from downtown. The city grew larger but not necessarily more urbane. In fact, the fifties were an ideal period for those who collected municipal trivia. A mayor of little note or notoriety, J. G. Tutler, won election in 1951; the main intellectual institution, San Diego State College, dismissed a professor as an accused Communist.[8] The El Cortez Hotel, which featured an elevator on the outside of the building, became the city's tallest building and main tourist attraction.

A 1956 film produced by the San Diego Convention and Tourist Bureau, *The Most Important Corner of the U.S.A.*, summarized the optimism of the time and the contentment of the citizenry:

> San Diego has moved with the strides of a giant—from sleepy border town to wartime boomtown and on to sophisticated and diversified wonderland of today . . . it is no surprise that those who visit San Diego for business or pleasure are startled by what they find: a metropolis of almost a half million people, their fresh and cheery homes sprawled over hills and canyons between the coastal mountains and the Pacific, interconnected by one of the most advanced freeway systems. Over these freeways they move in exploring the jobs of beneficent

climate or going about their work in building missiles, airplanes, electronic systems, in atomic research or in the vast Naval installations of the area.[9]

In 1959, Convair disrupted this idyllic state of prosperity when it laid off 21,000 workers due to the failure of its jet transport program and to cuts in the federal defense budget. The layoff once again emphasized San Diego's heavy dependence on military operations, and defense construction was a reliance that did not insure security. The aerospace industry alone accounted for 50,000 tenuous jobs. There seemed no way to forestall the coming bust.

The situation brought an imperceptible reaction from city government, which had little ability to control the area's economic destiny. San Diego's power structure chiefly resided in the hands of the business-finance community, and it was to that group that common citizens and elected officials alike looked for leadership.

The business community's response was a $30,000 study to investigate the best means of stimulating local business and resolving the problems associated with the absence of economic diversification. The principal recommendation was to build a convention center as a means of attracting more tourists. It was neither a novel idea nor a very popular one. Despite the endorsement of the city's business leaders, the electorate had already turned down five successive referenda for building such a center. The majority of citizens maintained a posture of rejecting outsiders—be they new businesses or tourists. Despite grave economic conditions and rising unemployment, antiurban sentiment held fast.

In 1962, the business community again sought to revive commercial enterprise in downtown San Diego. This time the commercial and industrial leaders formed an organization called San Diegans, Inc., which easily won recognition from the city council as the official representative of downtown interests.

The group commissioned a real estate firm to conduct still another study of the San Diego economy. The firm recommended the attraction of banks, offices, and thousands of hotel rooms to the central core as a major economic stimulant. The 1962 report sparked considerable enthusiasm for downtown development and resulted in the announcement of plans for a new city hall, a civic theater, and a convention center. The idea gained surprising support from the general public. Under the direction of an able city manager, Thomas Fletcher, the government borrowed more than $1 million from the city employees' pension fund to start construction.[10] Such action, planned and initiated by the city's leading businessmen and carried out by the municipal government, was proof that the city's future was now in the hands of its business and financial community rather than those of its elected officials.

Despite the optimism of the times, a continually sluggish economy dampened San Diego's precocious surge to a "great tomorrow." The aerospace industry cut back even further, but more important, many of the same persons who promoted downtown development simultaneously promoted the erection of several regional shopping centers in Mission Valley less than six miles away. Such large-scale commercial undertakings undermined the viability of the central business district, a fact made eminently clear when virtually every major department store relocated to the valley. Downtown revitalization or the need for an urban center seemed more a romantic dream than a committed reality. In the absence of a renewed core, the city continued to grow in the sprawl pattern that many urban commentators denounced as highly uneconomical and wasteful of land and public resources. A coalition of first families and environmentalists called for the drafting of a new city plan as a means to forestall the total suburbanization of the region.

The San Diego City Planning Commission submitted a technical study and schematic plan to the city council in June 1962. The central focus of the proposal was a series of strategies for shaping the city's physical pattern. The plan recommended a nineteenth-century urban configuration that would firmly establish downtown as the heart of the city. This attack upon sprawl was to be accomplished through official encouragement of high concentrations of commercial, governmental, and residential construction. Once established, this denser urban center would connect to freeways leading to outlying satellite communities, each of which would have its own nucleus of commercial facilities. This "visionary plan," in fact, was but a mirror of urban patterns in the congested Northeast. San Diegans thus gave serious consideration to deliberately recreating late nineteenth-century urban America (with freeways replacing streetcars) in the twentieth-century Southwest. Fortunately, there was very little interest in the study and it died quietly.[11]

By 1965, when it had become the sixteenth largest city in the United States, San Diego had expanded its physical boundaries to include 305 square miles. The city maintained an official policy of annexing available land adjacent to its boundaries in an attempt to forestall the sort of proliferation of incorporated suburban communities that had occurred elsewhere. Interest in the reconstruction of downtown diminished, and no significant new development occurred in the heart of the city. A few persons encouraged application for urban renewal funds as the final solution, but they met ridicule from an emerging coalition of conservatives who campaigned vehemently against federal programs that they alleged were antithetical to local self-determination.

Throughout the sixties, many San Diegans maintained a baffling outlook toward the federal government. The very prospect of an application for federal funds incurred vitriolic reaction. Given the fact that a great percentage of the population was sustained by some sort of federal largess connected to the military, the aerospace industry, or retirement, this rejection of federal funds resembled a child's rebellion against its parents. This somewhat schizophrenic attitude is documented most vividly in attempts to adopt a general city plan in the mid 1960s.

In 1964, a Citizens Committee of 100, composed mainly of representatives from the business community, involved itself in a revision of the earlier 1962 plan study. The committee initiated its efforts with the realization that a general plan of urban development was a prerequisite to obtaining federal funds for municipal revitalization. The committee completed its study, drafted a plan with the assistance of the San Diego City Planning Department, and submitted it to the city council on 22 April 1965. The council endorsed the plan and recommended use of federal urban renewal funds to combat urban blight in deteriorated portions of the city—specifically in the downtown area. The *San Diego Union* suggested the deletion of the term "renewal," but not before the area's ultraconservatives, under the banner of the Citizens Protective League, circulated a petition to nullify the council's actions. A referendum went before the voters on 21 September 1965 and the plan was defeated, 66,221 to 39,516, earning the city the singular distinction of being the only major city to vote upon and reject its general plan.[12]

Ironically, in the same election, voters approved a stadium to house a prospective baseball team. The stadium was heavily dependent on federal funds to build freeways to the ball park.

It was not until mid 1967 that the business community was able to regroup and mount another campaign for a general plan. This time the city's business leaders funded a professionally designed public relations program preparatory to submitting the plan to the council on 20 July 1967.

Frank Curran, a former longshoreman, held the mayor's office and with it a large measure of control over the council. Curran was a liberal Democrat, somewhat of a populist, and at times crude and inarticulate. In the minds of the public he represented a fatherly person whose main concern was for underprivileged kids. Yet, most observers agree that he retained office largely because of his relationship to power or, more particularly, his willingness to serve power, not to challenge or confront it. The "Mayor's council" adopted the plan of the economic elite, deleted references to urban renewal, and placed it on the November ballot for voter approval. Swayed by the public relations efforts of business and governmental leaders, the citizens approved the plan in the November election. The city could at last submit applications for federal assistance.

In late 1967, San Diego launched a series of community planning programs, which the federal government supported with over $2 million. The city hired planners from throughout the nation. Upon the request of a particular neighborhood, the city initiated a local planning program there and assigned planners to begin a community dialogue. This effort resulted in the most comprehensive planning process in the city's history. Hundreds of citizens attended endless meetings to discuss community problems, goals, and issues. Citizen participation became the city's badge of distinction. Many San Diegans thought the city had invented the grass-roots democratic process—a misconception seemingly endorsed when San Diego won an All American City award in 1967 for citizen involvement.

Elected officials, including the mayor, generally ignored the community planning movement except to make perfunctory appearances when it seemed politically advantageous to do so. Their true feelings remained hidden until March 1968 when the council, in a surprise move, voted to end the time-honored autonomy of the planning department by placing it under the city manager. The vote ensured that the autonomy of community planning groups would soon end as well. The motivation for such actions became clear later in the month when the council assembled the leaders of community planning. It was obvious that the council felt that this neighborhood "experiment in democracy" had gone too far. Planning groups were accused of butting in on zoning matters and of "fighting brush fires" instead of attending to general land-use planning. Citizen participants responded angrily to accusations that their efforts had created an unacceptable challenge to councilmanic power. Planning advocates alleged that the council's behavior stemmed from continued reliance upon campaign contributions from builders and developers who needed rezoning and other forms of developmental approval. The community planning groups, in this respect, represented a giant thorn in the side of developers who resented the review of their proposals by community groups that might object to their land-use plans. The leaders of community planning groups gathered for breakfast at a hotel across from city hall soon after the confrontation

with the council. At this meeting, they resolved to resist any political intrusions into their rights to participate in government. They
thought that they were on solid ground because community planning programs were federally funded, and Washington required citizen participation to be carefully monitored. Given the lack of local
political support, community planning could not emerge from a sort
of undercover role as a secret coalition between planners employed
in city hall and community people. The former leaked information
and worked with the latter to formulate strategies to stop political
intrusion into community planning.

Despite the merits ascribed to citizen planning, some individuals denounced the process as ineffective due to its emphasis upon
the production of planning documents and its apparent lack of concern for implementation and community action. Others alleged that
although political representatives were willing to accept federal
funds for such activities, they remained more interested in the rewards that new construction might bring to their political coffers
than in the cultivation of programs to rejuvenate and stabilize existing neighborhoods. In many respects, community planning became
a middle-class movement that recommended the maintenance of existing communities free from developmental pressures and un-
wanted change. At least twenty or more community plans appeared
recommending future land-use patterns that replicated existing
ones. In this regard, the goal of such plans was the maintenance of
the much desired status quo through rezoning. Each of the community plans was systematically adopted as part of the city's general
plan. Their emphasis upon "down-zoning" excluded growth from
existing neighborhoods and forced it outward to the suburban fringe.
Consequently, future plans for mass transportation and downtown
redevelopment had to be deferred because they relied upon high-
density development for support.[13]

The issues that absorbed community planning groups were decidedly different from those that most affected the city's minority
people. Members of the black community were involved throughout
the sixties in pressuring for more employment, adequate schools,
better housing, and more representation on elected and appointed
bodies. A host of reports documented the social and economic needs
of the black community, including the city's 1969 application for a
Model Cities grant. This document recorded widespread housing
shortages and community deterioration, continued deficiencies in
employment and social services, major problems of crime and delin-
quency, and a wholesale feeling of frustration.[14]

Nevertheless, elected officials and San Diegans in general evidenced minimal concern. It was frequently noted that despite its problems, southeast San Diego was not Watts. The fact remained that the black proportion of the population was small (less than 10 percent) and not highly visible given their relegation to one small neighborhood encircled by freeways. Moreover, the majority of the black leadership had consistently opted to work within the system, accepted a low profile, and managed to constrain the more radical elements of their community.

Initially, these same black spokesmen cooperated with the city in the development of the Model Cities program in the somewhat naive belief that the city was committed to the eradication of poverty in the southeast community. Through such efforts, some new housing went up and some older places underwent rehabilitation. A Community Educational and Cultural Arts Center took shape on federal surplus land, and area citizens banded together to stop a freeway that would have further divided their neighborhood. Such achievements were minimal at best. In the final analysis, those persons caught in the most dire straits of poverty remained unaffected. A public opinion survey conducted in late 1975 confirmed the fact that problems of the sixties, the very ones addressed by San Diego's war on poverty, continued on into the seventies. Bread and butter issues—issues of human survival—still plague southeast San Diego.[15]

The Chicano community, although growing, played a minimal role in community action efforts in the sixties. For the most part, Mexican Americans remained highly fragmented in leadership and politically passive. They were virtually unable to make their presence known until 20 July 1970, when 150 persons jammed the city council chambers carrying signs calling for justice, power, and equal treatment. Mayor Frank Curran, who chaired the meeting, had become highly skilled at placation. He stated that "no problem in our society is ever solved by throwing eggs at each other." He asked the protesting group to choose five or six representatives to discuss the issues with city administrators. The subsequent meetings generated more conflict than resolution. In fact, these gatherings mainly served to take the pressure off of the mayor and to allow him to turn his attention to issues associated with the burgeoning population.[16]

In mid 1970, Mayor Curran rejoiced when the Census Bureau released preliminary estimates indicating that San Diego had surpassed San Franscico and become the state's second largest city with 703,000 residents. Curran took the opportunity to jibe San Francisco mayor Joseph Alioto about his city's loss of rank. In a telegram to Alioto, Curran said, "My personal condolences to you on the occasion of becoming the third largest city in the State of California. Best regards from your older and bigger California City." The next day Curran received a telegram from Mayor Sam Yorty of Los Angeles inquiring whether he would like to become number one: "Los Angeles would be pleased to share some of its population provided you're willing to accept the pollution, traffic congestion and public service demands that go along with it."[17]

Yorty proved somewhat of an oracle. During the 1970s, San Diegans began to realize that becoming the fourth largest municipality in the twenty-four states west of the Mississippi had profound implications for their highly cherished environment. A local newspaper headlined, "San Diego Takes Lead as Boom Town, California," and added extensive comments about record increases in air pollution and traffic congestion and the widespread deterioration of the San Diego lifestyle.[18]

In 1971 Curran lost decisively to a young Republican, Pete Wilson, who had served three terms in the state assembly where he had championed environmental legislation. Wilson was obviously sensitive to the public's changing mood and realized that it was a politically opportune time to attack the growth ethic.

Even the conservative, business-oriented *San Diego Union* lashed out against builders and developers and the politicians who catered to them. The paper noted that local officials had consistently approved massive development projects that taxed city services, the environment, and the patience of residents. "Today," it noted, "we are entering a new age of questioning long-standing precedents and policies." Planning Director James Goff (whose predecessor, James Fairman, resigned over the absence of political commitment to community planning) optimistically asserted, "I think we've moved from the era of the developer's being king to a situation where the citizen is more important."[19]

Goff's pronouncements proved to be prophetic. In 1973, the city council placed a building moratorium on 50,000 acres of land threatened by development. The council imposed height limits on all new buildings near the ocean and placed steep areas in land conservation zones to protect against excessive cutting and filling. Environmental impact procedures went into effect citywide to review proposed developments and determine their negative impacts.

The builders panicked as they sensed an end to their power and to unbridled development. Their fears worsened when Mayor Wilson, who had recently served on a national urban development commission, began to campaign for the creation of a growth management plan similar to that instituted in Ramapo, New York. The Ramapo plan established limits on the amount and location of new housing based on the city's fiscal capabilities to construct public facilities and utilities. On numerous occasions the mayor decried the continued low-density sprawl of new development and urged the redirection of construction to vacant lands in existing communities already served with under-utilized schools and parks. Such planning drew support as a means of increasing the population adjacent to the central core. Such internal growth in turn would offer support to the downtown renewal efforts, a pet project of the mayor's. Interestingly, such development strategies contradicted ten years of grass-roots planning efforts devoted to down-zoning as a means of avoiding future congestion and maintaining existing community character.

Wilson successfully rode the issue of growth management through several elections. City councilmen and other office seekers hurriedly embraced the new ecological ethic. By the mid seventies San Diego had adopted a growth management plan that displayed the current disinterest in the community planning of the sixties. Citizen planning organizations felt betrayed by the possibility of increased development in their neighborhoods, which the management plan rationalized as an effective means of stunting suburbanization. Nevertheless the majority of San Diegans supported the plan as the only means of avoiding the specter of "Los Angelization."

Growth management and its progenitor Mayor Wilson did not remain in the limelight of popularity indefinitely. In November 1975, some three thousand labor union members paraded downtown protesting city growth policies that they claimed were responsible for double-digit unemployment. The public protest was held four days before council elections, and the mayor was hung in effigy. Construction industry representatives blamed growth control advocates for a loss of 8,100 construction jobs since 1973. They condemned the inability of city officials to attract new employment sources for the 72,000 persons unemployed, a total exacerbated by the continued influx of 30,000 persons a year. The director of the chamber of commerce, Lee Grissom, complained that outside companies wishing to locate in San Diego viewed city staff members as obstructionists and that bureaucrats and politicians were blatantly antiexpansionist.[20]

Despite such protests and allegations, the mayor was reelected over his opponent councilman Lee Hubbard, a building industry spokesman. The liberal *San Diego Magazine*'s chief political commentator, Harold Keen, saw Wilson's victory as initiating a renaissance in environmental consciousness, a movement in public involvement sufficient to propel the city toward greatness in the 1970s. He spoke of "a growing legion of intellectuals, ecologists, researchers, engineers, scientists and academicians who are bound to form a new establishment of 'do-gooders' best equipped to cope with the problems of the 1970s—pollution, noise, decay of older districts, ground, air and sea transportation, poverty, education and general planning to make life bearable in the urban crush."[21] At first, Keen seemed correct as Wilson proceeded to promulgate growth management as official city policy.

A series of newspaper articles appearing after the election noted that San Diegans elect politicians who put a high priority on the quality of life rather than economic expansion at least in the short run. Nevertheless, the local paper noted that the "finest City" may be in serious trouble since the economy is failing to grow as fast as community needs. "This situation," it observed, "is compounded by a shortage of business leaders and capital required to deal with economic problems and to create growth, jobs and opportunities for young persons entering the workforce."[22]

Initially Mayor Wilson was able to ignore such reports, given the fact that he was reelected by a landslide. However, he grew uncomfortable with his growing image as a champion of environmental causes. In fact, Keen inquired as to whether Wilson's aspirations to the California governorship could be sustained with such a characterization. Since the building and construction industries were stalwarts of the Republican party, their willingness to contribute to Wilson's political future as a liberal Republican was questionable.

The mayor's role as a growth manager held until the mid seventies. Again, due to outside economic forces, a metamorphosis in political philosophy occurred. The unemployment rate began to climb and housing costs skyrocketed. Small, stucco cottages, which represented the predominant form of shelter and the backbone of housing for low- and middle-income families, quadrupled in value. By the late seventies, the price of an average home had reached $100,000. Housing groups warned that given the tremendous increase in speculative investments flowing in from other American cities and foreign countries, San Diego's housing costs could reach astronomical heights that only the wealthiest could afford. By means of gentrification, the rich could push the poor out of the city. Indeed, the region could become totally affluent. Middle- and low-income people would certainly be dislocated. Dense development had become too costly. It was time for the "smokestack" people to take the limelight, and Mayor Pete Wilson knew it.

The late 1970s witnessed a shift toward conservative politics in San Diego as in the rest of the nation. Four avowed conservatives gained seats on the council in November 1978. While "fence jumping" on certain issues occurred—such as stopping a freeway from traversing the black community—the overall posture of the new council was one of fiscal restraint buttressed by widespread doubts about the performance and effectiveness of government. The council promptly nullified policies that either required environmental impact reviews or gave "excessive authority" to the planning department.

In late 1975, Mayor Wilson, once the chief advocate of government intervention, emerged as the darling of the "speculator-contractor set," maintaining that his position had been consistently misinterpreted by opponents. Acknowledging an inability to stop the influx of population, he declared that he stood for controlled growth, not no growth. His opponents, mostly Democrats such as Si Casady, who challenged him in the mayoral race of 1976, accused him of abdicating his commitment to environmental protection and selling city land to friends. Casady further questioned the economic viability of the mayor's Center City Redevelopment project. He also cited Wilson's alleged "deals" made with shopping-center promoter Ernest Hahn and his support of North City West, a development of monumental proportions, slated to accommodate 275,000 people. The mayor survived these charges and won reelection by arguing that the city must build to alleviate the problems caused by its homogeneous economic base, high unemployment, and astronomically high housing costs. Wilson reminded his detractors that the United States Constitution promises the right to free travel—the right of Americans everywhere to move to San Diego. Growth itself was inevitable. Wilson's backers began to refer to the growth management program of the 1970s as "managed sprawl."[23] The end of the 1970s saw Wilson further divest himself of any public vestiges of environmental liberalism. His platform switched from growth control to crime control.

Mayor Pete Wilson's state of the city address on 26 January 1979 exemplified his political metamorphosis. The mayor proclaimed, "We will not tolerate or stand for crime or violence in San Diego. We will win the war on crime whatever the cost." He noted that the city was already spending a whopping 45 percent of its general fund on public safety activities, of which police protection received the lion's share. He proceeded to recommend an increase in spending of $5 million for police manpower, construction of new police facilities costing $22 million, and support of a state bond issue to finance the construction of needed jails and prisons. These recommenda-tions were made despite the fact that the city's overall reported crime rate had declined from the previous year.

In the same address, the mayor also acknowledged the worsen-ing housing problem, noting that rents and home prices had risen alarmingly due largely to San Diego's population growth rate, which was triple the national average. He recommended the sale of city-owned lands to developers who would pass the savings on to low-income tenants, the development of mobile home parks on similar lands, and the issuance of tax-exempt municipal bonds to provide a fund for subsidized housing.[24]

The mayor's recognition of a housing problem in the midst of a law and order address failed to do justice to the growing dimensions of the problem. In the first five months of 1981, the price of an aver-age house in San Diego rose 2.8 percent to an alarming $128,000, while the number of building permits dropped to its lowest level in six years. The vacancy rate stood at less than 1 percent. The rate of foreclosures began to rise rapidly. The number of people need-ing emergency shelter far exceeded available facilities and the newspapers claimed that many people were being "driven into the streets."[25] Such issues proved particularly vexing as San Diego once again experienced a sluggish economy and the old palliatives were resurrected. The city fathers, particularly Mayor Wilson, urged the redevelopment of downtown. In mid 1981, they placed a referendum before the electorate to build a $224 million convention center as a critical first step. The referendum was defeated.[26]

A few months earlier, city officials cut a tape inaugurating a new light-rail transit system connecting downtown San Diego with Tijuana, Mexico. In many respects, this act represented San Diego's first acknowledgment of an exploding city-nation at its doorstep—a city with a population equal to that of San Diego (800,000). Despite the fact that there are over 34 million border crossings each year (70 percent of which are by Mexican citizens), economic and social ties had developed slowly.[27]

As to the future, a recent conference, "San Diego: The Year 2000," suggested that migration across the border will continue to increase and that the San Diego–Tijuana metropolis will grow to five million persons, the largest border concentration in the world. Furthermore, as one conference attendee noted:

. . . barring a complete militarization of the United
States–Mexico border and a naval blockade of the California
coast, both commuters and long distance migrants from the

interior of Mexico will be seeking work here in large numbers for the remainder of this century.[28]

It was evident from the conference that many San Diegans fear the prospects of large numbers of Mexicans migrating to their city in search of employment and housing especially at a time when both are in critically short supply. They are further irritated by the prospects of having to provide affordable health care, education, and shelter for such persons.

The director of a university-based Mexican studies program responded to such attitudes: "There are, of course, some who would like to enjoy all of the economic benefits of 'cheap,' readily available Mexican labor—as long as it leaves no 'social residue.'"[29] The massive migration of Mexicans projected by demographers and sociologists is occurring at a time in which large numbers of Americans are also migrating to Sunbelt San Diego. Many of them come in pursuit of a quiet, passive existence with few conflicts—one that represents an escape from the ponderous economic and social problems that they confront in midwestern and eastern cities. For many persons, San Diego personifies America's suburbia.

As a city unaccustomed to dealing with rapid social change, having a history of antiurbanism, and confessing to a lack of political and civic leadership, modern San Diego faces a rather herculean set of challenges with little optimism. Conflicts and confrontations will no doubt arise as affluent easterners run head-long against poor, if not destitute, migrants from Mexico who are searching for the basics of life, not the pleasures of its luxuries. Whether San Diego and San Diegans will at last be willing or able to meet the challenges of such potential problems and opportunities and work toward the creation of a true city—diverse in culture, employment, and opportunity—is highly problematic.

NOTES

1. See Henry Augur, "San Diego, a Study in Serenity," *Travel* (January 1941): 24–27.

2. Richard F. Pourade, *Rising Tide* (San Diego: Union Tribune Publishing Co., 1964).

3. C. McWilliams, "Boom Nobody Wanted," *New Republic*, 30 June 1941, 882–884.

4. *New York Times*, 7 October 1945.

5. Richard F. Pourade, *City of Dreams* (San Diego: Union Tribune Publishing Co., 1979).

6. "Along the Waterfronts: San Diego's Mission Bay," *American City* (August 1946): 93–94.

7. James Britton, "Comments," *Point*, 23 February 1951, 14.

8. *New York Times*, 19 May 1954.

9. *The Most Important Corner of the USA* (San Diego Visitor and Convention Bureau, San Diego, 1956, film).

10. *New York Times*, 13 January 1965.

11. Information on the history of the San Diego General Plan obtained from conversations with George Orman, Research Director, San Diego City Planning Department.

12. *Evening Tribune*, 5 November 1965.

13. The preceding description of the community planning movement is based upon the experiences of the author, who was employed as a planner in the San Diego City Planning Department from 1965–1969.

14. San Diego City Planning Department, *An Application for a Model Cities Program*, submitted to the Department of Housing and Urban Development, San Diego, California, 1969.

15. *San Diego, California: A Community Profile* (Hollywood, Calif.: Lotus Research of California, August 1975).

16. *Evening Tribune*, 21 July 1970.

17. Ibid., 24 November 1970.

18. Ibid., 27 October 1971.

19. Ibid., 3 December 1971.

20. Ibid., 7 January 1974.

21. Harold Keen, "Who's in Charge Here?" *San Diego Magazine* (February 1970): 107.

22. *San Diego Union*, 12 January 1981.

23. Harold Keen, "The Pete Paradox," *San Diego Magazine* (November 1979): 126–130.

24. Mayor Pete Wilson, *State of the City Address*, San Diego, California, 8 January 1979; *San Diego Union*, 31 March 1981.

25. *San Diego Union*, 5 May 1981.

26. Ibid., 7 May 1981.

27. Tore Tursland, "Economic Analysis of Mexican Citizen Activity in San Diego County" (San Diego Chamber of Commerce, San Diego, 1979).

28. *San Diego 2000 Conference Proceedings*, California Tomorrow, San Francisco, 7 February 1981.

29. Ibid.

CONTRIBUTORS

RICHARD M. BERNARD is associate professor of history and director of the Urban Affairs Program at Marquette University, Milwaukee, Wisconsin. He is the author of *The Melting Pot and the Altar: Marital Assimilation in Early Twentieth-Century Wisconsin* (1980) and *The Poles of Oklahoma* (1980).

BRADLEY R. RICE is associate professor of history at Clayton Junior College, Morrow, Georgia. He is the author of *Progressive Cities: The Commission Government Movement in America, 1901–1920* (1977).

DAVID L. CLARK is an instructor of history for UCLA Extension. He is the author of *Los Angeles: A City Apart* (1981) and *L.A. on Foot* (1972, revised and reprinted 1974 and 1976). He is presently writing a history of the relationship between UCLA and Los Angeles.

ANTHONY W. CORSO is chairman of the Management Program at St. Mary's College, Moraga, California. He was formerly director of the City Planning Program at San Diego State University and has worked as a city planner in San Diego and other California cities.

ARNOLD R. HIRSCH is assistant professor of history and urban and regional planning at the University of New Orleans. He is the author of *Making the Second Ghetto: Race and Housing in Chicago, 1940–1960* (forthcoming).

DAVID R. JOHNSON is associate professor of history at the University of Texas at San Antonio. He is author of *Policing the Urban Underground* (1979) and coeditor of *The Politics of San Antonio: Community, Progress, and Power* (1983).

BARRY J. KAPLAN is senior associate in Houston Research Services, a community research firm. He is an adjunct faculty member at the

West Houston Institute of the University of Houston and taught for seven years at the university's Central Campus.

BRADFORD LUCKINGHAM is associate professor of history at Arizona State University, Tempe. He is the author of *The Urban Southwest: A Profile History of Albuquerque, El Paso, Phoenix, and Tucson* (1982).

MARTIN V. MELOSI is associate professor of history at Texas A & M University, College Station. He is the author of *Garbage in the Cities: Refuse, Reform and the Environment, 1880–1980* (1981) and editor of *Pollution and Reform in American Cities, 1870–1930* (1979).

RAYMOND A. MOHL is professor of history at Florida Atlantic University, Boca Raton. He is the author of *Poverty in New York, 1783–1825* (1971), *The Paradox of Progressive Education* (1979), and *Steel City: Urban and Ethnic Patterns in Gary, Indiana, 1906– 1950* (forthcoming), as well as an associate editor of the *Journal of Urban History*.

GARY R. MORMINO is associate professor of history at the University of South Florida, Tampa. He is the author of *The Hill upon the City: An Italian-American Neighborhood, 1880–1950* (forthcoming).

HOWARD N. RABINOWITZ is associate professor of history at the University of New Mexico, Albuquerque. He is the author of *Race Relations in the Urban South, 1865–1890* (1978) and editor of *Southern Black Leaders of the Reconstruction Era* (1982).